Alison

The End of Wisdom

The End of Wisdom

A Reappraisal of the Historical and
Canonical Function of Ecclesiastes

MARTIN A. SHIELDS

Winona Lake, Indiana
EISENBRAUNS
2006

www.eisenbrauns.com

Library of Congress Cataloging-in-Publication Data

Shields, Martin A., 1965–
　　The end of wisdom : a reappraisal of the historical and canonical
　　function of Ecclesiastes / Martin A. Shields.
　　　　p.　cm.
　　Includes bibliographical references and index.
　　ISBN-13: 978-1-57506-102-3 (hardback : alk. paper)
　　1. Bible. O.T. Ecclesiastes—Commentaries.　2. Bible. O.T.
Ecclesiastes—Canonical criticism.　I. Title.
BS1475.53.S55　2006
223′.807—dc22

　　　　　　　　　　　　　　　　　　　　　　　　　　2005036745

Contents

Preface

Qoheleth's world is not a comfortable or a comforting one. He spends much of his time pondering the impact of death on all of life, only to conclude that death effectively invalidates life. Many readers find that Qoheleth's observation that the world makes no sense resonates with their own experience and cling to his exhortations to enjoy life. Yet even this joy is tainted by death and fate, for Qoheleth discovered that it is not possible to engineer circumstances in a way that will inevitably lead to joy, let alone hold onto it.

The danger we face as readers of Ecclesiastes is in becoming so caught up in Qoheleth's argument that we find ourselves sharing his conclusions. The danger is seeing in Ecclesiastes only Qoheleth's conclusions and forgetting that there is a bigger picture presented. This picture only comes fully into view against the backdrop of the remainder of the Bible, and the existence of this broader canvas is revealed by the words of Qoheleth's editor, the epilogist (writer of the epilogue), who frames Qoheleth's words with his own. It is this bigger picture that I wish to reveal in this book, for I suggest that it shows us how to understand the purpose of the book of Ecclesiastes and the reason for its inclusion in the Bible.

How are Qoheleth's words to be understood? One possible analogy can be found in modern politics. It is not uncommon for one political party, if it discovers potentially embarrassing information about its opponent, to "leak" the information in order to discredit the opposition in the eyes of the public. Leaks of this sort are particularly damning when they originate from within the opposition party and when they reveal double standards or hidden agendas—frequently far more damning than any logical argument could be.

Qoheleth's epilogist has obtained material likely to discredit his opponents, the members of the wisdom movement. This material takes the form of the words of Qoheleth, whose wisdom is beyond dispute and whose honesty cannot be called into question but whose conclusions cannot be reconciled with the remainder of the Bible. One could say that the epilogist "leaked" Qoheleth's words in order to discredit the sages and deter any would-be students of the sages from attaching themselves to the wisdom movement.

This book has its origins in my Ph.D. dissertation, submitted to the University of Sydney under the supervision of Dr. Ian Young. His suggestions and insights have contributed to and improved the final form of this work in many ways and have led me to consider matters that I would otherwise have neglected. I, however, bear sole responsibility for the shortcomings of the work.

I must also thank my wife, Susie, for her sustaining love, support, and patience over the years, as this work slowly came together. This work is dedicated to our boys, Simon and Wesley, in the hope that they may find more sense in this world than Qoheleth did.

Martin A. Shields
Sydney, Australia

Abbreviations

General

AB	Amplified Bible
Akk.	Akkadian
ANE	ancient Near East
Arab.	Arabic
ASV	American Standard Version
AV	Authorized Version
BA	Biblical Aramaic
BH	Biblical Hebrew
Copt.	Coptic version of the Old Testament
cs.	construct
DSS	Dead Sea Scrolls
ESV	English Standard Version
f.	feminine
imv.	imperative
inf.	infinitive
JB	Jerusalem Bible
KJV	King James Version
LXX	Septuagint
m.	masculine
MS(S)	manuscript(s)
MT	Masoretic Text
NAB	New American Bible
NASB	New American Standard Bible
NEB	New English Bible
NET	New English Translation
NIV	New International Version
NJPSV	New Jewish Publication Society Version
NRSV	New Revised Standard Version
NT	New Testament
pass.	passive
pf.	perfect
pl.	plural

ptc.	participle
RSV	Revised Standard Version
s.	singular
Symm	Symmachus (Jewish reviser of LXX to proto-MT, ca. A.D. 200)
SyrH	Syro-Hexaplar (Syriac translation of Origen's Hexapla)
v(v).	verse(s)
Vulg.	Vulgate

Reference Works

AB	Anchor Bible
ABD	Freedman, D. N. (ed.). *Anchor Bible Dictionary*. 6 volumes. New York: Doubleday, 1992
AF	*Archivo di Filosofia*
ANES	*Ancient Near Eastern Studies*
ANET	Pritchard, J. B. (ed.). *Ancient Near Eastern Texts relating to the Old Testament*. 3rd edition. Princeton: Princeton University Press, 1969
ATD	Das Alte Testament Deutsch
AUSS	*Andrews University Seminary Studies*
BDB	Brown, Francis, S. R. Driver, and Charles A. Briggs. *Hebrew and English Lexicon*. Peabody, Mass.: Hendrickson, 1979
Bib	*Biblica*
BKAT	Biblischer Kommentar: Altes Testament
BN	*Biblische Notizen*
BZAW	Beihefte zur Zeitschrift für die alttestamentliche Wissenschaft
CBQ	*Catholic Biblical Quarterly*
CBQMS	Catholic Biblical Quarterly Monograph Series
EvQ	*Evangelical Quarterly*
ExpTim	*Expository Times*
GKC	Kautzsch, E. (ed.). *Gesenius' Hebrew Grammar*. 2nd edition. Translated by A. E. Cowley. Oxford: Clarendon, 1910
GTJ	*Grace Theological Journal*
HAT	Handbuch zum Alten Testament
HKAT	Handkommentar zum Alten Testament
HSM	Harvard Semitic Monographs
HSS	Harvard Semitic Studies
HUCA	*Hebrew Union College Annual*
ICC	International Critical Commentary
ITC	International Theological Commentary
JBL	*Journal of Biblical Literature*

JHS	*Journal of Hebrew Scriptures* (http://www.jhsonline.org/)
JNES	*Journal of Near Eastern Studies*
JQR	*Jewish Quarterly Review*
JSOT	*Journal for the Study of the Old Testament*
JSOTSup	Journal for the Study of the Old Testament Supplement Series
JSS	*Journal of Semitic Studies*
KAT	Kommentar zum Alten Testament
KHC	Kurzur Hand-Commentar zum Alten Testament
LD	Lectio divina
LSJ	Liddell, Henry George, and Robert Scott. *A Greek-English Lexicon*. Revised and augmented by Sir Henry Stuart Jones. Oxford: Clarendon, 1940
NAC	New American Commentary
NCB	New Century Bible Commentary
NICOT	New International Commentary on the Old Testament
OBO	Orbis biblicus et orientalis
OBT	Overtures to Biblical Theology
OLA	Orientalia Lovaniensia Analecta
OLP	*Orientalia Lovaniensia Periodica*
OTG	Old Testament Guides
OTL	Old Testament Library
RHPR	*Revue d'histoire et de philosophie religieuses*
RTR	*Reformed Theological Review*
SBLSCS	Society of Biblical Literature Septuagint and Cognate Studies
SBT	Studies in Biblical Theology
TLZ	*Theologische Literaturzeitung*
TOTC	Tyndale Old Testament Commentary
TWOT	Harris, R. L., and G. L. Archer Jr. (eds.). 2 vols. Chicago: Moody, 1980
TynBul	*Tyndale Bulletin*
VT	*Vetus Testamentum*
VTSup	Vetus Testamentum Supplements
WBC	Word Bible Commentary
ZAH	*Zeitschrift für Althebräistic*
ZAW	*Zeitschrift für die alttestamentliche Wissenschaft*

Introduction

There is something perplexing, perhaps even surprising, about the book of Ecclesiastes.[1] Although Qoheleth's words exhibit a predominantly negative assessment of life, an assessment due largely to the inevitability of death, and although he sometimes appears to contradict himself, it is not these aspects of the book that are puzzling. It is, after all, not difficult to produce a text that has any or all of these features. What is most perplexing about Ecclesiastes is that a text of this sort is incorporated within a collection of writings that speak of a God who reveals and redeems, who chooses people and cares for them—themes not only absent from Qoheleth's words but frequently irreconcilable with them.

In spite of this, the majority of modern commentators spend very little time addressing the problem of Ecclesiastes' inclusion within the Bible, and when they do, the reasons offered are largely unconvincing. In the light of this problem, I intend to offer an interpretation of Ecclesiastes that both acknowledges the unorthodox nature of Qoheleth's words and manages to account for its acceptance among the canonical books of the Hebrew Bible.

Why Is It There?
Explanations for Ecclesiastes' Presence in the Canon

The problem of Ecclesiastes' presence in the canon has been apparent throughout the history of interpretation of the text. Indeed, the earliest recorded discussions of the book relate to this very issue. Since that time, a number of theories have been put forward to account for the presence of the work in the canon, although none has found unanimous support among the book's readers. Before proposing a new answer, however, I consider it worthwhile briefly to canvass previous approaches to the problem, for only then will the magnitude of the task be clear.

---

1. I shall adopt the convention whereby the title *Ecclesiastes* refers to the entire work, including the words of the epilogist, while *Qoheleth* refers specifically to the character to whom the bulk of the book is attributed and to his words.

"Traditional" Explanations

The two oldest explanations for Ecclesiastes' inclusion in the canon are probably the reasons most commonly recited in commentaries. The first claim is that the implied association with Solomon is supposed to have carried sufficient authority to overcome any objections to the work's inclusion in the canon. The difficulty with this justification, however, is clear: similar pseudonymous attributions in other texts—texts that were more orthodox than Ecclesiastes—proved to be insufficient reason for those texts to be accepted as canonical.[2]

The second traditional explanation for the inclusion of Ecclesiastes in the canon, which is usually offered in conjunction with the first, is that the conclusion of the epilogue—that one should fear God and keep his commands—was understood to redeem the work sufficiently to render it acceptable. This, certainly, appears to have been the outcome of the discussions concerning Ecclesiastes at Jamnia. Rabbi Akiba, for instance, said, "The wise men desired to withdraw the Book of Ecclesiastes because its language was often self-contradictory and contradicted the utterances of David. Why did they not withdraw it? Because the beginning and the end of it consist of words of the law" (*b. Šabb.* 30b).[3] However, that such a debate actually took place suggests not only that Ecclesiastes was widely held to have some claim to canonicity prior to this meeting but also that it was widely recognized as problematic. Thus even this testimony fails to account explicitly for the prior recognition that Ecclesiastes did have some place among the canonical books of the Hebrew Bible; it presents only one argument used to overcome objections to its place there.

Could both reasons together have been considered sufficient to accept Ecclesiastes? This appears unlikely, given the failure of works more consistently orthodox (rather than being orthodox only in the final couple of verses) to find acceptance. It thus appears likely that there were other factors that led to Ecclesiastes' being accepted as canonical—factors that had served to promote the work's acceptance among enough of its readership that there eventually arose a need to debate its canonicity.

Interpreting Qoheleth's Words as Orthodox

One other approach to understanding Ecclesiastes' presence in the canon is to attempt to demonstrate that the orthodox advice of the epilogist repre-

---

2. For example, the *Psalms of Solomon*; see G. Buchanan Gray, "The Psalms of Solomon," in *The Apocrypha and Pseudepigrapha of the Old Testament in English* (ed. R. H. Charles; Oxford: Clarendon, 1913).

3. William H. Green, *General Introduction to the Old Testament: The Canon* (London: Murray, 1899) 138.

sents an accurate summary of Qoheleth's teaching.[4] Roland Murphy, for example, objects to the notion that Qoheleth reflects a "crisis of wisdom" on the basis that the "viewpoint of the epilogist is important because it shows an assessment from people who were closer in time to him than we are."[5] For Murphy, the epilogue thus represents an early interpretation of Qoheleth's words, an interpretation that said, in effect, that Qoheleth's message could ultimately be summarized as "fear God and keep his commandments."

One problem with this view is that, by relegating the epilogue to little more than a reflection of an early interpreter of the book, Murphy treats the epilogue as both secondary to and less significant than the words of Qoheleth themselves. Furthermore, all attempts to find a reflection of Qoheleth's words in the epilogist's exhortation to fear God and keep his commandments have ultimately proved to be unconvincing. At the very least, they fail to account for the fact that Qoheleth's words are encapsulated by the summary statements that "everything is senseless."[6] The presence of this summary poses a substantial problem for scholars who would claim that Qoheleth is somehow presenting an orthodox message.

Dialogue in Ecclesiastes

Another approach to the problem of Ecclesiastes' presence in the canon is to identify competing viewpoints in the book and assign them to different voices. Thus, difficult or unorthodox statements can be interpreted as representing unorthodox thought, which is in turn answered or refuted by Qoheleth himself. Whybray, for example, comments on the presence of dialogue in Qoheleth's words:

> There can be no doubt that Qoheleth did employ this device. Some of his quotations (e.g., 1.15; 1.18) can be clearly recognized by their poetical form and their resemblance to sayings in the book of Proverbs, which cause them to stand out in the context of a prose passage. Such quotations are sometimes used to confirm a point (e.g., 1.18). In other cases they are used as a basis for Qoheleth's own critical comment (e.g., 2.14a, which is followed by the comment in 2.14b, which deprives it of much of its force).[7]

---

4. For example, see Michael A. Eaton, *Ecclesiastes* (TOTC; Leicester: Inter-Varsity, 1983) 156; Andrew G. Shead, "Ecclesiastes from the Outside In," *RTR* 55 (1996) 24–37.

5. Roland E. Murphy, "The Sage in Ecclesiastes and Qoheleth the Sage," in *The Sage in Israel and the Ancient Near East* (ed. John G. Gammie and Leo G. Perdue; Winona Lake, Ind.: Eisenbrauns, 1990) 271.

6. See my "Ecclesiastes and the End of Wisdom," *TynBul* 50 (1999) 118–24 for a critique of these approaches to reading Ecclesiastes.

7. R. N. Whybray, *Ecclesiastes* (OTG; Sheffield: Sheffield Academic Press, 1989) 25. See also Robert Gordis, *Koheleth: The Man and His World* (New York: Schocken, 1951) 95–108.

The most comprehensive application of this approach has come from T. A. Perry, who has argued that the entire work is an extensive dialogue between a pessimistic voice and a more measured presenter.[8]

While quite ingenious in his analysis of the text (although I disagree with his reading at many points), Perry faces a number of insurmountable difficulties. First, the reader is conditioned by the introduction to the work to hear only one voice, the voice of Qoheleth, son of David, king in Jerusalem. These, we are told, are his words. No other voice is identified, except for the voice of the epilogist, who introduces, concludes, and briefly interjects "said Qoheleth" into the words of Qoheleth. Perry argues that the "best solution seems to be that v. 1 is entirely said by the Presenter in order to introduce the theme that has made Kohelet famous: 'vanity of vanities.' "[9] The fact that the introduction refers to plural sayings rather than a single saying, however, makes this interpretation improbable.

The second, more serious, problem for Perry's approach is the absence of any explicit markers of dialogue. Perry's thesis supposes that dialogue could have been reliably encoded in a text without any of the usual indicators of change of voice as found elsewhere in the dialogue of the Bible. Perry has not been able to provide any example of an ancient text in which changes in speaker such as he is proposing can unequivocally be identified.[10] By contrast, there are numerous examples of texts that record dialogues in which changes in speaker are clearly and explicitly identified by the author, the book of Job being just one instance.

Skepticism in the Hebrew Bible

One more-recent approach to the problem of Ecclesiastes' presence in the Bible is to argue that there is a legitimate tradition of skepticism in the Hebrew Bible. Once this has been established, it is possible to argue that Ecclesiastes is an example of this tradition, albeit an extreme one, and thus not

---

8. T. A. Perry, *Dialogues with Kohelet* (University Park: Pennsylvania State University Press, 1993).

9. Ibid., 53.

10. Perry does provide a discussion of dialogue markers (see ibid., 186–97). The markers that Perry finds in Qoheleth, however, are far from unambiguous—each could be understood to have a function in the text other than to mark a change in speaker. The natural inference of the reader in most instances, given the work's opening attribution to a single author, would be that either Qoheleth's words were self-deliberative dialogue or else that Qoheleth's mind was uncertain and confused. Perry appeals to the Mishnah as an example of a text in which dialogue occurs without explicit indicators (ibid., x). It is not clear, however, that the Mishnah supports the case that Perry makes for reading Qoheleth as a sustained dialogue between well-defined, distinct characters.

ultimately as out of place as the reader may have been led to believe. In this case, Ecclesiastes is not unorthodox, because orthodoxy is far broader than otherwise acknowledged.[11] This approach has the distinct advantage of taking seriously the difficulties inherent in Qoheleth's words, difficulties that other approaches tend to gloss over or dismiss with improbable interpretations.

The problem with this view, however, is that the supposed tradition of skepticism or expressions of doubt elsewhere in the Hebrew Bible are not nearly as incessant or unremitting as the words of Qoheleth. Whybray explains this as a "development" of earlier doubts, as if Qoheleth's views are simply the logical result of taking these earlier doubts to the extreme.[12] This undermines the argument, however, for it does not follow that, because some expression of doubt or skepticism is accepted within the scope of "orthodox" thought, *all* expressions of doubt or skepticism can be acceptable. The simple truth is that, in spite of the existence of some expressions of doubt elsewhere in the Hebrew Bible, there is none that matches Qoheleth's words for a sustained denial of faith and doubt in the goodness of God.

In short, we do not know for certain why or how this book found its way into such esteemed company. All we can say is that the problematic nature of the work was widely recognized even in the earliest records of its interpretation and that there is no evidence that it was accepted as canonical because the readers of the work were so open-minded as not to be troubled by the contradictions between Qoheleth's words and the remainder of the Hebrew Bible.

A Solution to the Problem

It is clear that all of the explanations offered for Ecclesiastes' presence in the canon suffer from quite serious problems. My aim in the remainder of this

---

11. James L. Crenshaw, "Ecclesiastes: Odd Book In," *Bible Review* 6 (1990) 30–31; compare Whybray, *Ecclesiastes*, 59–60; James L. Crenshaw, *A Whirlpool of Torment: Israelite Traditions of God as an Oppressive Presence* (OBT; Philadelphia: Fortress, 1984); Robert Davidson, *The Courage to Doubt: Exploring an Old Testament Theme* (London: SCM, 1983). Whybray, for example, writes, "It has been argued that we need to view the Jewish religious tradition reflected in the Old Testament as being considerably more diverse than it was previously thought to be, and as having embraced a radical element from a quite early time. In this perspective the radicalism of Qoheleth would appear not as something quite new and outlandish, but as a development of earlier doubts about the purposes of God and dissatisfaction about the human condition which had already been voiced from time to time in opposition to the main, mainly optimistic, stream of Jewish religious tradition" (pp. 59–60). There are clearly difficulties in employing the term *orthodox* to biblical religion. Nonetheless, I shall continue to use the term as a convenient means of referring to the religious doctrines established throughout the Hebrew Bible outside Ecclesiastes.

12. Whybray, *Ecclesiastes*, 59–60.

book is to present an understanding of Ecclesiastes that can both acknowledge that the words of Qoheleth are incompatible with the orthodoxy of the remainder of the Hebrew Bible and still reconcile the book as a whole with that orthodoxy. The key to this reading is an understanding of the epilogue that sees the epilogist as using the words of Qoheleth to discredit the wisdom movement. Qoheleth is presented as the preeminent sage, both in the allusions to his Solomonic identity in the opening chapter of the book and in the opening words of the epilogue. This functions to overcome the tendency any orthodox reader would otherwise have to dismiss the words of Qoheleth as the insignificant outpourings of an embittered old sage.

Presented thus, the reader cannot dismiss Qoheleth as an aberration of the wisdom movement. Rather, he is a true representative of it. If this is so, the reader must question the value of a wisdom movement that presents ideas that are out of step with the remainder of the Hebrew Bible. If this is wisdom, then there is something fundamentally wrong with it. And this is precisely what the epilogist proceeds to assert. Beware of the sages, for they can lead you astray. Rather, choose the path of true wisdom: fear of God and obedience to his commands. As such, Qoheleth's words are akin to a leaked document from the inner realms of the wisdom movement. With little or no comment, the words themselves are sufficiently unorthodox to discredit the sages in the eyes of most readers. Qoheleth's words thus represent the zenith in the disjunction between religion and wisdom in ancient Israel.

Is this a viable solution to the problem of Ecclesiastes' presence in the Bible? To demonstrate that it is will require a number of steps, beginning with an overview of biblical attitudes to wisdom. This review will reveal a predominantly negative attitude toward wisdom in the Bible, a view that is appropriate if Ecclesiastes is understood to present wisdom in a negative light. Second, since this interpretation depends on the existence of an identifiable group of sages in ancient Israel, it is necessary to determine whether the existence of a group of this sort is historically viable. Third, because the perspective of the epilogist is critical to this reading of Qoheleth's words, we must examine the epilogue in detail. Finally, I will undertake a close reading of Qoheleth's words to determine whether my reading of the epilogue is consistent with them.

Wisdom in the Hebrew Bible

Wisdom Literature occupies a strange place in the Bible. Unlike the historical books or the prophets, it shows little awareness of or interest in the foundational redemptive acts of God as recorded in the Pentateuch. Furthermore, God, as portrayed in the Wisdom Literature, is not a free agent but appears to be bound by the rules of moral cause and effect that the sages supposed were foundational to the universe in which they lived. According to Proverbs 8, even God must operate within the confines dictated by the wisdom that orders the creation.

There is, of course, no reason to expect that there should be a consistent representation of the wise throughout the Hebrew Bible. Nonetheless, Qoheleth's words have traditionally troubled readers precisely because of their presence in these Scriptures and because they present a view of the world that appears diametrically opposed to the theistic framework upon which the Scriptures stand. If, as will be argued later, the epilogist presents Qoheleth's words precisely because they are representative of the wisdom movement's incompatibility with the belief system of the remainder of the Bible, we should not be surprised to find enmity to the sages expressed elsewhere in the canonical books. As will quickly become apparent, outside of the book of Proverbs, wisdom and those who practice it are almost universally decried. Clearly, an interpretation of Ecclesiastes as a book that condemns wisdom would place it firmly within the mainstream of biblical thought.

The Sage in the Historical Books

The Pentateuch

Although Genesis 3 does not use the term חכם ('wisdom, wise'), it contains the first wisdom language in the Hebrew Bible. Here we encounter the serpent who is described as ערום ('clever, wily' but also playing on the naked [ערום] man and woman, ערום being a term found elsewhere only in Job and Proverbs). Furthermore, the fruit forbidden to the man and woman is related to knowledge (דעת) and is seen by the woman as desirable to make one wise (שכיל, a term also common in the Wisdom Literature). This is a scene replete with wisdom terminology and concepts.

What is also clear is that all of the wisdom associations are aligned opposite God. Wisdom language is nowhere used of God in the narrative; rather, it is reserved for the serpent and its dealings with the humans. The serpent is the only character to which any attributes of wisdom are directly assigned, yet it is the serpent who questions God's instructions and implies that God has deceived the man and woman. It denies God's claim that death will follow consumption of the forbidden fruit. Once the fruit has been consumed, rather than elevating the humans to divine status, it brings enmity, pain, and toil into the previously idyllic relationships characterized in chap. 2 of Genesis.[1] Finally, the only recorded knowledge that the humans attain as a result of eating the fruit is the awareness that they are naked. There can be little doubt that wisdom here has very negative connotations.

Outside of the creation story, sages and nonprofessional wise people do not play a large part in the Pentateuch. Among the descendants of Abraham, only Joseph is described as חכם (Gen 41:39). However, Frymer-Kensky observes regarding this depiction that "it is noteworthy that the designation is made by Pharaoh. Within Israel's own system of values (as embodied in the Pentateuch), wisdom and knowledge are not held up as attributes to be emulated."[2] Not only does this attribution of wisdom to Joseph come from Pharaoh (as opposed to the narrator or some other more authoritative character such as God), but Joseph's wisdom is shown to reside only in his receptivity to divine revelation. In this respect the wisdom here ascribed to Joseph is fundamentally dissimilar to the wisdom of Qoheleth, who shows no awareness of authoritative revelation from God.

In Exodus, the majority of the wisdom language refers to technical skill, such as the skill required to engrave or embroider in the service of God (see Exod 7:11; 28:3; 31:3, 6; 35:10, 25–26, 31, 35; 36:2, 4, 8). The only other חכם language appears in reference to the Egyptians, who act in opposition to the Israelites (see Exod 1:10; 7:11).

Within the Pentateuch, it is only in Deuteronomy that we encounter wisdom in a positive light. Here it is designated as one of the attributes to be sought in prospective leaders over the tribes (see Deut 1:13, 15; 34:9). However, this positive representation of wisdom cannot be used as a basis for approving the speculative wisdom of Qoheleth, for the definition of wisdom in Deuteronomy is entirely foreign to Qoheleth:

---

1. See A. J. Hauser, "Genesis 2–3: The Theme of Intimacy and Alienation," in *Art and Meaning: Rhetoric in Biblical Literature* (ed. David J. A. Clines; JSOTSup 19; Sheffield: JSOT Press, 1982).

2. Tikva Frymer-Kensky, "The Sage in the Pentateuch," in *The Sage in Israel and the Ancient Near East* (ed. John G. Gammie and Leo G. Perdue; Winona Lake, Ind.: Eisenbrauns, 1990) 280.

See, I have taught you statutes and rules, as the LORD my God commanded me, that you should do them in the land that you are entering to take possession of it. Keep them and do them, for that will be your wisdom and your understanding in the sight of the peoples, who, when they hear all these statutes, will say, "Surely this great nation is a wise and understanding people." (Deut 4:5–6; ESV)[3]

This wisdom accords with the emphasis of the epilogist and later sages, for it ties wisdom to obedience to God's commandments. As McCarter noted, "the Deuteronomistic view sees the world as governed *ad hoc* by Yahweh, whose decisions are neither predictable nor in any way constrained by a cosmic system. Wisdom, then, is an understanding of divine will, and it is available only through special divine revelation, especially the Torah and prophetic oracles."[4] If Qoheleth knows of God's commands, his failure to refer to them can only be construed as a denial that they contain any value for the activity of life.

The Deuteronomistic History

Wisdom and the wise have both positive and negative associations throughout the Deuteronomistic History. Aside from the typical references to various skills under the wisdom rubric (see, for example, the wise woman of Tekoa in 2 Samuel 14, whose wisdom may well have related to her acting ability), there are a number of passages in which wisdom has clearly negative overtones (one example being the rape of Tamar in 2 Samuel 13), as well as a few in which it has positive overtones (such as the initial examples of Solomon's wisdom in 1 Kings 3).

In all of this, however, it is Solomon who dominates the presentation of wisdom, particularly in 1 Kings. Although Solomon's wisdom is presented positively in 1 Kings 3–10, the character of Solomon is tainted by his failings and apostasy as recorded in 1 Kings 11, problems that inevitably sullied his association with wisdom. At the very least, it is clear that even wisdom of the sort that Solomon possessed cannot guarantee that a person will remain faithful to the law of God.[5] McCarter writes: "Despite its preservation of this

---

3. See also the comments of Frymer-Kensky, in ibid., 280–85; P. Kyle McCarter Jr., "The Sage in the Deuteronomistic History," in ibid., 292–93.

4. McCarter, in ibid., 293.

5. A number of scholars suggest that Solomon's association with wisdom is more negative than positive. See G. E. Mendenhall, "The Shady Side of Wisdom: The Date and Purpose of Genesis 3," in *A Light unto My Path: Old Testament Studies in Honor of Jacob M. Myers* (ed. R. D. Heim, H. N. Bream, and C. A. Moore; Philadelphia: Temple University Press, 1974) 324–25; Martin Noth, "Die Bewährung von Salomos 'Göttlicher Weisheit,' "

tradition about Solomon's wisdom, however, the Deuteronomistic History does not present a wholly or even predominantly positive picture of the traditional wisdom of the sage. . . . Deuteronomistic thought did not accept the view that being a great sage was enough to be a great king, so that Solomon's reign is presented as a mixture of successes and failures."[6] The notion that Solomon's association with wisdom may be negative is enhanced by the observation that any discussion of wisdom in the Deuteronomistic History ceases with Solomon. Although Prov 25:1 suggests that there may have been ongoing influence by wisdom within Israel, particularly in Hezekiah's time, the record of Solomon's reign and downfall spells an end to the significance of wisdom in the Deuteronomist's historiographical record. Instead, the focus is consistently placed on obedience to the law and the word revealed by the prophets in determining the success of a monarch, rather than on individual wisdom.

The Sage in the Prophets

References to sages and wisdom in the prophetic books are concentrated in Isaiah and Jeremiah. Although Isaiah does speak positively of wisdom, it is only when God's wisdom is the subject (see Isa 11:2; 31:2; 33:6). When Isaiah (both First and Second Isaiah) speaks of human wisdom or the wise, he invariably condemns them. Human wisdom, according to Isaiah, has the propensity for deluding those who possess it (Isa 47:10; compare 5:21; 19:11–12) and will ultimately be confounded by God (Isa 29:14; see also Isa 10:13; 44:25).

Jeremiah, like Isaiah, praises wisdom when it is attributed to God (for example, Jer 10:12) but is even more scathing in his attack on human wisdom than Isaiah. For example, Jer 8:8–9 reads: "How can you say, 'We are wise, and the law of the Lord is with us,' when, in fact, the false pen of the scribes has made it into a lie? The wise shall be put to shame, they shall be dismayed and taken; since they have rejected the word of the Lord, what wisdom is in

---

in *Wisdom in Israel and the Ancient Near East* (ed. M. Noth and D. Winton Thomas; Leiden: Brill, 1955) 225–37; R. B. Y. Scott, "Solomon and the Beginnings of Wisdom in Israel," in *Studies in Ancient Israelite Wisdom* (ed. J. L. Crenshaw; New York: KTAV, 1976) 262–79; compare with Walter Brueggemann, "The Social Significance of Solomon as a Patron of Wisdom," in *The Sage in Israel and the Ancient Near East* (ed. John G. Gammie and Leo G. Perdue; Winona Lake, Ind.: Eisenbrauns, 1990) 128, who writes that "Solomonic wisdom is characterized by the Deuteronomist in ironic ways to show that it did not work."

6. McCarter, "The Sage in the Deuteronomistic History," 290.

them?" (NRSV).[7] With such a verbal attack, it is little wonder that opposition to Jeremiah appears: "Then they said, 'Come, let us make plots against Jeremiah—for instruction shall not perish from the priest, nor counsel from the wise, nor the word from the prophet. Come, let us bring charges against him, and let us not heed any of his words'" (Jer 18:18; NRSV).[8]

In both Isaiah and Jeremiah, the wise to whom the prophets address their invective are generally identifiable members of an official class, just as priests and even prophets apparently were. A number of scholars have identified the wise as politicians—members of the governing elite responsible for counseling the king and influencing national policy. McKane, for example, writes: "The wise against whom the pre-exilic Judahite prophets conducted a polemic were statesmen in the service of the kings of Judah on whose expertise and sagacity (*ʿēṣâ*) the kings relied for advice and policy."[9]

Further, Van Leeuwen has shown that the prophets (particularly Isaiah) employed some of the ideas found in Proverbs to attack the wise themselves (for example, Isa 5:21; compare with Prov 26:5, 12, 16).[10] For Van Leeuwen this suggests a chronology whereby Proverbs formed a foundation from which some of the sages had departed.[11]

---

7. M. Fishbane, *Biblical Interpretation in Ancient Israel* (Oxford: Clarendon, 1985) 32ff. has a useful discussion of the scribal associations of this and other passages.

8. It is clear from both this verse and the context of Jer 8:8–9 that his attack was directed at more than just the sages; it included the priest and even other prophets.

9. William McKane, "Jeremiah and the Wise," in *Wisdom in Ancient Israel: Essays in Honour of J. A. Emerton* (ed. John Day, Robert P. Gordon, and H. G. M. Williamson; Cambridge: Cambridge University Press, 1995) 142–51; see also idem, *Prophets and Wise Men* (London: SCM, 1965) 65–91; J. Fichtner, "Jesaja unter den Weisen," *TLZ* 74 (1949) 75–80; J. William Whedbee, *Isaiah and Wisdom* (Nashville: Abingdon, 1971) esp. 111–48; Joseph Jensen, *The Use of tôrâ by Isaiah: His Debate with the Wisdom Tradition* (CBQMS 3; Washington, D.C.: Catholic Biblical Association, 1973) 51–58; H. G. M. Williamson, "Isaiah and the Wise," in *Wisdom in Ancient Israel: Essays in Honour of J. A. Emerton* (ed. John Day, Robert P. Gordon, and H. G. M. Williamson; Cambridge: Cambridge University Press, 1995) 133–41.

10. Raymond C. Van Leeuwen, "The Sage in the Prophetic Literature," in *The Sage in Israel and the Ancient Near East* (ed. John G. Gammie and Leo G. Perdue; Winona Lake, Ind.: Eisenbrauns, 1990) 298–99.

11. However, Van Leeuwen apparently fails to consider the possibility that there was an evolutionary development in the wisdom movement of the sort that Proverbs might reflect a type of wisdom from one period of history, while the wisdom against which Isaiah speaks might reflect the wisdom of a different period. He does criticize those who see Proverbs as a later pious or religious development of the wisdom movement (ibid., 300 n. 26). The converse, however, could be true: Proverbs represents a naïve or primitive wisdom that later developed into the more speculative wisdom of Qoheleth and became the focus of attack

Both sages and prophets are presented as aspiring to influence political decisions within ancient Israel—the sages occupying official roles in government of advising the monarch, and the prophets claiming to speak on behalf
of God. It is not surprising that this should result in some degree of contention
and even animosity between the two groups, and this is reflected in the statements recorded in the prophetic books regarding the wise.[12] Uniquely, however, Qoheleth's words may represent the only record of the enmity that the
sages felt toward the prophets (see Qoh 5:3, 7).[13] For Qoheleth, and thus for
the wisdom movement, those who occupied religious or prophetic roles and
claimed to speak for God were fools. However, Qoheleth's words ultimately
discredited his own position in the eyes of the epilogist.

The negativity of the prophets toward the wise also lends some support to
the argument that the sages represented a specific, identifiable group in ancient Israelite society—at least at certain periods of history. It is unlikely that
prophetic invective would have been directed merely toward relatively incon-
spicuous individuals who could claim some degree of wisdom. Rather, the
wise people that the prophets criticized clearly held positions of influence in
society (for example, see Isa 44:25; Jer 8:8–9; 9:22[23]; 18:18), and thus
others may have aspired to join their ranks.[14]

The Sage in the Writings

Psalms

Although it has long been acknowledged that a number of the Psalms reflect concerns characteristic of Wisdom Literature (although scholars differ

---

by both the prophets and Qoheleth's epilogist. I am not suggesting, however, that there is
any evidence that Ecclesiastes can be assigned a date similar to Isaiah's or Jeremiah's.

12. For a discussion of these matters with specific reference to Isaiah, see Jensen, *The
Use of tôrâ by Isaiah*, 51–54. In particular he writes regarding the situation in which the
king was consulting sages for counsel:

> But if, during such deliberations, a prophet should stand up to claim that he knows what Yah-
> weh's *ʿēṣâ* is, a completely new situation is born for the wise man. His choices are limited: he
> can either accept the word of the prophet and be put out of business as a counsellor, or he can
> doubt the word of the prophet and try by every means to discredit his message. The temptation
> to the latter course would be very strong, especially for those convinced that their counsel was
> wise and would be effective, and the wise men of Isaiah's day seem to have succumbed to it.

13. Further evidence supporting this case can be seen in Qoheleth's repeated assertion
that the future is unknowable and unpredictable (e.g., Qoh 8:7; 10:14) and that the world
operates in a perpetual cycle that reveals no progress or purpose (e.g., Qoh 1:4–11).

14. It should also be noted that there is little to distinguish the clearly official position
associated with the sages in prophetic speech directed to nations outside Israel from the language used of the wise within Israel (see Isa 19:11–12; Jer 50:35; 51:57).

somewhat regarding which psalms these are), there are only a few direct references among the Psalms to wisdom or the wise. Furthermore, when wisdom is mentioned, it is frequently tied to obedience to the commandments of God, thus aligning it with the characteristic use of wisdom in Deuteronomy, where it is essentially reduced to heeding God's revealed will (see, for example, Ps 19:8[7]; 51:8[6]; 111:10; 119:98).[15]

From the perspective of Qoheleth's wisdom, Psalm 49 is the most interesting of the Psalms, for it reflects a number of motifs also found in the words of Qoheleth. Verses 11–13[10–12], for example, are strongly reminiscent of Qoheleth's own thinking about the finality of death (see Qoh 3:16–22):

> Surely one sees that even wise people die;
> fools and spiritually insensitive people all pass away
> and leave their wealth to others.
> Their grave becomes their permanent residence,
> their eternal dwelling place.
> They name their lands after themselves,
> but, despite their wealth, people do not last,
> they are like animals that perish. (NET)

Although Ps 49:11–13[10–12] may appear to reflect closely Qoheleth's own thinking about death, the psalm appears to offer some hope of distinction in death, some hope of redemption from Sheol. Verse 16[15] reads:

> But God will rescue my life from the power of Sheol;
> certainly he will pull me to safety. (NET)

Within this psalm, this expression of hope appears out of place. Craigie resolves this difficulty by treating this verse as a quotation of the misguided hope of the wealthy that the psalmist rejects,[16] but this reading is uncertain. First, other than the change to first-person speech, there is no indication of a quotation (such as the presence of some form of introductory formula along the lines of "the rich say"). Second, the psalmist earlier stated that the confidence of the wealthy lay in their wealth (Ps 49:7–8[6–7]), implying that they felt that through their wealth they could secure their redemption. Consequently it is best to treat these words as an expression of the psalmist's personal hope in redemption from Sheol.

---

15. J. K. Kuntz ("The Canonical Wisdom Psalms of Ancient Israel: Their Rhetorical, Thematic, and Formal Dimensions," in *Rhetorical Criticism: Essays in Honor of James Muilenburg* [ed. J. J. Jackson and M. Kessler; Pittsburgh: Pickwick, 1974] 212–13), for example, writes: "In all instances the sage manifests his willingness to subordinate himself to the divine will. . . . His task is to comprehend that will as it is revealed in the written Torah and his joy is to experience unmitigated delight in his thorough knowledge of the law."

16. Peter C. Craigie, *Psalms 1–50* (WBC 19; Waco, Tex.: Word, 1983) 360.

Regardless of whether this psalm does in fact express some hope that beyond death there remains some hope of redemption, and in spite of the parallelism with Qoheleth's own thoughts on death, the psalm cannot be said to
offer approval of Qoheleth's wisdom. The psalmist observes that death re-
duces all to the same level, but he does not proceed from this observation to
deny or contradict any of the fundamental teachings of the remainder of the
Hebrew Bible.

The Psalms, in the few places in which wisdom and the wise are mentioned, are less critical of the wisdom movement than the portions of the
Hebrew Bible reviewed above. However, they do not present a particularly
positive attitude toward human wisdom either, unless it is wisdom grounded
in obedience to God and thus a type of wisdom incompatible with the wisdom
of Qoheleth.

Proverbs

In some respects, the presentation of wisdom in Proverbs is unique in the
Hebrew Bible. Wisdom is presented here in an (almost) unequivocally positive manner.[17] Furthermore, when wisdom is treated positively elsewhere, it
is tied to obedience to the revealed commands of God. In Proverbs, by contrast, obedience is predominantly to the commands of the father (see, for example, Prov 2:1; 3:1; 4:4; 6:20). Although there is frequent use of the divine
name, YHWH, he is the creator, not the redeemer or lawgiver, in Proverbs. By
presenting wisdom utterances in an aphoristic form, the book of Proverbs
leaves itself open to naïve interpretations, simplistically concluding that there
is a simple corollary between action and consequence. A link is frequently
made, for example, between righteousness and wealth or gain on the one hand
and wickedness and poverty or loss on the other (see Prov 3:33; 10:3, 11, 16,
24; etc.). Any selective reading of this material will result in a view of wisdom that does not mesh with reality and that could feasibly result in the naïve
judgmentalism displayed by Job's friends.[18]

However, a fair reading of Proverbs must be more generous, for although
individual aphorisms tend to present a skewed picture of reality, they may be

---

17. There are a (very) few passages in Proverbs indicating that wisdom is not unequivocally good, such as Prov 3:7 (compare with Prov 17:28; 28:11).

18. Bruce K. Waltke ("Does Proverbs Promise Too Much?" *AUSS* 34 [1996] 325) correctly notes that the form lies at the heart of the problem: "Individual proverbs express
truth, but, restricted by the aphorism's demand for terseness, they cannot express the whole
truth. By their very nature they are partial utterances which cannot protect themselves by
qualification." See also Raymond C. Van Leeuwen, "Wealth and Poverty: System and Contradiction in Proverbs," *Hebrew Studies* 33 (1992) 28.

balanced with sayings elsewhere in the collection that present alternate, occasionally contradictory, views. The most blatant of these is Prov 26:4–5, which indicates that the aphorisms of Proverbs were not intended to be read as absolute moral laws but as stimuli to personal wisdom.[19]

Furthermore, Proverbs itself is not unequivocally positive in its presentation of wisdom but shows an awareness that the form can be misused:

> Like legs that hang limp from the lame,
>   so is a proverb in the mouth of fools.
> Like a thorn that goes into the hand of a drunkard,
>   so is a proverb in the mouth of a fool. (Prov 26:7, 9; NET)

Proverbs is even critical of the more speculative wisdom typical of Qoheleth, which abandons the foundational notion of fear of YHWH:

> Trust in YHWH with all your heart,
>   and do not rely on your own understanding.
>   (Prov 3:5; see also 26:12, 16; 28:26)

Thus, a holistic reading of Proverbs should produce a balanced form of wisdom in which there is no absolute law of moral cause and effect in the world and in which individual aphorisms are not treated as inflexible rules. This wisdom comes not simply from knowing many proverbs but from an understanding of when and where to apply them. This wisdom must ultimately be grounded in a theistic framework, which was itself foreign to the thought of Qoheleth.

Nonetheless, the inflexible and narrow application of the concepts of wisdom by Job's "friends" shows that wisdom of the sort found in Proverbs ultimately did lead (at least sometimes) to such an inflexible, narrow, simplistic understanding of the world. This point is noted by Farmer regarding Qoheleth: "we can see that he challenges the retributive expectations which surface in so many parts of the book of Proverbs. We can also see that Qohelet counters and denies the universal validity of many of the observations made by the wise who contributed to Proverbs."[20]

Of all the books in the Hebrew Bible, Proverbs is the most consistently positive in its treatment of human wisdom. This is hardly surprising, but given the predominantly negative attitude to wisdom elsewhere, we should find ourselves *less* surprised that Ecclesiastes, a text that we will see presents a predominantly negative attitude toward wisdom when viewed through the

---

19. See ibid., 25–36; Waltke, "Does Proverbs Promise Too Much?" 319–36.

20. Kathleen A. Farmer, *Proverbs and Ecclesiastes: Who Knows What Is Good?* (ITC; Grand Rapids: Eerdmans, 1991) 198.

eyes of the epilogist, finds a place in the Hebrew Bible and *more* surprised that Proverbs does.

Job

The narrative conflict of the Job story is predicated upon the notion that suffering is evidence of an action or behavior that offends God, a notion firmly founded in traditional wisdom thought (e.g., Prov 3:33–35; 10:2–17). The prologue asserts emphatically that Job is unmatched in his righteousness, yet he suffers. The friends all appeal to this presupposition, seeking to convince Job that he must acknowledge his sin (e.g., Job 4:7; 11:4–6; 15:17–35).[21] Furthermore, there are a number of indications that the friends are employing arguments from the wisdom tradition (see Job 15:18; 32:7; 33:33).[22] Ultimately, the arguments of the friends are shown by God in Job 42:7 to be false, whereas Job is said to have been right in his arguments.

Job's friends' repeated affirmation of and appeal to the fundamental logic of the wisdom movement, the doctrine of retribution, together with Job's repeated refusal to concede to their assertion that he is guilty of a hidden sin suggests that acceptance of this doctrine was deeply ingrained in the audience's beliefs. The narrator emphatically rebuts this belief by first establishing Job's innocence in the prologue, then by repeatedly presenting Job's plea of his own blamelessness, and finally (and most emphatically of all) by having God speak in Job's defense.

Thus, the book of Job functions to undermine the wisdom tradition, for it invalidates the presupposition that God will ensure that the righteous prosper and the wicked suffer. God is not bound by the rules established by the sage, and human wisdom is incapable of discerning the reasons for (at the very least) suffering. These points are stated eloquently in the poem of Job 28, which asserts that true wisdom is not available to humans but belongs to God alone. In taking this stance vis-à-vis the wisdom traditions, the book of Job concurs with the predominantly negative attitude toward wisdom found in the remainder of the Hebrew Bible and undermines the presuppositions of the sages.

---

21. See William J. Dumbrell (*The Faith of Israel* [Leicester: Apollos, 1988] 219), who writes, "Starting with the premise that God protects the lot of the righteous (4:1–6), Eliphaz and then Bildad and Zophar develop the inference that since Job is unprotected from adversity, he must be unrighteous."

22. Samuel Terrien notes that Job's friends are "thoroughly at ease" with the "most typical form of wisdom speech," the proverb, in "Job as a Sage," in *The Sage in Israel and the Ancient Near East* (ed. John G. Gammie and Leo G. Perdue; Winona Lake, Ind.: Eisenbrauns, 1990) 233.

Daniel

The book of Daniel, set as it is in a royal court and populated with advisers to the king (including the heroes of the story), has a strong focus on wisdom. Daniel and his three companions are selected precisely because they exhibit the attributes desirable in an adviser to the king (Dan 1:4). However, the author of the book of Daniel does not exalt wisdom in this presentation, for it is patently clear that the wisdom of Daniel and his friends comes from God (Dan 1:17). Furthermore, through repeated conflicts with the other sages in the royal court, it becomes apparent that the wisdom of Daniel far surpasses their wisdom (Dan 1:20). The wisdom of Daniel and his companions is rooted in their dependence upon God and their faithfulness to him. This is well expressed by Goldingay, who writes:

> God, the true God of Israel, is the source of the young men's insight and of Daniel's achievements in the Babylonians' own areas of expertise. There is no positive theology of pagan or secular learning here, but rather the assurance that it can be triumphed over. If there were two main attitudes to foreign wisdom in the postexilic period, Daniel belongs ultimately with the more exclusive, not the more open. . . . By allowing the young men to be open to alien wisdom but then portraying theirs as superior, Daniel makes the same points as Isa 47, perhaps even more strongly. It asserts that there is insight about life, history, and politics . . . that only God endows. . . . His involvement thus relativizes military power, political power, and the power of human wisdom.[23]

Thus, the treatment of wisdom in the book of Daniel finds close ties with the treatment of wisdom elsewhere in the Hebrew Bible. Wisdom that comes from God and is manifest in an obedient and faithful life, wisdom that is founded not on human ingenuity but on divine revelation—this is the wisdom of Daniel and his friends that is affirmed by the author of Daniel. By contrast, the wisdom that is based on human ingenuity without reference to God—wisdom like that of Qoheleth—is depicted as impotent and even evil, standing in opposition to God and his faithful servants.

Other Writings

Wisdom does not appear to be a major concern in the remaining writings of the Hebrew Bible. For example, although Canticles is often associated with the Wisdom Literature, it makes no mention of wisdom or the wise. Only in Chronicles is there any substantial reference to wisdom—and there once again in reference to Solomon. Chronicles, unlike Kings, does not highlight

---

23. John E. Goldingay, *Daniel* (WBC 30; Waco, Tex.: Word, 1987) 27.

the negative aspects of Solomon's reign and thus does not present his wisdom in an ambiguous light. However, this is largely a reflection of the Chronicler's differing priorities in recording the history of Israel: in the account of Solomon's reign, it draws attention to the construction and dedication of the temple to the exclusion of almost all other material.[24]

The Sage in Noncanonical Texts

Although most of the noncanonical texts (specifically the various apocalypses, pseudepigraphic, and deuterocanonical texts) reflect a period later than the bulk of the canonical material, they are of some interest in that they reveal the development of the wisdom movement beyond Ecclesiastes.[25] Examination of these texts quickly reveals that their presentation of the function of the sage bears little resemblance to the wisdom of Qoheleth. For example, Collins notes regarding the apocalyptic and pseudepigraphic literature:

> [T]he figures to whom the major apocalypses are ascribed, Enoch, Daniel, Ezra, Baruch, are sages or scribes. Daniel came to be regarded as a prophet already in antiquity (Matt 24:15; Josephus, *Antiquities* 10:11:7) but in the Hebrew Bible he is presented as a *maśkîl* and included among the wise men of Babylon (Dan 2:13). There is here a certain blurring of the distinction between sage and prophet, and the apocalyptic sages bear greater resemblance to Ezekiel or Zechariah than to Sirach or Ecclesiastes, but they are sages nonetheless.[26]

However, Daniel is the only one of these characters who is specifically identified as a sage—the remainder are all scribes. Although this may reflect a blurring of these categories, the distinction is worth mentioning because it could also reflect a diminution in the significance and prestige of the sages in Israel. Furthermore, the fact that these characters bear a closer resemblance to prophetic figures than to traditional wisdom figures such as Qoheleth may be attributed to a triumph of the prophetic vision over the sage's counsel.

---

24. As Dumbrell (*The Faith of Israel*, 276) observes: "The most significant event of his reign is the dedication of the temple, and the major moments connected with it—the transfer of the ark (chap. 5) and Solomon's prayer of dedication (7:1–3)—are both marked by divine epiphanies. As he does with David, the Chronicler in his presentation of Solomon ignores almost everything which is noncultic."

25. While I am deliberately avoiding entering the debate over the date of composition of Ecclesiastes, most scholars agree that it does reflect a period earlier than most of the noncanonical texts that fall in these categories.

26. John J. Collins, "The Sage in the Apocalyptic and Pseudepigraphic Literature," in *The Sage in Israel and the Ancient Near East* (ed. John G. Gammie and Leo G. Perdue; Winona Lake, Ind.: Eisenbrauns, 1990) 343.

The deuterocanonical literature, however, does preserve not only characters depicted as sages but also literature that directly emulates Wisdom Literature. Nonetheless, in both Sirach and the Wisdom of Solomon, the emphases of the sages shifted to obedience to God and the Law, as Gammie writes: "In the era following the Exile, Israel's sages came more and more to venerate the Torah. . . . Ben Sira shows himself to be very much in this tradition, which celebrates the Torah," and further: "Similarly, like the authors of the wisdom psalms Ben Sira taught that the keeping of the commandments was the way to wisdom (Sir 6:37, 23:27)."[27] Indeed, the Wisdom of Solomon goes further by actively criticizing the type of wisdom typical of Qoheleth and other sages by ascribing it to "the ungodly" and describing their reasoning as "unsound" (Wis 1:16–2:24).

Thus the later sages come to reflect the priorities of both Qoheleth's epilogist and Deuteronomy, wherein true wisdom is ultimately a reflection of one's obedience to the revealed will of God in the Law.

Conclusion

In spite of its brevity, this survey has been sufficient to demonstrate that Spina's observations regarding wisdom are valid:

> [E]ven if most that has been identified as wisdom *is* wisdom, that in no way diminishes the fact that wisdom is frequently depicted in a negative light in the Bible. When taken as a whole, it is not nearly as upbeat or nobly humanistic as has sometimes been claimed. In addition, when one considers that Job and Qoheleth are also negative in the sense that both reject the possibility of securing one's existence and guaranteeing one's future by means of wisdom, then the amount of positive wisdom is reduced even further. Some scholars have even questioned whether Solomon's association with wisdom is to be viewed positively or negatively, though for the most part the canonical form of the text seems to indicate a positive connection.[28]

---

27. John G. Gammie, "The Sage in Sirach," in ibid., 360. See, for example, Sir 38:34b (Greek).

28. Frank A. Spina, "Qoheleth and the Reformation of Wisdom," in *The Quest for the Kingdom of God: Studies in Honor of George E. Mendenhall* (ed. H. B. Huffman, F. A. Spina, and A. R. W. Green; Winona Lake, Ind.: Eisenbrauns, 1983) 271. For further discussion of this matter, see James L. Crenshaw, "Method in Determining Wisdom Influence upon Historical Literature," *JBL* 88 (1969), which Spina uses on his p. 271. Other useful references on this matter are: Mendenhall, "The Shady Side of Wisdom: The Date and Purpose of Genesis 3," 323–24; McKane, *Prophets and Wise Men*; and Jensen, *The Use of tôrâ by Isaiah*.

The presentation of wisdom in the Hebrew Bible can largely be divided into two categories. First, there is divine wisdom, originating with God, revealed through prophetic speech or encoded in the Law, and manifest through obedience to the word of God. This wisdom is consistently given a positive presentation and is achieved more through obedience than through philosophical contemplation.

Second, there is human wisdom, wisdom that rests solely in the application of human intellect to the problems of life in the world. This even encompasses the analysis of Job's suffering by his companions, and even more so does it describe the attempts that Qoheleth makes to comprehend his world. This wisdom, although represented as being based on theistic presuppositions, is almost universally presented negatively. The consistent message of the Hebrew Bible is that inquiry of this kind is bound to fail, for God alone has access to this information.

This background information is vital if we are to arrive at an understanding of the place of Ecclesiastes in the canon. The interpretation of Ecclesiastes proposed here fits well with the presentation of wisdom throughout the remainder of the Hebrew Bible. It will become apparent that Qoheleth is a prime example, even the preeminent example, of the failure of human wisdom. He is praised by the epilogist for his forthright account of the inadequacies and limitations of wisdom. Then, declaring the bankruptcy of the wisdom movement in light of Qoheleth's admissions, the epilogist points to an alternative wisdom and claims access to the answers for which Qoheleth searched in vain—answers revealed by God. Thus, although Qoheleth stands in stark contrast to and even denounces the type of wisdom approved by the remainder of the Hebrew Bible, obedience to God, Ecclesiastes as a whole affirms this sort of wisdom.

The Wise in the Hebrew Bible

A clear prerequisite for the notion that Ecclesiastes presents some form of polemic against the wisdom movement is that there must have been, at the point in Israel's history corresponding to the composition of the work, a wisdom movement to criticize. Unfortunately, establishing the existence of a group of wise people or sages is not without its difficulties. Whybray, for example, has written that

> [T]he question remains whether it can be convincingly argued that Qohelet was a "wisdom writer" in the sense that he belonged to an exclusive guild of "wise men" which had preserved its corporate identity throughout the centuries since the time of the early Judean monarchy. There seems to be no concrete evidence for this. . . . It is not at all certain that the authors of these books would have seen themselves as belonging to a single class distinct from all other Israelites, except in the sense that they were all educated men.[1]

---

1. Whybray, *Ecclesiastes* (OTG; Sheffield: Sheffield Academic Press, 1989) 57–58; see also Van Leeuwen, "The Sage in the Prophetic Literature," in *The Sage in Israel and the Ancient Near East* (ed. J. G. Gammie and L. G. Perdue; Winona Lake, Ind.: Eisenbrauns, 1990) 297. Whybray appears to have become more equivocal on the issue since his work on the topic in 1974 (R. N. Whybray, *The Intellectual Tradition in the Old Testament* [BZAW 135; Berlin: de Gruyter, 1974] chap. 3), which was itself a considerable about-face from his view in 1965 (R. N. Whybray, *Wisdom in Proverbs* [SBT 45; Naperville, Ill.: Allenson, 1965]). See also Lester L. Grabbe, *Priests, Prophets, Diviners, Sages: A Socio-historical Study of Religious Specialists in Ancient Israel* (Valley Forge, Pa.: Trinity, 1995) 175–76. Rather than Qoheleth's being critical of a wisdom movement (or, in Whybray's words, "wisdom tradition"), Whybray (*Ecclesiastes*, 58) suggests that "it may be more fruitful to regard [Qoheleth] as an independent thinker who set himself to make a critical examination, not just of a distinct 'wisdom tradition', but of his own native religious tradition as a whole—that is, of the main religious tradition enshrined in the Jewish Scriptures. There is ample evidence of this." This is rather unlikely, however, given Qoheleth's failure to engage that tradition at anything beyond the most fundamental level (e.g., see below, p. 146). Blenkinsopp has responded to Whybray's claim that חכם never refers to a member of an identifiable class of specialists by noting that "Whybray was surely mistaken in supposing that a tradition can be sustained and transmitted without institutional grounding" (Joseph Blenkinsopp, *Sage, Priest, Prophet: Religious and Intellectual Leadership in Ancient Israel* [Library of Ancient Israel; ed. Douglas A. Knight; Louisville: Westminster/John Knox, 1995] 11). Blenkinsopp goes on to note that the likelihood that חכם is used to refer to a class of intellectuals (usually teachers) increases toward the later period of Israel's history.

However, the task of demonstrating the existence of these sages is somewhat less daunting than Whybray indicates. If the epilogist attacks the sages, it is only necessary to establish the existence of the sages at the time the epilogist wrote, not throughout the history of ancient Israel. Although it is impossible to demonstrate this with absolute certainty, there is evidence that, at the time of Ecclesiastes' composition, there was an identifiable wisdom movement of some form.

Ecclesiastes' Sitz im Leben

In our attempt to establish the identity of the sages referred to in the epilogue of Ecclesiastes, we face two quite difficult problems. First, Ecclesiastes lacks any readily identifiable historical references (such as regnal years for monarchs or explicit references to international events), which complicates the task of finding a place for the book in history. Second, we need then to reconstruct some of the details of the social history of Ecclesiastes' time from sources external to Ecclesiastes, and these are (at best) rather thin on the ground for any period of Israel's history.

Qoheleth's Language

Most attempts to date Ecclesiastes focus on its language.[2] Scholars have offered numerous (not necessarily mutually exclusive) accounts of the unusual Hebrew found in Ecclesiastes. They have argued for Aramaic influence (even arguing that Qoheleth was translated from an Aramaic original), similarities with Mishnaic Hebrew, the presence of Persian loanwords, and even Phoenician and Greek influence on Ecclesiastes' language.[3] Any or all of these con-

---

2. A number of comprehensive analyses of Qoheleth's language have appeared in recent years, including Choon-Leong Seow, "Linguistic Evidence and the Dating of Qohelet," *JBL* 115 (1996) 643–66; B. Isaksson, *Studies in the Language of Qoheleth: With Special Emphasis on the Verbal System* (Studia Semitica Upsaliensia 10; Stockholm: Almqvist & Wiksell, 1987); Daniel C. Fredericks, *Qoheleth's Language: Re-evaluating Its Nature and Date* (Lewiston, N.Y.: Edwin Mellen, 1988); A. Schoors, *The Preacher Sought to Find Pleasing Words: A Study of the Language of Qoheleth* (OLA 41; Leuven: Peeters, 1992); Ian Young, *Diversity in Pre-exilic Hebrew* (Tübingen: Mohr, 1993) 148–54. These studies question the tendency of recent commentators to assign a third-century date.

3. *Aramaic influence* has been identified in Qoheleth's use of both Aramaic loanwords and Aramaic syntactical features. Among those who have argued for an Aramaic original are Frank Zimmerman, "The Aramaic Provenance of Qohelet," *JQR* 36 (1945–46) 17–45; Charles C. Torrey, "The Question of the Original Language of Qoheleth," *JQR* 39 (1948–49) 151–60; H. L. Ginsberg, *Studies in Koheleth* (New York: Jewish Theological Seminary, 1952). *Similarities with Mishnaic Hebrew* have been identified by S. R. Driver, *An Introduction to the Literature of the Old Testament* (9th ed.; Edinburgh: T. & T. Clark / New York: Scribner's, 1913) 474–75. *Persian loanwords* identified include פרדס (Qoh 2:5) and

clusions have consistently prompted scholars to date the book in the postexilic period, any time from the late fifth century B.C.E. to around 150 B.C.E.[4]

Recent studies have questioned the value of this sort of analysis for determining the date of the original composition of any ancient text for which we do not have an autograph. Daniel Fredericks, for example, has questioned the use of linguistic arguments to establish a late date for Ecclesiastes.[5] Ian Young has examined the various linguistic factors usually considered indicative of a late date and found the evidence far more ambiguous than most are willing to admit.[6] Furthermore, Longman has correctly noted that "so little is known about the transmission of the biblical text during its earliest stages that we cannot rule out linguistic updating. The so-called late forms may not in fact have been original to the book but may reflect the updating of vocabulary and grammar by later scribes so their contemporaries could understand the book better."[7]

Consequently, although the general consensus is that Ecclesiastes' language points to a postexilic provenance for the work, this conclusion is hardly certain, and we must explore other means in order to identify Ecclesiastes' Sitz im Leben more precisely.

פתגם (Qoh 8:11). However, both the value of these words for determining a date and their Persian provenance are questioned by Young (*Diversity in Pre-exilic Hebrew*, 70–71, 161–62). Mitchell Dahood has argued that *Phoenician influence* is apparent in Qoheleth ("The Phoenician Background of Qoheleth," *Bib* 47 [1966] 210–12; "Canaanite-Phoenician Influence in Qoheleth," *Bib* 33 [1952] 30–52, 191–221; "The Language of Qoheleth," *CBQ* 14 [1952] 227–32; "Qoheleth and Northwest Semitic Philology," *Bib* 43 [1962] 264–82; "Canaanite Words in Qoheleth 10,20," *Bib* 46 [1965] 349–65), but his arguments have been ably refuted by others, including James R. Davila, "Qoheleth and Northern Hebrew," *Maarav* 5/6 (1990) 69–87; and Choon-Leong Seow, *Ecclesiastes* (AB 18C; New York: Doubleday, 1997) 15–16. Seow concludes that there is no compelling evidence for Phoenician influence, even though it cannot be ruled out entirely.

4. The discovery of fragments of Qoheleth among the DSS, which are dated to around 150 B.C.E., provide this *terminus ante quem* (see Seow, "Linguistic Evidence and the Dating of Qohelet," 643). Most recent commentaries date the work to the third century B.C.E. (see ibid., 644 n. 7 for references); some other suggested dates include: 450–350 B.C.E. (idem, *Ecclesiastes*, 21) and 250–225 B.C.E. (Crenshaw).

5. Fredericks, *Qoheleth's Language* (Lewiston, N.Y.: Edwin Mellen, 1988).

6. Young, *Diversity in Pre-exilic Hebrew*, 148–54; idem, "Late Biblical Hebrew and Hebrew Inscriptions," in *Biblical Hebrew: Chronology and Typology* (ed. Ian Young; JSOTSup 369; Sheffield: Sheffield Academic Press, 2003) 276–311; idem, "Concluding Reflections," in ibid., 312–17. In the latter essay, Young constructs a history of the Hebrew language in which Qoheleth's language could plausibly be preexilic.

7. Tremper Longman III, *The Book of Ecclesiastes* (NICOT; Grand Rapids: Eerdmans, 1998) 10. One should note, however, that there is no clear evidence of updating with respect to Ecclesiastes.

Historical References in Ecclesiastes

Another means to locate Ecclesiastes historically is to identify any apparent historical references in the text, and scholars have found a number of references. The first portion of the text to make historical allusions is chap. 1, where there are various indications that Qoheleth should be identified with Solomon. The epilogist initially identifies Qoheleth as "the son of David, king in Jerusalem" (Qoh 1:1), after which Qoheleth himself claims to have been king in Jerusalem (Qoh 1:12) and to have obtained greater wisdom than all in Jerusalem before him (Qoh 1:16). Subsequently, Qoheleth sets out to explore what is done under the heavens (Qoh 1:13), a task that includes vast building projects and other tasks that are immediately reminiscent of the reign of Solomon (see 1 Kings 6; 9–10).

It is no surprise, then, that Qoheleth has traditionally been identified with Solomon. The only other king in the Davidic dynasty with any recorded wisdom associations is Hezekiah (see Prov 25:1). For Qoheleth's words to have originated with either of these kings, a preexilic date for the book would be required.

However, identifying Qoheleth with either of these two kings is problematic. Qoh 1:16 appears to indicate that there were many generations prior to Qoheleth in Jerusalem, which was not true for the biblical Solomon.[8] Qoh 1:12 suggests that Qoheleth, while having been king at some point in his life, was no longer ruling. Neither Solomon nor Hezekiah is recorded as being overthrown or having abdicated. Furthermore, Qoheleth's claim to be wiser than all in Jerusalem who had preceded him would be a bold claim indeed from the mouth of Hezekiah (given the renown of Solomon's wisdom, any claim to have greater wisdom than he would not likely be accepted by the reader). Finally, the failure of Qoheleth or the epilogist to identify Qoheleth suggests that the function of these allusions was not to identify Qoheleth unequivocally with a well-known historical figure.

Consequently, the vast majority of scholars agree that Qoheleth was neither Solomon nor Hezekiah (nor, for that matter, any historical king).[9] Rather,

---

8. It is not true unless pre-Israelite monarchs in Jerusalem are to be included, which might be considered consistent with the supposed "international" nature of the wisdom movement. Seow, however, points out that the expression "surpassing all who were over Jerusalem before me" is common in royal propaganda, and thus Qoheleth's use is formulaic (Seow, *Ecclesiastes*, 124).

9. Few exceptions exist, even among conservative scholars. Those who do maintain this identity include Walter C. Kaiser, *Ecclesiastes: Total Life* (Everyman's Bible Commentary; Chicago: Moody, 1979); R. J. Kidwell, "Ecclesiastes," in *Ecclesiastes and Song of Solomon* (ed. R. J. Kidwell and Don DeWelt; Joplin, Mo.: College Press, 1977).

these allusions to Solomon served some other purpose and cannot be used to date the work to preexilic times. Probably the best explanation for the implied identification of Qoheleth with Solomon is an attempt to establish Qoheleth's credentials as a sage and to undermine any tendency the reader might have to dismiss the troubling words of Qoheleth as the cynical ramblings of an embittered but insignificant old sage. This matter will be considered more fully in the next two chapters.

There are other portions of Ecclesiastes that have been identified as historical references or allusions. Perhaps the most widely recognized candidate is Qoh 4:13–16:

> A poor but wise youth is better than an old but foolish king who no longer knows how to receive advice, for he came out of prison to reign. Then a poor man was also born under his reign. I saw all the living who walked under the sun with the second youth, who had come to stand in place of [the first]. There was no end to all these people before whom he went, although those who would come after would not rejoice in him. So this, too, is senseless, and [like trying to] direct the wind.

The principal difficulty in attempting to align this information with any particular historical figure, however, is that the information is too vague to be used to make a convincing identification. Qoheleth speaks of a poor, wise, young man released from prison, who ultimately becomes king, apparently replacing an old, foolish king.[10] The fact that Qoheleth again refers to a youthful king in Qoh 10:16 enhances the impression that this is a historical allusion, despite the fact that the descriptions of the two kings increases the likelihood that Qoheleth is not referring to the same individual in these passages. Although some scholars attempt to identify references to people who were historical in Qoheleth's time, such as Joseph and Pharaoh,[11] there are problems with all of these proposed identifications.[12]

---

10. For a full discussion of the interpretation of this passage, see pp. 154–157.

11. See James L. Crenshaw (*Ecclesiastes* [OTL; London: SCM, 1988] 112), who notes that this anecdote echoes the story of Joseph and warns that the text lacks sufficient historical detail to confirm any definite link. Graham S. Ogden ("Historical Allusions in Qoheleth IV 13–16?" *VT* 30 [1980] 309–15; idem, *Qoheleth* [Readings; Sheffield: JSOT Press, 1987] 70–74) is more certain that the Joseph story stands behind Qoheleth's words. Ultimately, the information is not specific enough to allow for an explicit identification (nor a detailed rebuttal of a specific identification). Most commentators note that Qoheleth's words are not entirely clear (see Crenshaw, *Ecclesiastes*, 112), and it is certainly not clear that Joseph's Pharaoh was foolish or that Joseph rose to the position of king. Finally, it is not clear how an identification with historical figures would contribute to the meaning of this text.

12. See Seow, *Ecclesiastes*, 190.

Nonetheless, it remains possible that this text refers to people and events familiar to the audience and roughly contemporaneous with them, thus providing a possible clue to dating the work. However, despite numerous attempts to make an identification,[13] scholars have been unable to reach any agreement. If this text ever did contain a historical reference (and there is no particular necessity for it to have done so), the lack of detail has obscured its identification from modern readers. The referent is now lost to us.

The other passages with possible historical references (Qoh 9:13–15; 10:16–17) have similar difficulties. If these texts have real historical referents, they are too vague for the modern audience to identify them. Besides Qoheleth's rather ambiguous words, the lack of information external to Ecclesiastes that is available regarding the history of the period surrounding the exile hampers us in making a determination.[14] Furthermore, there is no guarantee that the incidents described in these verses were even roughly contemporaneous with Qoheleth—he could have been referring to events that had taken place a considerable time before he wrote. Finally, there is no clear indication that these are not merely hypothetical events invented by Qoheleth in order to illustrate a point. Consequently, we are forced to arrive at the conclusion that Qoheleth makes no reference to events that can be used to date his work.

Aside from dating Qoheleth based on references to identifiable historical events, we may be able to determine a date based on some of the subject matter under discussion. Of particular interest in this regard is the advice that Qoheleth offers relating to behavior in the royal court (e.g., Qoh 8:2–5; 10:20). The inclusion of these instructions implies the existence of a royal court in which the advice would prove beneficial. The relevance of this piece of information is explained by Ian Young, who notes that "the most important difference between pre-exilic Jerusalem and post-exilic Jerusalem was quite simply that in pre-exilic Jerusalem there was a king, whereas in post-exilic Jerusalem there was not."[15]

---

13. Seow (ibid.) notes various proposals for referents contemporaneous with the composition of Ecclesiastes: Cyrus and Astyages, the High Priest Onias and Joseph the Tobiad, Antiochus III and Ptolemy Philopater, Ptolemy Philopater and Antiochus Epiphanes, Antiochus Epiphanes and Alexander Balas, Antiochus Epiphanes and Demetrius I, Ptolemy IV and Ptolemy V, Herod and his son Alexander, and so forth. For further discussion, see K. D. Schunk, "Drei Seleukiden im Buche Kohelet?" *VT* 9 (1959) 192–201.

14. Seow describes the period following the exile as "a 'dark age' in the history of Israel on account of the paucity of information on it" (Seow, *Ecclesiastes*, 21). The information that is available from either pre- or postexilic Israel does not provide a sufficiently detailed picture for us to make precise historical associations with allusions in Qoheleth.

15. Young, *Diversity in Pre-exilic Hebrew*, 146–47.

Qoheleth's advice regarding behavior in the royal court therefore points either to a preexilic date or to a postexilic setting outside Jerusalem.[16] There are a number of details indicating that Qoheleth should be tied to a setting in Jerusalem. First, the Solomonic fiction of the opening two chapters binds Qoheleth to the monarchy in Jerusalem (and specifically to the Davidic line). Second, Qoh 4:17 refers to the "house of God" in which sacrifices are offered, indicative of the temple rather than a synagogue.[17] This combination of details suggest that the most reasonable inference to be made from the text is that Qoheleth was located in Jerusalem, which means that most likely Ecclesiastes is set in a preexilic context. This, at least, appears to be where the author would have us place Qoheleth.

Parallels to Qoheleth's Thought

The final approach commonly employed in attempting to date Ecclesiastes is to identify texts, both from Israel and from elsewhere, that echo the sentiments expressed by Qoheleth. Scholars have identified thoughts and ideas similar to Qoheleth's in texts both from the ancient Near East and from Greece.

Greek Parallels

Prior to the discovery of numerous wisdom texts from the ancient Near East, scholars identified parallels between Qoheleth's thoughts and various

---

16. C.-L. Seow noted (in private correspondence) the existence of local "kings" in the Persian Empire, including in the region of Syria–Palestine, such as the kings of Sidon, Tabnit and Eshmunazar, in the fifth century B.C.E. (both of whose tomb inscriptions employ the phrase "under the sun"). Persian imperial documents also referred regularly to local rulers as kings. Seow also noted that the reference to an all-powerful king in Qoheleth 8 finds its closest parallel in the Aramaic proverbs of Aḥiqar found in Elephantine in the late fifth century (although Aḥiqar's date is disputed, Greenfield notes indications that the proverbs were compiled during the reign of Esarhaddon, well before the exile and in a context in which comments regarding the monarchy were appropriate; see Jonas C. Greenfield, "The Wisdom of Ahiqar," in *Wisdom in Ancient Israel* [ed. John Day, Robert P. Gordon, and H. G. M. Williamson; Cambridge: Cambridge University Press, 1995] 49–50).

17. R. B. Y. Scott, *Proverbs, Ecclesiastes* (AB 18; New York: Doubleday, 1965) 200 (although, on p. 227, Scott suggests that the temple here referred to may not necessarily be in Jerusalem). Scott goes on to note that "the incidental references to weather phenomena in relation to agriculture (xi 3–4, xii 2) are appropriate to the Palestinian climate, less so to the better-watered Phoenicia, and not at all to Egypt or Mesopotamia where great rivers provide abundant water for the irrigation of crops." For other indications of Palestinian provenance, see the references in Young, *Diversity in Pre-exilic Hebrew*, 146.

segments of Greek philosophy, particularly Epicureanism.[18] Although scholarly acceptance of Greek influence on Qoheleth is waning,[19] there are still
proponents. Otto Kaiser, for example, writes that, "if it is not really marked,
the influence of Greek-Hellenistic writing and thought is certainly demon-
strable."[20] Fox notes the general impression of Greek influence on the work
as follows: "Qohelet's affirmation of individual experience, in particular the
experience of pleasure, seems to bear a significant similarity to Hellenistic
popular philosophy, whose central purpose was to find a way to individual
happiness by the use of human reason alone."[21]

There are, however, a number of difficulties with the theory of Hellenistic
influence on Qoheleth. Proponents often presuppose that Ecclesiastes was
composed in the Hellenistic period and thus assume that Qoheleth would inevitably have come across Greek ideas.[22] They tend to dismiss any direct dependence on Greek works but conclude, based on perceived parallels between
aspects of Qoheleth's thought and Greek philosophical literature, that Qoheleth was influenced in a general way. These studies generally proceed from
a supposed date for Qoheleth rather than identifying parallels and proceeding
from there toward determining a date.

Another problem for proponents of Greek influence is that ideas similar to
Qoheleth's existed in the ancient Near East that date in some instances to before the nation of Israel.[23] If parallels to aspects of Qoheleth's thought are
found this early, a date in the Hellenistic period is hardly necessary.[24] If Qo-

---

18. In addition to Epicureanism, scholars have identified echoes of Theognis, Me-
nander, Euripides, Pindar, and Homer, as well as Stoic thought. See N. Lohfink, "Der Bibel
skeptische Hintertür: Versuch, den Ort des Buchs Kohelet neu zu bestimmen," *Stimmen der
Zeit* 198 (1980) 17–31; idem, "Zu einigen Satzeröffnungen im Epilog des Koheletbuches,"
in *Jedes Ding Hat Seine Zeit . . .* (ed. Anja A. Diesel; Berlin: de Gruyter, 1996) 131–47.
The fact that Greek parallels have long been noticed is due to the widespread availability of
Greek philosophical literature, whereas many parallels from the ancient Near East have
only come to light in the last century.

19. A number of modern commentaries do not even discuss Greek influence as a possibility; see, for example, Seow, *Ecclesiastes*; and Crenshaw, *Ecclesiastes*.

20. Otto Kaiser, "Qoheleth," in *Wisdom in Ancient Israel: Essays in Honour of J. A.
Emerton* (ed. John Day, Robert P. Gordon, and H. G. M. Williamson; Cambridge: Cambridge University Press, 1995) 84.

21. Michael V. Fox, *A Time to Tear Down and a Time to Build Up: A Rereading of Ecclesiastes* (Grand Rapids: Eerdmans, 1999) 7.

22. For example, R. Braun, *Kohelet und die frühhellenistische Popularphilosophie*
(BZAW 130; Berlin: de Gruyter, 1973).

23. See, for example, George F. Held, "Parallels between The Gilgamesh Epic and
Plato's Symposium," *JNES* 42 (1983) 131–41.

24. Other important studies on supposed Hellenistic influence in Ecclesiastes include
Martin Hengel, *Judaism and Hellenism* (Philadelphia: Fortress, 1974); Reinhold Bohlen,

heleth were independently dated to the Hellenistic period, a good case could be made for Greek influence. It is not clear, however, that the parallels alone can establish a late date for the work.

Mesopotamian Parallels

Although Qoheleth's thought has often been linked with various early Greek philosophical ideas, many of these apparently distinctive ideas have also been found in older writings from elsewhere in the ancient Near East. Scholars have identified a number of Mesopotamian and Egyptian texts that reflect some of the ideas found in Qoheleth. Nonetheless, in many cases the similarities with Qoheleth have been overstated. A brief review of some of these parallels will demonstrate that there was a long-standing intellectual tradition in the ancient Near East, the existence of which confirms that there is no need to tie Qoheleth to an exclusively Hellenistic background.

The *Dialogue of Pessimism* records a discussion between a master and his servant about what is good in life. Their discussion ultimately despairs of finding an answer, although death is suggested as an option.[25] The genre of the text is unclear, however, and unlike Ecclesiastes the dialogue contains comedic elements and may have been intended for performance by actors.

The *Babylonian Theodicy* contains another dialogue, this time between a voice of orthodoxy and a suffering friend.[26] The text suggests that the limits of human knowledge are to blame for our inability to understand contradictions in the world.[27] Although often cited as a parallel to Ecclesiastes,[28] this text more closely resembles Job. Ultimately, however, it differs from both of these works in that it blames human evil on the gods.[29]

The only Mesopotamian text consistently referred to by its opening line in Akkadian is *ludlul bēl nēmeqi* 'I will praise the lord of wisdom', a hymn of

"Kohelet im Kontext hellenistischer Kultur," in *Das Buch Kohelet: Studien zur Struktur, Geschichte, Rezeption und Theologie* (ed. Ludger Schwienhorst-Schönberger; Berlin: de Gruyter, 1997) 249–73; and O. Loretz, *Qohelet und der Alte Orient: Untersuchungen zu Stil und theologischer Thematik des Buches Qohelet* (Freiburg: Herder, 1964), who places Qoheleth's thought squarely in a Semitic context.

25. W. G. Lambert, *Babylonian Wisdom Literature* (Oxford: Clarendon, 1960 [reprinted, Winona Lake, Ind.: Eisenbrauns, 1996]) 139–49; *ANET*, 437–38; compare with Seow, *Ecclesiastes*, 64; Young, *Diversity in Pre-exilic Hebrew*, 143.

26. Lambert, *Babylonian Wisdom Literature*, 63–91; *ANET*, 601–4. The text takes the form of an acrostic poem, which reads, "I *Saggil-kīnam-ubbib*, the priest, am an adorant of the god and the king" (see n. 68 below, p. 41).

27. The relevant lines are 84, 256–57, and 267–75.

28. See Crenshaw, *Ecclesiastes*, 51–52; Roland E. Murphy, *Ecclesiastes* (WBC 23A; Dallas: Word, 1992) xlii; Seow, *Ecclesiastes*, 63.

29. See Murphy, *Ecclesiastes*, xlii.

praise to Marduk.[30] At one point it does complain that the wicked and the righteous receive the same reward, but otherwise its similarity to Ecclesiastes is insignificant.[31]

Seow notes that small portions of *Ahiqar* find echoes in Qoheleth's words.[32] In particular, there are parallels to Qoheleth's advice regarding behavior in the presence of the king in Qoh 8:1–5 (compare Ahiqar 1.1.84–90) and Qoh 10:20 (compare Ahiqar 1.1.80–82), and Qoheleth's warning about moderation in Qoh 7:15–16 (compare Ahiqar 1.1.147). This final parallel is significant because it undermines the case made by some scholars that here Qoheleth clearly reflects Greek thought.

Qoheleth's observation that the memory of those who have died soon passes away (Qoh 1:11; 2:16) and that human beings make no lasting contribution in the world (Qoh 1:9) is echoed in the Sumerian "Poem of Early Rulers."[33] This text includes references to the famed Gilgamesh to make the point that even the achievements of the most renowned people are eventually brought to nought.

Scholars widely agree that the most striking parallel to the thought of Qoheleth is found in the words of Siduri in the *Epic of Gilgamesh*.[34] Siduri advises Gilgamesh with these words:

> O Gilgamesh, where are you wandering?
> The life that you seek you never will find:
> when the gods created mankind,
> death they dispensed to mankind,
> life they kept for themselves.

---

30. Lambert, *Babylonian Wisdom Literature*, 21–62.

31. See Seow, *Ecclesiastes*, 63; Murphy, *Ecclesiastes*, xlii; Crenshaw, *Ecclesiastes*, 51.

32. See Seow (*Ecclesiastes*, 62–63), who goes on to claim that the author of Qoheleth may have been familiar with the Aramaic version of the *Proverbs of Ahiqar*. References to Ahiqar are from B. Porten and A. Yardeni (eds.), *Textbook of Aramaic Documents from Ancient Egypt* (3 vols.; Jerusalem: Israel Academy of Sciences and Humanities, 1986–1993) vol. 3, §1.1.

33. See B. Alster, "The Sumerian Poem of Early Rulers and Related Poems," *OLP* 21 (1990) 6–7. Andrew R. George also refers to this in *The Babylonian Gilgamesh Epic: Introduction, Critical Edition and Cuneiform Texts* (2 vols.; Oxford: Oxford University Press, 2003) vol. 1, chap. 3, and has elsewhere described it as a "wisdom text that preaches the pleasure of beer-drinking in the face of mankind's inescapable doom" (see http://www .britac.ac.uk/institutes/iraq/bsain7.html).

34. See, for example, *ANET*, 90; Crenshaw, *Ecclesiastes*, 51; Murphy, *Ecclesiastes*, xliii; Seow, *Ecclesiastes*, 64–65; Young, *Diversity in Pre-exilic Hebrew*, 143. The oft-quoted words of Siduri are preserved only in the Old Babylonian version of the epic, although similar sentiments are found in the words of Uta-napishti to Gilgamesh in the standard Babylonian version.

But you, Gilgamesh, let your belly be full,
enjoy yourself always by day and by night!
Make merry each day,
dance and play day and night!
Let your clothes be clean,
let your head be washed, may you bathe in water!
Gaze on the child who holds your hand,
let your wife enjoy your repeated embrace![35]

The Epic's tale of a hero who seeks to outmaneuver death but ultimately fails to do so echoes Qoheleth's repeated complaint that death is the ultimate injustice, depleting life of any possibility of meaning. Furthermore, the notion that human fate is ultimately determined by the whims of unpredictable gods finds similar expression in both works. Nonetheless, there are enough differences between the works that direct dependence is difficult to establish.

Tremper Longman notes a number of parallels between Ecclesiastes and a genre of texts that he labels "fictional Akkadian autobiographies."[36] However, these texts contain parallels not to Qoheleth's thought but to the structure of his work. If Qoheleth did deliberately emulate the style of these texts, doing so does not require a late date for Ecclesiastes.

Egyptian Parallels

In addition to these Mesopotamian parallels to the thought and structure of Ecclesiastes, a number of Egyptian texts express sentiments similar to Qoheleth's. Of course, when they address the theme of death (one major theme in Qoheleth's thought), we must remind ourselves that the Egyptian texts reflect a highly developed tradition regarding the afterlife, a tradition that is quite distinct from the Mesopotamian and Israelite traditions.

The *Songs of the Harper* are tomb inscriptions that can be cited as having parallels to the thought of Qoheleth because they question the reality of an afterlife and exhort the living to enjoy their lives while they may.[37]

The *Dispute of a Man with His Ba* records a dialogue between a man who despairs of life and his *ba* 'soul', which tries to convince him that, in spite of

---

35. Gilgamesh iii 1–13 from Andrew George, *The Epic of Gilgamesh* (Penguin Classics; rev. ed.; London: Penguin, 2003) 124; see also *ANET*, 90; Seow, *Ecclesiastes*, 64.

36. Longman, *The Book of Ecclesiastes*, 17–20; Tremper Longman III, *Fictional Akkadian Autobiography: A Generic and Comparative Study* (Winona Lake, Ind.: Eisenbrauns, 1991).

37. A. Lichtheim (ed.), *Ancient Egyptian Literature* (3 vols.; Berkeley: University of California Press, 1971–80) 1.196–97; *ANET*, 467; see also Crenshaw, *Ecclesiastes*, 51; Grabbe, *Priests, Prophets, Diviners, Sages*, 164; Murphy, *Ecclesiastes*, xliii; Seow, *Ecclesiastes*, 62.

its drawbacks, life is still better than death.[38] One part of this discussion contains an exhortation to enjoy life while he can.

A number of didactic texts have been preserved, some quite old, that are parallel to certain aspects of Ecclesiastes in varying degrees.[39] One of the oldest, *The Instruction of Ptah-hotep*, contains advice quite reminiscent of Qoheleth's:

> Follow your heart as long as you live,
> Do no more than is required,
> Do not shorten the time of "follow-the-heart,"
> Trimming its moment offends the *ka*.
> Don't waste your time on daily cares
> Beyond providing for your household;
> When wealth has come, follow your heart,
> Wealth does no good if one is glum.[40]

The Complaints of Khakheperre-Sonb records a man's discussion with his heart about the troubles in the land, concluding that "none is wise enough to know."[41] While this is reminiscent of Qoheleth's thought, it is also vague enough to reflect the sentiments of Job or a number of the prophets in the Hebrew Bible.

Papyrus Insinger is a late (ca. first century C.E.) text that considers the hiddenness of God and his determination of fate, with an emphasis on moderation; these ideas are cited as parallels to some portions of Qoheleth's thought.[42] The value of these parallels has been questioned, however, and the late date precludes locating Qoheleth in any historical context.[43] Other late Egyptian texts such as *Ankhsheshonq* also contain vague parallels to Qoheleth, but these similarities are too superficial to be particularly useful in understanding Qoheleth.[44]

---

38. Lichtheim (ed.), *Ancient Egyptian Literature*, 1.163–69; *ANET*, 405–7; see also Grabbe, *Priests, Prophets, Diviners, Sages*, 164; Murphy, *Ecclesiastes*, xliii; Seow, *Ecclesiastes*, 62.

39. Seow cites a number of structural parallels to Qoheleth in Egyptian works with epilogues that consider the work of the sage retrospectively, in *Ecclesiastes*, 60–61.

40. Lichtheim (ed.), *Ancient Egyptian Literature*, 1.66; also Seow, *Ecclesiastes*, 60–61.

41. Lichtheim (ed.), *Ancient Egyptian Literature*, 1.145–49; also Seow, *Ecclesiastes*, 62.

42. Lichtheim (ed.), *Ancient Egyptian Literature*, 3.184–217; also Crenshaw, *Ecclesiastes*, 51.

43. See Seow (*Ecclesiastes*, 61), who quotes Lichtheim as having pointed out that "Qohelet's point of view is quite different from Papyrus Insinger's."

44. On *Ankhsheshonq*, see Lichtheim (ed.), *Ancient Egyptian Literature*, 3.159–84; Crenshaw, *Ecclesiastes*, 51; Seow, *Ecclesiastes*, 61–62.

Having surveyed all of the above texts, we must conclude that there is still no text from either Mesopotamia or Egypt that is comparable with more than a few of the words and ideas of Qoheleth. That a number of these supposed parallels are also often cited as reminiscent of Job is indicative of the rather vague associations that we are able to make between the Israelite and international works. We may conclude that, with such relatively minor similarities, Ecclesiastes is unlikely to have been dependent on any of the above works. However, the existence of these parallels to aspects of Qoheleth's thought does significantly weaken the case for its dependence on Greek thought. In the end, we find that all aspects of Qoheleth's thought that some scholars consider indicative of Hellenistic influence may actually reflect literature and thinking in the ancient Near East long before the Hellenistic period.

Israelite Parallels

The most striking parallel with Qoheleth in Israelite writings is Wisdom of Solomon 1:16–2:11. The relevant portion of this text reads:

> Short and sorrowful is life, and there is no remedy when a life comes to
>   its end,
> and no one has been known to return from Hades.
> For we were born by mere chance,
> and hereafter we shall be as though we had never been,
> for the breath in our nostrils is smoke,
> and reason is a spark kindled by the beating of our hearts;
> when it is extinguished, the body will turn to ashes,
> and the spirit will dissolve like empty air.
> Our name will be forgotten in time,
> and no one will remember our works;
> our life will pass away like the traces of a cloud,
> and be scattered like mist that is chased by the rays of the sun and overcome
>   by its heat.
> For our allotted time is the passing of a shadow,
> and there is no return from our death,
> because it is sealed up and no one turns back.
> Come, therefore, let us enjoy the good things that exist,
> and make use of the creation to the full as in youth. (NRSV)

These words from the Wisdom of Solomon are strongly reminiscent of Qoheleth's own words but differ in that they are attributed to the ungodly. A number of scholars conclude that these words were aimed directly at Qoheleth,[45]

---

45. See Longman, *The Book of Ecclesiastes*, 99; William Horbury, "The Christian Use and the Jewish Origins of the Wisdom of Solomon," in *Wisdom in Ancient Israel: Essays*

which if true would indicate a date for Qoheleth that was prior to the Wisdom of Solomon. This book, however, is usually assigned a date considerably later than any suggested for Ecclesiastes, and so the parallel is ultimately of little assistance in directly dating Ecclesiastes. Nonetheless, the text is valuable, if only to illustrate the impact on later sages of wisdom such as Qoheleth's and to undergird my thesis that Qoheleth's epilogist employed Qoheleth's words to discredit the sages (although more subtly than the Wisdom of Solomon).[46]

Barton has found indications that Sirach was literarily dependent on Ecclesiastes,[47] but Whitley has concluded that Ecclesiastes shows signs of dependence on Sirach.[48] The only direct thematic parallel to Sirach in Ecclesiastes appears in the closing words of the epilogue, "fear God and keep his commands" (Qoh 12:13; compare Sir 43:27). However, Sirach also reflects a movement against the type of wisdom represented by Qoheleth, as I will show below. The case for dependence is based on a number of verbal parallels between the two works, which otherwise present markedly different perspectives.[49] Many of these verbs also find parallels in other texts of the Hebrew Bible. Thus, the case for direct dependence in either direction is rather weak, as Murphy notes: "On the strength of these and other associations it is not possible to prove

---

in Honour of J. A. Emerton (ed. John Day, Robert P. Gordon, and H. G. M. Williamson; Cambridge: Cambridge University Press, 1995) 195; F. Delitzsch, *Commentary on the Song of Songs and Ecclesiastes* (trans. M. G. Easton; Edinburgh: T. & T. Clark, 1877) 212. Gerhard von Rad sees the association as "uncertain" (*Wisdom in Israel* [trans. James D. Martin; London: SCM, 1972] 238). Michael V. Fox (*Qohelet and His Contradictions* [JSOTSup 71; Sheffield: Almond Press, 1989] 149) argues against any direct interaction. P. W. Skehan ("Wisdom and Ecclesiastes," in *Studies in Israelite Poetry and Wisdom* [Washington D.C.: Catholic Biblical Association, 1971] 213–36) discusses the merits of literary dependence and decides that the data are too vague. Nonetheless, the words from Wisdom of Solomon reflect a period when the sentiments of Qoheleth were being questioned rather than endorsed.

46. Loretz (*Qohelet und der Alte Orient*, 196–212) lists numerous themes that Ecclesiastes shares with other biblical and extrabiblical texts (such as joy, life and death, fear of God, royalty, etc.), highlighting the strong connection between Ecclesiastes and the remaining biblical wisdom tradition. Qoheleth's conclusions on these matters, however, frequently differ from the others'.

47. G. A. Barton, *A Critical and Exegetical Commentary on the Book of Ecclesiastes* (ICC; Edinburgh: T. & T. Clark, 1908) 59–60; cf. Young, *Diversity in Pre-exilic Hebrew*, 151.

48. Charles F. Whitley, *Koheleth: His Language and Thought* (BZAW 148; Berlin: de Gruyter, 1979) 122–31.

49. Murphy lists the most significant verbal parallels as being Qoh 3:11 and Sir 39:16; Qoh 3:13 and Sir 5:3; Qoh 8:1 and Sir 13:25; Qoh 7:28 and Sir 6:6; Qoh 3:1 and Sir 4:20 (emended); Qoh 12:13 and Sir 43:27; Qoh 12:14 and Sir 13:25; Qoh 10:11 and Sir 12:13; Qoh 3:20 and Sir 40:11.

dependence in either direction. The data are simply ambiguous, and some of the similarities could easily derive from a common source."[50]

The fact that many of the same Near Eastern parallels cited for Ecclesiastes are also cited for Job shows that Job shares similarities with Ecclesiastes. Job questions the value of traditional wisdom in accounting for his predicament and ultimately concludes that some answers are unavailable to the human mind. In spite of some broad similarities, however, Ecclesiastes' differences from Job are more striking still.

Another striking parallel with Ecclesiastes is Psalm 49, because it agrees with Qoheleth's identification of death as the great leveler of all humanity. However, there is little possibility of finding a historical context for this psalm or a related potential setting for Ecclesiastes.[51]

Conclusion

It is clear from this brief survey of material that the apparently distinctive thoughts of Qoheleth echo ideas that had found expression throughout the ancient Near East well before the period of the Exile. We have, however, been unable to establish a precise historical setting for Ecclesiastes. Ancient literary parallels to Ecclesiastes do not help us to refine the historical context for Qoheleth because they are only parallel in rather broad linguistic, structural, or philosophical ways. What is clear, however, is that a postexilic date for Qoheleth is neither mandated nor excluded by the evidence.

Ecclesiastes' Place in Israelite Wisdom

It is clear from these various attempts to date Ecclesiastes that it is impossible to reach a precise conclusion about the historical origins of the text. Even if we could, we still would lack much information (either biblical or extrabiblical) about the time periods. Rather than abandon the task altogether, however, we may be able to determine Ecclesiastes' position in the progression of thought apparent in the wisdom writings preserved from ancient Israel. We may then be able to assign Ecclesiastes a date relative to other texts rather than to a point in the history of Israel. In doing so, we may also find ourselves able to establish a hypothetical historical context for Ecclesiastes that adequately accounts for Qoheleth's words and the inclusion of the work in the canon.

The above discussion of Israelite parallels to Qoheleth's words revealed that the Wisdom of Solomon and, to a lesser extent, Sirach may have been

---

50. Murphy, *Ecclesiastes*, xlvi.
51. Psalm 49 is discussed in more detail above, p. 13.

reacting to the wisdom of Qoheleth. Furthermore, their emphatic association of wisdom with Torah places them in a different context from the Wisdom Literature of the Bible, which lacks the great redemptive themes so prominent in all other literary genres of the Hebrew Bible.[52] The Wisdom of Solomon and Sirach, then, may be understood as a reaction against the wisdom of Qoheleth and thus logically as appearing after Ecclesiastes, during the move against that form of wisdom.

At the other end of the spectrum stands the book of Proverbs. As noted previously, the terse nature of the work, predominantly consisting of short aphorisms divorced from any broader hermeneutical context, promotes naïve interpretations of the wisdom contained therein. One possible, and historically likely, consequence of this is the perception that Proverbs justifies belief in a simplistic, highly ordered world, in which wisdom and righteousness are rewarded and folly and wickedness are swiftly punished. A few brief examples can serve to demonstrate:

> For the upright will abide in the land,
> and the innocent will remain in it;
> but the wicked will be cut off from the land,
> and the treacherous will be rooted out of it. (2:21–22)

> Honor the LORD with your substance
> and with the first fruits of all your produce;
> then your barns will be filled with plenty,
> and your vats will be bursting with wine. (3:9–10)

> The fear of the LORD is the beginning of wisdom,
> and the knowledge of the Holy One is insight.
> For by me your days will be multiplied,
> and years will be added to your life. (9:10–11)

> The LORD does not let the righteous go hungry,
> but he thwarts the craving of the wicked. (10:3)

> The blessing of the LORD makes rich,
> and he adds no sorrow with it. (10:22) (all from NRSV)

In these aphorisms, the notion of an underlying order maintained by God is readily apparent and unquestioned. Furthermore, parallels can be made between Proverbs' understanding of the world and Job's counselors' understanding. Thus, in the book of Job, a battle is portrayed between men who endorse "traditional" wisdom (which could have derived from a simplistic

---

52. Grabbe (*Priests, Prophets, Diviners, Sages*, 160) notes that, for "Ben Sira, the main concern of wisdom is the Torah of God."

reading of Proverbs) and the sage who is forced to reconsider and even deny this wisdom in the face of the circumstances of life. The book of Job concludes with God's condemnation of the simplistic position and endorsement of the understanding of Job, marking a movement from naïveté to a more sophisticated wisdom that accounts for the realities of everyday life.

Although the book of Job questions aspects of traditional wisdom and therefore promotes an evolved form of wisdom, it does not go as far as Qoheleth. Qoheleth's wisdom goes so far as to doubt the goodness of God, as Longman notes: "reading Qohelet's statements about God in context leads one to side with those scholars who characterize Qohelet's God as distant, occasionally indifferent, and sometimes cruel."[53]

Thus, both Job and Ecclesiastes can be read as reactions to a particular use of the wisdom presented in the book of Proverbs, with Ecclesiastes being the more extreme of the two. By contrast, the later Sirach and Wisdom of Solomon appear to react to the wisdom of Qoheleth, which had shifted too far from orthodoxy to be readily acceptable. This ordering of the books allows us to construct a logical flow of thought through the Wisdom Literature of ancient Israel, beginning with Proverbs (or, at least, wisdom similar to the wisdom found in parts of Proverbs), moving to Job which reacts against it, and then to Ecclesiastes, which reacts more strongly, and on to the counteraction of Sirach and Wisdom of Solomon, which seek to return the wisdom movement to a position under the umbrella of the Law.[54]

Finally, if the understanding of the epilogue (and so of Ecclesiastes in its entirety) that I propose is valid, then Ecclesiastes itself marks the turning point in the history of wisdom in Israel. The epilogist uses Qoheleth's words to demonstrate that the teachings of the sages were, at that time, incompatible

---

53. Longman, *The Book of Ecclesiastes*, 35. Compare the comments of Leo Perdue: "Confidence in the beneficence of God was replaced by a deep-seated terror and final resignation before an unknowable God whose uncontested decrees determined the fates of human creatures. Indeed, God remains the *deus absconditus*, dwelling within the heavenly regions, separated and removed from human habitation and understanding of the wise" ("Cosmology and the Social Order in the Wisdom Tradition," in *The Sage in Israel and the Ancient Near East* [ed. John G. Gammie and Leo G. Perdue; Winona Lake, Ind.: Eisenbrauns, 1990] 469).

54. In reality it overstates the case to assert that Proverbs should be considered the earliest point on this trajectory of wisdom. The book of Proverbs, by its very nature, need not have existed in its entirety to have triggered the use of wisdom against which I suggest that later sages reacted. Any wisdom material similar to Proverbs (much of which appeared throughout the ANE at times considerably earlier than any of the material in the Hebrew Bible would normally be dated) could have triggered the reaction evident in Job and Ecclesiastes.

with the religion of Israel. Although the words of Qoheleth may represent the thoughts of the sages in their most extreme reaction against the apparent naïveté of Proverbs, the epilogist uses these words to condemn the position that the sages had moved to and to call them back to the words of the Law—fear God and keep his commands (Qoh 12:13). It is certainly true that the sages who came after Qoheleth, among whom were Sirach and the author of the Wisdom of Solomon, propounded a wisdom that adheres closely to the religious traditions of Israel.

Ecclesiastes' Use of חכם

The question of whether the term חכם 'wise' refers to a member of an identifiable group of (semi-)professional wise people, a sage, can only be answered through an examination of the use of the term in context. This task must ultimately focus on the use of the term in Ecclesiastes, and particularly its use by the epilogist, for it is in this historical context that the group must be identified. Whether or not the wise were an identifiable social group prior to Qoheleth's time is ultimately irrelevant if the final editor of Ecclesiastes was primarily writing to discredit the sages in a different social and historical context.

Whybray has claimed that the term חכם in the Hebrew Bible *never* refers to a professional class of sages.[55] With regard to use of the word by Qoheleth, it is clear that Whybray is largely correct—in almost all instances, the adjective חכם does not refer to an identifiable class but merely to people who possess wisdom, as opposed to those who do not. This usage is particularly clear in statements about the wise that are contrasted with statements about the foolish (e.g., 2:14–19; 6:8).[56]

However, as a general proposition encompassing all references to the wise, Whybray's assertion has not been widely accepted.[57] Indeed there are strong

---

55. Whybray, *The Intellectual Tradition in the Old Testament*, 49–50; cf. Grabbe, *Priests, Prophets, Diviners, Sages*, 175–76.

56. It is interesting also to note the instances in which the adjective חכם is preceded by the definite article in the Hebrew Bible. While there are no such instances in Proverbs, Ecclesiastes contains a number of them (2:14, 16, 19; 8:1, 17; 9:1). Although this may reflect little more than the compositional idiosyncrasies of the authors, it could also be indicative of a shift in the way of identifying the wise between the time of the two works.

57. See, for example, Blenkinsopp (*Sage, Priest, Prophet*, 11), who notes that "Whybray was surely mistaken in supposing that a tradition can be sustained and transmitted without institutional grounding." See also Fox (*Qohelet and His Contradictions*, 330–32), who identifies other instances in which חכמים refers to members of an identifiable class rather than just wise individuals (such as Prov 22:17; 24:23a). Grabbe, who agrees with Whybray's conclusion, fails to discuss specific passages in his analysis.

indications within the book of Ecclesiastes that the term is sometimes used with a technical meaning pointing to a professional, or at least distinctly identifiable, social group.

First, Qoh 12:9 records that Qoheleth taught the people.[58] Although neither the precise context of this teaching nor the identity of "the people" is established, the assertion itself suggests that more is being claimed for Qoheleth than merely that he was a wise person. He apparently held some type of teaching position in his capacity as wise man. Second, v. 11 of the epilogue parallels the "words of the wise" with the "[words of the] masters of the collections," an expression that implies a formal group that was responsible in some way for the collection and preservation of Wisdom Literature.

A third indicator that חכם in Ecclesiastes is used, at least sometimes, to refer to an identifiable group is the title (or, less likely, name) קהלת 'Qoheleth' itself.[59] The meaning of the word is most likely a 'gatherer' of people, wealth, or wisdom.[60] As such, קהלת appears to have been a title bestowed on one whose task related to the collection and dissemination of wisdom materials, perhaps even a title conferred on one who was a "master of collections" (Qoh 12:11). The use of this title is suggestive of an official position.

In light of these considerations it appears likely that, at least by the time of the composition of Ecclesiastes, the term חכם could have been used in reference to a member of an identifiable group of intellectuals who were involved in some form of instruction.

Sages in the Ancient Near East

The Bible alludes to the international status of the wisdom movement (e.g., 1 Kgs 5:10[4:30]). If we can establish unequivocally that within the social structures of Israel's neighbors the proponents of wisdom were recognized as an identifiable group serving in teaching (or other) roles, then we

---

58. The Piel of למד 'teach' is used in a number of contexts. Often it refers to YHWH as teacher (Isa 48:17; Jer 2:33; 32:33; and numerous times in the Psalms). It is used of teaching in family contexts (Jer 9:14, 20; Cant 8:2) as well as between peers (Jer 31:31). It may refer to a more formally identified teacher in Prov 5:13; Ezra 7:10; and 2 Chr 17:7–9 (see Dan 1:1–4 where it is used with reference to a Mesopotamian setting).

59. Two factors indicate that קהלת is better understood as a title rather than a name. First, it appears with the article in Qoh 7:27; 12:8. Second, the qōṭelet form (Qal f. ptc.) is elsewhere used to designate an occupation (see Ezra 2:55, 57; Neh 3:57, 59).

60. See Seow (*Ecclesiastes*, 95–97), who argues for a gatherer of wisdom. On the basis of the use of both verbal and nominal forms of קהל elsewhere in BH, it is most likely that the title refers to one who gathers people in order to teach them wisdom. See pp. 110–11 for further discussion of the meaning of קהלת.

may be able to help identify the setting for the Wisdom Literature of the Hebrew Bible and to find support for the argument that the sages were an identifiable group in Israel.

There are immediate difficulties in making comparisons between Israel and its neighbors, however. First, there are problems of comparative linguistics. Wisdom Literature in the Hebrew Bible is marked by the use of a distinctive vocabulary, a vocabulary that is unparalleled in texts that deal with similar subject matter from either Egypt or Mesopotamia.[61] Second, there were substantial differences between Israel and its neighbors both in the size and in the type of administration and government, differences that impose constraints on the extent to which parallels can be drawn.

Nonetheless, the parallels between Wisdom Literature in Israel and various didactic and reflective texts from both Egypt and Mesopotamia suggest that the people who were responsible for their composition and preservation shared at least some common ground. Consequently, there is value in briefly examining the contexts in which these texts originated.

Sages in Egypt

In Egypt the terms *sage* and *scribe* were almost interchangeable, as Ronald Williams notes: "The sages were all learned scribes, steeped in the texts usually designated as wisdom literature, and in many cases authors or compilers of such works."[62] The Egyptian state had developed a vast administrative system and civil service, both of which employed scribes in a range of tasks, including advising the pharaoh, serving in religious institutions, and educating the next generation of civil servants. Specific terminology was used to refer to the sages (in earlier times, the expression *rḫ-[ꜣ]ḫt* 'one who knows things', and in later times, *rmt-rḫ* 'wise man').[63] The numerous references in the Hebrew Bible to the sages of Egypt show that there was widespread awareness of their position in the Egyptian administration.[64]

---

61. Note Lambert's comment that "'Wisdom' is strictly a misnomer as applied to Babylonian literature. As used for a literary genre the term belongs to Hebraic studies" (Lambert, *Babylonian Wisdom Literature*, 1). Nonetheless, there is evidence for literary forms in both Sumerian and Akkadian literature that closely correspond to the Wisdom Literature of the Hebrew Bible. And, although the existence of such literature supports the case that an identifiable group responsible for its composition and preservation must have existed, it does not prove it.

62. Ronald J. Williams, "The Sage in Egyptian Literature," in *The Sage in Israel and the Ancient Near East* (ed. John G. Gammie and Leo G. Perdue; Winona Lake, Ind.: Eisenbrauns, 1990) 25; cf. Grabbe, *Priests, Prophets, Diviners, Sages*, 164.

63. See Williams, "The Sage in Egyptian Literature," 27; Grabbe, *Priests, Prophets, Diviners, Sages*, 164.

64. See Gen 41:8; Exod 7:11; Isa 19:11, 12.

Given the variety of employment opportunities for the sages, it is not surprising that formal schools existed in which the next generation of scribes was prepared for service.[65] The complex writing system and the specific qualifications required for the various jobs demanded more formal training than could be expected in a home setting. There is evidence that the didactic texts often designated Wisdom Literature were used in the training of the students.

Sages in Mesopotamia

Akkadian attests no term that is broadly parallel in meaning to the Hebrew word חכם, which can be applied to magicians, craftsmen, or intellectuals. Rather, there are several terms that Ronald Sweet has identified as occupying the same semantic field as the Hebrew term.[66]

Sweet's analysis indicates that, while some of the Akkadian terminology can be applied to wise people in general, there are terms that were specifically applied to certain classes of the king's subjects. Among the people commonly described in the terminology of wisdom language, scribes probably came the closest to paralleling the type of sage who would have been responsible for compiling material such as the words of Qoheleth (as also in Egypt). Sweet summarizes the situation as follows: "Is the one passage quoted in which a wise man acts as a teacher sufficient evidence for believing that a distinct professional group of wisdom teachers existed in Mesopotamia? Hardly. Nor are the texts that refer to wise counsellors sufficient to support the idea of a distinct class of professional counsellors. Both sets of evidence are better subsumed under the more general heading of scribe."[67] The texts from Mesopotamia that are generally categorized as Wisdom Literature are usually anonymous (with the exception of *The Babylonian Theodicy*, which is in the form of an acrostic and identifies the author as a "priest" and "adorant" of the god and the king[68]),

---

65. What is more surprising, and perhaps relevant to the discussion of the presence of schools (or even a school) within Israel, is the fact that Egyptian Wisdom Literature rarely mentions the school. See James L. Crenshaw, "The Sage in Proverbs," in *The Sage in Israel and the Ancient Near East* (ed. John G. Gammie and Leo G. Perdue; Winona Lake, Ind.: Eisenbrauns, 1990) 210.

66. See Ronald F. G. Sweet, "The Sage in Akkadian Literature: A Philological Study," in ibid., 45–65.

67. Ibid., 64.

68. 'Priest' renders Akk. *mašma(š)šu* and refers to a priest in charge of oaths and exorcisms. 'Adorant' renders Akk. *karibu*, from a verb meaning 'to bless [someone]'. See K. Riemschneider, *An Akkadian Grammar* (trans. Thomas A. Caldwell, John N. Oswalt, and John F. X. Sheehan; 3rd ed.; Milwaukee: Marquette University Press, 1977) general vocabulary, p. 18b; John Huehnergard, *A Grammar of Akkadian* (HSS 45; Atlanta: Scholars Press, 1997 [3rd printing; Winona Lake, Ind.: Eisenbrauns, 2000]) 501a.

and the contents do not specifically locate them in the royal court or even in administrative centers.

Nonetheless, there is evidence in the biblical record that there were men in Mesopotamia who could be identified as wise who occupied some form of official, probably administrative, position. For example, Jeremiah lists the sages (חכמים) alongside other readily identifiable leaders, such as שרים 'princes', פחות 'governors', סגנים 'prefects', and גבורים 'mighty men'.[69] This suggests that, from the Hebrew perspective, there was an identifiable (and clearly quite official) class of sages in the Mesopotamian administrative hierarchy, even if the precise Akkadian term for this position remains unclear.[70] In turn, this fact increases the likelihood that the Hebrew word חכם could elsewhere, at least in some contexts, be understood to refer to an official position.

Sages in Ugarit

We may assume that Ugarit reflected the situation in Israel more closely than either Egypt or Mesopotamia. Ugarit employed an alphabetic cuneiform script that was similar to the consonantal Hebrew script, which would have required considerably less training to master than the more widely used syllabic cuneiform writing system. Furthermore, in terms of size, Ugarit, like Israel, would have required a less complex administrative structure than the major centers of power in the ancient Near East.

Texts from Ugarit indicate the availability of some form of school system there with curriculum that included the teaching of literacy skills. The many texts discovered there reveal that Akkadian and Hurrian also played a significant role in the urban correspondence and record-keeping, from which we have been able to determine that there were close ties between Ugarit and Mesopotamia.[71]

These strong Mesopotamian links make it difficult to identify Ugaritic sages comparable to sages in the Hebrew Bible. Nonetheless, the presence of a significant didactic tradition increases the likelihood that teachers would have fit the role. Most likely, the "sages" of Ugarit were at least a subset of the scribal community, and as teachers, a readily identifiable group in the society.

---

69. See Jer 50:35; 51:57.

70. For Mesopotamian education and the part in it played by the scribe, see Samuel Noah Kramer, *The Sumerians: Their History, Culture, and Character* (Chicago: University of Chicago Press, 1963) 229–48.

71. See Loren R. Mack-Fisher, "A Survey and Reading Guide to the Didactic Literature of Ugarit: Prolegomenon to a Study on the Sage," in *The Sage in Israel and the Ancient Near East* (ed. John G. Gammie and Leo G. Perdue; Winona Lake, Ind.: Eisenbrauns, 1990) 67–80; idem, "The Scribe (and Sage) in the Royal Court at Ugarit," in ibid., 109–15.

Sages in Israel

Parallels are often drawn between the sort of sages in Egypt and Mesopotamia and sages in ancient Israel. The value of these parallels have, however, been called into question. Israel was a considerably smaller state, with a relatively small bureaucracy and a relatively simple writing system. Furthermore, the ambiguity inherent in the term חכם, due to its broad semantic range, complicates the task of identifying allusions to professional sages.

The clearest presentation of the wise as an identifiable (and somewhat elite) group in Israelite society appears in Sirach. Here the sage is depicted as an adviser to great men or kings (Sir 39:4; compare Prov 14:35; 25:15), as distinguished from and superior to people employed in more mundane, everyday tasks, such as farming (see Sir 38:24–25). It is clear that men who pursued wisdom required the time and financial independence to do it. Sirach also contains the earliest unequivocal evidence for a school in Israel (Sir 51:23), an institution for the training of people with the time, money, and inclination to become sages.

Prior to Sirach, the position of sage in Israel is not as clear, partly because of a lack of specificity in the term חכם. Furthermore, evidence for the existence of schools whose teachers would have formed a readily identifiable social group aptly described as sage is not compelling. Crenshaw notes that there is incontrovertible evidence for the existence of educational institutions in the nations surrounding Israel as far back as the first millennium, if not earlier.[72] The existence of these schools, however, is usually associated with the complex writing forms of the societies. From within Israel, although there is no lack of conjecture, there are no hard data pointing to the existence of formal educational institutions. Furthermore, Israel had adopted a simple alphabetic script that would have been relatively easy to master and may not have required extensive education.[73]

In spite of the fact that there is no hard evidence for educational institutions in Israel prior to the reference in Sirach, some scholars maintain that their existence can be reasonably inferred. Various indications support this claim. First, the preservation of ancient texts, including the collation of collections of wisdom material such as Proverbs, suggests the existence of a group dedicated at least in part to this work.

---

72. See James L. Crenshaw, *Education in Ancient Israel* (New York: Doubleday, 1998) 85–86.

73. See Crenshaw (ibid., 91–92), who believes that Isa 28:9–13 and 50:4 reflect the existence of schools in some form.

Second, the progressively complex demands of administration in an increasingly complex domestic and international setting may have prompted the establishment of training for employees in the government. The need for training would have been all the greater in situations in which contact with foreign governments or trading firms demanded knowledge of foreign languages and scripts.

Third, there are some texts that may be understood as alluding to formal educational settings, although none of them requires this interpretation. For example, Isa 28:9–13 may ridicule techniques employed to teach students the alphabet.

In addition to these vague indications of the presence of schools of some form in ancient Israel, André Lemaire adduces a number of inscriptions from the Palestinian region as evidence: abecedaries, word lists, apparent sample letters, and what appear to be exercises in reading foreign languages.[74] Ultimately, however, Lemaire's inscriptional evidence remains insufficient to convince many scholars of the presence of schools within Israel. The reason for this is primarily its fragmentary nature. To date we have not recovered large numbers of texts that are uncontestably practice texts in any location in Palestine or any direct reference to the existence, organization, and operation of formal pedagogical institutions. Without evidence of this sort, it remains unclear whether the extant materials are the result of school activity or are merely the work of an individual or even a family group. Furthermore, as pointed out by Crenshaw, the Palestinian material claimed to support the existence of educational institutions lacks any marks of correction by teachers, which are a characteristic feature of Egyptian and Mesopotamian texts.[75]

If there were schools in ancient Israel, the remains suggest limited literacy, pointing to a quite restricted school system at best.[76] Furthermore, if there were schools, we have no clear information about the nature of the schools and the qualifications of the teachers and students. Consequently, we find

---

74. André Lemaire, *Les écoles et la formation de la Bible dans l'ancien Israël* (OBO 39; Göttingen: Vandenhoeck & Ruprecht, 1981); idem, "Education (Israel)," *ABD* 2.305–12; cf. Crenshaw, *Education in Ancient Israel*, 100–108. Graham I. Davies ("Were There Schools in Ancient Israel?" in *Wisdom in Ancient Israel: Essays in Honour of J. A. Emerton* [ed. John Day, Robert P. Gordon, and H. G. M. Williamson; Cambridge: Cambridge University Press, 1995] 199–211) also argues for the existence of schools on the basis of inscriptional evidence.

75. Crenshaw, *Education in Ancient Israel*, 106.

76. On literacy in ancient Israel, see Ian Young, "Israelite Literacy: Interpreting the Evidence (Part 1)," *VT* 48 (1998) 239–53; and "Israelite Literacy: Interpreting the Evidence (Part 2)," ibid., 408–22.

little support for the case for an identifiable body of sages prior to Sirach based on the existence of schools.

However, there are good indications that in some instances there was at least an elite societal group of "the wise," if not an actual profession. Perdue argues that "the social knowledge produced by traditional sages points to intellectuals who either possessed political power and wealth or were supported by those who did. Certainly the invitation to take up wisdom, which included acquiring the elite skills of reading and writing, demarcated sages and their tradition from everyday Israelite and Jewish society."[77] The term חכם is also used with clear reference to professionals in the service of foreign governments (e.g., Gen 41:8; Exod 7:11). Then, the instructions in Deut 1:13–15 may have set a precedent for giving positions of authority to men recognized as possessing wisdom. Jer 18:18 lists the חכם who offers עצה 'counsel' alongside the priest and prophet, suggesting that if this sage was not a member of a professional class, he was at least as readily identifiable as the priest and prophet (see Isa 19:11). Fox also argues that the superscriptions of various sections of the book of Proverbs (Prov 1:6; 22:17 [LXX]; 24:23) are indicators of the existence of an identifiable group of sages.[78]

Some of the Wisdom Literature appears to be directed generally toward people who were entering service in the royal court. For example, Qoh 8:2–5 would be of little relevance to the vast majority of the population but of particular importance to men and women serving in central government positions.[79] This specialized wisdom suggests some sort of formal context involving training and instruction by employed teachers. Finally, the very preservation of the wisdom material testifies to a group with an interest in its preservation and the ability to preserve it.

Conclusion

It is likely that the term חכם served as a label for people who displayed a degree of proficiency in any of a wide range of skills including but not confined to literary and intellectual abilities, as well as for people who were officially recognized for their wisdom. Moreover, at a number of points in the history of Israel there was apparently a close association between scribes and sages, no doubt due to their common interest in literary activity.

---

77. Perdue, "Cosmology and the Social Order in the Wisdom Tradition," 476.

78. Fox, *Qohelet and His Contradictions*, 331–32.

79. See Young, *Diversity in Pre-exilic Hebrew*, 147; Perdue, "Cosmology and the Social Order in the Wisdom Tradition," 476–78.

Although the evidence overall is somewhat ambiguous, the best indication for the existence of sages as an identifiable group in Israelite society, for the purposes of this study, comes from Ecclesiastes itself. There are clear examples in Qoheleth's words of wisdom terminology applied simply to people who possessed some degree of intellectual nous, but the epilogue is almost certainly using wisdom terminology in reference to a specific group whom the audience could identify: the sages.

The epilogue (as we will see in the next chapter) suggests that a group of sages had been established by the time that the epilogist created the book of Ecclesiastes. It is to this group at this particular point in history that I have applied the designation *wisdom movement*. I have deliberately avoided using terms such as *wisdom tradition* to refer to this group, because a title of this sort implies that this group had extensive historical antecedents. While I am not ruling out the possibility that a group did indeed exist well before the epilogist's time, the claim is ultimately unessential to my interpretation of Ecclesiastes.

The understanding of Ecclesiastes proposed below requires only two prerequisites to be viable. First, there must have been, at the time of composition by the epilogist, a group actually identified by the adjective חכם. Second, this group had to have been responsible for the composition or collection of wisdom material—material that was designed for the instruction of others, whether oral or written. The precise setting in which instruction took place is of little significance. Based on the discussion above, we may assume that taking these two fundamentals as our working presuppositions is not unreasonable.

The Epilogue

There is widespread agreement that the final six verses of the book of Ecclesiastes (12:9–14) form an epilogue to the words of Qoheleth recorded in the body of the work. Although it is commonly recognized that the voice of the epilogist also intrudes into the work in Qoh 1:1–2; 7:27; and 12:8, only in 12:9–14 do we find the thoughts of the epilogist about Qoheleth. Consequently, I exclude 12:8 from the epilogue proper for, despite the fact that it appears alongside the epilogue and contains a third-person reference to Qoheleth rather than the characteristic first-person speech found in the body of the work, it is nonetheless a quotation of Qoheleth's own words.

The short epilogue to Qoheleth's words, Qoh 12:9–14, is foundational to understanding the book of Ecclesiastes as a whole. Here the epilogist, who is effectively the author of the work, expresses his own thoughts on Qoheleth and the wisdom movement of his time. Only from this perspective is it possible to proceed to identify the relationship of Ecclesiastes to its world and to the remainder of the canon.

The Nature of the Epilogue

There has been a tendency for interpreters of Ecclesiastes to downplay or overlook the significance of the epilogue in their interpretation of the work and to focus instead on the words of Qoheleth himself.[1] This appears to have been the result of at least two factors. First, the epilogue is brief and somewhat enigmatic. Aside from the difficulties in reading it (see in detail below), its relative brevity causes many interpreters to overlook it or at least to assume that it does not significantly affect the message of the work as a whole.

The other factor contributing to the lack of attention given to the epilogue is its assumed secondary nature. This assessment of the epilogue derives from historical-critical scholars' identification of one, two, or even more later hands as responsible for the epilogue (see further in the next section). The epilogue has generally been judged as an attempt to soften the unpalatable words of Qoheleth and to present a less heterodox view that fits more comfortably with the remainder of the Hebrew canon. Consequently, the epilogue has been judged secondary, and interest has focused on the words of Qoheleth.

---

1. For example, C. Hassell Bullock (*An Introduction to the Poetic Books of the Old Testament* [Chicago: Moody, 1979] 220), who devotes only a brief paragraph to the epilogue.

Recently, however, writers have recognized the shortcomings of this approach. There are no extant copies of Ecclesiastes that do not include the epilogue as we have it.[2] There is no evidence that Ecclesiastes ever existed in any form other than the form in which it appears in the biblical canon. Consequently, we must consider the epilogist to be the author of the book of Ecclesiastes.[3]

There are several justifications for this assertion. It is the epilogist who shaped and presented the work in its final form. Although his hand is only explicitly evident in the prologue, epilogue, and 7:27, it is likely that he was responsible at least for the selection and arrangement of material presented in the book.[4] Indeed, it is possible that Qoheleth never did exist as an independent person but is merely a persona that was created by the epilogist to present the conclusions that he wanted to evaluate in the epilogue.[5] At least it was the epilogist, as the final redactor of the material, who approved the overall content of the work as it stands and recognized it as a literary unit that suited his intentions.

The historical-critical approach basically assumes that later redactors of Ecclesiastes were not willing to tamper with the contents of the work but

---

2. Only two partial copies of Ecclesiastes have been found at Qumran. 4QQoh[a] is the older (ca. 175–150 B.C.E.) and larger, preserving portions of chaps. 5–7. 4QQoh[b] is later (dated to the middle or latter half of the first century B.C.E.) and only preserves two small fragments of chap. 1. Neither copy is extensive enough to assist us in determining whether the epilogue is original.

3. See Michael V. Fox, "Frame-Narrative and Composition in the Book of Qohelet," *HUCA* 48 (1977) 83–106; idem, *A Time to Tear Down*, 365.

4. Although there are some women who were called wise in the Hebrew Bible (e.g., the wise woman of Tekoa—see p. 9 above; see also Proverbs 31) and a few literary associations between wisdom and the feminine (e.g., Proverbs 8), it is nonetheless highly probable that the epilogist was male. Consequently, I use the masculine pronoun to refer to the epilogist.

5. Fox, *Qohelet and His Contradictions*, 311–21. J.-M. Auwers similarly writes: "At the extreme, the epilogist could be the real author of the entire book and Qoheleth a purely fictional character set in an ill-defined past, a lightweight figure whom the author could transform at will (identifying him initially with Solomon, then abandoning that guise, concluding that 'Qoheleth was a sage'), a simple 'narrator' whom the author would make responsible for expressing daring ideas," in *Qohelet in the Context of Wisdom* [ed. A. Schoors; Leuven: Leuven University Press, 1998] 282); translation is mine. Original: "À la limite, l'épiloguiste pourrait être l'auteur réel de tout le livre et Qohèlèt, un personnage purement fictif relégué dans un passé mal défini, un être de plume que l'auteur métamorphoserait à son gré (l'identifiant tantôt à Salomon, abandonnant ensuite ce travestissement pour dire, finalement, que 'Qohèlèt fut un sage'), un simple 'narrateur' à qui l'auteur ferait endosser la responsabilité d'une pensée audacieuse" ("Problèmes d'interprètation de l'épilogue de Qohèlèt").

merely satisfied themselves with penning a few words of postscript in order to achieve their ends, no matter how little it accorded with the content of the preceding text. However, this assumption is somewhat anomalous, given that for so many other books in the Bible the proponents of this hermeneutic are happy to allow redactors to significantly alter all aspects of the texts. This sort of approach defies logic. A more consistent approach to Ecclesiastes is to recognize that any redactors of an earlier recension would have been willing to remove portions of the text that did not meet with their approval or to rearrange the text to suit their purposes.

The epilogue should, then, be treated as an integral part of the finished work of Ecclesiastes. The epilogist is—in a literary sense—the implied author of the entire book, and this invests the words of the epilogue with particular significance in shaping meaning for the book as a whole. The epilogist has chosen to append his remarks regarding Qoheleth and the wisdom movement to the record of Qoheleth's words, and it is only at this final point in the work that the reader grasps the full function of and intent for the entire work. The relative silence of the epilogist until the end has resulted in a text that draws the reader into Qoheleth's world, to accompany him on his discovery of the inadequacies of wisdom and to read about the true nature of the wisdom movement. By the end, the reader sees that wisdom cannot answer its own fundamental questions, and, even when it offers some benefit, it is fragile and easily undermined. Only at this point does the epilogist speak to affirm the veracity of Qoheleth's findings and to offer a way out of the darkness, from which wisdom by itself cannot escape.[6]

The Authorship of the Epilogue

Although I have argued above that the final editor of Ecclesiastes should ultimately be considered the author of the entire work, the issue of the authorship of the epilogue warrants a more detailed discussion. There are a number of opinions about the author of the epilogue, but they can be divided roughly into three categories.

First there are scholars who argue that Qoheleth himself was the author of the epilogue. Duane Garrett is a recent exponent of this position, arguing that

> [T]reating the conclusion as a secondary epilogue, either as a pious gloss or as part of an emerging canon consciousness, decapitates the entire work. Everything Ecclesiastes has affirmed up to this point—the sovereign freedom of God, the limits of human wisdom, thoughts on the use and abuse of

---

6. Possible reasons for the epilogist's choosing to place his words at the end rather than the beginning of the work are discussed below, p. 108.

wealth and power, and the brevity and absolute contingency of human life—all lead to the command to fear God.

For us the "meaninglessness" of life which the Teacher so ruthlessly exposed would seem to lead to despair or nihilism; for him it is an incitement to true piety. The insignificance of all that is done under the sun leaves him awestruck and silent before God.[7]

This position has little in its favor. The epilogue marks a change from Qoheleth's characteristic first-person speech to a third-person speech about Qoheleth and the wisdom movement. The most natural inference to be made from this change is that the epilogue was not authored by Qoheleth himself. Inference is a fundamental part of the reading process: in order for the reader to arrive at conclusions that contradict natural inferences, he or she must be given unambiguous contextual signals, which simply are not present in the epilogue.[8]

The validity of inferring that Qoheleth was not the author of the epilogue is further enhanced by the fact that, as will be shown below, the epilogue is somewhat critical of the sages—including Qoheleth himself. Furthermore, the third-person reference in Qoh 7:27 is more difficult to explain as self-referential speech by Qoheleth, because it would have been superfluous.[9] Someone other than Qoheleth has at least played a part in the formation of the book of Ecclesiastes. Finally, the epilogue introduces concepts foreign to the thought of Qoheleth in the rest of the body of the work, most notably the exhortation to "fear God and keep his commandments" in v. 13.[10]

Harold Fisch contends that to attribute to someone other than Qoheleth the authorship of the epilogue undermines the supreme irony of having the final words of the work invert the argument of the book.[11] However, the use of

---

7. Duane A. Garrett, *Proverbs, Ecclesiastes, Song of Songs* (NAC; Nashville: Broadman, 1993) 345; see also H. Carl Shank, "Qoheleth's World and Life View," in *Reflecting with Solomon* (ed. Roy B. Zuck; Grand Rapids: Baker, 1994) 71–73; Ardel B. Caneday, "Qoheleth: Enigmatic Pessimist or Godly Sage," *GTJ* 7 (1986) 21–56; Leland Ryken (Tremper Longman III and Leland Ryken, *A Complete Literary Guide to the Bible* [Grand Rapids: Zondervan, 1993] 269), who sees Qoh 12:9 as the writer's "self-portrait."

8. For a useful discussion of the role of inference in reading and understanding texts, see Susan S. Lanser, "(Feminist) Criticism in the Garden: Inferring Genesis 2–3," *Semeia* 41 (1988) particularly pp. 70–71.

9. See Fox, "Frame-Narrative and Composition in the Book of Qohelet," 84.

10. See the discussion below, beginning on p. 95.

11. Harold Fisch, *Poetry with a Purpose: Biblical Poetics and Interpretation* (Bloomington: Indiana University Press, 1988) 175. For further discussion on Qoheleth's use of irony, see Izak J. J. Spangenberg, "Irony in the Book of Qohelet," *JSOT* 72 (1996) 56–69.

irony by Qoheleth does not necessitate an ironic reading of the epilogue, and an appeal to this possibility is not sufficient to overcome the problems associated with maintaining that Qoheleth authored the epilogue. Consequently, the vast majority of scholars agree that the epilogue is the work of someone other than Qoheleth.[12]

The second position regarding the authorship of the epilogue is that the epilogue is the work of a single author who was not Qoheleth. This is essentially the position I follow because it provides an interpretation that is consistent with the evidence. The change to third-person speech about Qoheleth,[13] the unenthusiastic appraisal of the wisdom movement—including Qoheleth's teachings (an attitude that I shall argue is characteristic of the entire epilogue, not merely the final half)—and the presentation of a more orthodox alternative all point to the identity of the epilogist as someone other than Qoheleth.

At this point, the question naturally arises whether Qoheleth was a real person or was a persona created by the epilogist to make his point. Certainly the predominant view of scholars has been that Qoheleth did exist and that he was the author of the bulk of the material in the book—although many of his claims, particularly early on, are considered to be fictional, and his true identity is uncertain. The alternative is that Qoheleth was a persona created by the epilogist, with whom all the material in the book originated. This view accounts for the fact that the claims about Qoheleth in the opening chapters of the book do not present him as an entirely credible historical figure. The claim that he was king (but apparently no longer king), his vast wealth, his unmatched wisdom, and other descriptions make it difficult to align Qoheleth with any known historical figure. The frequent conclusion that the allusions are to Solomon has two main problems: no accounts of Solomon's reign suggest that he ever relinquished the throne, nor were there a number of monarchs reigning in Jerusalem prior to Solomon (as implied in Qoh 1:16).

Ultimately, there is no way to prove the historical existence or nonexistence of Qoheleth. This is not a great problem, because interpretation of the work does not rest on proving the existence of Qoheleth. To us as readers, it is clear that the epilogist intends to treat Qoheleth as a real person, and, in order to understand his meaning, we ought to follow his lead.

---

12. R. N. Whybray (*Ecclesiastes* [OTG; Sheffield: Sheffield Academic Press, 1989] 23) goes so far as to say that "it is indisputable that the book has been edited by someone other than Qoheleth."

13. For discussion on the likelihood of Qoheleth's employing third-person speech about himself, see Fox, "Frame-Narrative and Composition in the Book of Qohelet," 84; and Longman, *The Book of Ecclesiastes*, 7.

The third position regarding authorship of the epilogue is that more than one author wrote it.[14] The multiple-author view is generally based on the perception that the epilogue contains contradictory assessments of Qoheleth and the wisdom movement: portions of the epilogue appear favorably disposed toward Qoheleth, but other parts are antagonistic. As I will demonstrate below, the difficulties inherent in any reading of the text suggest that the variations in attitude toward Qoheleth may be exaggerated by some scholars. Furthermore, if a later editor had disagreed with the assessment of Qoheleth as recorded by a previous editor, why wouldn't he simply have removed the words of the previous editor rather than adding a contradiction? As I noted above, unless there is overwhelming evidence to support the presence of conflicting views in the epilogue, we should not assume that ancient editors were so simple and naïve as to be blind to having introduced outright contradictions into the works they were editing.

Given the considerations outlined above, I conclude that the most reasonable approach to the epilogue, and indeed to the entire book of Ecclesiastes, is to treat it as a single unit that comprised the introduction, body of the work, and epilogue, and this single unit met with the approval of the epilogist, who can reasonably be considered the author of the work.

The Structure of the Epilogue

The epilogue is commonly divided into two sections—12:9–11 and 12:12–14.[15] Scholars who make this division commonly offer two justifications for their understanding. First, the repetition of the term יתר 'and the rest/remainder' in vv. 9 and 12 is claimed to mark the beginning of new subsections. Second, most scholars understand vv. 9–11 to endorse Qoheleth's words and to praise Qoheleth as a sage, while vv. 12–14 are understood to be more critical

---

14. The greatest number of "authors" proposed for the epilogue is (to my knowledge) four; see M. Jastrow, *A Gentle Cynic Being the Book of Ecclesiastes* (Philadelphia: Lippincott, 1919) 254. O. Eissfeldt (*The Old Testament: An Introduction* [New York: Harper and Row, 1965] 493, 499) and H. Hertzberg (*Der Prediger* [KAT 17/4; Gütersloh: Mohn, 1963]) identify three separate voices. The more common disjunction of the epilogue into two parts (12:9–11 and 12–14) is posited by (for example) A. Lauha, *Kohelet* (BKAT 19; Neukirchen-Vluyn: Neukirchener Verlag, 1978) 217–23 and W. Zimmerli, *Das Buch des Predigers Salomo* (ATD 16/1; Göttingen: Vandenhoeck & Ruprecht, 1962). Seow has recently divided the epilogue into 12:9–13a and 13b–14 (*Ecclesiastes*, 38). Crenshaw states that 12:9–11 is "sympathetic" to Qoheleth, whereas 12–14 is "cool and dismissive," but he goes on to quote part of v. 11 as evidence of the epilogist's "cool and dismissive" attitude; see Crenshaw, "Ecclesiastes: Odd Book In," 28–29.

15. E.g., Kaiser, "Qoheleth," 85.

of Qoheleth and to provide an orthodox word in an attempt to make the work more palatable to the reader.[16]

In addition to basing a division on the repetition of the term יתר, Ogden offers three further points.[17] First, vv. 9–11 speak about Qoheleth in the third person while vv. 12–14 use imperative verbs (second person). Second, Ogden argues that the construct דברי 'words/sayings of' is used in a different way in vv. 10 and 11 from דבר 'thing/matter' in v. 13. Third, Qoheleth is the subject of vv. 9–11, whereas vv. 12–14 address the faithful in their search for wisdom. Ogden's arguments are far from compelling, however. Most significantly, only vv. 9–10 refer to Qoheleth; v. 11 explicitly moves to address sages in general, and v. 12 appears to build on v. 11 (see the discussion below). Ogden's other observation regarding variation in the use of דבר cannot realistically be taken as the mark of a new section, for not only is the term quite common but the semantic variation is understood by its use in differing grammatical constructions (appearing in construct in vv. 9–11 but in the absolute state in v. 13).

The supposed variation in attitude toward Qoheleth's words is the one element of the epilogue that has prompted most writers to regard the epilogue as the work of more than one person. However, this analysis does not represent best the content of the passage. The presumption that vv. 9–11 offer a positive evaluation of Qoheleth (and indeed of the broader wisdom movement) is not as plainly borne out by the text as many suppose. Further, if the pronoun המה 'them' in v. 12 has an antecedent, it ties v. 12 to the preceding verses, further undermining the argument for multiple, independent epilogues.

In view of these considerations, the apparent pattern created by the repetition of יתר may not be compelling enough to dictate a bipartite structure for the epilogue. When יתר is used elsewhere in Ecclesiastes, it does not mark a new section (see 2:15; 6:8, 1; 7:11, 16). We must be careful not to allow purely lexical patterns to determine the structure of a narrative and then base our reading of the text on that structure, which is thus allowed undue control over the meaning.[18] The effect of this is the subordination of grammatical and semantic elements to lexical patterns, potentially skewing the meaning.

---

16. See Svend Holm-Nielsen, "On the Interpretation of Qoheleth in Early Christianity," *VT* 24 (1974) 169–70.

17. Ogden, *Qoheleth*, 208.

18. This is my principal criticism of the work of Andrew G. Shead on the epilogue. See his *Ecclesiastes 12:9–14: Reading the Epilogue as an Epilogue* (M.Th. diss., Australian College of Theology, 1995); idem, "Ecclesiastes from the Outside In." For further discussion of Shead's approach, see my "Ecclesiastes and the End of Wisdom," 121–24.

The following representation of the basic structure is derived from the detailed grammatical and semantic analysis of the epilogue that follows. The justification for this structure appears in the sections below, which also provide a detailed analysis of the text.

> 12:9–10   A biographical comment about Qoheleth
> 12:11–12   Warnings about the teaching of the sages
> 12:13–14   The conclusion to the matter

Interpreting the Epilogue

Having discussed the nature and structure of the epilogue, we now turn to the text itself. Unfortunately, the task of interpreting the epilogue is beset by difficulties. There are a number of hapax legomena and rare or obscure terms, as well as grammatical difficulties and ambiguities. These factors contribute to the obstacles we as readers face when attempting to understand the function of Ecclesiastes in the biblical canon.

Before proceeding, I will make some preliminary comments regarding methodology. My goal in this chapter is to understand the received text and to appeal to emendation and alteration only as a last resort. When difficulties arise with the text, I prefer to opt for a solution that requires only a change in the Masoretic pointing and punctuation rather than in the consonantal text, because the vowel points represent a layer of tradition considerably younger than the consonantal text itself (with the *matres lectionis*).

Furthermore, the aim is to understand the significance of the text in its original historical context—at least insofar as possible. I am not offering a "contemporary" reading without reference to historical factors that control the meaning. I seek to posit a plausible understanding of the function of this text as originally composed for a specific historical context. Because there is little external historical information regarding this context, much of the detail of the situation, the Sitz im Leben of the text, will need to be reconstructed from the text itself, although whenever data external to Ecclesiastes are available for establishing a context, I will take them into consideration.

Qoheleth 12:9–10: A Biographical Comment

[9]Furthermore, because Qoheleth was a sage he constantly taught knowledge to the people. He listened to, researched, and corrected many wisdom sayings. [10]Qoheleth sought to find pleasing words, but very honest words of truth were written.

The epilogue opens with a few brief biographical comments about Qoheleth. Murphy claimed that v. 9 describes Qoheleth's activity rather than his book,[19] but the words of Qoheleth recorded in Ecclesiastes cannot be distinguished from his teaching and research activities. Indeed, v. 10 indicates that the epilogist here seeks to provide the reader with background information on Qoheleth in order to explain the pertinence of the words of Qoheleth that he has previously recorded. Those words were from one who taught extensively, researched comprehensively, and wrote honestly.

Verse 9

ויתר שהיה קהלת חכם

Furthermore, because Qoheleth was a sage . . .

The opening clause of the epilogue presents two difficulties. First, the significance of the term ויתר followed by a relative pronoun must be determined. Second, although it is clear that Qoheleth is described as being a חכם, it is not immediately clear whether this word is here being used as a technical term referring to a class of sages or court officials, or whether it is merely being used to describe Qoheleth as a wise man.

The lexical and syntactical problems associated with this first clause of the epilogue revolve around the meaning of the term יתר and the function of the relative pronoun ש. Part of the difficulty in understanding the expression lies in the rather infrequent use of the noun יתר, which appears outside of Ecclesiastes only in 1 Sam 15:15 and Esth 6:6. What is more, nowhere else is the noun followed by the relative pronoun. The relative is itself problematic: there is no apparent referent for it and it is unlikely that it functions here as a conjunction.[20] Four different solutions have been proposed by various scholars.

The first solution understands the expression ויתר ש- as an idiom used to introduce a statement of the form "in addition to a is b."[21] In support of this interpretation, Gordis appeals to the Mishnaic expressions יותר מש- and יותר ממה ש-, both of which mean 'beyond the fact that . . .'. The LXX employs περισσὸν 'furthermore' at this point, which may also be understood to lend support to this argument.

---

19. Murphy, *Ecclesiastes*, 125.

20. On the use of the relative pronoun as a conjunction, see Bruce K. Waltke and M. O'Connor, *An Introduction to Biblical Hebrew Syntax* (Winona Lake, Ind.: Eisenbrauns, 1990) 333–35.

21. Gordis, *Koheleth: The Man and His World*, 351; Fox also cites Podechard, Barton, and most other commentators as appealing to this meaning (Fox, *Qohelet and His Contradictions*, 322).

This solution, however, is not entirely adequate, because the Mishnaic expressions do not completely parallel the expression as it appears here; the Mishnaic phrases quoted by Gordis include the preposition מן 'from', which frequently conveys a comparative sense, a sense clearly present in the Mishnaic phrases. The absence of this preposition in Qoh 12:9 means that this interpretation of the opening of the epilogue is far less likely.[22]

Second, Fox argues that יתר here ought to be understood as a conjunction meaning 'furthermore', used to introduce new information about Qoheleth. Fox does not understand the new information to be the statement that Qoheleth was a חכם but, rather, that he constantly taught knowledge to the people.[23]

Fox explains the relative to be a "nominalising pronoun" as it is used in Cant 1:7; 3:1 (see also Qoh 5:4; Neh 2:10) and quite frequently in BA.[24] The clause with the relative אשר in Qoh 5:4 is similar in grammatical structure and may be compared with our clause as follows:

| 5:4 | לא־תדר משתדור ולא תשלם | אשר | טוב |
| 12:9 | היה קהלת חכם | ש | ויתר |

Third, it is possible to render the relative pronoun in the normal sense by understanding the verse along the lines of 'And [this is] an additional thing that Qoheleth was: a sage'. Although this interpretation has the advantage of relying on the most common meaning for the relative, the clause becomes rather clumsy because the relative is actually redundant. The English equivalent becomes something like this: 'and another thing that Qoheleth was was a sage'.

Finally, Seow suggests that the particle ש should not be understood as a relative at all but in a causal sense, which is reflected in his rendering of the opening words of the epilogue: "Additionally, because Qoheleth was a sage. . . ." Seow cites the use of ש as 'because' in Qoh 8:14; Cant 1:6; 5:2, and of אשר (also 'because') in Qoh 4:9.[25] The use of ὅτι in the LXX's otherwise rather literal rendering of this verse also tends to support this interpreta-

---

22. Fox, ibid., 322.

23. Idem, *A Time to Tear Down*, 350–52.

24. Fox has not made this clear in his works to date but has explained his understanding of the relative pronoun to me in private correspondence. This type of usage is quite common in Aramaic; see such passages as Dan 2:8–9. Fox (ibid., 350) offers a literal translation of the opening of v. 9 as "and something remaining is (the fact) that Qohelet was a sage."

25. Seow, *Ecclesiastes*, 383. Seow ("Linguistic Evidence and the Dating of Qohelet," 661) also makes the comment that "ש־ is used in Qohelet in a variety of ways, including as a conjunction introducing a subject of an object clause, or even a purpose clause (1:7; 2:13, 14, 15, 24; 3:13, 14; 5:14, 15; 8:14; 9:5; 12:9)."

tion. Furthermore, Seow understands ויתר to be separated from the remainder of the clause, as indicated by the disjunctive accent in the MT.

As far as the meaning of the clause is concerned, Shead is correct in stating of the first two suggestions that there "is not much to distinguish the two options," although he prefers the first option, based on the fact that "it requires a less harsh ellipsis to render ויתר."[26] This is a rather dubious means of making a decision, because in Fox's own rendering (second option) there is *no* ellipsis (the ellipsis only appears in Shead's own attempt to render along Fox's lines). Shead also overlooks the fact that the first explanation of the grammar is entirely without parallel anywhere in ancient Hebrew writing. Fox's interpretation is clearly superior to the first option, although the relative then makes little contribution to the sentence at all. In light of all these considerations, Seow's causal understanding is ultimately the simplest solution and accounts well for the presence of the particle.

In spite of the grammatical difficulties of this clause, most scholars agree that additional information about Qoheleth is being provided by the epilogist. At this level, Fox's interpretation substantially agrees with the position he criticizes: both positions understand the text to be telling us that Qoheleth taught the people knowledge and that this is to be understood as information added to what has already been gleaned from Qoheleth's words by the reader. The difference emerges in the fact that Fox understands the epilogist's identification of Qoheleth as a sage (as opposed to a wise person) as also being part of the additional information being presented. The causal reading of ש in this clause indicates that the additional information about Qoheleth was that, as a sage, he constantly taught knowledge to the people.

This brings us to the significance of the description of Qoheleth as חכם. The meaning of the term חכם is the other major issue facing the interpreter of the opening clause of the epilogue.[27] Once again there are two alternatives: either Qoheleth is being described as wise; or else he is being described as a member of a professional class of sages, at least some of whom may have been members of the royal court.

Whybray has argued that the term חכם does not designate a member of a specific class but refers to any person possessing the virtue of wisdom.[28] In support of this reading is the fact that this appears to be the way in which the

---

26. Shead, *Ecclesiastes 12:9–14: Reading the Epilogue as an Epilogue*, 44.

27. For further discussion, see p. 38.

28. See Whybray, *The Intellectual Tradition in the Old Testament*, 47–48; idem, *Ecclesiastes* (NCB; Grand Rapids: Eerdmans, 1989) 170. Shead also adopts this position, in *Ecclesiastes 12:9–14: Reading the Epilogue as an Epilogue*, 44.

term is used elsewhere by Qoheleth, suggesting that the epilogist conformed to Qoheleth's pattern of usage.

Fox argues, however, that Whybray has pushed his case too far.[29] Fox notes a number of passages in the Wisdom Literature in which חכם most likely refers to a specific group of people within society. Fox argues that חכמים in Qoh 12:11 refers to a specific class of sages and that this is borne out by the parallel expression בעלי אספות ('masters of collections').[30] Furthermore, it appears to be redundant for the epilogist merely to comment that Qoheleth was a wise person in v. 9, for this has been made clear by all that has gone before. It makes more sense if we are being informed that Qoheleth was himself a member of the sages. Indeed, if the epilogist is referring just to anyone who is 'wise' חכם, he is then certainly making unjustifiable generalizations about these people in vv. 11–12. The reference to making books in v. 12 suggests a focus on literary activity, from which we may infer that the word חכם is being employed specifically to refer to a group of people who produced such works (if this is not the case, the reference to making books is reduced to an aside with no specific connection to the remainder of the epilogue or to the words of Qoheleth recorded by the epilogist).[31] In addition, to be able "constantly [to] teach knowledge to the people," as Qoheleth is said to do, and to do this because one is a חכם, suggests that this term is most likely being used to refer to a specific category of people in society.

Although this choice appears to be relatively insignificant, the decision about which way to read the term חכם here has ramifications for the interpretation of the entire work and its function in the canon of Scripture. If this term refers to a specific group in society, the epilogue makes comments about this group and their activities (such as making books) and may be seen as either endorsing or criticizing these activities. If, on the other hand, חכם is understood as only making the assertion that Qoheleth himself was a wise person, the warnings of the epilogue must be applied to wisdom and wise people in general. On balance, however, it is likely that the epilogist is using חכם to refer to a specific class in society, not merely to any wise person in society.

---

29. Fox, *Qohelet and His Contradictions*, 330–32.

30. See p. 74 below for further discussion of this expression.

31. The idea of producing books here, however, need not be a direct reference to the scribal task of writing the text but can be understood as the broader task of composing the words that constitute the text of the book. Others who understand חכם to refer to a member of a specific class include Murphy, *Ecclesiastes*, 125; and Seow, *Ecclesiastes*, 384.

עוד למד דעת את העם

he constantly taught knowledge to the people

The relationship of this clause to the previous is not easy to determine. The Masoretic accents suggest that this begins a new clause (placing the *'atnah* under the previous word, חכם). The difficulty centers on the use of the adverb עוד (literally 'more'). The term usually expresses continued action and as such is understood to be indicating that Qoheleth constantly taught the people knowledge—that is, this was his regular practice.[32] Gordis, on the other hand, understands עוד to mean 'additionally', thus making the activity of teaching knowledge to the people an exceptional one for a חכם.[33]

Gordis's interpretation depends heavily upon the validity of his explanation of the opening clause. As we have seen above, however, his explanation does not stand up to close scrutiny. Because the particle ש is most appropriately understood in a causal sense, this clause functions to explain the consequences of Qoheleth's identification as a sage.[34] The information is being provided precisely because Qoheleth is a sage.

What we are told in this clause, however, raises two further questions: what was the content of the knowledge that Qoheleth taught, and to whom did he teach it?

The term דעת 'knowledge' is used by the epilogist to describe what Qoheleth taught to "the people." In spite of the fact that דעת has a broad semantic range, it is nonetheless predominantly associated with the Wisdom Literature (almost two-thirds of all occurrences of דעת in Biblical Hebrew appear in Proverbs, Job, and Ecclesiastes). Furthermore, in Wisdom Literature it is frequently used parallel to חכם (e.g., Qoh 1:16, 18; 7:12). Thus it is reasonable to conclude that the type of knowledge that Qoheleth taught related to the concerns of the wisdom movement—knowledge that was intended to improve one's life by providing guidance in choosing appropriate behavior in all matters of life.

Turning to the second question—various views about the identity of the students of the sages exist. Some hold that the sages specifically operated in the royal courts, others suggest that there were wisdom schools, while still others suggest that people from all walks of life benefited from the teachings of the sages. I must point out, however, that the epilogist uses the noun עם,

---

32. Fox (*Qohelet and His Contradictions*, 322) cites Qoh 7:28; Gen 46:29; Ruth 1:14; and Ps 84:5 as examples of such usage of this term.

33. Gordis, *Koheleth: The Man and His World*, 351–52; cf. BDB, 729a.

34. Otherwise, we would be left with a hanging introduction: "Additionally, because Qoheleth was a sage. . . . He also. . . ."

which does not usually refer to specific subclasses of society but commonly refers to the 'people' in general.[35]

Seow claims that teaching the public was clearly part of the "job description" of the Israelite sage: "Yet, the sages in Israel, whatever one may assume about their social location, surely did not regard teaching of the public as something extraordinary (cf. Sir 37:23). Public instruction was not what one did 'besides being a sage' (so JB)."[36] This argument is not convincing, however. There are strong indications that, by the time of Sirach, the wisdom movement had been quite comprehensively reformed, whereas the book of Ecclesiastes originated at a time when the wisdom movement had moved away from the theological ideals established to some extent in Proverbs.[37] Seow does not explain why the epilogist felt it necessary to include the information that, as a sage, Qoheleth also taught wisdom to the people. Furthermore, the fact that the epilogist has to tell the reader that Qoheleth constantly taught knowledge to the people suggests that this was information that the reader did not expect and that was not immediately associated with the activities of a sage. Seow may be correct in stating that "the sages were supposed to teach the public, even humanity in general, not just the elite," but the fact that the epilogist made this explicit implies that many sages of Qoheleth's time had forsaken this responsibility.

Thus it is likely that the epilogist is highlighting Qoheleth as an exceptional sage. He was exceptional because, unlike many of his contemporaries, he felt that part of his role as a sage was to teach the public. And this is not the only point the epilogist is making in this statement. It is also apparent that the epilogist felt that a sage ought to teach the public and that, by making this statement about Qoheleth, he may well have been casting aspersions on the credentials of some of his contemporaries.

---

35. The use in some editions of the LXX of λαός 'people' to render עַם suggests that 'people' was the understanding adopted by the translators of the LXX. See Colin Brown (ed.), *The New International Dictionary of New Testament Theology* (3 vols.; Grand Rapids: Zondervan, 1976) 2.796–99; Seow, *Ecclesiastes*, 384; Auwers, "Problèmes d'interprétation de l'épilogue de Qohèlèt," 270, who states that "In Qoh 12:9, the word עַם undoubtedly indicates, as opposed to חֲכָם, those who did not study in the schools of wisdom" [original: "En Qo 12,9, le mot עַם désigne sans doute, par opposition à חֲכָם, ceux qui n'ont pas étudié dans les écoles de sagesse"]. Others who recognize עַם as a reference to the general populace include N. Lohfink, *Kohelet* (Neue Echter Bibel; Stuttgart: Echter-Verlag, 1980); Crenshaw, *Ecclesiastes*, 190.

36. Seow, *Ecclesiastes*, 383.

37. Refer to the discussion beginning on p. 38.

ואזן וחקר תקן משלים הרבה

He listened to, researched, and corrected many wisdom sayings

This portion of v. 9 explains some of Qoheleth's activities as a sage. To understand precisely what is being said, we need to take a close look at all of the terms to understand their significance in the epilogist's view of Qoheleth and the sages in general.

The first verb, אזן, is a hapax legomenon and has frequently been understood as meaning 'weigh': Qoheleth would here be described as one who 'weighed' proverbs. This understanding is based on the apparent cognate noun מאזן 'balances, scales' as well as on an apparent Arabic cognate.[38] However, Michael Fox is correct in rejecting this common interpretation of the term. There are more appropriate terms in BH for 'weigh'; and if the sense intended here was 'judge', then there are other terms that were normally used to express that notion.[39] Furthermore, Seow points out that the idiom "to weigh words," in the sense of evaluating them, is not attested anywhere in Biblical Hebrew or anywhere else in the ANE.[40]

The term is better understood to be a denominative form derived from the noun אזן 'ear', with the meaning 'listen' or, perhaps, 'analyze'. This interpretation is supported by the LXX (which employs the noun οὖς 'ear'), Syriac, Targum, and other ancient versions.[41] Listening is one of the activities characteristic of the wise according to Prov 1:5–6, 2:2, 4:20, 5:1, and numerous other passages. Considering that the remainder of this verse claims that Qoheleth corrected the wisdom of others (see below), it is appropriate that Qoheleth is here described as one who listened to the wisdom of others. Qoheleth analyzed the wisdom of others and then sought to correct its deficiencies himself.

The asyndetic juxtaposition of the verbs חקר 'research' and תקן 'correct' suggests that the verbs should be read as an instance of hendiadys. Ginsberg observes that the syntax here indicates that the first two verbs function as adverbial modifiers of the third. The problem with this view is that in each of the other ten appearances of this type of construction in BH the most straightforward reading of the text is to tie the first two verbs together and have the third

---

38. See BDB, 24b; Auwers, "Problèmes d'interprètation de l'épilogue de Qohèlèt," 270.

39. Fox, *Qohelet and His Contradictions*, 323.

40. Seow, *Ecclesiastes*, 384. Seow goes on to point out that the noun מאזנים is properly related not to the root אזן but to יזן, from a hypothetical Proto-Semitic root *wzn* (cf. Arab. *wazana* 'to weigh').

41. See also F. J. Backhaus, "Der Weisheit letzter Schluß!" *BN* 72 (1994) 35; N. Lohfink, "Les épilogues du livre de Qohélet et les débuts du canon," in *"Ouvrir les Écritures": Mélanges offerts à Paul Beauchamp* (ed. P. Bovati and R. Meynet; LD 162; Paris: Cerf, 1995) 86–87.

begin a new asyndetic clause.[42] There are no instances in which Ginsberg's proposed understanding of the construction easily fits the context.

Another alternative proposed by scholars such as Michael Fox is to follow some ancient manuscripts and insert the conjunction ו prior to תקן to overcome the difficulties.[43] Taking into consideration the other instances of this construction, I find this emendation unnecessary; a similar meaning can be derived from the asyndetic construction.

The verb חקר appears only here in the Piel but generally means 'search' in the sense of 'investigate, research, discover' rather than in the sense of 'seek something' (for which the use of the verb בקש, as in the next verse, would be more common). The term is used as a reference to the activities of the wise in Job 5:27, 29:16, and Prov 28:11 and is an appropriate description here of the activity of Qoheleth.

The term תקן appears only in Ecclesiastes (1:15; 7:13; 12:9), although the Aramaic cognate appears in Daniel (Dan 4:36). Many scholars render תקן as 'composing' in this verse, but this is quite difficult to justify, and better understandings are available.[44] The previous two appearances in Ecclesiastes refer to something that exists but is 'bent' (עות) and cannot be straightened, implying that Qoheleth's task as described here was to "straighten" preexisting

---

42. The construction verb-*waw*-verb-verb, with the verbs all agreeing in gender and number, appears in BH in 1 Kgs 8:47; Isa 37:27; Hos 5:14; Mic 1:8; Pss 3:6; 35:15; 95:6; Job 3:13; 5:18; 36:11; and Qoh 12:9. It also appears in BA in Dan 3:11. If we read this text as in these other instances, we would have: 'he listened [or analyzed] and he investigated, and he corrected many proverbs'. Lohfink's rendering appears to reflect this understanding: "after gathering and examining them, he corrected many proverbs" [original: "après les avoir rassemblés et examinés, il a corrigé beaucoup de proverbes"]; see Lohfink, "Les épilogues du livre de Qohélet et les débuts du canon," 141–42 (translation mine).

43. Fox, *Qohelet and His Contradictions*, 310, 322–23.

44. The word תקן is understood to mean 'compose' by Gordis, *Koheleth: The Man and His World*, 350, 352; Fox, *Qohelet and His Contradictions*, 310, 322–23; Eric S. Christianson, *A Time to Tell: Narrative Strategies in Ecclesiastes* (JSOTSup 280; Sheffield: Sheffield Academic Press, 1998) 103 n. 18; Lauha, *Kohelet*, 217–18; Backhaus, "Der Weisheit letzter Schluß!" 32–33; L. Di Fonzo, *Ecclesiaste* (La Sacra Bibia; Turin: Marietti, 1967) 328–30; K. von Galling, "Der Prediger," in *Die Fünf Megilloth* (HAT 18; Tübingen: Mohr, 1969) 123; D. Michel, *Qohelet* (Darmstadt: Wissenshaftliche Buchgesellschaft, 1988) 168; Cristoph Dohmen, "Der Weisheit letzter Schluß? Anmerkungen zur Übersetzung und Bedeutung von Koh 12,9–14," *BN* 63 (1992) 13–14. Fox offers no justification for this reading, although others appeal to the use of the term in Sir 47:9 or a supposed Akkadian cognate, overlooking the use elsewhere in Ecclesiastes. The LXX does not appear to render this term explicitly. Seow (*Ecclesiastes*, 385) indicates that in postbiblical Hebrew the term had a range of meanings in addition to 'straighten, repair', including 'to fix in place, set in order, prepare, establish, introduce, improve', although our best clue here is Qoheleth's own use of the term and the immediate context.

wisdom sayings that he considered "bent." The term עות in the Piel or Pual usually means 'pervert, corrupt'. Because elsewhere in Ecclesiastes תקן is used as an antonym for עות, it is best to read תקן in the epilogue as referring to the correction of preexisting wisdom sayings rather than the composition of new sayings.[45] If this is the case, Qoheleth is here described by the epilogist as a corrector of the words of other sages.[46]

This clause is the only place in which the term משל 'proverb' appears in Ecclesiastes. Although some scholars have considered the term to be a reference to the book of Proverbs, suggesting that the epilogist is implying that Qoheleth was in some way responsible for the book of Proverbs, the claim cannot stand up to scrutiny.[47] The contents of Proverbs are significantly different from the recorded words of Qoheleth, making it unlikely that the two share a common source. Furthermore, the argument presumes much about the dating and formation of both the book of Proverbs and the book of Ecclesiastes, as well as the early designation of Proverbs by this term. Considering that the term משל was a common term in Wisdom Literature and referred to a broad variety of wisdom utterances, it is unnecessary to see here a reference to any specific work.

The word משל often refers to the short aphorisms characteristic of some portions of the Wisdom Literature (notably much of the book of Proverbs), but it ought not to be restricted to this meaning. The epilogue is not claiming that Qoheleth corrected aphorisms, exclusive of any other forms of Wisdom Literature. The Hebrew Bible elsewhere uses this same term to refer to parables, riddles, or allegories (for example, see Ezek 17:1–24), or to the oracles of Balaam (Num 23:7, 18; 24:3, 15); it is used in parallel with the term שנינה

---

45. See Auwers, "Problèmes d'interprètation de l'épilogue de Qohèlèt," 270–71; Lohfink, "Les épilogues du livre de Qohélet et les débuts du canon," 141–42. Seow (*Ecclesiastes*, 385) also admits that this verb may include the notion of 'repairing, improving'. Fishbane (*Biblical Interpretation in Ancient Israel*, 32) states that, "although the basic meaning of the Biblical Hebrew verb תקן is 'to correct', it is found with the developed scribal sense 'to edit' both in the contemporary Aramaic milieu to which 'Ecclesiastes' was so indebted and in rabbinic Hebrew." Fishbane's argument tends to overlook the previous use of the verb by Qoheleth in favor of extrabiblical references but is worth noting for his acknowledgment of the basic meaning of the term.

46. Longman (*The Book of Ecclesiastes*, 277) states that "it appears that [Qoheleth] studied proverbs and did not invent new ones. This coincides with what we encounter in 1:12–12:7."

47. See F. Hitzig, *Der Prediger Salomo's* (Leipzig: Weidmann, 1847) 217; Barton, *A Critical and Exegetical Commentary on the Book of Ecclesiastes*, 197–98; E. Podechard, *L'Ecclésiaste* (Paris, 1912) 475–76; and especially Gerald H. Wilson, "'The Words of the Wise': The Intent and Significance of Qoheleth 12:9–14," *JBL* 103 (1984) 175–92.

'byword' (Deut 28:37; 1 Kgs 9:7; and elsewhere), and even to refer to the speeches of Job (see Job 13:12; 27:1; etc.).[48]

It is more likely that the term משל here refers to all of Qoheleth's wisdom compositions, including—but not necessarily limited to—all the words recorded by the epilogist in the body of this book. Consequently, the epilogist claims here that all of the words of Qoheleth recorded in this book operate in some way to correct the teachings of the other sages, who were probably Qoheleth's contemporaries.

Adopting this perspective sheds light on the words of Qoheleth recorded in the contents of the work. Qoheleth's words are not the result of his isolated reflections but are his truthful correction of the thoughts of other sages.[49] Thus, while other sages may have offered their own answers to the speculative questions posed throughout Ecclesiastes, Qoheleth reconsidered the questions addressed by these sages together with their answers and concluded repeatedly that their solutions were incorrect. Because Qoheleth deduced that the answers to the questions were not available to the sages, it must be that other sages did offer answers—answers that enticed their students with their pleasing nature (as we shall see below).

Verse 10

בקש קהלת למצא דברי־חפץ

Qoheleth sought to find pleasing words . . .

Verse 10 concludes the epilogist's description of the activities of Qoheleth. Although the terminology of v. 10 is straightforward, we must answer two questions regarding the first clause in order to arrive at the epilogist's meaning: What are דברי־חפץ? And did Qoheleth succeed in finding them?

It is clear that the expression דברי־חפץ in v. 10 describes the nature of the words that Qoheleth sought. The problem for interpreters is that, in reference to language, חפץ 'delight' can function on two levels: it may refer to aesthetic form or it may refer to meaning.

Even a cursory reading of Qoheleth reveals that the meaning of his words cannot easily be described as "pleasing."[50] Additionally, the activity of the sages in the ancient world was generally considered to be of a noteworthy literary nature—a point reflected in the clear linguistic shaping of Qoheleth's

---

48. See *TWOT*, 1.533–34.

49. With reference to the emphasis on the truthfulness of Qoheleth's words, see my comments on p. 67 below.

50. See Crenshaw (*Ecclesiastes*, 191), who notes that "many readers have not concurred in the statement that Qohelet's observations are both pleasing and trustworthy."

own words. This leads most scholars to suggest that דברי־חפץ refers not to the meaning of Qoheleth's words but to an aesthetic assessment of their rhetorical form.[51] The epilogist, on this understanding, is suggesting that Qoheleth invested some time and effort in presenting his wisdom in a style that was pleasing to the hearer, even if the message itself was not necessarily pleasant. Gordis suggests that there may even be in this statement a veiled criticism: "as though to say that Koheleth had strained unduly after literary effect."[52]

However, to rule out entirely the possibility that דברי־חפץ could refer to the meaning of Qoheleth's words would be unfortunate for a number of reasons. First, the epilogist does not claim that Qoheleth *succeeded* in producing דברי־חפץ (a point discussed in detail below). Second, Qoheleth is presented throughout the body of the work as beginning his investigations with positive expectations of a fruitful outcome, only to be frustrated at every turn and repeatedly driven to the conclusion that גם־זה הבל ('this, too, is senseless'). This leaves the reader with the impression that, although Qoheleth sought to find a "pleasing" answer, in the end he could not do so and maintain his integrity. Third, Qoheleth himself never explicitly reveals a desire to present his findings in an aesthetically pleasing manner; his concern always appears to be to record the truth as he finds it. The fact that Qoheleth's writings do reveal a degree of literary design does not dictate that this term must refer to the aesthetic quality of his words. Qoheleth himself makes it clear that he strove to find answers to the questions he considered (see 1:12–13; etc.).

Thus, although it is possible for the expression דברי־חפץ to refer to the aesthetic appeal of Qoheleth's words, I contend that the epilogist is almost certainly using the expression to refer to the pleasing meaning that Qoheleth was seeking in answer to his questions.[53]

The manner in which the epilogist has expressed himself in v. 10 has opened the way for scholars to debate at length whether or not Qoheleth

---

51. See Gordis, *Koheleth: The Man and His World*, 352; Crenshaw, *Ecclesiastes*, 191; Whybray, *Ecclesiastes* (NCB), 171; Murphy, *Ecclesiastes*, 125; Christianson, *A Time to Tell*, 104. See also the scholars listed by Auwers, "Problèmes d'interprètation de l'épilogue de Qohèlèt," 273. An exception is Brevard Childs (*Introduction to the Old Testament as Scripture* [London: SCM, 1979] 585), who writes that "the phrase 'pleasing words' (v. 10) is not an aesthetic description, but rather portrays his writings as 'fitting' and 'appropriate.'"

52. Gordis, *Koheleth: The Man and His World*, 352.

53. Unfortunately, the expression דברי־חפץ does not occur elsewhere in BH. Graham Ogden accepts both options when he describes Qoheleth's words as "both elegant in form as well as able to convey deep and satisfying meaning"—although I disagree with him about how successful Qoheleth was in producing pleasing words. See Ogden, *Qoheleth*, 209; see also Seow, *Ecclesiastes*, 385.

successfully found דברי־חפץ. Looking at other instances of a finite form of the verb בקש followed by an infinitive does not help us to decide whether Qoheleth succeeded in finding דברי־חפץ. The word בקש 'sought' followed by an infinitive means 'sought to do something' without success in Exod 2:15; 4:24; Deut 13:10; 1 Sam 19:2, 10; 2 Sam 21:2; 1 Kgs 11:40; 19:10, 14; Jer 26:21; Ps 37:32; 40:15; Esth 2:21; 3:6; and 6:2. However, the construction means 'sought to do something' with success in Gen 43:30; 1 Sam 14:4; 1 Kgs 11:22; Zech 6:7; and 12:9.

Some of the remaining instances of this construction in Biblical Hebrew could fit into either of these categories, but the passages listed above represent the majority of the occurrences in the Hebrew Bible. The most feasible conclusion, based on this sample of the uses of the construction, is that the phrase refers to a desire without predetermining the nature of the outcome.[54] However, most of the instances of this construction (בקש + infinitive construct) appear in narrative in which the success or otherwise of the seeking is determined only later in the narrative; thus, it would be inappropriate to disclose the outcome of the story and would undermine the rhetorical construction of the narrative as a whole. In the epilogue of Ecclesiastes, however, the story has already been told—the words of Qoheleth have been recorded and read by the time the reader arrives at this statement. Both reader and epilogist already have the available data to decide whether or not Qoheleth had succeeded in finding דברי־חפץ. Because the text does not simply tell us that Qoheleth *found* דברי־חפץ, the epilogist must be insinuating that Qoheleth failed to find pleasing words. Furthermore, it is plainly quite difficult to reconcile the words of Qoheleth recorded in the body of the work with the description דברי־חפץ. Consequently, it is highly likely that the epilogist is indicating that Qoheleth failed to find דברי־חפץ.

However, it also appears unlikely that the epilogist is critical of Qoheleth's failure to find דברי־חפץ.[55] He is probably only referring to Qoheleth's initial aim of attempting to answer the questions he was considering. Qoheleth did not set out to find depressing, painful truths. Rather, he was forced to these conclusions by the weight of the evidence before him and by his own honesty. The fact that he did not find what he sought indicates not his failure but his integrity—instead of falling back on easy answers and pleasing words (as perhaps other sages had done), Qoheleth preferred to state the truth. This appears to be the point made by the second clause of v. 10.

---

54. Similar comments could also be made about the use of the verb בקש by itself, such as in Qoh 7:25–29 and 8:17, where the success of the quest is not evident from the presence of the verb.

55. Contra Longman, *The Book of Ecclesiastes*, 278.

וכתוב ישר דברי אמת

but very honest words of truth were written

The verb כתוב is vocalized in the MT as a Qal passive participle, a vocalization that is generally dismissed as erroneous on the basis that it is too awkward, although this reading is supported by the LXX.[56] Most scholars emend the verb and read it as either a Qal perfect (כָּתַב) or Qal infinitive absolute (כָּתוֹב), rendering the result as 'and/but he wrote'.[57] Of these, the infinitive reading requires less manipulation of the text (leaving the consonantal text intact), and on that basis may be preferred.

Reading כתוב as an infinitive has prompted Longman to see in this second clause an instance of verbal ellipsis, reading it with an implied בקש supplied from the opening to the verse. Consequently, Longman understands the epilogist to be asserting that, not only did Qoheleth seek to find pleasing words, he also sought to write words honestly—but he failed in both tasks.[58] This interpretation is, however, rather less generous toward Qoheleth than the words of the epilogist suggest. In spite of the widespread acceptance of the infinitive reading of כתוב, it is by no means certain (as I will demonstrate below). Perhaps more damaging to this reading is the fact that, in almost all instances in which the Piel of בקש is followed by an infinitive construct, the preposition ל is prefixed to that infinitive.[59] The absence of ל from the second clause in contrast to its presence in the first clause, in addition to the general expectation that ל ought to be present, make Longman's elliptical reading unappealing.

However, in spite of the preference among modern readers of the text to emend this verb, preserving the Qal passive participle does not present as great a problem as most scholars suppose. A similar construction appears in Ezek 2:10, which reads וכתוב אליה קנים והגה והי 'written on it were words of lamentation and mourning and woe'. In this verse, the subject of the participle appears at the end of the clause, with the verb first. Following this example, Qoh 12:10 may be understood as indicating that ישר דברי אמת were written by Qoheleth. Furthermore, read this way, the lack of a finite verb in the clause subordinates it to the previous clause and suggests that the conjunction ו should be understood as disjunctive—"*but* ישר דברי אמת were written."

---

56. The LXX renders כתוב by γεγραμμένον 'it is written'.

57. See Murphy, *Ecclesiastes*, 123; Fox, *Qohelet and His Contradictions*, 310, 323–24; Ogden, *Qoheleth*, 209; Crenshaw, *Ecclesiastes*, 191; Longman, *The Book of Ecclesiastes*, 275 n. 65; etc. Seow (*Ecclesiastes*, 385) notes that the active does appear in a few Hebrew MSS. These probably reflect attempts to simplify (or correct) the Hebrew and are thus unlikely to be original.

58. Longman, *The Book of Ecclesiastes*, 278.

59. The exceptions appear in Exod 4:24 and Jer 26:21 (the infinitive verb in both instances is the Hiphil inf. cs. of מות 'die'), and Ps 27:4.

This naturally forces us to determine what it was that Qoheleth wrote. The relationship between ישר and דברי אמת is difficult. Gordis's solution is to understand ישר as an "adverbial accusative" meaning 'honestly'.[60] Although this attenuates the difficulty, precedent for reading ישר in an adverbial sense is lacking in Biblical Hebrew. The word ישר is generally parsed as a noun meaning 'straightness, uprightness'. Furthermore, there is no apparent reason for the epilogist to be concerned with *how* Qoheleth wrote as opposed to *what* he wrote. Fox offers a more plausible solution to the difficulty, reading ישר as a bound form, similar to קשט 'truth' in Prov 22:21.[61] Following this pattern, Fox reads the expression as a superlative: "the most honest words of truth."

These considerations show that both clauses in v. 10 offer descriptions of Qoheleth's words. The first explains what Qoheleth sought to find—"pleasing words"—and the second recounts what Qoheleth actually wrote—"the most honest words of truth."[62] This contrast is established by repeated reference to Qoheleth's words with alternate modifiers—דברי־חפץ in the first clause and דברי אמת in the second. While the implication of the first clause is that Qoheleth did not succeed in finding pleasing words, the second clause makes the unequivocal assertion that he wrote the truth. This parallelism, together with the subordination of the second clause to the first, suggests that the reason Qoheleth failed to find "pleasing words" was his commitment to declaring the truth—when faced with the choice of writing pleasing words or truthful words, Qoheleth chose to tell the truth.

Summary

Qoheleth, according to the opening verses of the epilogue, was a sage—a member of a scholarly group of Israelite society. However, Qoheleth was not merely another sage; he was exceptional. In keeping with the Solomonic associations in the opening chapters of the book that allude to Qoheleth's exceptional standing among the wise, the epilogist informs us that Qoheleth was a sage whose efforts and integrity exceeded those of his contemporaries.

Not only did his audience include more than just the intellectual elite of the wisdom community (the people in general, as indicated by העם in v. 9), he also corrected the conclusions of other sages, preferring to speak honestly rather than offering pleasing advice of dubious truthfulness. The fact that Qoheleth felt the need to correct the work of other sages indicates that there were problems within the wisdom movement. Thus Qoheleth is portrayed as preeminent

---

60. Gordis, *Koheleth: The Man and His World*, 353; see also Longman, *The Book of Ecclesiastes*, 275 n. 66; Schoors, *The Preacher Sought to Find Pleasing Words*, 45–46.

61. Fox, *Qohelet and His Contradictions*, 324.

62. The singular form of the expression דברי אמת appears in Ps 119:43 (cf. Ps 45:5).

among the sages. When Qoheleth's conclusions differed from other sages', Qoheleth was to be believed because his credentials far surpassed theirs.

Given this portrayal of Qoheleth, I now want to consider why Qoheleth corrected the words of other sages. Qoheleth's response is summarized by the refrain that recurs throughout his work: הכל הבל. This conclusion, which relates to the frustration of hopes or ambitions by the inevitable fate of all living things—death—when understood as a correction to the wisdom of others, implies that other sages had offered more "pleasing" words about the various matters that Qoheleth examines. Although Qoheleth sought to find pleasing words, he could not honestly offer them to his audience. Qoheleth's words reflect the application of wisdom to the question of the value of life, for he acknowledged no other means to find an answer. Thus, his words show only that wisdom could not reveal the answer to its own fundamental question.

Qoheleth 12:11–12:
Warnings about the Teaching of the Sages

[11] The words of the wise are like the goads,
and like the cattle-prods are [the words of] masters of collections,
which are used by a lone shepherd.
[12] And in addition to these things, my son, beware of the excessive production of writings—for this never ends, and of excessive study—it exhausts the body.

The opening words of v. 11 signal a shift in focus for the epilogist. While vv. 9–10 offer specific information about Qoheleth the individual, v. 11 speaks of the sages (or wise people) in general.[63] Furthermore, the epilogist does not comment further on Qoheleth the individual. What has been said about Qoheleth to this point must, therefore, have been sufficient to make his point, although his point becomes clearer in the remaining verses of the epilogue.

Verse 11

Verse 11 is a proverbial tricolon that appears to employ parallelism typical of this literary form. The inclusion of a saying of this sort, along with the use of בני 'sons of' in v. 12, indicates that the epilogist is probably writing from within the wisdom tradition. The extent of the quotation, however, is not entirely clear. The placement of the Masoretic *'atnaḥ* accent under the word אספות 'collections' suggests either that the final three Hebrew words ('which

---

63. See Ogden, *Qoheleth*, 209–10. Scholars almost universally agree that Qoheleth's words are in view here, but many fail to deal adequately with the shift from Qoheleth, overlooking the consequences of this and the subsequent verses.

are used by a lone shepherd') are an addition to the original saying, or that the complete saying is in the form of a poetic tricolon. The alternative is to read the entire verse as a bicolon in which the second colon is substantially longer than the first. The precise relationship of the final three words to the remainder of the verse will be discussed in greater detail below.

דברי חכמים כדרבנות

The words of the wise are like the goads

The first colon of v. 11 is a simile describing the words of the sages, which are likened to דרבנות (here translated 'goads'). The colon raises two specific questions: Are 'the wise' here referred to a specific, identifiable group or merely wise people in general? And what is the meaning of the term דרבנות?

Although it is tempting to assume that חכמים refers to the same class of sages that Qoheleth belongs to in v. 9, it may be that this term takes on a broader reference here. This colon refers not just to the wise but more specifically to the "words of the wise." In so doing, the text is not referring to a specific group of people but to a specific group of words—whether in written or oral form. Extant Wisdom Literature from Israel and other places in the ancient Near East reveals a variety of sources for wisdom, ranging from the home to the royal court. This indicates that the wise people who composed the literature were both professional sages and nonprofessional members of the broader community (although the long-term preservation of the wisdom material probably was the work of professional sages and scribes).

Having said this, we can adduce evidence in support of the case that the "wise" here, those who were the source of the "words of the wise," may actually have been members of the class of sages. The parallel expression בעלי אספות 'masters of collections' in the second colon, if taken to share the same referent as the noun חכמים 'wise' in the first, is unlikely to encompass all people responsible for the composition of words of wisdom. Nonetheless, this expression presents its own difficulties, which will be examined in more detail below.

The significance of the expression "words of the wise" here is not ultimately bound up with the identification of the wise but with the identification of the material classified as the "words of the wise"—the Wisdom Literature. The use of this expression here indicates that the epilogist and his audience were readily able to identify a genre of this sort and were familiar with the material. There is, however, no indication of the precise material that constituted this classification for the epilogist apart from Qoheleth's words themselves. The suggestion that the words here refer to the other canonical Wisdom Literature found in the Hebrew Bible can be no more than speculation because it rests on a whole range of assumptions relating to the date and dissemination of those works as well as the date of Ecclesiastes.[64] What we can say about this expression is that it refers to specific Wisdom Literature (I use the term loosely to encompass both oral and written material) that was circulating contemporaneously with Qoheleth's own teachings and that was likely the subject of some of Qoheleth's correctional work (see above on v. 9).

The final point to make regarding this expression is that it also includes the words of Qoheleth recorded in the body of the book. This is clear from vv. 9 and 10, in which Qoheleth and his words are established as being not only among the words of the sages but preeminent among them. This ought not to obscure the fact, however, that the epilogist has here moved beyond exclusive consideration of Qoheleth's words to addressing the wisdom movement more broadly.

The words of the wise are likened to דרבנות 'goads'. BDB treats the term as the feminine plural of דרבנה, a hapax legomenon. As such, the meaning of the term is not immediately clear and neither is the ultimate meaning of the simile. The choice of this unusual word may have been prompted by poetic considerations because the root (דרב) is a play on the noun דבר ('word').[65] In addition, paronomasia is exhibited in the repeated endings and prefixes of the

---

64. Sheppard has suggested that this may refer to literature explicitly associated with Solomon (so Proverbs and Ecclesiastes): Gerald T. Sheppard, "The Epilogue to Qoheleth as Theological Commentary," *CBQ* 39 (1977) 188–89. Farmer assumes that the biblical books of Proverbs and Ecclesiastes are the result of the work of a single editor and that the expression "words of the wise" refers specifically to these two canonical books (*Proverbs and Ecclesiastes*, 3–4, 196). Farmer depends on Wilson's argument in favor of this position ("'The Words of the Wise': The Intent and Significance of Qoheleth 12:9–14," 175–92). Wilson makes several points in his attempt to bind Ecclesiastes to Proverbs in such a way that any independent interpretation of either work is inadequate. First, Proverbs can legitimately—based on the titles introducing each section—be labeled "words of the wise" (p. 179). Second, the titles in Proverbs are indicative of the type of editorial process supposedly described in Qoh 12:9–10 (p. 179). Third, the superscriptions of both books bear some similarities, specifically the association with Solomon, not to speak of the uniqueness of having superscriptions at all (pp. 179–80). Fourth, Wilson observes some parallels between Prov 1:2–8 and Qoh 12:9–14, including: both employ the phrase דברי חכמים; Qoh 12:9–11 reflects the learning and skill that would be the outcome of Prov 1:5–6; the phrase "fear of Y HWH" opens Proverbs and closes Ecclesiastes. Wilson's arguments are, however, far from compelling. The first two points above merely indicate that both Proverbs and Ecclesiastes were the products of the wisdom tradition. They are not a sufficient basis for asserting a direct literary connection between the two works. The final points that Wilson makes depend heavily on a specific interpretation of Ecclesiastes' epilogue that cannot easily be justified; many of the difficulties are detailed in the exegetical discussion below.

65. See Wilfred G. E. Watson, *Classical Hebrew Poetry: A Guide to Its Techniques* (JSOTSup 26; Sheffield: JSOT Press, 1984) 239–41; Perry, *Dialogues with Kohelet*, 172.

successive terms כדרבנות and כמשמרות. Metrical considerations may also have played a part in the choice of terminology.[66]

Scholars have suggested a number of cognate terms in an attempt to clarify the meaning of דרבנות. Dahood cites Ugaritic *drb*, which is found associated with words such as 'knife' and 'spear'.[67] More commonly, the Arabic term *dariba* (which is almost certainly a cognate of the Ugaritic term) is cited, meaning 'to be sharp'.[68] That the term might connote "sharpness" is further supported by the parallel משמרות 'cattle-prods' in the second colon. The problem with identifying these Arabic and Ugaritic terms as cognates with the Hebrew is that both Ugaritic *drb* and Arabic *dariba* would normally be cognate with a (hypothetical) Hebrew root **zbr*.[69] Furthermore, the parallelism between this colon and the next does not require that the terms דרבנות and משמרות be synonymous.

Comparative Semitic grammar postulates that the correct Arabic cognate with the Hebrew root *drb* is *dariba*, which means 'to train, to be(come) accustomed', and is frequently associated with the training of animals.[70] In Biblical Hebrew, the closest term is דרבן in 1 Sam 13:21, where the term appears to apply to some type of agricultural tool (which could easily include an implement used in the training of animals).[71] In light of these considerations, I contend that the usual rendering 'goad' or 'ox-goad' best fits the context (particularly the reference to a shepherd at the end of the verse) and is compatible with the Arabic cognate and the appearance of the similar term in 1 Samuel.[72]

The question of why the words of the wise should be likened to a goad, a device used to train and direct animals, awaits an analysis of the remainder of the saying. Thus we turn to the second colon.

וכמשמרות נטועים בעלי אספות
and like the cattle-prods are [the words of] masters of collections

---

66. Refer to the comments in n. 85.

67. See Seow, *Ecclesiastes*, 387.

68. See Whitley, *Koheleth*, 102; BDB, 201.

69. See Sabatino Moscati, *An Introduction to the Comparative Grammar of the Semitic Languages* (Wiesbaden: Harrassowitz, 1980) 28–30, 43.

70. See Gordis, *Koheleth: The Man and His World*, 353; Seow, *Ecclesiastes*, 387.

71. The meaning of דרבן in 1 Sam 13:21 is also difficult, although the context suggests that it refers to some type of agricultural tool (appearing as it does in a list of agricultural implements).

72. This interpretation is also supported by the rendering τὰ βούκεντρα in the LXX which, although also a hapax legomenon, is clearly a compound of βοῦς 'ox' and κέντρον 'goad'.

The second colon of this wisdom saying reverses the order of the first, creating a simple chiastic pattern. This colon presents two particular difficulties of its own. First, there is the problematic combination of feminine-plural and masculine-plural gender in the first two words, as well as the meaning of this expression. Second, the meaning of the expression בעלי אספות is not at all clear.

The word משמרות (here rendered 'cattle-prods') is a feminine plural form of the noun משמר. The noun appears nowhere else in this form in Biblical Hebrew, although it is generally assumed that it is an alternate form of מסמר (which itself only appears four times, always plural) and is usually rendered 'nail' (see Isa 41:7; Jer 10:4; 1 Chr 22:3; 2 Chr 3:9). Seow claims that the term may actually refer to any nail-like object, although the only support for this is late.[73] Nonetheless, the possibility remains that the epilogist used the term metaphorically. Given the relative obscurity of the term, we are justified in allowing him some degree of semantic ambiguity.

The noun משמרות is followed immediately by a Qal passive participle, נטועים, which may be rendered literally as 'those that are implanted'. This is usually understood as an attributive adjectival use of the participle (or else as an attributive relative participle, which however is usually marked by the presence of the definite article on the participle), and so the phrase is commonly rendered as "implanted nails."[74] However, the immediate difficulty with this understanding is the discordant gender—we would normally expect the gender of a noun and participle to agree.[75]

One solution is to read the noun in the construct state, which would overcome the grammatical difficulty of the verse. Although this resolves the problem of gender, the meaning of the resulting expression is unclear. What does "like nails of implanted things" mean? The solution to this problem could be to emend נטועים to נוטעים and read it as a Qal participle (not passive), in which case the expression could be rendered 'like stakes of planters' (assuming that משמר could be used to refer to some type of stake used to guide the

---

73. Seow, *Ecclesiastes*, 387. The term only appears four times in Biblical Hebrew, and 'nail' appears to be a perfectly adequate rendering in each case. Seow appeals to M. Jastrow, *A Dictionary of the Targumim, the Talmud Babli and Yerushalmi, etc.* (London: Luzac / New York: Putnam's, 1903) 809 to support the claim that מסמר can refer to any nail-like object. However, the relevance of this later evidence to the use of the term by the epilogist is difficult to establish.

74. For a discussion of the uses of the participle in instances such as these, refer to Waltke and O'Connor, *An Introduction to Biblical Hebrew Syntax*, 619–23.

75. This pattern of f. pl. noun followed by m. pl. ptc. (or pass. ptc.) does appear elsewhere in BH in Jer 22:14 and 2 Chr 29:28.

growth of crops or vines). While this interpretation solves the grammatical difficulties and relies only on a relatively trivial alteration of the text, it raises further problems of its own. It presumes that planters of crops used nails or stakes for some purpose, and, although one may assume that they were used to tie plants to or to guide sowers in the planting of seeds, these suggestions are largely conjectural and lack substantial archaeological or textual verification.[76] Finally, the subsequent reference to מרעה אחד in the final colon suggests that an interpretation with pastoral rather than agricultural imagery is more appropriate.

Seow suggests that משמרות should be read as a masculine plural.[77] This is quite possible because a number of prominent masculine Hebrew nouns take feminine-plural endings.[78] In general, however, these are commonly used words in the language, and it is less likely for rare or obscure terms to exhibit such exceptional behavior. Further, most irregular terms do not appear with both ות- and ים- plural endings, as does מסמר. This noun appears in masculine-plural form in Isa 41:7 and 1 Chr 22:3, but in feminine-plural form in Jer 10:4 and 2 Chr 3:9 (however, it is likely that these texts reflect the existence of two distinct singular nouns, one masculine and one feminine). This points to some degree of ambiguity in the gender of this noun, although it is surprising that here the expression does not adopt the masculine form.

It is clear that there is no wholly satisfying solution to this problem. The best solution appears to be to treat the participle as an attributive adjective, and trace the anomalous gender to the influence of the feminine-plural form of דרבנות in the previous colon.[79]

Interpretations of the words בעלי אספות (here 'masters of collections') can generally be separated into two groups, which divide over the understanding of the first term, בעלי. The second word, אספות, is a hapax legomenon (although the singular אספה appears in Isa 24:22, the pointing suggests that the

---

76. There is evidence, for example, for the use of some form of trellis in the growing of grape vines in ancient Israel (see Carey Ellen Walsh, *The Fruit of the Vine: Viticulture in Ancient Israel* [HSM 60; Winona Lake, Ind.: Eisenbrauns, 2000] chap. 3). Unfortunately, the nature of these stakes is such that there is little likelihood of finding direct archaeological evidence for them.

77. Seow, *Ecclesiastes* 387. Shead (*Ecclesiastes 12:9–14: Reading the Epilogue as an Epilogue*, 51 n. 60) argues that מסמר has "common" gender.

78. For example: שם (pl. שמות); אב (pl. אבות); חלום (pl. חלמות).

79. Gary Rendsburg (*Diglossia in Ancient Hebrew* [New Haven, Conn.: American Oriental Society, 1990] chap. 3) presents a number of examples of gender incongruence throughout BH, demonstrating that, although incongruence is not the norm, there is clear precedent for leaving the words in the epilogue unaltered. It is also likely that וכמשמרות ought to be read as definite, parallel with כדרבנות in the previous colon.

underlying word here is different) derived from the root אסף meaning 'to gather, remove'. The noun אספה has thus been understood as 'assembly' (of people) or else 'collection' (of wisdom sayings). The fact that this expression is parallel to דברי חכמים suggests understanding אספות as referring to a collection of wisdom sayings.

As noted above, בעלי is typically understood in one of two ways. The first interpretation of the word is 'members of', in which case the full expression refers to individual elements in a collection of wisdom material.[80] Although this meaning does not appear to fit easily with the common use of בעל 'lord, master' elsewhere in the Hebrew Bible, proponents of this interpretation argue that Gen 14:13 and Neh 6:18 demonstrate that it does indeed lie within the semantic range of this term. In Gen 14:13, the expression בעלי ברית refers to participants in a covenant. In Neh 6:18, the expression בעלי שבועה refers to participants in a vow. Fox, however, correctly points out that the parallel is not complete, for the participants in a covenant or a vow do exercise some control over their participation (so maintaining the notion of mastery otherwise inherent in the term בעל), while the sayings that constitute a collection of wisdom material are entirely passive and can in no way be said to exercise mastery over the collection.[81]

The second interpretation of בעל is that the word refers to those who organize the collections, making the expression בעלי אספות parallel in meaning to חכמים in the first colon of the saying. Fox appeals to Rabbinic Hebrew usage, in which expressions such as בעלי מקרא mean something like 'experts in Scripture', understanding the expression here as 'experts in collections' and again seeing it as parallel to the wise in the first colon.[82] Although this may illuminate the meaning, the expression can be understood without resort to later usage if 'collections' is read as a reference to wisdom material (and, given the context, any other reference would seem inappropriate).

In order for this second interpretation to make sense of these words in their present context, the second colon of the saying is understood to be elliptical, omitting the word דברי, which appeared in the first colon. Consequently this expression would read as '(words of) masters of collections'. Gordis objects to this interpretation, regarding this passage to be insufficiently poetic for such a reading.[83] It is not entirely clear how Gordis arrives at this assessment,

---

80. For example, Delitzsch, *Commentary on the Song of Songs and Ecclesiastes*, 434; Barton, *A Critical and Exegetical Commentary on the Book of Ecclesiastes*, 198; Gordis, *Koheleth: The Man and His World*, 353; Hertzberg, *Der Prediger*.

81. Fox, *Qohelet and His Contradictions*, 324.

82. Ibid.; idem, *A Time to Tear Down*, 354.

83. Gordis, *Koheleth: The Man and His World*, 353.

for we are clearly dealing with a wisdom saying, and wisdom sayings typically employ any of the whole range of poetic devices in spite of their brevity.
The parallelism that is arguably the most identifiable feature of Biblical Hebrew poetry is readily apparent in the cola of this saying, appearing not only
at the semantic level, but also the grammatical (the inverted word order of the
two verbless cola presenting a neat chiasm). Furthermore, other features of
Biblical Hebrew poetry are also present: rare terminology, unusual word order, and imagery. Finally, ellipsis is not a literary device confined to poetic
texts in the Hebrew Bible. It is clear that Gordis's objection to this interpretation cannot be sustained.

The evidence clearly favors understanding the second cola to be likening
the words of the masters of collections (an expression that functions as an epithet for the sages, paralleling חכמים in the first colon) to implanted nails or
stakes of some form. The precise meaning of the similes in these two cola can
only be properly determined, however, once the meaning of the remaining
words of v. 11 and their relationship to the first two cola have been determined.

נתנו מרעה אחד

which are used by a lone shepherd

The relationship of these final three words in v. 11 to the preceding words is
not entirely clear. It is possible to read them as an extension of the second colon only, or else as a third colon that refers generally back to the subject matter of the previous two cola in their entirety. This uncertain relationship to the
preceding cola has prompted Whybray, among others, to suggest that these
words may form an addition to the saying, which originally consisted only of
the portion of the verse prior to these words.[84]

It is unlikely, however, that these words should be read as part of the second colon, because doing so undermines the parallelism between the first two
cola. It is preferable to read these words as a third colon, so that v. 11 takes the
form of a poetic tricolon, exhibiting an A/A′/B structure.[85]

This observation highlights the problem of determining the subject of the
verb נתן (in Qal, 'to give'; in the Niphal, 'use'; for the latter, see pp. 81–82).
The subject could feasibly be either the "implanted nails," the "(words of)

---

84. Whybray, *Ecclesiastes* (NCB), 172. The absence of any relative particle, noted by
Whybray, need not indicate a new sentence; omissions of this sort are particularly common
in Biblical Hebrew poetry.

85. See Longman, *The Book of Ecclesiastes*, 279. For other examples of this form of
tricolon, and discussion, see Watson, *Classical Hebrew Poetry*, 180–81. Although the subject of meter in BH poetry remains a point of contention among scholars, this verse, read as
a tricolon, demonstrates some degree of metrical balance (particularly if meter is determined by word-counting or stress-counting, for which a 3/4/3 pattern can be identified).

masters of collections," or both together.[86] Each of these solutions has found some support, although arguments generally depend on one's identification of the מרעה אחד ('lone shepherd'). Consequently, we must discuss the meaning of this expression before we return to the question of the subject of the verb that opens this colon.

The מרעה אחד has been variously identified as Moses, Solomon, Qoheleth, and God.[87] The majority of modern commentators argue that the "one shepherd" is a reference to God, based on the imagery of God as a shepherd elsewhere in the Hebrew Bible. Shead has also suggested that the similarity between רעה and רעות (from the expression רעות רוח 'a plan for [the] wind', Qoh 4:6; see pp. 114–15 below) is "perhaps the most compelling reason for taking 'one shepherd' to be God."[88] Those who make this identification generally proceed to draw two conclusions. First, the subject of the verb נתן is the "words of the wise/masters of collections" rather than the "nails" or "goads," because nails and goads are clearly not given by God but are descriptions of the nature of the words given by God to the sages. Second, this text becomes an assertion of the divine origin and authority of the Wisdom Literature.

Although this explanation of the passage is superficially appealing, it is ultimately inadequate in a number of ways. First, if this verse is asserting the divine origin and authority of Wisdom Literature, it is claiming far more than the majority of proponents of this view acknowledge. In general, these scholars claim that this verse affirms either the inspiration of Qoheleth's words alone or, at most, the canonical Wisdom Literature.[89] This saying, however, evidences no such restrictions, quite markedly departing from the specific focus on Qoheleth in vv. 9–10 of the epilogue to focus on the "words of the

---

86. Shead (*Ecclesiastes 12:9–14: Reading the Epilogue as an Epilogue*, 53) asserts that the subject of the verb encompasses all these elements—the "words," the "goads," and the "nails." This conclusion, however, rests on an identification of the shepherd that is refuted below.

87. See Gordis, *Koheleth: The Man and His World*, 354; Murphy, *Ecclesiastes*, 125; Eaton, *Ecclesiastes*, 154–55; J. Stafford Wright, "Ecclesiastes," in *The Expositor's Bible Commentary* (ed. Frank E. Gaebelein; Grand Rapids: Zondervan, 1991) 1196; Ogden, *Qoheleth*, 210; Childs, *Introduction to the Old Testament as Scripture*, 586. Whybray (*Ecclesiastes* [NCB], 172) is unhappy with the identification of the shepherd as God but feels that no better alternative has been offered. Shead (*Ecclesiastes 12:9–14: Reading the Epilogue as an Epilogue*, 53–55) argues that the reference is to both Solomon and God.

88. Ibid., 55.

89. Shead (ibid., 55–56) overlooks the difficulty that his identification of מרעה אחד as God has on his understanding that דברי חכמים refers to the "general wisdom tradition" (p. 51) by only discussing the implications this identification has for Qoheleth's words (see especially pp. 55–56). Gordis (*Koheleth: The Man and His World*, 354) simply asserts, without citing any supporting evidence, that the reference is to the canonical Wisdom Literature.

sages" in general. Attempts by some scholars to restrict the reference of this expression to the canonical Wisdom Literature are less than convincing.[90] Furthermore, the fact that Qoheleth is described by the epilogist as one who corrected the teachings of other sages clearly indicates that the epilogist could not have accepted the position that the words of all of the sages were divinely inspired.[91]

Second, the argument that the use of the term 'shepherd' (רעה) would instantly evoke in the audience a reference to God is difficult to sustain. A close examination of instances in the Hebrew Bible in which the shepherd metaphor is unequivocally applied to God reveals that the identification of God and shepherd was probably not automatic.[92] Every text that identifies God as a shepherd makes the connection quite explicit.[93] I conclude, therefore, that it is unlikely that the unqualified term here in the epilogue would have been understood this way. Furthermore, the only other instances of the expression רעה אחד are in Ezek 34:32 and 37:24, where the reference is to the messianic David—*not* to God.

Shead suggests that the use of the similar term רעות 'a plan' (see pp. 114–15) in the expression רעות רוח almost certainly prompted the epilogist to use the epithet רעה 'shepherd' to refer to God to remind the reader of that earlier key phrase.[94] Shead claims that רעות רוח refers to something only God could achieve (despite the fact that Qoheleth himself does not make this point when using the expression). Shead proceeds to conclude that "the implication of this for the meaning of the epilogue is that what humans cannot control, God can. Thus the fact that Qoheleth's wisdom comes from God serves as a reassurance that despite its painfulness, it is both trustworthy and effective." There are a number of obstacles to Shead's argument, chief among them being the fact that Qoheleth himself never makes a connection between the expression רעות רוח and God. Furthermore, the epilogue is not suggesting that the shepherd is somehow able to do something that is impossible for mortal humans to do—otherwise the identity of the shepherd would be incontrovertible. This

---

90. See the discussion on p. 70.

91. Refer to the discussion on p. 62.

92. Passages that refer to God metaphorically as a shepherd in the Hebrew Bible are Gen 48:15; 49:24; Ps 23:1; 28:9; 80:1; Isa 40:11; Jer 31:10; Ezek 34:12; Mic 7:14. Shead (*Ecclesiastes 12:9–14: Reading the Epilogue as an Epilogue*, 55) claims that Jer 17:16 refers to God as shepherd of his people. The meaning of this text is problematic, but if it is to be read as describing anyone as a shepherd, it is clearly a reference to Jeremiah, not to God.

93. See Fox, *Qohelet and His Contradictions*, 325.

94. Shead, *Ecclesiastes 12:9–14: Reading the Epilogue as an Epilogue*, 55–56. The phrase רעות רוח appears in Qoh 1:14, 17; 2:11, 17, 26; 4:4, 16, and elsewhere.

saying is only making the point that the shepherd is the source of either the words of the wise or the goads and nails. The issue of what is possible or impossible is entirely irrelevant to the epilogue.

Third, the claim that רעה should be understood as a metaphor for God fails to account adequately for the presence of the adjective אחד. Whybray states that "this apparent assertion of the oneness of God also seems to be made with no obvious reason."[95] Shead argues that אחד is used here in the sense that "*one* person can make a difference for good or ill" based on the usage of this word throughout the body of the work. From this assertion he concludes that "the shepherd is the one source of truly effective wisdom."[96] This highlights a mistake that Shead makes fairly frequently: he transfers from another occurrence (or other occurrences) in the book not only the meaning of the term he is examining but its entire context. In this instance, rather than note that Qoheleth occasionally uses אחד to highlight the fact that he is referring to one as opposed to many, Shead incorporates into the term אחד considerable semantic baggage. Consequently, Shead proposes a meaning for the verse that overlooks its immediate context in favor of contexts found elsewhere in the book.[97]

Furthermore, we are dealing here with an epilogue in which we hear a different voice from the voice that has spoken throughout the body of the work, which may also suggest that the use of a term in the epilogue need not be constrained too tightly by its use in the body of the work. The adjective אחד is itself quite common in BH and does occasionally function as an indefinite article, as well as sometimes being used to highlight the isolation of its subject. These uses are not common, but to argue that in one place a less-common meaning for a term is inappropriate because it does not appear elsewhere is to allow statistics, rather than context, to control meaning. If we argue purely from statistics, the meaning of any word would only be the meaning that most commonly appears! Language simply does not work this way.

One other possible explanation for the presence of אחד is that it has been included to clarify for the reader that the shepherd *is* God. So, rather than

---

95. Whybray, *Ecclesiastes* (NCB), 172.

96. Shead, *Ecclesiastes 12:9–14: Reading the Epilogue as an Epilogue*, 54.

97. Shead (ibid.) also claims that Qoheleth's usage of the verb נתן supports his claim that the shepherd ought to be identified as God. He argues that, "although the words of the wise may not be seen as God's gift elsewhere, the word נתן is a 'favourite' of Eccl, with God being the giver in 11 out of 24 occurrences. Six of these come in the positive refrain. Thus there is a hint that these words are God's gift to enable enjoyment of life." This argument is not at all convincing; if God is the giver in 11 out of 24 occurrences of נתן, then it is more likely that God is not the subject of the verb!

merely referring to a shepherd, the epilogist (or the author of the saying) has emphatically indicated that this is a reference to "the one shepherd," that is, God. This explanation, however, would be far more convincing if the expression were definite (in which case the text would read מן־הרעה האחד 'from the one shepherd') rather than indefinite. The indefiniteness of the expression makes it less likely that the epilogist is here referring to God.

Finally, to argue that this saying proclaims the divine inspiration of wisdom, particularly the divine inspiration of Qoheleth's words, fails to account for the negative assessment of wisdom and the wisdom movement in the remainder of the epilogue. Although it is already apparent from the epilogue's assertion that Qoheleth corrected the wisdom of others (see v. 9), this evaluation by the epilogist will become more apparent as we examine the concluding verses.

These considerations indicate that the phrase מרעה אחד cannot reasonably be identified as God. Furthermore, the identification of the shepherd with any other specific historical figure—such as Moses, Solomon, or Qoheleth—can be ruled out, for it is not clear how any of these figures could be said to have "given" the "words of the sages" or alternatively the "goads" or "implanted nails." In addition to this, the text is too vague about the identity of the shepherd to permit any identification.

Having eliminated the possibility that מרעה אחד should be understood as a metaphorical description of a specific historical figure or of God, we are forced to conclude that this expression refers to a shepherd.[98] There are two immediate corollaries that follow from this observation.

First, the adjective אחד is not here employed to highlight a particular shepherd out of all possible shepherds. Besides this understanding of the adjective, there are two possible interpretations. The first is to understand אחד as roughly equivalent to the indefinite article in English. In this case the reference would be to any shepherd rather than to a particular shepherd. This colon would thus be elaborating on the first two so that, as Seow says, "*any* herder would use whatever it takes to move the herd in the desired direction."[99]

However, a second possible interpretation of אחד also presents itself. The adjective may be employed to highlight the isolation of the nonspecific shepherd; in this case, we have a reference to "a lone shepherd." Although the notion of isolation is usually denoted by לבדו in Biblical Hebrew, there are a few notable instances in which אחד is used to highlight the isolation of a char-

---

98. Others who reach this conclusion include Fox, *Qohelet and His Contradictions*, 325–26; and Seow, *Ecclesiastes*, 387–88.

99. Ibid., 388; cf. Fox, *Qohelet and His Contradictions*, 325–26.

acter or object.[100] Read this way, the "goads" and "implanted nails" would be "given" by a shepherd who worked alone, as opposed to working with a group of shepherds.[101] A lone shepherd would presumably experience greater difficulties in restraining and directing a herd than would a group of shepherds working together, so he would be more likely to require various accoutrements to achieve his end. Thus the "goads" and "implanted nails" would function to assist the lone shepherd in controlling the herd.[102]

While this reading is lexically and grammatically plausible, we lack information about specific herding practices in ancient Israel to allow us to evaluate this proposal adequately.[103] Without further information, this suggested understanding of the text can be no more certain than the alternative reading, in which the reference is simply to *any* shepherd.

The second corollary to the identification of מרעה אחד as a shepherd is that the subject of the verb נתן cannot be the "words of sages" or "(words of) masters of collections." This is because it would be absurd to suggest that all wisdom—the words of sages—originated from the compositional activities of itinerant pastoralists. Rather, the subject of the verb must be (at least) the "implanted nails." Furthermore, because of the parallelism of the first two cola, it is likely that the saying should correctly be understood as stating that the "goads" of the first colon and the "implanted nails" of the second are the dual subjects of this verb.

This observation raises the question of precisely how the verb נתן should be understood in this context. Although the basic meaning assigned to the term by BDB is 'to give, put, set', it exhibits a considerably diverse semantic

---

100. See 1 Kgs 19:4; Ezek 33:24; 1 Chr 29:1.

101. There is evidence that shepherds could either operate alone or in groups in the ANE; see, for example, J. N. Postgate, "Some Old Babylonian Shepherds and Their Flocks," *JSS* 20 (1975) 2: "A shepherd might work on his own, or if he accepted more sheep than he could pasture himself, he might employ 'under-shepherds.'" For more discussion of Old Babylonian shepherds, see F. R. Kraus, *Staatliche Viehhaltung im altbabylonischen Lande Larsa* (Amsterdam, 1966).

102. Goads would be used to move the herd in the desired direction. If the phrase "implanted nails" is not a reference to nails implanted in the end of sticks (so making the expression virtually equivalent to "goads") but to immovable, fixed nails, it may be a reference to some method by which the shepherd tethered the herd to prevent them from straying when they stopped to rest.

103. Limited information about herding practices in the ancient world can be found in Gerhard J. Botterweck, "Hirt und Herde im Alten Testament und im alten Orient," in *Die Kirche und ihre ämter: Festgabe J. Frings* (ed. W. Corsten; Cologne: Bachem, 1960) 339–52; Kenneth E. Bailey, *Poet and Peasant and Through Peasant Eyes: A Literary-Critical Approach to the Parables in Luke* (combined ed.; Grand Rapids: Eerdmans, 1976, 1980) 149–50; and J. Jeremias, *The Parables of Jesus* (2nd ed.; London: SCM, 1963) 133–34.

range in its numerous occurrences in Biblical Hebrew.[104] Fox has noted that
this verb has the meaning 'to stick, pierce' in Deut 15:17 and suggests that
this is appropriate in the present context, where the "goads" (possibly together with the "implanted nails") function to direct the herd by being stuck
into the sides of the animals.[105] Further to this understanding, if the expression משמרות נטועים refers to nails firmly embedded in such a way that they
are immovable, then the verb נתן would describe the application of the goads
to the animals as well as the act of setting the nails (or stakes) firmly in place.

These observations help to clarify the text. The words of sages are likened
to goads and implanted nails employed in some fashion by a shepherd. Various functions for the "implanted nails" have been suggested. A number of
scholars understand the nails to be implanted in the sense that they are firmly
embedded, immovable, and so the words of the sages "can be conceived as
giving strength and firmness, and perhaps providing a foundation for life's activities, a basis for a responsible life style."[106]

While there is no agreement about the precise significance of the "implanted nails," the use of goads is well understood. Goads were used by the
herder to direct the herd by prodding and poking the animals to compel them
to move in the desired direction. Furthermore, the parallelism between the
first two cola of v. 11 suggests that the "implanted nails" should best be understood to function similarly to the goads in the first colon—the nails being
implanted in the end of a wooden stake thus creating a goad.[107] A shepherd

---

104. BDB, 678–81.

105. Fox, *Qohelet and His Contradictions*, 326. Other instances of נתן that may have a
similar sense include Lev 24:20 and Deut 30:7. Although Shead argues that נתן is a "favorite" term of Qoheleth, the Niphal form only appears here and in Qoh 10:6. Furthermore, the
verb is so common in Biblical Hebrew that a particularly strong case would need to be made
to invest it with some special significance in Ecclesiastes. Indeed, Shead's analysis of Qoheleth's "favorite" terms fails to account for the effect of Qoheleth's use of repetition and
thus skews the statistics associated with counting the terms used in this way. See Andrew G.
Shead, "Reading Ecclesiastes 'Epilogically,'" *TynBul* 48 (1997), particularly pp. 70–76.

106. Murphy, *Ecclesiastes*, 125; cf. Whybray, *Ecclesiastes* (NCB), 172; Gordis, *Koheleth: The Man and His World*, 350.

107. See Seow (*Ecclesiastes*, 387), who writes, "We should think here of spikes or
nails implanted at the end of sticks to be used as prods (so Rashbam: 'like nails driven
firmly and inserted in the ends of sticks'). Technically, an ox-goad (*malmēd*) consists of a
wooden handle with a specific type of iron tip (*dorbān*) properly set. But there were probably also improvised prods, made with pieces of wood, with nails or the like implanted in
them." See also Fox, *Qohelet and His Contradictions*, 324–25. Eben Scheffler ("Archaeology and Wisdom," *Old Testament Essays* 10 [1997] 464–66), in an article supposedly about
the manner in which archaeology has shed light on some wisdom texts, states that "the
driving in of nails could be painful initially, but if the nails are firmly fixed they have the

would presumably employ a goad to prompt the herd to move in a desired direction. Consequently, this saying is asserting that the words of the wise also prompt the hearers to respond in a particular manner—they direct and guide the hearer to follow a path proposed by the sage.

In keeping with their presumption that the first half of the epilogue presents a favorable evaluation of both Qoheleth and the other sages, most scholars understand this saying to be praising the wisdom of the sages despite the painful similes employed. Seow explains his understanding of the intent of the saying by saying: "The words of the wise may hurt; they are not what one may choose to hear. Yet in the end, they are better for one's well-being (compare 7:5)."[108] This explanation finds some substantiation in the common declaration in Proverbs that through being disciplined one may learn wisdom and ultimately benefit.[109]

Scrutinized closely, however, the saying is more ambiguous than most acknowledge. If the path set out by the sages is good, then being directed along that path would no doubt also be good. However, the saying is not drawing any conclusions about the worth of the advice of the sages; it certainly does not conclude that this advice is "better for one's well-being." If the path set out by the sages is *not* good, then this saying must stand as a warning *against* heeding the wisdom of the sages, lest it direct us down that path. The wisdom of the sages could, according to this saying, be used to manipulate and ultimately lead the student astray![110] Unlike the assertions of Proverbs that wisdom and benefit are derived from the pain of discipline, the epilogist demonstrates no interest in describing the outcome of the pain inflicted by the words of the wise. Given the negative evaluation of the sages implied by the need for Qoheleth to correct their wisdom (see v. 9) and the additional negative statements in the subsequent verses, it is better to read in this saying something of this negativity toward the words of the sages.

Adding to this is a further incentive to read the saying negatively rather than positively. Sheppard suggests that this verse closely parallels Prov 22:17–19: "Incline your ear, and hear the words of the wise[men], and apply

---

function of keeping the object together." Scheffler, however, provides no evidence (archaeological or otherwise) to back up this interpretation.

108. Seow, *Ecclesiastes*, 393. Seow's proposed parallel in Qoh 7:5 differs from 12:11 in that it explicitly claims that the rebuke of the wise is better than the songs of fools. Many scholars recognize that the similes here express something of the painful nature of the words of the sages, including Ogden, *Qoheleth*, 210.

109. See Prov 3:11–12; 6:23–24; 12:1; 13:1, 24; 19:18, 25; 21:11; 23:13–14; 28:23; 29:17.

110. By "student" I mean only to refer to someone who sought the wisdom of the sages; I am not using the term in any technical sense.

your mind to knowledge; for it will be pleasant if you keep them within you, if all of them are ready on your lips. That your trust may be in YHWH I have made them known to you today."[111] What Sheppard's comparison highlights, however, is not the similarity but the difference between the epilogue and Proverbs. The similes chosen by the epilogist do not depict the wisdom of the sages as working through gentle instruction or parental advice. There is no hint that keeping their wisdom with you will be pleasant. Rather, the image here is one of coercion, amd the sages' words function as a harsh and painful means to constrain and manipulate the path of the student.[112] These harsh terms used to describe the effects of wisdom material on the student of wisdom also present a sharp contrast to the desirable words that Qoheleth is said to have sought in the previous verse.

Verse 12

Many scholars argue that v. 12 begins a second section of the epilogue.[113] The above analysis of vv. 9–11 clearly demonstrates that basing this assertion on the supposed variation in attitude toward Qoheleth is not borne out by the text itself. The opening verses of the epilogue are clearly not as positive toward Qoheleth and (in particular) the sages as many presume. Verse 12 includes a warning (marked by the verb זהר) in addition to a clear link to the preceding saying (ויתר מהמה). Dividing the epilogue at this point obscures this transition and is not warranted.

ויתר מהמה בני

And in addition to these things, my son . . .

The imperative הזהר is usually read as part of the opening clause as though this were a warning against adding to these words. It is, however, better associated with the next clause (see discussion below). The reappearance of the term ויתר (see v. 9) is also cited as evidence that a new section is beginning, but this tends to invest too much significance in a lexical pattern. Rather, the

---

111. Sheppard, "The Epilogue to Qoheleth as Theological Commentary," 180. Compare also passages such as Prov 4:20–22 and 8:34–36, which also suggest that acquiring wisdom is a pleasant experience.

112. Longman comments that "the metaphors of goads and embedded nails, while usually understood positively, are better understood as negative. Goads and nails are painful!" R. B. Dillard and Tremper Longman III, *An Introduction to the Old Testament* (Grand Rapids: Zondervan, 1994) 254; cf. Longman, *The Book of Ecclesiastes*, 280. Fox also highlights the painful nature of the words of the sages (Fox, *Qohelet and His Contradictions*, 324–25).

113. See the above discussion of more general points relating to the bipartite division of the epilogue, p. 52.

term here functions to indicate that the epilogist has more to say about the sages and their words.[114]

The more significant question regarding these opening words is the referent of the pronoun הֵמָּה. Two options present themselves. First, the pronoun may serve an introductory function, referring to what is about to be said: 'and in addition are these things . . .'.[115] The exclusion of הִזָּהֵר from this clause on syntactical grounds restricts the clause to the force of a simple connective (which is one possible function if the pronoun is read as having an antecedent referent; see below), meaning 'and in addition are these things, my son . . .'. Constrained in this way by the removal of the imperative to the subsequent clause, one finds that the significance of the preposition מִן before the pronoun הֵמָּה 'these things' is unclear, a problem resolved by the second option: assigning an antecedent referent for the pronoun.

Two possibilities present themselves as antecedent referents for the pronoun. It may refer to the "words of the wise" in v. 11,[116] or it may function as a *neutrum* having a nonspecific reference to all that has been said to this point.[117] When the antecedent is considered to be the "words of the wise," this verse is understood to begin with a warning against adding to the words found in this book (taking הִזָּהֵר as part of the opening clause in v. 12 so that the clause reads, "Beware of anything in addition to them"), thus affirming the completeness and sufficiency of the text (and perhaps the inadequacy of alternatives).[118] Seow adduces an impressive list of ancient works that include a similar closing formula.[119]

---

114. Fox argues that, as in v. 9, וְיֹתֵר should be read alone rather than as part of the expression וְיֹתֵר מֵהֵמָּה (see Fox, *Qohelet and His Contradictions*, 326–27). Seow, however, points out that יוֹתֵר מִן is well attested in Classical Hebrew (Choon-Leong Seow, "'Beyond Them, My Son, Be Warned': The Epilogue of Qoheleth Revisited," in *Wisdom, You Are My Sister* [ed. Michael L. Barré; Washington, D.C.: Catholic Bible Association, 1997] 135 n. 42). Furthermore, the fact that הִזָּהֵר is best read as part of a subsequent clause undermines Fox's position.

115. Fox (*Qohelet and His Contradictions*, 310) takes this position and renders the text "At the same time, my son, of these things be wary. . . ."

116. See Murphy, *Ecclesiastes*, 124; Seow, *Ecclesiastes*, 388.

117. The *neutrum* is usually represented by a feminine pronoun in BH; see Waltke and O'Connor, *An Introduction to Biblical Hebrew Syntax*, §16.3.5c. Whybray appears to endorse this position by saying, "The phrase . . . is simply an announcement of a further piece of advice. It does not refer to the teachings of the wise mentioned in v. 11." See Whybray, *Ecclesiastes* (NCB), 173.

118. See Eaton, *Ecclesiastes*, 155; Farmer, *Proverbs and Ecclesiastes*, 196; Seow, *Ecclesiastes*, 388.

119. Ibid.

This interpretation faces at least two objections. First, הזהר is grammatically better associated with the next clause of v. 12 (a point I shall argue in more detail below), so that the text reads only "in addition to them" and is not a warning in itself. Second, unlike most of the parallels adduced by Seow, the referent is not just the words of Qoheleth but the more vague "words of the wise." Once again, one must presume too much about the existence of a body of wisdom writings at the time of the writing of the epilogue to give this position credence. Murphy's claim that the referent must be restricted to Qoheleth's words is not borne out by the text because the expression "words of the wise" in v. 11 contrasts with the narrower focus on Qoheleth explicit in the first two verses of the epilogue.[120]

Consequently, the best understanding for the pronoun המה is that it functions as a *neutrum*, simply introducing a point that follows what has already been said.[121]

The appearance of the vocative בני is characteristic of wisdom writings in the Hebrew Bible and throughout the ANE.[122] The use of the expression here suggests that the author of the epilogue himself writes from within the wisdom tradition, in spite of the fact that the content of the epilogue suggests that he has become disenchanted with it.[123] Furthermore, the use also suggests that the work is aimed at students of the sages. This correlates well with the use of Qoheleth's words by the epilogist (he has acknowledged that Qoheleth

---

120. Murphy, *Ecclesiastes*, 125. Murphy does acknowledge the improbability that the expression "words of the wise" refers to a specific corpus of wisdom texts. Seow attempts to overcome the problem by stating that the "warning is probably formulaic" and so concludes that the expression "words of the wise" refers specifically to Qoheleth's words (Seow, *Ecclesiastes*, 393). As noted above, in order to reach this conclusion, Seow must overlook the significant difference between this text and the parallels that he has identified.

121. See Gordis, *Koheleth: The Man and His World*, 354. If הזהר is included in the first clause of v. 12, this understanding of the pronoun as a *neutrum* would suggest that v. 12 opens with a warning against interpreting the "words of the wise" as being anything more than goads and sharp sticks rather than as an affirmation of their authority and finality.

122. See, for example, Prov 1:8, 10, 15; 2:1; 3:1.

123. Contra Tomáš Frydrych (*Living under the Sun: Examination of Proverbs and Qoheleth* [VTSup 90; Leiden: Brill, 2002] 222), who writes that "the epilogist is not a sage, he is a theologian whose primary interest is in the cult and the revelation that it provides." There are at least two types of wise person in the Hebrew Bible: those whose wisdom is demonstrated by their observance of God's laws (e.g., Deut 4:6) and those like Qoheleth who are frequently criticized by the prophets and the authors of the biblical material. This issue was reviewed above, in the opening chapters of this book. Fox ("Frame-Narrative and Composition in the Book of Qohelet," 99) correctly states that, by using this terminology, "the epilogist thus implicitly identifies himself as a wise-man, a wisdom teacher."

was a sage) to reach conclusions, make observations, and provide warnings about the teachings of the sages.

הזהר עשות ספרים הרבה אין קץ

beware of the excessive production of writings—for this never ends

The Niphal imperative הזהר is almost universally understood to be part of the opening clause of v. 12. Understood this way, the second clause begins with the infinitive עשות 'to produce' and contains no finite verb. The result is also difficult to decipher because the function of the infinitive construct verb is not immediately apparent. By contrast, including the imperative verb "beware" with this clause results in an unambiguous warning against the authorial work that the epilogist apparently associates with the sages.

Furthermore, in every other instance in the Hebrew Bible in which an imperative verb is immediately followed by an infinitive construct, the two are bound together both grammatically and semantically.[124] This reading is reflected in the LXX, which presents a quite literal rendering of the Hebrew for the entire epilogue and also binds the warning to the words about making many books.[125]

Read this way, the second clause becomes a warning from the epilogist to the reader, rather than a mere observation about the production of books. The reader is warned either against making ספרים הרבה 'many books' or against the 'excessive production of "books" '.[126] These two possible interpretations rest on differing understandings of the function of the Hiphil infinitive absolute הרבה. Most scholars understand הרבה to function here adjectivally (as

---

124. The construction imv. + inf. cs. occurs only in Isa 1:16, 17; 23:16; Jer 15:15; 18:20; Ps 33:3; Qoh 12:12. See my "Re-examining the Warning of Eccl. xii 12," *VT* 50 (2000) 123–27.

125. The LXX verse division places the words καὶ περισσὸν ἐξ αὐτῶν 'and more of them' in v. 11 and begins v. 12 with the words υἱέ μου φύλαξαι ποιῆσαι βιβλία πολλά 'My son, beware of making many books'. Although verse divisions are of only limited value in understanding the text, they do reflect an early stage of the understanding of the structure of the text. Septuagint Greek also frequently ties imperative and infinitive verbs together, a fact that supports the claim that the imperative of φυλάσσω 'beware' ought to be read as part of the second clause. Also of interest is the fact that the verb φυλάσσω is often followed by ποιεω 'make' in the LXX, and in five other instances the construction is also imperative plus infinitive, as it is here (Exod 23:15; Deut 6:3, 24:8; Josh 1:7, 22:5); however, in those instances the meaning is something like 'be careful to observe . . .', which is not appropriate here. The LXX can be understood to support the interpretation of the Hebrew text described above.

126. As Seow points out, the translation 'books' for ספרים is anachronistic, and perhaps the less-specific word 'writings' does more justice to the historical reality, in which texts were composed in various forms, most commonly perhaps scrolls. See Seow, *Ecclesiastes*, 389, for more detailed discussion.

reflected in the former option),[127] although infinitive absolutes do commonly function adverbially, as reflected in the second option.[128] In the final analysis, there is little to distinguish the two alternatives, except the context, which reveals the meaning of the warning.

Because this warning follows a criticism of the activities of the sages and their words, the activity against which the epilogist here warns the reader cannot reasonably be understood to be anything other than an activity of the sages; to suggest otherwise divorces these words from the remainder of the epilogue and trivializes them.[129] Consequently, this is a warning against the excessive production of books, with which the sages, at least from the perspective of the epilogist, occupied their time. The epilogist thus warns the reader against being caught up in the work of the sages.

The implicit association between the sages and the production of books is probably also an indication of the close association between the sages and the scribes.[130] This association is only elsewhere explicit in the Hebrew Bible in Jer 8:8, although by NT times it appears that the association between professional sages and scribes was more readily accepted (see, for example, 1 Cor 1:20). Nonetheless, the focus of this warning is clearly not against those who merely write books but specifically against the sages who record their wisdom in books. This association between sages and authors further enhances the case that the חכמים who are the subject of the epilogue are professional wise people, for they have both the knowledge and the time to produce literary works (and apparently to keep producing them), and they are literate.

---

127. The word הרבה is understood adjectivally by (among others) Fox, *Qohelet and His Contradictions*, 310, 327; Murphy, *Ecclesiastes* 123; the NRSV; the NASB. See the arguments of Judah Goldin, "The End of Ecclesiastes: Literal Exegesis and Its Transformation," in *Biblical Motifs: Origins and Transformations* (ed. Alexander Altmann; Cambridge: Harvard University Press, 1966) 145–46.

128. Waltke and O'Connor, *An Introduction to Biblical Hebrew Syntax*, 582–83; cf. Seow, *Ecclesiastes*, 389. The word הרבה, as an inf. cs., is an exception because it does appear to have been used adjectivally in a number of instances; see BDB, 915b.

129. Wilson ("'The Words of the Wise': The Intent and Significance of Qoheleth 12:9–14," 177) comments that "Both *ʿăśôt sĕpārîm* and *lahag* fit well with the description of the work attributed to Qohelet in 12:9." It is also interesting to note Josephus's later criticism of the Greeks: "For we have not an innumerable multitude of books among us, disagreeing from and contradicting one another, [as the Greeks have,] but only twenty-two books" (*Ag. Ap.* 1.8).

130. Fishbane (*Biblical Interpretation in Ancient Israel*, 29–32) draws parallels between Qoh 12:9–14 and ANE scribal activity, noting that עשות ספרים is similar to an Akkadian scribal expression and may be a technical expression meaning 'to compose' or 'to compile' books, an idiom specifically associated with scribal schools. Kaiser ("Qoheleth," 83) states that "we should probably picture [Qoheleth] as a scribe who also worked as a teacher, recording the results of the discussions which he led in school."

This statement closes with two words that function to explain the epilogist's warning: אֵין קֵץ. This same expression occurs a total of five times in the Hebrew Bible, three of which are found in Ecclesiastes.[131] In each of its other appearances, the expression refers to something that continues perpetually, never reaching a conclusion, never finishing. Fox, however, argues that, if this text is merely saying that the production of many books never ceases, then these words are not saying very much at all, and it is not clear why we should be warned about the activity. Rather, Fox argues that the epilogist's aim here is to indicate that "making many books is a thing of no purpose."[132]

Although Fox is correct in noting that the task is a "thing of no purpose," this does not preclude the task's also being endless. Producing wisdom texts is endless because the sages can never find the answers they are looking for. The search will never reach a satisfying conclusion and thus cannot end; equally, it can have no purpose because its aim is inaccessible. Qoheleth has himself provided ample evidence to support this assertion, with his utter failure to reach any conclusion other than that all is הבל—"people are not able to discover the work which is done under the sun. In so much as people seek earnestly, they will not find [it]. Even if the sage plans to know, he will not find [it]" (Qoh 8:17). Qoheleth's conclusion is that the answers cannot be found, and so here the epilogist warns against getting caught up in the search, for there is no end to it.

ולהג הרבה יגעת בשר

and of excessive study—it exhausts the body

Verse 12 concludes with a clause that parallels the previous clause by repeating הרבה. The first word, להג, is often identified as a noun meaning 'study', based on its similarity with the Arabic *lahija* 'to be devoted, attached; apply oneself assiduously'.[133] Understood this way the term is unique within BH. Furthermore, this understanding is not reflected in any of the ancient versions,[134] which appear to read the term as a form of the root הגה 'meditate, speak'. Finally, the presence of the infinitive absolute and the parallelism with the first clause imply that להג is itself a verbal form.

Consequently some scholars have suggested emending the form here to either the infinitive construct form להגות (which is not attested elsewhere and

---

131. See Isa 9:6; Job 22:5; Qoh 4:8, 16; 12:12.

132. Fox, *Qohelet and His Contradictions*, 327.

133. BDB, 529b; Gordis, *Koheleth: The Man and His World*, 354; Murphy, *Ecclesiastes*, 124; and apparently also Ogden, *Qoheleth*, 212.

134. The LXX reads μελέτη 'meditation'; the Vulg. reads *meditatio* 'meditation'. In addition, both the Talmud (*b. ʿErub.* 21b) and *Qoheleth Rabbah* understand the word in this sense.

for which the required textual corruption to the MT's להג is difficult to explain) or להגה (which is also not attested elsewhere but resulted from simple haplography that gave rise to the extant reading). Seow notes that there are examples of III-weak verbs which, in infinitive construct, take a final ה instead of ת, thus offering some support for correcting the text here to read an infinitive construct form of הגה.[135] However, the examples that Seow cites are all for common verbs, and common words in all languages tend to exhibit greater deviation from the norm than obscure terms. It would indeed be unusual for a more obscure term such as הגה—which nowhere else appears as an infinitive construct—to exhibit such deviation. Furthermore, the preposition ל appears to be superfluous to the meaning of the clause as well as destructive to the obvious parallels with the previous clause.

Thus, the better explanation for the term להג is to adopt the original suggestion outlined above: to read it as an infinitive construct form of the root להג, which is cognate with Arabic *lahija*. This requires no emendation of the consonantal text,[136] reinforces the parallelism with the previous clause, and makes good sense in the context. The parallelism of the entire verse can now be illustrated clearly, highlighting the function of the text as providing two warnings (through the ellipsis of הזהר in the second clause):

		הזהר
Beware		
of the excessive production of writings—for this never ends	עשות ספרים הרבה אין קץ	
and of excessive study—it exhausts the body	ולהג הרבה יגעת בשר	

The meaning of להג is suggested not only by the Arabic cognate but also by the parallelism with עשות ספרים in the first clause and the contextual constraint that the task in view must describe the work of the sages. In light of these considerations, 'study' appears to be a reasonable rendering, referring to the sages' research, which they presumably wrote down (the subject of the first warning). Thus, the second clause warns against excessive study, in particular the research undertaken by the sages.

The impact of the warning is heightened by the inclusion of the consequences of the actions, as in the first clause. In this instance, the consequence of excessive study is said to be יגעת בשר 'exhausts the body'. The construct

---

135. See Seow, *Ecclesiastes*, 389–90.
136. Assuming להג to be a Qal inf. cs., we would expect the form לְהֹג.

noun יגעת 'exhaustion, weariness' is not attested elsewhere in BH, although other forms of the root יגע are reasonably common.[137] The point the epilogist is making here is that the excessive study the sages undertook resulted only in exhaustion. Once again the words of the epilogist are marked by their negativity.

Summary

Verses 11 and 12 of the epilogue record two sets of warnings, each consisting of two parts. The first warning is against the teachings of the sages, the second against the research work upon which those teachings are based. The epilogist begins by warning that the sages' words are painful and manipulative. Although most commentators on this verse claim that the epilogist is making the point that the pain the sages' students must go through will ultimately lead them to good, the epilogist does not make this point. Nothing is added to the observation that the words of the sages are painful and manipulative. Nothing, that is, except for the warnings in v. 12 that alert the reader to the futility of the activities of the sages. The position that, through pain, a good end will come is excluded, for the activities of the sages have no end.

In v. 12 the epilogist offers the reader two warnings about the activities of the sages (their study and writing in the pursuit of wisdom). We are told that they have no positive outcomes, only negative ones. First of all, the study of the sages results only in exhaustion (see Qoh 2:21–23), and second, the work of composing and recording wisdom never ends, for it never reaches its goal. Furthermore, these warnings are rooted in the words of Qoheleth presented by the epilogist for our consideration. Qoheleth frankly stated and restated his observations about the inaccessible nature of the answers that the sages sought, about the endlessness of the search for wisdom, and about the weariness of the task.

Qoheleth, however, never offered a viable alternative. Qoheleth's own conclusion was little more than "make the most of what life serves up to you."[138] His words stand only as a warning against pursuing the path that he pursued so fruitlessly. The epilogist is not content with this state of affairs and moves to point the reader toward an alternative, and it is this alternative that we find presented in the final two verses of the epilogue.

---

137. An adjective form appears in Qoh 1:8, while a verbal form appears in Qoh 10:15. The former verse begins with Qoheleth's observation that כל־הדברים יגעים 'all things are exhausting'.

138. See the discussion of the meaning of such texts as Qoh 2:24; 3:12–13; and 5:18–20 in the next chapter.

The assessment made in vv. 11 and 12 of the work of the sages raises one question that demands attention: Are Qoheleth's words and activities as a sage to be included in the warnings about the endlessness of making books and the weariness of the sages' research? Although some argue that the epilogist does not have Qoheleth's words in view when he makes these warnings and criticisms, there are a couple of good reasons for thinking so.

First, the epilogist has not excluded Qoheleth's words from the words of the wise that are the focus of these verses. The opening two verses of the epilogue portrayed Qoheleth as preeminent among the sages and as being honest and bold enough to correct the words of other sages, even when the truth could not be conveyed in pleasing terms. Rather than distinguishing Qoheleth from the sages, the epilogist has closely aligned Qoheleth with the sages. The epilogist ultimately affirms Qoheleth's words only insofar as he, unlike other sages, realized the futility of the task of the wisdom movement, and he was willing to admit it.

Second, the various warnings and criticisms made by the epilogist fit well with the words of Qoheleth recorded by the epilogist. When the epilogist warns against the futility of the task of the sages, Qoheleth attests to this futility in his own experience and in the results of his search for wise answers to the questions that life poses. Qoheleth does not, as the epilogist does, move beyond the futility of his task to find an alternative form of wisdom rooted in the commandments of God, and so remains among the ranks of the sages against whom the epilogist felt the need to warn his readers.

The exclusion of Qoheleth's words from among those criticized by the epilogist is often based on the interpretation of the opening of v. 12 as extolling the sufficiency of Qoheleth's words (or of the "words of the wise" to which the epilogist has referred). The problems with this position, discussed above, undermine the basis for excluding Qoheleth from among the warnings of v. 12. In view of these considerations it is preferable to adopt the position that the epilogist includes Qoheleth's own words among these warnings.[139] Indeed, that the epilogist's warnings so precisely correspond to Qoheleth's words indicates that they provided the evidence upon which these warnings are based.

Qoheleth 12:13–14:
The Conclusion to the Matter

The end of the matter, everything has been heard. Fear God and keep his commandments, for this applies to everyone. For God will bring every deed into judgment—including every hidden deed, whether good or evil.

---

139. See Gordis, *Koheleth: The Man and His World*, 350.

The final two verses of the epilogue are marked off from the remainder of the epilogue by the introductory clauses, which indicate that some form of conclusion has been reached, and by the move away from warning the reader about the sages and their teaching to more positive advice on how to live.

Verse 13

סוף דבר

The end of the matter

The noun סוף is usually understood to be a synonym of קץ and to be of Aramaic derivation. It appears in the similar Aramaic expression סופא די־מלתא in Dan 7:28 (although there, it is in the emphatic state). Seow notes a number of later but similar expressions that refer to the end of a verse or book.[140] These are not good parallels, however, for the epilogist simply uses the vague דבר rather than the more specific terms used in the texts that Seow has cited. Were this expression truly analogous to these later texts, the epilogist would have had to be more specific about what was ended by this statement.

Qoheleth uses the synonyms סוף and קץ twice, and the epilogist uses them once (סוף in 3:11 and 7:2; and 12:13 by the epilogist; and קץ in 4:8 and 16; and 12:12 by the epilogist). There appears to be no semantic significance to the variations, and each may have the nuance of "goal" in at least one of their occurrences. If the use of סוף in this verse has this nuance, the epilogist is claiming that the point to which everything has been leading, the ultimate purpose for quoting extensively from Qoheleth's words and then offering comment on them in the previous words of the epilogue, is now to be stated.

This clause is universally translated as though the expression were definite, so the absence of the definite article in Hebrew is surprising. Barton has argued that the absence of the article suggests that a technical expression or an idiom is being used.[141] Although there is no evidence to support this claim—the expression does not appear elsewhere in BH (nor, for that matter, does the expression קץ דבר)—treating the expression as idiomatic appears to be the best explanation for the absence of the article on either word.

The expression clearly marks some form of conclusion. It is sometimes taken to refer back to the entire work, marking the end of the original text of the book of Ecclesiastes.[142] However, it may also be understood to introduce

---

140. Seow, *Ecclesiastes*, 390; see also Barton; Crenshaw, *Ecclesiastes*, 192. Barton took this expression to be a marker of the end of the original work, to which a pious glossator appended the final two verses.

141. Barton, *A Critical and Exegetical Commentary on the Book of Ecclesiastes*, 200 (see Seow, *Ecclesiastes*, 390).

142. Barton, ibid., 199; Seow, ibid., 394. Seow also notes the frequent use of the expression "it is finished" at the end of Egyptian wisdom texts and concludes that what follows in

the epilogist's own final conclusion to the work. In view of the epilogist's critical stance toward the teachings of the sages, and in view of the nature of the
advice found in the words that follow—advice that cannot be reconciled with
Qoheleth's own advice, this latter approach makes best sense of the text. The
epilogist here presents a stark contrast to his assessment of the task of the
sages offered in the previous verses. Unlike the sages, whose work could reach
no conclusion (אֵין קֵץ), the epilogist is now presenting a conclusion, a decisive
statement advising the reader how to live. Furthermore, unlike Qoheleth, the
epilogist has definite advice. While Qoheleth's only conclusion had been that
all is הבל and that, consequently, we must simply accept (in Shakespearean
terms) the slings and arrows of outrageous fortune and make the most of life,
the epilogist has specific, positive advice to impart to the reader.

הכל נשמע

everything has been heard

The verb נשמע has variously been explained as a Qal cohortative, a Niphal
participle, and a Niphal perfect.[143] The first option is improbable, because it
requires that הכל be understood as the direct object of the verb, despite the
lack of the object marker את on the definite noun (compare with the next
clause, which opens with the words את־האלהים, and the subsequent clause,
which opens ואת־מצותיו), while the word order tends to suggest, more naturally, that הכל is the subject of the verb. The remaining two possible interpretations are semantically closer, although the verb is probably best understood
as a Niphal perfect.[144]

This clause stands in apposition to the previous and expands on the point
made by the epilogist in that clause. The end of the matter has been reached.
Everything has been heard. The epilogist thus asserts that no more needs to be

---

Ecclesiastes is "simply tacked on at the end." However, no similar conclusion occurs elsewhere in BH; the parallel to the Egyptian material may only be superficial, and interpreting
the expression on this basis may therefore be premature. In keeping with the approach outlined at the beginning of this chapter, I maintain that the entire work met with the approval
of the final editor, and so I reason that the remainder of the epilogue is integral with the entire work.

143. Reading נשמע as a Qal cohortative is principally reflected in the Vulgate's *audia-
mus* and is still suggested by some modern scholars, such as Whybray, *Ecclesiastes* (NCB),
173. Those who understand it to be a Niphal participle include Seow, *Ecclesiastes*, 390; and
Murphy, *Ecclesiastes*, 124. The pausal form of the Niphal pf. 3ms is identical with the participle, indicating that only context can determine between the two options. Most modern
readings understand the verb to be Niphal perfect.

144. The Niphal pf. 3ms form appears 17 times elsewhere in BH, while the participle
appears only 3 times.

said about the sages or their teaching, no more warnings are necessary, no more evidence needs to be presented against them. The point has been made: the teachings of the sages are dangerous, manipulative, misleading. Their task is futile and cannot reach a conclusion. Thus the epilogist proceeds to close the work with positive words of advice—words that outline a way of life that is in direct contrast to the teaching of the sages.

את האלהים ירא

Fear God

The epilogist has not mentioned God up to this point, but, in keeping with the usage of Qoheleth, here he uses the word with the definite article.[145] Although the use of the article on אלהים is not confined to Ecclesiastes, the clear preference for this form over the inarticular form is characteristic of Qoheleth.[146] Much debate has taken place regarding the relationship between Qoheleth's God and the God of the remainder of the Hebrew Bible, and an increasing number of readers concur with Lauha's conclusion that *sein Gott ist nicht der Gott des israelitischen Glaubens* ('his God is not the God of Israelite belief').[147] Stephan de Jong has attempted to refute this assertion by demonstrating that the characteristics attributed to God by Qoheleth can be found elsewhere in the Hebrew Bible.[148] De Jong's arguments fail on two accounts, however. First, although he demonstrates a number of areas of equivalence, when he argues that God outside Qoheleth acts deterministically according to "non-moral standards," the evidence he adduces is not convincing.[149] Second, he fails to recognize that much of what is unique in Qoheleth's presentation of God lies not in what is said but in what is not said.[150] This point will come to

---

145. Qoheleth prefers the form האלהים, which he uses in 31 out of 39 references to God (not counting this instance in the epilogue).

146. The word אלהים appears approximately 2,602 times in BH, of which only 376 are articular. In Ecclesiastes, the word appears 40 times, 32 of which are definite. Many of the other instances of האלהים in BH are in specific constructions (where the word is more often articular than not), such as in 2 Kings 1–11 in the construction איש האלהים 'man of God'. The significance of Qoheleth's distinctive usage is unclear.

147. Lauha, *Kohelet*, 17; cf. D. Michel, *Untersuchungen zur Eigenart des Buches Qohelet* (BZAW 183; Berlin: de Gruyter, 1989) 276, 289; and Michel, *Qohelet*, 97–100.

148. Stephan de Jong, "God in the Book of Qohelet: A Reappraisal of Qohelet's Place in Old Testament Theology," *VT* 42 (1997) 154–67. See also Roy B. Zuck, "God and Man in Ecclesiastes," in *Reflecting with Solomon: Selected Studies on the Book of Ecclesiastes* (ed. Roy B. Zuck; Grand Rapids: Baker, 1994) 217–18.

149. De Jong, "God in the Book of Qohelet: A Reappraisal of Qohelet's Place in Old Testament Theology," 156, 166.

150. Seow (*Ecclesiastes*, 146) summarizes some of the characteristics of Qoheleth's God: "This God described by Qohelet is very present and very active in the cosmos, always

the fore when we consider the significance of the epilogist's call to keep God's commandments.

Distinct from the discussion of Qoheleth's understanding of God is the issue of the epilogist's understanding of God. It is readily apparent that the epilogist's brief comments do not permit the construction of a comprehensive theology, yet there are some important points that can be made. First, the epilogist's statements about God—particularly regarding keeping his commandments and the expectation of divine judgment—reflect an understanding of God that is not echoed in Qoheleth's words (a point to be considered more completely below). These comments more closely reflect Deuteronomistic thought than wisdom thought and tie the epilogist to traditional Yahwism more closely than to the sages about whom he comments.

Second, the use of the form האלהים by the epilogist rather than the more normal, inarticular form is clearly reminiscent of Qoheleth's own distinctive usage. The fact that the epilogist has employed it in his orthodox statement about keeping the commandments suggests that he thinks that Qoheleth is speaking about the God of Israel, despite his unorthodox and troubling words. Despite the fact that Qoheleth demonstrated no knowledge of God's revelation to or election of the people of Israel, his observations were intended to be about the God of Israel.

The fear of God was mentioned specifically by Qoheleth in 3:14; 5:7, 7:18, and 8:12–13, and the phrase is typical of Wisdom Literature.[151] What is not entirely clear, however, is whether Qoheleth uses the expression with the same nuances that it carries elsewhere in the Hebrew Bible and whether this statement by the epilogist reflects comments already made by Qoheleth or stands in opposition to or modifies them.[152]

---

giving . . . and doing/making. . . . But the deity never speaks and never deals directly with individuals or with nations (unlike YHWH). It is a transcendent and inscrutable God of whom Qohelet speaks."

151. A number of scholars have argued that these references to the "fear of God" should be attributed to a pious glossator and should not be considered original (e.g., Barton, *A Critical and Exegetical Commentary on the Book of Ecclesiastes*, 199; cf. Wilson, "'The Words of the Wise': The Intent and Significance of Qoheleth 12:9–14"). The above examination reveals, however, that, although the terminology is reminiscent of the "fear of Yahweh" terminology used elsewhere in the Hebrew Bible, Qoheleth uses the expression with a significantly different nuance, so the need to attribute the words to a glossator is obviated.

152. Regarding the "fear of Yahweh" elsewhere in the Hebrew Bible, Muntingh has shown that in Isaiah this phrase "includes fear but also reverence, faith and love." See L. M. Muntingh, "Fear of Yahweh and Fear of the Gods according to the Books of Qohelet and Isaiah," in *Studies in Isaiah* (ed. W. C. van Wyk; Pretoria West: NHW, 1980) 143–58.

I have already argued that the epilogist has deliberately indicated that the God both he and Qoheleth refer to is the same God (through his use of Qoheleth's terminology). This observation could be seen as support for the assertion that the concept "fear of God" is the same for the epilogist and Qoheleth. Closer consideration of Qoheleth's references to the "fear of God" reveals that Qoheleth provides bases for this fear. In Qoh 3:14 it is clear that God's works are designed to inspire fear in people. Qoh 5:5–6[6–7] indicates that people are to fear God because he can destroy their work if they fail to fulfill a vow. In Qoh 7:18 the fear of God is expressed by avoiding being either overly righteous or overly wicked, for neither righteousness nor wickedness guarantees a desirable or undesirable outcome; avoiding both may be more beneficial.

In 8:12–13 Qoheleth contends that those who fear God will be better off than those who do not; in this he reflects traditional wisdom thinking. Gordis claims that these words are being quoted by Qoheleth, who does not believe them to be true. Thus, he proceeds to refute them in what follows.[153] Gordis's argument centers on Qoheleth's use of the verb ידע in 8:12. This verb has been examined in greater detail by Isaksson,[154] who notes that in general Qoheleth uses the perfect form to indicate knowledge that he has acquired as a result of searching and studying. Consequently, the use of a participle here may indicate that Qoheleth is referring to knowledge that is generally accepted and widely promulgated, the serious shortfalls of which he is aware. It appears likely, then, that to some degree Qoheleth disputes the traditional basis for fearing God by revealing exceptions to the rule. This awareness of exceptions not covered by the traditional formulation supports the claim that Qoheleth's concept of the fear of God may differ from the epilogist's.

Although there is insufficient data upon which to build a comprehensive understanding of Qoheleth's concept of the fear of God, his must ultimately differ from the epilogist's (and, indeed, the concept in the remainder of the Hebrew Bible), for Qoheleth fears a distant, unknown God, whereas the epilogist fears a God who has revealed his will in his commands to his people.[155]

---

153. Gordis, *Koheleth: The Man and His World*, 297; cf. Murphy, *Ecclesiastes*, 85. Fox rejects Gordis's argument that there are no indications that other people are being quoted; Qoheleth, rather, is stating a general principal that he believes is true, but he is aware of exceptions to the rule (see Fox, *Qohelet and His Contradictions*, 253).

154. Isaksson, *Studies in the Language of Qoheleth*, 67; cf. Seow, *Ecclesiastes*, 288; Longman, *The Book of Ecclesiastes*, 219.

155. See Muntingh's summary of Pedersen's conclusion on this matter: "In the other books of the OT one reads that one has to fear and love God, but for Qohelet it is only fear." Muntingh, "Fear of Yahweh and Fear of the Gods according to the Books of Qohelet and

This difference in views clearly has implications for the manifestation of one's fear of God. For the epilogist, the fear of God clearly manifests itself in the keeping of God's commands. For Qoheleth, who makes no reference to these commands, the fear of God cannot be demonstrated in this manner.

ואת מצותיו שמור

and keep his commandments

This clause is grammatically parallel with the previous clause, both taking the form of a direct object followed by an imperative verb. The parallelism serves to tie the two together as one combined instruction from the epilogist to the reader.

God's commands are nowhere mentioned by Qoheleth. In fact, the noun מצוה appears only once in Qoh 8:5, in reference to the command of a king. Although the majority of scholars consider this statement by the epilogist to be at odds with the words of Qoheleth that the epilogist records,[156] Shead has argued that "the words of Qohelet, when boiled down to their basic essence, are 'fear God and keep his commands.'"[157] Shead's interpretation does not

---

Isaiah," 144. For more on the "fear of God" in Qoheleth, see E. Pfeiffer, "Die Gottesfurcht im Buche Kohelet," in *Gottes Wort und Gottes Land: Hans-Willhelm Hertzberg zum 70. Geburtstag* (ed. Henning Graf Reventlow; Göttingen: Vandenhoeck & Ruprecht, 1965) 133–58; J. Pedersen, "Scepticisme Israélite," *RHPR* 10 (1930) 361. O. Kaiser ("Qoheleth," 91) comments that "The 'fear of God' in Qoheleth, then, is understood more broadly than in the second epilogist's legalistic sense, and its consequence is not so certain. If the epilogist has eschatological judgement in mind in xii 14, then he has left Qoheleth's thinking far behind." Seow (*Ecclesiastes*, 56) discusses extensively the impersonal nature of Qoheleth's God: "it is not an immanent deity of whom Qohelet speaks. This deity does not relate personally with anyone. In Ecclesiastes, God does not enter into a covenant with anyone. Indeed, this God is wholly transcendent, and the distance between God and humanity is stressed." Seow proceeds to tie this remoteness to Qoheleth's concept of the "fear of God" (p. 57).

156. So, for example, Murphy says, "The epilogue is obviously putting forth an ideal which has been developed elsewhere and which is not a concern in Ecclesiastes" (Murphy, *Ecclesiastes*, 126); Fox writes, "The author puts Wisdom in perspective: Wisdom is all very fine, he says, but once we have heard what the sages have to say, we must remember that what really counts is fear of God and obedience to him" (Fox, *Qohelet and His Contradictions*, 328). Whybray understands the epilogist to be attempting to claim that the meaning of Qoheleth's teaching is "fear God and keep his commands," in order to provide an orthodox reinterpretation of the work (Whybray, *Ecclesiastes* (NCB), 173). Seow recognizes that the perspective of the epilogist is nowhere represented in the words of Qoheleth but argues that, because Qoheleth nowhere denies the importance of obedience to divine commands, the words of 12:13 do not contradict the content of the book (Seow, *Ecclesiastes*, 394–95).

157. Shead, "Ecclesiastes from the Outside In," 31; see also Farmer, *Proverbs and Ecclesiastes*, 196–97; and Caneday, "Qoheleth: Enigmatic Pessimist or Godly Sage?" (p. 89 in Zuck), who claims that "Qoheleth's whole approach was governed by foundational presuppositions: his firm beliefs that God had revealed Himself through the biblical themes

flow immediately from the meaning of the epilogue but is principally based on structural considerations and the perception of various "word chains" in the epilogue.

However, Shead's argument is not compelling. The conclusion that v. 13 provides a summary of Qoheleth's teaching is based not only on Shead's identification of various "word chains" but also on his subsequent investiture of these chains with special meanings without demonstrating that the meanings are consequent upon the existence of the word chains. Particularly important to Shead's argument is the significance of the word chain that he identifies as based on the noun דבר:

> there is a four-fold repetition of 'word' (דָּבָר). More than anything else in the first half of the epilogue, Qohelet's wisdom is described as one of 'words'. It is therefore highly significant that the narrator should choose to use דָּבָר in vs. 13 (literally, 'the end of the word; the all is heard'). Like so much of his thought, this points in two directions, the general and the specific. On a general level, vs. 13 gives the reader 'the final word', namely, the statement about fearing God. But specifically, it is a pointed reference back to the 'words' of Qohelet (and other sages) which tells us that when Qohelet has had his say, it all amounts to 'fear God and keep his commands'.[158]

It is not at all clear how the word chain formed by the fourfold repetition of דבר leads us to the conclusion that Shead reaches. Why, for example, should not the epilogist's "final word" be the one that supplants all of the previous words of the sages? A conclusion of this sort appears to be more in keeping with the meaning of the epilogue. Shead makes the decision to invest the word-chain with one specific meaning over and above other possibilities without discussing or acknowledging alternatives.

Furthermore, if Qoh 12:13 is intended to be a summary of Qoheleth's teaching, it is difficult to explain why Qoheleth never mentioned God's commandments or used any of the related legal terminology, such as תורה, חקה, and עדה. Instead, at numerous points where he could have reached this conclusion, if it had reflected his thinking, he instead concluded that all is הבל.

Although the command to fear God and keep his commands is not alluded to directly in the Wisdom Literature, it is strongly reminiscent of Deuteronomistic thought.[159] Fearing God and keeping his commands is explicitly

---

of creation, the fall of man, and the ensuing history of redemption. . . ." Hubbard points out that Jerome also argued that v. 13 summarized Qoheleth's teachings (David Hubbard, *Ecclesiastes, Song of Solomon* [Mastering the Old Testament 15B; Dallas: Word, 1991] 253).

158. Shead, "Ecclesiastes from the Outside In," 30.

159. Job 23:12 and (probably) Prov 19:16 also refer to God's commands (מצוה), but they do not tie them to the fear of God.

mentioned in Deut 5:29; 6:2; 8:6; and 13:5, and indirectly in 2 Kgs 17:37; Dan 9:4; and Neh 1:5. Thus, the epilogist's instruction directly reflects Israelite orthodoxy and stands in stark contrast to the words of Qoheleth that he has quoted. Within the wisdom tradition, these sentiments are not explicitly expressed until the work of Sirach.[160]

כי זה כל האדם

for this applies to everyone

The final clause of v. 13 is difficult, principally because of its enigmatic brevity. Perry's solution, which ties this clause to the opening clause of the next verse, will be discussed in detail below (under v. 14). Both the LXX and the Vulgate offer quite literal translations, which do little to resolve the difficulties faced in interpreting the clause, and the expression appears nowhere else in BH.

The expression כל־האדם elsewhere clearly refers to 'every person' (see Qoh 3:13; 5:19; 7:2). Most commentators recognize that the expression is elliptical, although precisely how the ellipsis should be completed is considered difficult to prove.[161] Because the conjunction כי normally has a connective function, this clause is probably understood as an expansion or explanation of the previous clause. Thus, it is best understood as offering a justification for the epilogist's assertion that fearing God and keeping his commands should stand as the final word after all the words of the sages have been dismissed. The epilogist thus makes the point that these tasks—fearing God and keeping his commands—apply to everyone, not merely people outside the wisdom circles but also the wise. The epilogist maintains that all are subject to these imperatives.

This statement by the epilogist also appears to denigrate the *works* of the sages by excluding their advice from what is considered necessary work in life. Furthermore, the *words* of the sages, against which the epilogist has previously warned the reader, are not considered essential for human beings, whereas fearing God and keeping his commands (words) *are* essential. In order to emphasize this point further, the epilogist offers one final reason that fearing God and keeping his commands are essential, as opposed to heeding the advice of the sages, in the final verse of the book.

---

160. See Sir 23:27, and see the discussion of Sheppard, "The Epilogue to Qoheleth as Theological Commentary," 182–89.

161. See Seow, *Ecclesiastes*, 390–91; Fox, *Qohelet and His Contradictions*, 329; Gordis, *Koheleth: The Man and His World*, 355.

Verse 14

כי את כל מעשה האלהים יבא במשפט

For God will bring every deed into judgment

The final verse of the epilogue has traditionally been understood as serving to substantiate the epilogist's exhortation to fear God and keep his commands by offering justification for the validity of the advice. Perry argues, however, that the absence of an article following the particle את at the opening of the clause is particularly problematic for this interpretation and proposes that מעשה be read as a construct form and האלהים be read as part of the object of the verb יבא (as it is in the same expression in Qoh 8:17, 'every work of God').[162] The subject of the verb is provided in the final clause of v. 13, and so Perry renders the entire sentence: "For this is man's usual pursuit: namely, to pass judgment upon every one of God's actions, even all the hidden ones, whether for good or evil."[163] While some aspects of Perry's interpretation are appealing, it also raises some difficulties. First, the connection between the final clause of v. 13 and the beginning of v. 14 proposed by Perry is unlikely. His explanation depends on a "dialogical" use of the particle כי, but both his argument for this sort of dialogical use of כי in BH and his explanation of the specific use in this context are flawed. Perry attempts to prove that כי is occasionally used in the MT as "indicating a shift in the narrative voice from the narrator to another party."[164] However, in each instance in which such a shift in narrative voice is unambiguously present (some are not unambiguous[165]), there are also other indicators of the shift, such as change of person or use of another form of the verb אמר. Furthermore, it is not clear how Perry moves from identifying the כי at the beginning of v. 14 as "dialogical" to his final rendering, which appears to invest the word with an epexegetical function.

Second, Perry proposes a difficult reading of the final clause of v. 14, אם־טוב ואם־רע. This clause most plainly reads 'whether good or evil', not, as Perry renders it, 'whether *for* good or evil'. The expression best explains the scope of the "deeds" that are brought under judgment, rather than the consequences

---

162. For discussion of the article prefixed to אלהים, see p. 95.

163. Perry, *Dialogues with Kohelet*, 171–74.

164. Ibid., 192.

165. In some examples, Perry cites texts in which a speaker appears to quote from a popular saying (e.g., Jer 18:18; ibid., 193) with approval. These examples, however, are fundamentally different from the use that Perry advocates in Ecclesiastes, where כי is claimed to introduce contrary points of view. The absence of even one unambiguous dialogical marker in Ecclesiastes (aside from the words of the frame-narrator) and the explicit identification of only one author of the words of Qoheleth are major stumbling blocks to his interpretation.

of bringing them under judgment. In his attempt to avoid concluding that God's deeds may be either good or evil, Perry must resort to a difficult and ultimately unjustified reading of the text.

Third, it is not at all clear how this verse, read as Perry suggests, fits with the remainder of the epilogue, even on Perry's own interpretation. Having just exhorted the reader "not to waste any more time, but to proceed to more useful activities such as fearing the Lord,"[166] why would the epilogue then go on to state that every person brings God's deeds under judgment? Perry also fails to explain how a human being is able to pass judgment on the hidden works of God (something that seems to be required by the final clause, in Perry's interpretation).

Fourth, Perry must make כל־האדם the subject of the verb. Although this is grammatically acceptable, the noun האלהים appears to be a more appropriate subject, standing as it does immediately prior to the verb, with no easily identifiable alternate antecedent. Perry must propose an ellipsis in order provide a subject for the verb.

Fifth, although the expression יבא במשפט (a form of the verb בוא followed by the preposition and noun) only appears a few times in BH, it always (elsewhere) has God as the one bringing the judgment (see Isa 3:14; Ps 143:2; Job 14:3; 22:4; Qoh 11:9). While this fact alone cannot discount Perry's interpretation, it does increase the likelihood that the traditional interpretation is correct.

Ultimately, Perry's objection to the traditional understanding of the verse cannot be sustained, for as Gordis has indicated, there is considerable precedent for a direct object that lacks a definite article to follow the object-marker את.[167] Furthermore, the expression "every deed" could be an ellipsis meaning "every deed *of theirs*" (referring back to כל־האדם). In fact, ellipsis may have prompted the use of the object marker in the phrase without the appearance of a definite article.[168] This and the warning by Qoheleth in 11:9 (compare 3:17) that God will bring a person's deeds under judgment provide sufficient support for the traditional interpretation.

The epilogist's reference to judgment provokes us to ask whether he shared the same view of judgment as Qoheleth. Murphy has argued that there

---

166. Ibid., 173.

167. "The absence of the article in מעשה after את is paralleled in many passages of early Hebrew (cf. Ex. 21:28, את איש; I Sam. 24:5, את כנף; II Sam. 4:11, את איש צדיק; 5:24, את קול צעדה; 18:18, את מצבת; Ez. 16:32, את זרים). This erratic use of the article becomes more pronounced under the influence of Aramaic, where the determinative status, which contains the article, loses its meaning and becomes virtually equivalent to the absolute" (Gordis, *Koheleth: The Man and His World*, 355).

168. Nouns with object suffixes are treated as grammatically definite in spite of having no article.

is at least some distinction between Qoheleth's understanding of judgment and the epilogist's:

> Does he mean by "judgment" the same thing that Qoheleth did? The manner in which this is introduced by v 13 suggests that he shares the views of Sirach and another generation. The emphasis on divine judgment is not strictly contradictory to Qoheleth's views, but it is hardly possible that he would have expressed himself in this way. He recognized God as judge but nowhere does he attempt to explain this, much less to motivate human action on the basis of divine judgment. For him the judgment of God is a total mystery.[169]

Qoheleth has not had much to say about the matter of divine judgment, although in 3:17 and 11:9 he affirms the idea that God will judge (it is unlikely, however, that he is referring to an eschatological judgment, particularly considering his comments in 3:19–21).[170] However, the nature of God's judgment does not appear to conform to traditional expressions. Although Qoheleth fails to explain the basis of God's judgment (probably because he cannot determine what the basis is), his association of the theme of God's judgment with observations about the apparent lack of justice (see 3:19–21; 8:10–17) and with the declaration that everything was הבל (see in particular Qoh 3:19) suggests that he felt that God will judge but that the basis and outcome of that judgment were inscrutable.

In contrast to Qoheleth's view of judgment, then, stands the view of the epilogist, who has unambiguously tied God's judgment to obedience to the commands of God. The epilogist's argument that divine judgment provides a motive for obedience to God's commands demonstrates his belief that justice will ultimately be done. Furthermore, it is more likely that the epilogist, rather than Qoheleth, anticipated some form of eschatological judgment, for this appears to be the only solution to Qoheleth's problem with the lack of justice in this world.[171]

---

169. Murphy, *Ecclesiastes*, 126; cf. Longman, *The Book of Ecclesiastes*, 283.

170. By contrast, Caneday ("Qoheleth: Enigmatic Pessimist or Godly Sage" [in Zuck, "God and Man," 109]) claims that "Qoheleth, throughout his book, had repeatedly raised the motif of eschatological judgment to motivate obedient behaviour despite the fact that rotters advance in prosperity and live long in this world while the righteous flounder in their struggles and succumb early to the curse of death. . . . The final judgment serves as a chief orientation to which Qoheleth directs his readers to steer them through the labyrinths of this meaningless life." Bold and unequivocal statements like these are impossible to reconcile with the actual words spoken by Qoheleth.

171. See Longman, *The Book of Ecclesiastes*, 283; C. D. Ginsburg, *The Song of Songs and Coheleth* (New York: KTAV, 1970 [1861]) 478.

The expression כל־מעשה appears previously three times in the words of
Qoheleth (2:11; 8:9, 17): twice with reference to human deeds, once with reference to God's. What is particularly interesting, however, is the prominence
of this expression in Deuteronomy (appearing in 2:7; 11:7; 14:29; 15:10;
16:15; 24:19; 28:12; 30:9). The epilogist has again used terminology that is
reminiscent of the Law (see comments on v. 13, p. 98), a tendency that reflects his apparent intention of promoting orthodoxy over the heterodox conclusions of the wisdom movement, revealed in the words of Qoheleth.

על כל נעלם אם טוב ואם רע

including every hidden deed, whether good or evil

The final clause of the epilogue further elucidates the nature of God's judgment, which itself serves as motivation for the exhortation to fear God and
keep his commands because the preposition על indicates the basis for the
judgment.[172] Thus, although the epilogist has specifically mentioned that God
will judge all deeds, here he makes explicit the fact that God's judgment will
include things that are hidden, both good and evil.

This emphatic reference to God's judgment of things that are hidden (although the writer does not say from whom these things are hidden) is probably parallel to the final expression, אם־טוב ואם־רע, with both serving as an
expansion of כל־מעשה (rather than being an explanation of the scope of the
hidden things). The placement of the *'atnaḥ* between the two parallel expressions supports this reading of the verse.

Given that the epilogist has already stated that God will bring all deeds
into judgment, the reference to "hidden things," although technically superfluous, is included to highlight one specific aspect of the judgment that God
will bring to bear on all deeds. The most likely explanation for his reference
to hidden deeds is his overall evaluation of the wisdom movement.[173] The
epilogist ascertained that the wisdom movement was embroiled in error and
deception—facts that motivated his acclamation for Qoheleth, who corrected
the wisdom of other sages (v. 9) and chose to speak honestly rather than con-
cocting "pleasing words" to endear himself to his audience (v. 10). The epilogist's response was to warn against the pointless activities of the sages
(having employed Qoheleth's own teachings to demonstrate that in general

---

172. See Seow, *Ecclesiastes*, 391; Waltke and O'Connor, *An Introduction to Biblical
Hebrew Syntax*, §11.2.13e, p. 218.

173. Although Qoheleth himself did not use this terminology, he did find many things
to be hidden from him (see Qoh 8:17). These findings reflect the message of Job's hymn to
wisdom (see particularly Job 28:21, which also uses the Niphal of עלם). Nevertheless, these
hidden things cannot reasonably be said to form the basis for judgment.

the teachings of the wisdom movement were pointless) and now proceeds to inform the reader that all things will be brought under judgment. The reference to what is hidden may thus refer to the apparently deceptive (and this may include self-deception) character of much of the wisdom movement at the time these words were written.

The expression אם־טוב ואם־רע not only to refers to the universal scope of the judgment—no deed will escape the judgment of God—but also emphasizes the moral element that underlies the judgment of these deeds. A comparable statement appears only once elsewhere in the Wisdom Literature, in Prov 15:3, "The eyes of Yahweh are in every place, watching the evil and the good," again emphasizing the scope of Yahweh's vision together with a moral element. Also of interest, in light of the close association between Qoheleth and Solomon established in the opening chapters of the book (and possibly exploited in the opening of the epilogue), is the use in 1 Kgs 3:9, where Solomon prays for wisdom to distinguish between good and evil. This request by Solomon reflects a more traditional understanding and application of wisdom: wisdom facilitates judgment and is ultimately based on application of the Law. The epilogist, by contrast, implies that the sages, who ought to have been using their wisdom to apply the Law, as Solomon had initially sought to do, would have their own deeds brought under God's judgment.

Finally, the epilogist's focus on God's judgment functions to redress the doubts that Qoheleth himself expressed about the appearance of justice in the world. Gordis has correctly observed this in saying that "v. 14 seems specifically directed against Koheleth's doubts about retribution, to which he has given so much attention (cf. 8:9 to 9:3)."[174]

The Epilogue and Sirach

A number of scholars have noticed close parallels between the epilogue and Sirach. Gerald Sheppard highlights two specific similarities between Qoh 12:13–14 and Sirach. First, "an editorial device like that in v 13 occurs in Sir 43:27."[175] Second, Sirach—unlike either Proverbs or the words of Qoheleth—explicitly advises observation of God's commands and ties this to divine judgment (see Sir 1:26–30). Sheppard concludes: "we find that only Sirach has exactly the same ideology as Qoh 12:13–14, a perspective not expressed in the body of Qoheleth itself. We must conclude that the redactor of Qoh 12:13–14 either knew of Sirach or fully shared in a similar, pervasive

---

174. Gordis, *Koheleth: The Man and His World*, 351.
175. Sheppard, "The Epilogue to Qoheleth as Theological Commentary," 187.

estimate of sacred wisdom."[176] Sheppard (along with others) apparently maintains that Sirach's work influenced the final redactor of Ecclesiastes. Ultimately, however, this interpretation of the function of vv. 13–14 fails to account for the understanding of the remainder of the epilogue expounded above. In light of my exposition of the epilogue above, a more fitting interpretation would be the reverse. As I have previously demonstrated, the notion that true wisdom is reflected in obedience to God's commands appears in Deuteronomy; the epilogist did not need to borrow it from Sirach. Furthermore, the profoundly different direction in which the sages appear to have moved by the time of Sirach may well have been influenced by the reformative work of Qoheleth's epilogist and others who shared his concerns about the wisdom movement of his day.

The Relationship of the Epilogue to Qoheleth's Words

The principal objection to the interpretation of Ecclesiastes that I have espoused is probably that it undermines the message and impact of Qoheleth's words by effectively contradicting them. If the epilogist's aim was to discredit the wise, then surely the critique would be more extensive than a mere six verses at the end of the text.[177] If the epilogist was intending to invert the conclusions of Qoheleth and the other sages, why did he present so much of Qoheleth's work? Certainly this strategy appears to be unparalleled in the extant literature of the ancient Near East.

This is a serious issue and requires a response. The views of previous scholars who have claimed that the epilogue is at least *partially* critical of Qoheleth (and few have made the case that the epilogue is so consistently critical of the wisdom movement, including Qoheleth, as I have) have been rejected at precisely this point. Nonetheless, a quite reasonable answer to this criticism can be provided: the epilogist uses Qoheleth's own conclusions and observations to criticize the sages and their teachings in the epilogue.

For example, there are a number of passages throughout Ecclesiastes that reflect the futility of the sages' task (e.g., Qoh 1:2–11; 3:15; 7:23–25; 8:16–17). That Qoheleth's conclusion may be summarized by declaring everything to be הבל indicates that Qoheleth, together with all sages, could not make sense of the world. It is inherently senseless to the observer, without revela-

---

176. Ibid.

177. So Fox (*A Time to Tear Down*, 371), who writes that "the author of the epilogue basically supports Qohelet's teachings. Otherwise he could have refrained from writing, editing, or transmitting the book."

tion from God. Their task was ultimately futile, and Qoheleth has shown from his own research that it is futile. The world of the sages makes no sense; there is no order to be discovered, no means by which a wise person can influence the outcome of his or her own life.

The painful nature of the teachings of Qoheleth also comes through in many passages (e.g., Qoh 1:12–18; 2:1–26; 3:16–22; 4:1–3; 9:11–12). This, too, is reflected in the epilogue's assertion that the words of the wise are like goads and nails.

Thus Qoheleth's words are the evidence that the epilogist uses to substantiate his criticism of the sages. The choice of Qoheleth's words (as opposed to any other sage's) is also explained in the opening verses: Qoheleth was not afraid to speak the truth, even if it meant he could not write the pleasing words that he desired to write. By noting that Qoheleth revised the conclusions of other sages, the epilogist has informed the reader that not all of the sages could be trusted and has cast doubt on the integrity of the sages whose conclusions are "pleasing."

Furthermore, by presenting Qoheleth as the foremost sage in the line of Solomon himself, the epilogist has based his criticisms on the observations of the preeminent sage, thereby placing them beyond dispute by other sages. By extolling the greatness and integrity of Qoheleth in the opening two verses of the epilogue, the epilogist has shown that his words cannot easily be dismissed but that in fact they represent the heart of the wisdom movement as opposed to the "public face" of the wisdom movement.

The epilogist does not contradict Qoheleth; indeed, both Qoheleth and the epilogist are critical of the wisdom movement in their own ways. The fundamental difference between them is that Qoheleth admits knowledge of no alternative to the way of wisdom. For Qoheleth, once wisdom has shown itself inadequate for determining value in life, there is no viable alternative. By contrast, the epilogist points the reader to an alternative: obeying the commandments of God. Qoheleth's admission of wisdom's failure is thus in keeping with the perspective of the epilogist and ultimately proves (contra Seow and others) that the way of wisdom pursued by him and his contemporaries is *not* compatible with the call to obedience to the commandments of God.[178]

---

178. See Seow (*Ecclesiastes*, 396), who writes:

Without contradicting Qohelet, then, the redactor calls attention to an important dimension to be considered when all is said and done: that it is possible to hold the perspective of sages like Qohelet together with the central tenets of Israelite faith. Radical Wisdom in the end need not be seen as contradictory to the call to obedience. And, indeed, it is the possibility of such a hermeneutical move that assured the acceptance of Ecclesiastes into the canon (see *b. Šabb.* 30b).

See also Fox, *A Time to Tear Down*, 373.

The Position of the Epilogue

To claim that the epilogist has used Qoheleth's words to criticize the wisdom movement is to raise one more issue. The epilogist has chosen to express his own position only at the very end of the work rather than to provide an introductory note preparing the reader for both the words of Qoheleth that follow and the conclusions drawn from those words in the epilogue. One possible objection to the understanding of Ecclesiastes offered in this book is that there is danger that the typical reader will be so dismayed by Qoheleth's heterodox views that he or she may give up reading before the end of the work and so never discover the alternative perspective offered by the epilogist. Given this possibility, would it not have been more appropriate for the epilogist to have included or written a prologue of the sort that no epilogue was needed?

The question of an epilogue over a prologue or a combination of both is ultimately a rhetorical one. The choice made by the epilogist was based on the nature of the intended audience. If the intended audience of this work had been devout religious people with little interest in the wisdom movement—an audience sympathetic to the epilogist's position—a prologue setting out the intention of the work would indeed have allayed their concerns over the troubling nature of Qoheleth's words. If, however, the intended audience was favorably disposed toward the wisdom movement, such as prospective students attracted to the life of the sages and having at least some familiarity with their work, a prologue that revealed the work to be one that was critical of the sages might have deterred them from reading it in its entirety.[179] Beginning with the words of Qoheleth—a character presented as the foremost sage—served to entice such a reader further into the work. Moreover, coming from an insider to the wisdom movement, Qoheleth's words carried more weight for this audience than the words of an outsider.

We must also remember that Ecclesiastes does in fact begin with the words of the epilogist, who introduces the work with a summary of Qoheleth's teaching: all is הבל. At this stage of the work, however, the significance of this summary is somewhat enigmatic. In this way, the introduction raises the audience's curiosity and draws the readers into the words of Qoheleth. At the end of the work, the same summary statement recalls the failure of wisdom revealed by Qoheleth and leaves the audience prepared to hear the final words of the epilogist.

---

179. The appearance of the typical wisdom form בני 'my son' in Qoh 12:12 suggests that the epilogist does indeed have an audience of this sort in mind.

Conclusion

The epilogist thus employed Qoheleth's words to reveal the true state of the wisdom movement and to shock the audience, which most likely consisted of prospective students who were favorably disposed toward the sages, into a critical stance regarding them. The explicit warnings against the sages, their teachings, and their practices all serve to enhance this effect. Finally, the epilogist offered an alternative to the way of the sages by pointing the readers back to the commands of God and warning that all will have to account for their deeds. The sages offered no means to escape this judgment, but the epilogist showed that escape may be found in obedience, not the misguided wisdom of the sages. It is thus clear that, in the case of the epilogue to Ecclesiastes, Salyer is mistaken when he writes: "As important as the frame is for this book, it must not be allowed to replace the portrait which it holds. As Christianson's study shows so well, an artistic/literary frame is not meant to replace its contents. Having been an artist myself, I cannot imagine a frame being more important than any work of art whose beauty a frame is supposed to augment, not eclipse."[180] In Ecclesiastes, the epilogue proves to be an essential part of understanding the message of the book. It is not possible to interpret the work correctly by excluding either the words of Qoheleth or the words of the epilogist.

On this understanding, Qoheleth's words may be likened to a "leaked" document. It is not uncommon in the modern world for one party to obtain a secret document from its opposition and leak it to the media with the intent of undermining the opponent in the eyes of the public. The epilogist has done exactly this with the words of Qoheleth, and in case his shocking and unorthodox conclusions have been insufficient to condemn the wisdom movement in the mind of the readers, the epilogist has added brief notes at the end to highlight the dangers in thinking like Qoheleth and to propose an alternative. If Qoheleth's message is that there is no sense to be found in the world, the epilogist's message is that sense can only be found in fearing God and keeping his commandments.

---

180. Gary D. Salyer, *Vain Rhetoric: Private Insight and Public Debate in Ecclesiastes* (JSOTSup 327; Sheffield: Sheffield Academic Press, 2001) 372 n. 110. By contrast, David Dickinson warns on the BBC's Antiques Web site that "we often spend so much time clocking [*sic*] the canvas, we neglect to look closely at the frame. This can sometimes be the real work of art and worth more than the picture itself" (see http://www.bbc.co.uk/antiques/buyers_guides/pictures.shtml).

The Words of Qoheleth

The ultimate test for the interpretation of the epilogue expounded in the previous chapter is whether it accounts for the words of Qoheleth themselves. If Qoheleth's words offered traditional wisdom that accords with the rest of the Hebrew Bible, it would be difficult to see them as adequate grounds for criticism by the epilogist. A similar problem would arise if Qoheleth's words affirmed orthodox religious teaching. Indeed, the interpretation of the epilogist's words as a criticism of and warning against the wisdom movement is only viable if Qoheleth's words demonstrate that wisdom is futile and is not compatible with the ideas and beliefs reflected throughout the remainder of the Hebrew Bible. In this chapter, my examination of Qoheleth's words will focus primarily on understanding how they relate to the understanding of the epilogue revealed in the previous chapter.

There is widespread agreement that many of Qoheleth's statements challenge, undermine, or even fully contradict doctrines firmly established elsewhere in the Hebrew Bible. The presence of this contradictory material readily supports the case that the epilogist employs Qoheleth's words in order to undermine the wisdom movement, confronting the reader familiar with orthodox teaching with his incompatible teachings.

Beyond these obviously troubling statements, however, are other words in Ecclesiastes that do not obviously contradict orthodox teaching or that even appear to affirm it. For many scholars these passages redeem Qoheleth and demonstrate that his teachings are ultimately compatible with the remainder of the Hebrew Bible. Others insist that the presence of these passages indicates a progression in Qoheleth's thought from the unorthodox to the orthodox. Either way, the presence of this material requires particular attention if the thesis that the epilogist is using Qoheleth's words to undermine the credibility of the sages is to stand.

Qoheleth 1:1

The words of Qoheleth, son of David, king in Jerusalem.

The book of Ecclesiastes opens with an identification of the author of the words that form the bulk of the text, designating him קהלת. The fact that this term is used with the definite article in Qoh 7:27 and 12:8 indicates that it functions as a title rather than a name.[1] Traditionally, this appellation has been translated as the title of some religious functionary, such as, in English, 'the preacher' or, in German, 'der Prediger'. This understanding follows from both the canonical context of the word and the later development of the Greek term ἐκκλησία 'gathering, church' to designate a religious rather than a secular gathering.

However, the marked absence of references to the major religious tenets of ancient Israel in Qoheleth's words reveals the inappropriateness of this religious interpretation of the title. The root meaning of the term is 'gathering', and most commentators agree that Qoheleth was given this designation because of his work in gathering, whether it was gathering wealth, gathering people for instruction in wisdom, or gathering משלים ('proverbs') in his work as a sage. Linguistically, the second option is to be preferred, because the verb קהל is elsewhere always used in reference to gathering people,[2] and the nominal forms almost always refer to gatherings of people.[3]

Although the text does not use the name *Solomon* explicitly, there is no real doubt that the audience is meant to identify Qoheleth with Solomon. Qoheleth is said to have been king in Jerusalem (1:1), the son of David (1:1), wiser than any predecessor (1:16), possessor of vast wealth and resources (2:8), initiator of great building works (2:4–6), and someone who had many concubines (2:8).[4] Consequently the implied identification with Solomon is almost indisputable, and this identification further undermines any case for attributing a religious title to Qoheleth. Rather, Qoheleth is identified with Israel's preeminent sage, the authoritative wise man whose wisdom exceeded that of all others.

This implicit identification between Qoheleth and Solomon serves to lend authority to the words that follow the introduction. In view of the startling

---

1. The Qal feminine participle is used elsewhere to designate an occupation (see Ezra 2:55, 57; Neh 7:57, 59), although Seow also points out that a number of names for males are (apparently) grammatically feminine (C.-L. Seow, *Ecclesiastes* [AB 18C; New York: Doubleday, 1997] 96). Qoh 7:27 MT reads אמרה קהלת, but this should almost certainly be corrected to אמר הקהלת 'says Qoheleth'.

2. The root קהל appears in verbal forms 39 times (counting the *Qere* reading in 2 Sam 20:14) in the Hebrew Bible, always with reference to gathering people. There are numerous synonyms for the verb קהל in BH, including אסף, לקט, קבץ, קשש, בצר, קוה, and כנס; these terms are not confined to the gathering of people (see Gen 31:46, which uses לקט of stones; Gen 41:35, which uses קבץ of food; etc.).

3. There are 134 nonverbal occurrences of קהל in the Hebrew Bible, of which only the form קהלת is not clearly a reference in some way to a gathering or assembly of people.

4. Some have suggested that Qoheleth's words about not finding one woman in 1,000 in 7:28 may allude to Solomon's 1,000 wives and concubines mentioned in 1 Kgs 11:3, although the interpretation offered below makes this unlikely.

and unsettling observations made by Qoheleth, an appeal to authority appears necessary so that the words are not simply dismissed as the erroneous ramblings of an embittered old sage who has long since lost his way.[5]

Excursus:
The Meaning of הבל in Ecclesiastes

Qoheleth uses the term הבל numerous times, often to close a discussion of one topic or another with the conclusion that this too is הבל. It is thus readily apparent (and widely acknowledged) that this term is central to Qoheleth's message. Furthermore, all agree that, whatever the precise meaning of the term, it is thoroughly negative.

Attempts to define precisely what Qoheleth meant by the term הבל have been numerous and diverse, except for broad agreement that it is negative. Although the term literally means 'vapor, breath', it is used metaphorically in almost all of its 73 appearances in the Hebrew Bible.[6] Of these, 13 times it is used in reference to idols.[7] In Jer 16:19 and Zech 10:2, הבל appears parallel to the term שקר 'lie, falsehood'. In some instances, the term is clearly used to highlight transience (for example, see Job 7:16),[8] while in others the notion appears to be more the worthlessness or unreliability of whatever is being discussed.[9]

To understand what Qoheleth means by הבל, however, we must use Qoheleth's own words as our primary source of information. The term appears 38 times in Ecclesiastes, and 30 of these are in the words of Qoheleth (the

---

5. As B. Childs (*Introduction to the Old Testament as Scripture* [London: SCM, 1979] 584) writes:

> In its canonical form the identification [of Qoheleth with Solomon] assures the reader that the attack on wisdom which Ecclesiastes contains is not to be regarded as the personal idiosyncrasy of a nameless teacher. Rather, by his speaking in the guise of Solomon, whose own history now formed part of the community's common memory, his attack on wisdom was assigned an authoritative role as the final reflections of Solomon. As the source of Israel's wisdom, his words serve as an official corrective from within the wisdom tradition itself. Once this point was made, the literary fiction of Solomon was dropped.

Although I agree with Childs's assessment of the significance of the veiled identification between Qoheleth and Solomon, there is no indication that Qoheleth's intent was to criticize the wisdom movement. Rather, this was the use that the epilogist made of Qoheleth's words.

6. See BDB, 210b–211a. T. Longman (*The Book of Ecclesiastes* [NICOT; Grand Rapids; Eerdmans, 1998] 62 n. 24) notes that Isa 57:13 contains the only undisputed use of הבל in a nonmetaphorical sense in the Hebrew Bible.

7. See Deut 32:21; 2 Kgs 17:15; Ps 31:7; 57:13; Jer 2:5; 8:19; 10:8, 15; 14:22; 16:19; 51:18; Jonah 2:8; Zech 10:2.

8. See also Ps 39:5–12[4–11]; 62:10[9]; 78:33; Job 21:34; Prov 31:30 (cf. Prov 21:6).

9. See Deut 32:21; 1 Kgs 16:13, 26; 2 Kgs 17:15; Isa 30:7; Jer 2:5; 8:19; 10:15; Lam 4:17; etc. See Seow, *Ecclesiastes*, 100–101.

remaining 8 occur in the epilogist's frame narrative). Although a consensus on the meaning of this term continues to elude scholars, many of the various suggestions are semantically very close to each other. Furthermore, it is likely that no English term will exactly match the semantic range of the Hebrew term and that different English words will convey the meaning of הבל at different points in Qoheleth's arguments.

The term has traditionally been rendered 'vanity' in English, although this rendering is no longer in favor because 'vanity' has undergone a decisive semantic shift away from meaning "empty" to meaning "self-pride."[10] Other translation suggestions include 'fleeting' or 'transitory', 'futile', 'senseless', 'incomprehensible', 'mystery' or 'enigma', 'meaningless', and 'absurd'.[11] The latter suggestion, from Fox, encounters the distinct problem that 'absurd' in English is shifting to mean 'ludicrous, laughable', meanings that Fox eschews.[12]

In order to clarify the situation, we must turn to Qoheleth and hear what he has to say. Typically, Qoheleth culminates a number of observations with the conclusion that they are הבל. On a few occasions he expands on the הבל conclusion by offering either an additional or a parallel statement. In order to gain further insight into Qoheleth's understanding of הבל, we shall first examine these parallels and then look further at the observations that move Qoheleth to conclude that a matter is הבל.[13]

---

10. See BDB, 210b–211a; R. E. Murphy, *Ecclesiastes* (WBC 23A; Dallas: Word, 1992) lviii; and many of the English versions (e.g., the NRSV and the NASB, which also uses 'futile' in some instances).

11. For 'transitory', see D. C. Fredericks, *Coping with Transience: Ecclesiastes on Brevity in Life* (The Biblical Seminar 18; Sheffield: Sheffield Academic Press, 1993) chap. 1; cf. Barry G. Webb, *Five Festal Garments: Christian Reflections on the Song of Songs, Ruth, Lamentations, Ecclesiastes and Esther* (New Studies in Biblical Theology 10; ed. D. A. Carson; Leicester: Apollos, 2000) 100. For 'futile', see J. L. Crenshaw, *Ecclesiastes* (OTL; London: SCM, 1988) 28, 57; cf. R. B. Y. Scott, *Proverbs, Ecclesiastes* (AB 18; New York: Doubleday, 1965) 202. For 'senseless', see Victor Hamilton, "הבל," *TWOT* 204–5; and M. V. Fox, *A Time to Tear Down* (Grand Rapids: Eerdmans, 1999) 30–31 n. 5. For 'incomprehensible', see D. Hubbard, *Ecclesiastes, Song of Solomon* (Mastering the Old Testamen 15B; Dallas: Word, 1991) 21. For 'mystery' or 'enigma', see ibid., 44; Graham S. Ogden, "Vanity It Certainly Is Not," *Bible Translator* 38 (1987) 301–7; cf. Seow, *Ecclesiastes*, 47, 59. For 'meaningless', see Longman, *The Book of Ecclesiastes*, 64–65. For 'absurd', see M. V. Fox, *Qohelet and His Contradictions* (JSOTSup 71; Sheffield: Almond, 1989) 31–32.

12. Ibid., 31–32; compare idem, *A Time to Tear Down*, 31 n. 5, where Fox states, "Since 'absurd' in common usage has connotations of the ludicrous, in a translation for popular use another gloss, such as 'senseless,' might be more appropriate."

13. Further discussion on most of the passages that I am considering here follows in the detailed exegesis of the text below.

רעות רוח *'A Plan for [the] Wind'*

The expression רעות רוח appears parallel with הבל in Qoh 1:14; 2:11, 17, 26, 4:4; 6:9 and stands on its own in 4:6. In addition, the apparently similar expression רעיון רוח appears parallel with הבל in 1:17, 2:22, 4:16. Consequently, this is the most common parallel phrase employed by Qoheleth and thus perhaps the most significant for delineating Qoheleth's understanding of הבל.

Unfortunately, the meaning of the phrase רעות רוח is not straightforward. It appears nowhere in the Hebrew Bible outside Qoheleth. The problem lies in the meaning of the term רעות. The precise derivation of the term is disputed, with four semantically distinct homomorphic roots attested in BH as possibilities. Thus the root form רעה can mean 'to feed, shepherd, tend, herd', 'to associate with', 'to strive', or 'to desire'.[14] To complicate matters further, the noun form can also be derived from the root רעע, meaning either 'to do evil' (see, for example, Qoh 1:13) or 'to break'.

The nominal form רעות appears in 6 other places in BH (Exod 11:2; Isa 34:15, 16; Jer 9:19; Zech 11:9; Esth 1:19), in contexts where it is almost certainly derived from רעה II and means 'neighbor'. It is quickly apparent that this meaning does not fit Qoheleth's usage.

Hos 12:2[1] is often cited as a text that can illuminate our understanding of Qoheleth's use of this expression.[15] Hosea reads:

Ephraim herds the wind	אפרים רעה רוח
and pursues the west wind all day long	ורדף קדים כל־היום

Here the expression רעה רוח is parallel with ורדף קדים, suggesting that the appropriate meaning of רעה here is something like 'pursue, chase'.[16] This appears to tie the term רעה (and with it, Qoheleth's רעות) to the root רעה I, 'to feed, shepherd, tend, herd', in which case the expression רעות רוח may refer to attempting to control the wind as a shepherd controls a flock of animals.[17] This meaning is acceptable in the Hosea parallelism and is derived from רעה I.

---

14. BDB, 944–46.

15. See Longman, *The Book of Ecclesiastes*, 81; Fox, *Qohelet and His Contradictions*, 49; Seow, *Ecclesiastes*, 121–22.

16. Longman (*The Book of Ecclesiastes*, 81) warns that the terms cannot be treated as synonyms based on the characteristic of biblical parallelism that second and subsequent lines develop the first line in some way. In Hos 12:2, however, the development has already occurred in the addition of the phrase "all the day" in the second line. So perhaps it is safe to treat the terms as essentially synonymous after all.

17. One common understanding comes from רעה III 'to strive', in the sense of "to strive [to catch] the wind," or "like striving [to grasp] the wind" (see NET). The difficulty with this

The only other parallel appears in Ecclesiastes. The expression רעיון רוח shows up in 1:17; 2:22; 4:16, apparently as a direct synonym to the expression רעות רוח. The word רעיון is not attested elsewhere in BH but does appear in BA in Dan 2:29, 30; 4:16; 5:6, 10; and 7:28 with the meaning 'pleasure, will, ambition, desire'.[18] The LXX renders both expressions in Ecclesiastes alike, as προαίρεσις πνεύματος, which is usually explained as meaning 'choosing of wind' but which may better be understood as 'a plan for the wind'.[19] The expression thus seems to refer to the impossibility of determining the course of the wind (a suitably ambiguous explanation meaning either controlling the course of the wind or else determining the course the wind will take).

In order to determine the meaning of this expression more precisely, we must consider its contexts in Ecclesiastes as used by Qoheleth. It appears first in 1:14, where it functions as a summary of Qoheleth's findings regarding the value of what is done under the sun, which he discusses in greater detail in the subsequent section. That entire section depicts his search to determine what value there is in all his labor and his conclusion that there is none (Qoh 2:11). For Qoheleth, then, his labor is profitless; it is not 'mysterious' like the course of the wind but 'futile', as is attempting to control the course of the wind or attempting to pursue the wind.

Qoheleth's conclusion to this section, 2:24–26, is not as clear. In light of the futility of labor, Qoheleth commends making the most of it, enjoying it if possible. However, even enjoyment is beyond human capacity, for it only comes from the hand of God.[20] Although the expression is possibly used here to refer to the enigmatic nature of securing God's approval, previous usage suggests otherwise. Thus it is preferable again to interpret 2:26 as referring to the futility of attempting to extract enjoyment from work, because enjoyment ultimately comes only from God.

---

reading is arriving at a sensible meaning for the text (as indicated by the explanatory additions in the translations quoted). Ultimately, the Hosea parallel suggests that Qoheleth means something impossible to achieve related to the wind.

18. See Seow, *Ecclesiastes*, 121. Seow also notes the Phoenician cognate *rʿt* and suggests that the Hebrew here is probably an Aramaic loanword (although he does not explain why the existence of a Phoenician cognate indicates an *Aramaic* loan).

19. Seow (ibid.) offers the usual translation of προαίρεσις as 'choosing', but LSJ provides a broader semantic range for the term, including 'purpose, plan, or scope of action' and 'deliberate course of action, plan'. This suggests that the expression may have been understood as a reference either to the futile act of attempting to control the wind or else the impossible task of finding the plan of the wind.

20. Note that, although Qoheleth speaks of God's approval in 2:26, there is no indication that he knows of any means of securing such approval. See my "Ecclesiastes and the End of Wisdom," *TynBul* 50 (1999) 119–21.

'Futile' works as the meaning of רעות רוח in Qoh 4:4 as well. The verse again turns to discussion of human labor, identifying rivalry as the predominant motivating factor in human endeavors. For Qoheleth, motivation of this sort only increases the futility of the tasks that occupy people. The remaining instances of רעיון or רעות רוח (Qoh 4:16; 6:9) are a little unclear because in both instances the antecedent of זה ('this') is not immediately clear.

In summary, the expressions רעות רוח and רעיון רוח as used by Qoheleth are best understood as expressions of futility. They generally appear together with the הבל declaration and in discussions on the value to be found in human labor.

אין יתרון תחת השמש *'There Is No Gain under the Sun'*

The clause אין יתרון תחת השמש appears once, in Qoh 2:11, and is parallel with both Qoheleth's הבל conclusion and the expression רעות רוח. The term יתרון appears only in Qoh 1:3; 2:11, 13; 3:9; 5:8[9], 15[16]; 7:12; 10:10, and 11. The noun means 'surplus, advantage' and is included by Dahood with other economic terms used by Qoheleth,[21] but the term as used by Qoheleth cannot be restricted to this setting. Indeed, Qoheleth's use of this term in 2:11—declaring that there is no יתרון amidst all the material wealth he had accumulated—itself highlights the fact that the term cannot be confined to a purely economic context.

The conclusion that there is no advantage appears as an answer to the question that Qoheleth originally raised in Qoh 1:3 (compare Qoh 3:9; 5:15 [16]), which is, "What gain is there for a person in all his toil at which he toils under the sun?" Traditional wisdom maintained that the one who labors is clearly better off than the one who is indolent (note Proverb's use of עצל 'sluggard' in 6:6, 9; 13:4; 15:19; 19:24; 20:4; etc.) and that in nature there is an underlying order that can be perceived and from which one can benefit.[22] Furthermore, the belief that hard labor pays a dividend to the laborer functions as the background to Qoheleth's quest. For Qoheleth, the discovery that there is no perceivable dividend from labor signaled a disruption to the expected order in the universe. Traditional wisdom portrayed the universe as reflecting a sensible, moral, and discernible underlying order, but Qoheleth found that no such order existed.

---

21. See M. Dahood, "Canaanite-Phoenician Influence in Qoheleth," *Bib* 33 (1952) 221; R. Gordis, *Koheleth: The Man and His World* (New York: Schoken, 1951) 205; compare with Seow (*Ecclesiastes*, 103), who also cites an Aramaic papyrus from Egypt that uses the term in an economic context.

22. This fundamental precept of the wisdom movement in Israel is noted by numerous scholars. For example, see James L. Crenshaw, *Old Testament Wisdom: An Introduction* (rev. ed.; Louisville: Westminster John Knox, 1998), in particular, comments on pp. 10, 50.

Qoheleth's use of this expression thus extends the meaning of הבל beyond mere futility to the collapse of the moral world order that formed the basis for the inquiries of the sages. Toil may prove to have no advantage and be futile, but the world view that there must be some underlying order, some sense to the world that the sages could discern was obviated by Qoheleth's discovery that the world makes no sense.

רעה רבה *'A Great Evil'*

This clause appears parallel to הבל in Qoh 2:21 (see also רע in 2:17). Scholars have rendered the adjective רעה here by a range of English glosses from 'evil' to 'tragedy'.[23] Similar expressions appear elsewhere in Deut 31:17 and 21 (both in the plural) and with a predicative use in Gen 6:5; Joel 4:13[3:13]; and Ps 34:20[19]. Whether the term carries a moral sense, however, can only be determined from the context. Elsewhere Qoheleth uses רעע terminology 31 times,[24] and in a number of instances he uses it in contexts that clearly require the stronger sense of the word. For example, in 4:3 Qoheleth states that it is better never to have existed than to have witnessed the רע that is done under the sun. In Qoh 5:15[16] it is the undiscriminating nature of death that is described as רעה; death comes to all and unravels any work they have done, paying no attention to whether it was for good or evil. However, Qoheleth's use of this terminology does not always demand the more severe interpretation. For example, in Qoh 7:3 רע is used to describe the appearance of the face and is usually rendered 'sad, troubled' rather than 'evil'.

In the immediate context of Qoh 2:21, Qoheleth has been prompted to make this statement by the observation that he must leave the fruits of his toil to the ones who come after him, whether they are wise or foolish (so 2:18–21). For this reason he hates (שנא) life (2:17), and despairs (יאש) of all his labors (2:20). This use of negative and emotive terminology throughout the section together with the emphatic רבה to modify רעה suggest that it is appropriate to understand רעה here as also being strongly negative, or 'evil'.

Thus in Qoheleth's examination of wisdom and folly (2:12), which began with the observation that wisdom is better than folly, wisdom's benefit was undone by the inability of the wise person to guarantee that any gains from wisdom would not be squandered when they were inevitably handed on to a

---

23. For 'evil', see Longman, *The Book of Ecclesiastes*, 104–5; Fox, *Qohelet and His Contradictions*, 185; for 'tragedy', see Seow, *Ecclesiastes*, 118.

24. See Qoh 1:13; 2:17, 21; 4:3, 8, 17[5:1]; 5:12[13] (×2), 13[14] (×2), 15[16]; 6:1, 2; 7:3, 14, 15; 8:3, 5, 6, 9, 11 (×2), 12; 9:3, 12 (×2); 10:5, 13; 11:2, 10; 12:1. The epilogist also uses this language once in 12:14.

successor. The fact that Qoheleth describes these circumstances as רעה רבה clearly indicates his disapproval. The situation is wrong, it is unfair, and Qoheleth finds the situation offensive, and he uses strong language of disapproval to reinforce the הבל statement. Thus הבל here is best understood to reflect the senselessness of a world that permits such immoral outcomes.

עניןֵ רע הוא *'An Evil Task'*

The clause עניןֵ רע הוא appears juxtaposed to הבל in Qoh 4:8. The context is somewhat similar to that of the above passage. In this case, however, the problem is not the inability to determine who will benefit from one's arduous labor and accrued wealth but the fact that there is no one to benefit from it. In spite of this, there is no end to the toil and (apparently) no opportunity to enjoy the fruit of one's labor.

Although the circumstances described by Qoheleth could conceivably be described as 'futile', this understanding does not fit the parallel clause, עניןֵ רע הוא.[25] Rather, this expression again highlights the absence of any discernible moral order to the world. The ceaseless work that is for no apparent benefit may well be futile, but it is the unfairness of the circumstances that Qoheleth appears to highlight.

חלי רע הוא *'A Sickening Evil'*

The expression חלי רע הוא appears once, in Qoh 6:2 (although a similar expression, רעה חולה 'sickening evil' appears in 5:12[13], 15[16]). Once again a phrase that is parallel to הבל is associated with the question of who benefits from the wealth of a rich person. The identity of the beneficiary is again beyond the ability of the wealthy person to determine and is described by Qoheleth as a נכרי 'stranger'. The expression חלי רע appears elsewhere only in the plural in Deut 28:59, where it refers to a severe illness. In the Ecclesiastes context, the expression must be understood metaphorically, likening the situation described to a disease: once again the real world inverts Qoheleth's understanding of what is right. In this context, understanding הבל as 'futile' makes little sense; rather, the meaning is decidedly the senselessness of the sickening situation that Qoheleth describes.

Qoheleth's Use of הבל

This examination of expressions parallel to הבל in a number of passages has revealed that Qoheleth uses the term to describe circumstances that invert

---

25. The noun עניןֵ only appears in Ecclesiastes in BH, although it is attested in post-biblical Hebrew. Seow notes that, for Qoheleth, "*'inyān* is associated with restlessness, obsession, worry, and human inability to find enjoyment" (*Ecclesiastes*, 121).

his sense of what is right and undermine the traditional expectation in wisdom circles that there is a discernible order to the universe. A number of the parallels to הבל and contexts in which it falls also incorporate the notion of futility. However, this nuance may reasonably be subordinated to the meaning "senseless." The failure of the world to adhere to a sensible order and thus our inability to predict outcomes render our actions futile. Because so far my observations have been based on expressions used by Qoheleth that are parallel to הבל, I must now demonstrate that the understanding of הבל as "senseless" fits with Qoheleth's use of the term in other situations.

We begin with Qoh 3:16–21, where Qoheleth again records his observations about the inversion of justice in human affairs. While he affirms the traditional belief in divine justice (3:17), he also observes that it is undermined by the fact that all share the same fate—indeed the very same fate that befalls the animals. For Qoheleth, it is this common fate that ultimately foils everything and is unjust. The use of הבל to describe this situation accords with our understanding of the term above as describing the failure of traditional wisdom's expectations regarding the underlying order and justice of the universe.

Qoh 5:9[10] is usually interpreted as a "typical moralizing proverb";[26] it is an observation that the love of money and property is insatiable, and thus, pursuing them is futile. This interpretation, however, does not do justice to Qoheleth's words.[27] Qoheleth makes a number of observations relating to riches and wealth throughout this section (Qoh 5:7[8]–6:12), all of which suggest that he is objecting to the inability of the one who loves money to be satisfied with his or her wealth. Thus, he is not merely describing the futility of the situation but, more specifically, its senselessness.

Verses 10–11[11–12] recount two reasons that the rich cannot enjoy their riches. First, increasing wealth (lit., 'good things') is of questionable benefit to the owner. Second, while the laborer sleeps soundly, the rich cannot similarly enjoy their sleep.

In v. 12[13] Qoheleth highlights what he considers to be a 'sickening evil' (רעה חולה). This is the situation in which riches are protected (שמר, usually rendered 'hoarded') by their owner, only to cause him harm (רעה). Although it may appear that Qoheleth is sickened by the hoarding of wealth, this fails to explain why he would then have a problem if the owner was hurt in some way—surely that would be the just outcome! I think, instead, that Qoheleth is troubled by the fact that the one who carefully accumulates wealth is harmed by it rather than being able to enjoy it. This is made clear from the subsequent

---

26. Gordis, *Koheleth: The Man and His World*, 251.

27. For further discussion, see below, pp. 167–69.

verses, which lament the loss of wealth through 'bad investment' (עִנְיַן רָע). A pejorative translation of שָׁמַר as 'hoarded' in many versions is unjustified in the context and ultimately misleading. The word is better understood as referring to the care with which the rich person has accumulated wealth. This parallels the "love" of money described in Qoh 5:9[10].

Qoheleth proceeds to state what is good in his opinion (Qoh 5:17–19[18–20]): to be able to enjoy what one has. In v. 18[19] this is applied specifically to the wealthy person. In Qoheleth's opinion, it is good for a rich person to enjoy the wealth that God has given, but this happens only as a gift from God. The contrasting situation—in which God has not enabled the rich person to enjoy his or her wealth—is described in the subsequent verses (Qoh 6:1–2) as 'evil' (רָעָה). For Qoheleth, this 'evil' also is ultimately traceable to God.

Thus the context supports the argument that what is הבל in Qoh 5:9[10] is not the insatiability of the person who loves wealth but the injustice of the situation in which one who loves money is not satisfied by it. Again Qoheleth is using הבל in the context of overturned moral order: what should be (at least in Qoheleth's view) is displaced by what is but should not be.

The inversion of justice is also the theme of Qoh 8:14 (compare Qoh 7:15). Once again, the situation anticipated by traditional wisdom teaching, that wise and righteous acts are rewarded but foolish and evil acts are punished, is not reflected in the real world.

Finally, הבל in Qoh 11:10 is used to describe the nature of youth and forms the basis for Qoheleth's encouragement to enjoy one's youth. This verse is problematic for those who insist on a single English equivalent for הבל throughout Qoheleth, for any meaning here other than 'fleeting, temporary', or something similar is difficult to justify.[28]

Conclusion: The Meaning of הבל in Ecclesiastes

Clearly, Qoheleth has chosen the term הבל to summarize his observations because it has sufficient semantic diversity to function validly in disparate

---

28. Longman, who has argued consistently that הבל ought to be rendered 'meaningless', here admits, "This may, however, be the one verse where the temporal aspect of the root is emphasized. In other words, the verse may be saying: 'for youth and vitality are transient'" (see Longman, *The Book of Ecclesiastes*, 261–62). Fox, who consistently argues for 'absurd' (by which he means 'senseless'; see above) renders this clause 'for youth and life's prime are fleeting', explaining that this "is the only quality of youth that makes pleasure-seeking urgent" (see Fox, *Qohelet and His Contradictions*, 278–79).

Fredericks, on the other hand, argues that transience is the primary notion behind Qoheleth's use of הבל (D. C. Fredericks, *Coping with Transience* [Sheffield: Sheffield Academic Press, 1983] chap. 1). However, this interpretation is overly strained and ultimately unconvincing at many points in Qoheleth's writing.

contexts. If one nuance can be said to be more prominent than another, it is that the underlying order of the universe is ultimately inaccessible. Furthermore, the sages' traditional claim that the world is just and that it rewards those who deserve to be rewarded is not borne out in Qoheleth's experience. When used this way, הבל as 'meaningless' is close to what Qoheleth is saying: whatever meaning one would expect to find in the world is not to be found. There is no discernible reason that some are permitted to enjoy their lives and others are not.

However, in some respects 'meaningless' is not quite adequate. Qoheleth is not content with this situation—quite the reverse. Qoheleth's observations are not detached and clinical: rather, they anger him (as attested by the frequent use of strongly emotive parallel language such as 'sickening', 'evil', etc.). 'Senseless' may come closer to expressing Qoheleth's intent in many instances.

Finally, we note that Qoheleth plays on the ambiguity of the term הבל. He finds it serves well in instances where the notion of transience is to the fore (Qoh 11:10) or where futility appears to be the significant point he wishes to make (Qoh 1:14; 4:4). Even in these texts, the underlying failure of the world view of the wisdom movement to offer realistic answers to the problems of life reflects the senselessness of Qoheleth's world.

The one irrefutable aspect of Qoheleth's use of the term הבל is its clearly negative connotation. This fact undermines any attempt to find a message in Qoheleth's words that is consistent with the remainder of the Hebrew Bible. The Hebrew Bible describes idols as הבל but certainly not "everything." For example, Qoheleth observes that human toil produces no discernible advantage and is thus senseless, whereas Proverbs insists that there is value in human endeavor (see, for example, Prov 14:23).[29] Qoheleth observes that all too often justice is inverted, the wicked receive the rewards of the righteous and vice versa, evil triumphs over good, and the wicked live long, full lives but the righteous do not. The expectation that a sage could comprehend and apply the same wisdom that God used in creating and running the universe— an expectation that was foundational to the whole wisdom enterprise—is dashed by the reality that Qoheleth faces. Qoheleth uncovers the disturbing truth: the sage cannot understand the world, and the supposed advantages of wisdom are compromised.

---

29. Prov 14:23 uses the noun עצב 'pain' in reference to arduous labor (cf. Isa 14:3). See also Prov 6:6–11; 10:4; 12:14; 15:19; 19:15; 21:25; 24:30–34; 28:19. Qoheleth's attitude toward labor and toil is more closely reflected by Ps 127:2 (which, like Prov 14:23, uses עצב in reference to painful labor).

Qoheleth 1:2

"Utterly senseless," says Qoheleth. "Utterly senseless, everything is sense-less."

Qoheleth's words are bracketed by the epilogist's summary statements in Qoh 1:2 and 12:8 that all is הבל. This fact alone undermines the claim that there is any real progression evident in Qoheleth's thought, for from the epilogist's perspective, the הבל claim is presented as a consistent and accurate summary of all of Qoheleth's words. Whatever is to follow is now inevitably to be fil-tered through this all-encompassing statement about Qoheleth's thought. We readers should not expect that Qoheleth will fulfill wisdom's promise of pro-viding answers, for we stand warned in these opening words. The greatest sage declares it: even the wisest can make no sense of this world.

Qoheleth 1:3

What gain is there for a person in all his toil at which he toils under the sun?

It is not readily apparent whether Qoh 1:3–11 presents the words of Qoheleth or the words of the epilogist in continuing his introduction to the work. The sudden change to first-person speech in v. 12 is striking and suggests that the preceding verses could reasonably be understood as introductory. If they are more words from the epilogist, they nonetheless summarize Qoheleth's mes-sage further instead of presenting the epilogist's personal views. The distinc-tion between Qoheleth and the epilogist's summarizing of Qoheleth is so subtle that it has little impact on our understanding of the passage. This is particularly true in light of our conclusion that the epilogist was the ultimate author of the entire work and that even Qoheleth's first-person speech was selected by the epilogist to serve his purpose.

This section begins with a rhetorical question: מה יתרון לאדם בכל עמלו שיעמל תחת השמש. Key to understanding this question is determining the meaning of the word יתרון, a term unique to Qoheleth.[30] The verb יתר is rela-tively common in BH (appearing 106 times) and means 'to surpass, exceed, be additional'. In the discussion of the meaning of הבל above, I noted that the meaning of יתרון is 'surplus, advantage'.[31] It refers to a positive gain or bene-

---

30. Qoheleth uses the term in 1:3; 2:11, 13 (twice); 3:9; 5:8[9], 15[16]; 7:12; 10:10, 11. The question posed in 1:3 is itself closely paralleled by questions in 3:9 and 5:15[16]. Qo-heleth also uses related forms: יותר 'more' (2:15; 6:8, 11; 7:11, 16; 12:9, 12), a term that appears elsewhere only in 1 Sam 15:15 and Esth 6:6; and מותר 'profit, advantage' (Qoh 3:19), which appears elsewhere only in Prov 14:23 and 21:5. Consequently, it is fair to say that this vocabulary is characteristic of Qoheleth.

31. See above, p. 116.

fit; here Qoheleth is asking what may be gained from all the עמל at which human beings toil under the sun.[32]

The word עמל is also used often by Qoheleth, the nominal form appearing 26 times and the verbal form 9 times. Scholars are not certain whether Qoheleth invests this term with a specific nuance to differentiate it from the noun מעשה, which itself appears 21 times (the two appear together in 2:11 and 4:4). Most agree, based on the usage of the term outside Ecclesiastes, that עמל draws attention to the arduous, laborious nature of the labor in view.[33] We can see that Qoheleth is casting his first question in a negative light, for people do not merely work but *toil*. This emphasis on the negative heightens the sense that this labor ought not to be in vain—surely such arduous toil must have a purpose?

Qoheleth concludes this question with the expression תחת השמש 'under the sun', which appears nowhere else in the Hebrew Bible but appears frequently in Qoheleth's words.[34] It is also attested in a number of ancient Near Eastern texts dating back to the 12th century B.C.E.[35] The use in these texts, as well as Qoheleth's own usage, suggests that the expression draws a distinction not so much between this world and another location (such as this world as opposed to the heavens or Sheol) as between the world of the living and the realm of the dead. Seow explains thus:

> In the ancient Near East, the light of the sun is equated with life and its blessings, while the deprivation of its rays means death. To be under the sun ... is the same thing as "to see the sun," a metaphor for living. . . . Thus, "under the sun" is simply the realm of the living—"this world" as opposed to the netherworld (which is without the sun). . . . Whereas "under the heavens" refers to the universality of human experiences everywhere in the world (i.e., it is a spatial designation), "under the sun" refers to the temporal universe of the living.[36]

Fox argues that the phrase is not restrictive but expansive—not highlighting the limitation of Qoheleth's investigation to the physical world as

---

32. The MT reads אדם 'man, human being' as definite, which is in keeping with Qoheleth's general usage of אדם (which appears without inseparable prepositions with the article 31 times but without only 6 times). It is apparent that little exegetical significance can be read into most of these uses of the article.

33. See Gordis, *Koheleth: The Man and His World*, 205; Fox, *Qohelet and His Contradictions*, 54–57; Seow, *Ecclesiastes*, 104.

34. Qoheleth uses this phrase 29 times: 1:3, 9, 14; 2:11, 17, 18, 19, 20, 22; 3:16; 4:1, 3, 7, 15; 5:12, 17; 6:1, 12; 8:9, 15 (2×), 17; 9:3, 6, 9 (2×), 11, 13; 10:5.

35. See Seow, *Ecclesiastes*, 105–6 for a list of ANE references.

36. Ibid., 105.

opposed to heaven or the netherworld but emphasizing the breadth of Qoheleth's inquiry, which covers the entire realm of human experience.[37] Fox
argues that understanding the expression as restrictive undermines Qoheleth's
argument by admitting the possibility of advantage beyond the present life.
However, while Qoheleth remains both agnostic and skeptical about the afterlife, he does make vague reference to it (see Qoh 3:18–21), so we cannot entirely exclude the possibility that Qoheleth is using the phrase תחת השמש to
restrict the scope of his investigation.

The use of this phrase has prompted a number of commentators to claim
that Qoheleth seeks to draw a contrast between life lived "under the sun"
without reference to God and the life of faith. Thus Eaton claims:

> For much of the time the argument leaves God out of account. Then dramat-
> ically the Preacher introduces God and all changes. The 'under the sun' ter-
> minology falls into the background or lapses altogether (2:24–26; 11:1–
> 12:14); instead he refers to the 'hand of God' (2:24), the joy of man (2:25;
> 3:12; 5:18, 20; 9:7; 11:7–9), and the generosity of God (2:26; 3:13; 5:19).
> Ecclesiastes is thus an exploration of the barrenness of life without a practi-
> cal faith in God. Intermingled with its pessimism are invitations to a differ-
> ent outlook altogether, in which joy and purpose are found when God is
> seen to be 'there' and to be characterized supremely by generosity.[38]

There are insurmountable problems with this claim, however, that will be
highlighted at the appropriate points below in this examination of Qoheleth's
words. In this regard, Longman's observation is particularly salient: "Qohelet's frequent use of the phrase *under the sun* highlights the restricted scope of
his inquiry. His worldview does not allow him to take a transcendent yet immanent God into consideration in his quest for meaning. In the Bible this
viewpoint is unique to Qohelet."[39] For Qoheleth there is only one mode of existence—existence "under the sun." If there is another, Qoheleth only vaguely
admits it as a possibility and then claims no knowledge of it. In fact, the overwhelmingly negative assessment of death as the ultimate injustice in life suggests that Qoheleth's apparent uncertainty about the afterlife in Qoh 3:21 is a

---

37. Fox, *Qohelet and His Contradictions*, 170.

38. M. A. Eaton, *Ecclesiastes* (TOTC; Leicester: Inter-Varsity Press, 1983) 45; see also
p. 58; see also Joseph Azize, "Considering the Book of Qohelet Afresh," *ANES* 37 (2000)
183–214; and H. C. Leupold (*Exposition of Ecclesiastes* [Columbus: Wartburg, 1952] 42–
43), who paraphrases Qoheleth's words here in this way: "Let us for the sake of argument
momentarily rule out the higher things."

39. Longman, *The Book of Ecclesiastes*, 66; cf. Shields, "Ecclesiastes and the End of
Wisdom," 118–21.

momentary lapse in his general line of argument, which is firmly bound to this life as the only realm in which rewards and profit may be found.

Ogden notes that Qoheleth's inquiry into the advantage of work is the "programmatic question for the entire book."[40] The recurrence of this question in Qoheleth's work (with minor variations) suggests that this is a reasonable conclusion.[41] However, it is essential to distinguish between the words of Qoheleth and the book as a whole, shaped and authored by the epilogist. With this in mind, we can designate advantage in labor as the programmatic question for Qoheleth but not necessarily for the epilogist who is ultimately the true author of the work. Answering the question of the advantage of labor may help us understand the meaning of Qoheleth's own words but cannot define the function of the work in its entirety.

Furthermore, this question was actually the same for all of Israel's wisdom authors—they sought to understand what actions ultimately benefit the wise person, as Crenshaw has noted: "Wisdom is a particular attitude towards reality, a worldview. . . . It asks what is good for men and women, and it believes that all essential answers can be learned in experience. . . . The one God embedded truth within all of reality."[42] Qoheleth stands firmly within the wisdom tradition in posing this question. The task of the sage was to divine, through intelligence, observation, and experience, just how one could benefit from the arduous task of living and laboring under the sun.

If this question places Qoheleth within the context of the wisdom tradition, his answer sets him at odds with it. In traditional wisdom, hard work is rewarded and laziness leads to one's downfall.[43] By Qoh 2:11, however, Qoheleth reaches the conclusion that there is no benefit to be found in all one's labor and that it is all senseless (הבל). More immediately, Qoheleth hints at this finding by observing the endless and unchanging nature of the world, upon which the toil of human beings has no perceptible bearing.

Qoheleth 1:4–11

[4] A generation passes away and a generation comes,
　　but the earth is forever the same.
[5] The sun rises and the sun sets,
　　tirelessly returning to its place and rising from there.

---

40. G. S. Ogden, *Qoheleth* (Readings; Sheffield: JSOT Press, 1987) 28, 22–26.

41. Refer to n. 30.

42. J. L. Crenshaw, *Old Testament Wisdom* (Louisville: Westminster John Knox, 1998) 10.

43. See Prov 6:6, 9; 13:4; 15:19; 19:24; 20:4; etc.

⁶ Blowing to the south and around to the north,
        round and round goes the wind, along its paths the wind returns.
⁷ All the rivers flow into the sea,
        but the sea is never full.
To the place where the rivers are flowing,
        there they shall flow again.
⁸ All [these] things are weary.

A man will never finish speaking,
        [his] eye will never be satisfied with seeing,
        and [his] ear will never be filled with hearing.
⁹ Whatever has happened will happen [again],
        and whatever has been done will be done [again].
        There is nothing entirely new under the sun.
¹⁰ There might be something of which one could say, "Look at this, it is new,"
        but it has already been in the ages which were before us.
¹¹ There is no remembrance of the former things,
        and even for those things yet to come
        there will be no remembrance of them by people who come after them.

In 1:4–11 Qoheleth reflects on the immutable character of the natural world. Although the relationship between this section and the preceding verse is not immediately apparent, both are commonly understood to demonstrate that individuals have no lasting impact on their world, so the notion that there may be some profit in their toil is undermined. As Fox explains: "All this is meant to show that, by analogy and *a fortiori*, man's toil cannot be expected to affect the course of events."[44]

In this sense, vv. 4–11 provide an answer to the question raised in v. 3. The poem, however, is not phrased simply as an answer to the query—that will have to wait until Qoheleth recounts his quest and its results in Qoh 1:12–2:26. If Qoh 1:3 does function as a "programmatic question" to introduce the words of Qoheleth as a whole, then it is not surprising that a complete answer is not immediately forthcoming. These words thus function as the *introduction* to Qoheleth's attempt to answer the question raised in v. 3. They do not, however, provide a complete or specific answer.

There is some debate over the precise meaning of some of the cola within the poem. Recent discussion has focused on the terms דוֹר 'generation' and אֶרֶץ 'earth' as used in v. 4. Although דוֹר is generally understood to refer to a

---

44. Fox, *A Time to Tear Down*, 165; cf. Longman (*The Book of Ecclesiastes*, 66), who writes, "Qohelet now hints at the reason why human beings see no profit to their exertions. Nothing ever changes except perhaps the time. In the midst of apparent activity, the earth remains the same."

single generation of humanity, Ogden has argued that it should instead be understood as referring to the cycles of nature.[45] The term אָרֶץ has traditionally been understood as a reference to the earth, but Fox has argued that it should instead be understood as a reference to humanity as a whole (as opposed to a specific generation of humanity), a usage with precedents in Gen 11:1; 1 Kgs 2:2; and Ps 33:8.[46]

As indicated in the translation above, הלך 'walk, go, pass' can be understood as representing death figuratively, which is appropriate in this context of the coming and going of generations and in Qoheleth's broader context of death.[47]

It is difficult to relate v. 8 to its context or to understand its meaning. The usual translation of the adjective יגעים as 'wearisome' actually inverts the meaning it has elsewhere ('weary'; see Deut 25:18; 2 Sam 17:2). The weariness here probably refers to the endless repetition of the world previously described, not the effect that this has on observers. What follows is also difficult and usually requires considerable expansion by commentators before the meaning can be elucidated. In my translation I have opted to emend the MT's יוכל 'can, is able' to יכל[ה] from כלה 'to be complete, at an end, finished'. The alteration is minor, and this clause then parallels the two subsequent clauses about the insatiability of the eye and ear. The MT is also unclear about precisely what it is that a man (אִישׁ) is unable to tell.

However, the overall meaning of the passage is largely undisputed.[48] In spite of the ebb and flow of all aspects of life, the net result is that nothing changes. There is ultimately no contribution that can be made to the world, nothing new that anyone (including, of course, the sages themselves) can offer. Qoheleth here implies that, at the very least, humanity as a whole cannot profit from the toil of the individual. Whether the individual can profit is a question that Qoheleth will investigate in the next section.

---

45. Graham S. Ogden, "The Interpretation of *dôr* in Ecclesiastes 1.4," *JSOT* 34 (1986) 91–92.

46. Fox, *A Time to Tear Down*, 166.

47. See Qoh 3:20; 6:6; 9:10; 12:5; BDB, 234a; Seow, *Ecclesiastes*, 106.

48. There are a number of scholars who attempt to interpret this poem as positive rather than negative, including N. Lohfink ("Die Wiederkehr des immer Gleichen: Eine frühe Synthese zwischen griechischem und jüdischem Weltgefühl in Kohelet 1,4–11," *AF* 53 [1985] 125–49), who praises the eternal stability of the cosmos. Ogden (*Qoheleth*, 30–34) is also more favorable in his interpretation than most. However, the negative context together with the comment about forgetting past generations undermine this interpretation. Ogden argues that the poem serves as Qoheleth's justification for the quest that he subsequently records because "we cannot depend on answers from the past; each generation must itself face the question of life and meaning" (p. 34). According to this reasoning, perhaps we should ignore Qoheleth's conclusions, because they themselves belong in the past.

Qoheleth's conclusion here is clearly at odds with the remainder of the Hebrew Bible. As Seow points out, Ps 102:26–28[25–27] states that even the heavens and the earth will not endure forever.[49] Qoheleth perceives a complete lack of purpose in history, but this runs contrary to the previous expectation—that God would work within history to achieve his ends. This belief was particularly prominent retrospectively, in the record, when God established covenants with the people of Israel and the house of David, and prospectively, in the writings of the prophets.

Furthermore, the assertions that there is nothing new and that nothing is remembered by future generations (Qoh 1:9–11) clash with the biblical record of the exodus, which depicts unique events in history and explicitly requires all subsequent generations to remember them. The outlook of the sages revealed here by Qoheleth is clearly incompatible with faith in the God who intervenes in human history as depicted in the remainder of the Hebrew Bible.

Qoheleth 1:12–2:26

The remainder of chap. 1 and all of chap. 2 record Qoheleth's search to identify and understand what there is of value under the sun. The opening reflections in Qoh 1:12–18 summarize Qoheleth's findings, which are more fully explored in the second chapter. The overall structure of this section can be summarized as follows:

A	1:12–15	What is done under heaven
B	1:16–18	Wisdom, knowledge, madness, and folly
A´	2:1–11	What is done under the sun
B´	2:12–23	Wisdom, madness, and folly—and death
C	2:24–26	Conclusion

Of particular significance in this section are the concluding words, in which Qoheleth discusses the role of God in human toil in connection with terms such as "joy." This has prompted many readers to conclude that Qoheleth has reached a conclusion compatible with the view presented elsewhere in the Hebrew Bible. However, a closer examination of this text will demonstrate that this perception is incorrect.

---

49. Seow, *Ecclesiastes*, 106. The impermanence of the heavens and the earth is also implied in passages such as Isa 66:22.

Qoheleth 1:12–18

[12] I am Qoheleth. I was king over Israel in Jerusalem.

[13] I set my mind to investigate and explore with wisdom all which is done under the heavens. (It is an evil task that God has given to human beings to be occupied with!) [14] I saw all the work that was done under the sun and realized that everything is senseless and [like] controlling the wind. [15] Whatever is crooked is not able to be straightened, and whatever is missing is not able to be counted.

[16] I said to myself, "I am now greater and wiser than all who were over Jerusalem before me," and my mind has seen vast wisdom and knowledge. [17] I set my mind to know wisdom and knowledge, madness and folly. I realized that this too was chasing the wind. [18] For with much wisdom is much frustration, and increasing knowledge increases pain.

The opening section presents a brief overview of Qoheleth's conclusions. Qoheleth states the two avenues of his inquiry: investigating all that is done under heaven (1:13);[50] and investigating wisdom, madness, and folly (1:17). Without offering details (which Qoheleth saves for the more extensive discussion in chap. 2), he summarizes his conclusions on these matters: they are all futile (הבל).[51] In each instance he offers a proverb about the two matters under investigation.

Of particular interest is what these verses reveal about Qoheleth's understanding of God. Although the work with which human beings are occupied is futile (1:14), it is God who has assigned us this work. It is upon this realization that Qoheleth finds justification for describing the tasks that occupy human beings as רע.[52] Although the term רע spans a wide semantic range, from

---

50. M. M. Kline ("Is Qoheleth Unorthodox?: A Review Article," *Kerux* 13 [1998] 22–31) argues for an eschatological understanding of the expression "under the heavens" based on the use of the phrase in eschatological contexts elsewhere in the Hebrew Bible. His argument is unconvincing because he cannot identify any instance where the phrase includes eschatological overtones not explicitly introduced in its immediate context, yet he requires it in Qoheleth. The examples he provides all use this phrase as a reference to the location and breadth of the judgment of which the passages speak (e.g., Gen 6:17).

51. For a discussion of the meaning of the phrases here used by Qoheleth, refer to the excursus, beginning on p. 112.

52. Contra Seow (*Ecclesiastes*, 121), who claims that "the 'it' refers to the task Qohelet set for himself (the search by wisdom), not to 'all that has been done under the heavens.'" The text, however, more clearly favors the common interpretation: Qoheleth's research is always an individual task (so it is always described in 1st-person-singular terms), whereas the subject of his observations is always universal ("everything that is done under the heavens" and "all the deeds that have been done under the sun"). Thus, when Qoheleth mentions the task set by God for all human beings, the universal scope of the statement ties it directly to the work done under heaven, not the task that Qoheleth has set himself in understanding

'severe' to 'evil', Qoheleth's conclusion warrants an understanding more toward the negative end of this range.[53] Thus Qoheleth portrays God as the ultimate source of the work that occupies human beings, and because this work is pointless and has no redeeming value, it can justifiably be described as evil. This ascription of evil to God does not sit comfortably with the world view of much of the remainder of the Hebrew Bible.[54]

Verse 15 expresses Qoheleth's frustration at the immutability of a fundamentally flawed world. In 7:13, it becomes clear that Qoheleth attributes these flaws to God, who has made things crooked. In the present context of his search to discover an advantage in his toil, however, it anticipates the impending failure of his task, as Bernon Lee has observed: "The proverb describes the results of his quest; the world is crooked and bereft of any permanent advantage for the wise."[55]

Qoheleth concludes his second area of investigation, the investigation of "wisdom, knowledge, madness, and folly" (1:17), with a statement of the disadvantages of wisdom: "in much wisdom is much frustration, and the one who adds knowledge adds pain." This negative assessment again stands at odds with the consistently positive evaluation of wisdom in Proverbs and later (noncanonical) wisdom texts. Furthermore, given Qoheleth's repeated conclusion that there is nothing better than to enjoy one's work, the assertion that wisdom is inevitably coupled with pain constitutes a disincentive to fol-

---

that work. Furthermore, one cannot argue that the singular הוא ענין רע 'it is an evil task' points to Qoheleth's task, because the expression כל־אשר נעשה 'all that was done' is also singular. This interpretation I present above is lent support by Qoheleth's words elsewhere, such as Qoh 3:9–11.

53. See Longman, *The Book of Ecclesiastes*, 80; Murphy, *Ecclesiastes*, 11. Contrast this reading (רע) with the more insipid rendering found in most English versions: 'unhappy' (NRSV), 'grievous' (NASB), etc.

54. There are, however, a few other passages that indicate some relationship between God and evil, in particular 1 Sam 16:14, 23; 18:10; 19:9; but see also Deut 6:22; Josh 23:15; and Ezek 14:21. In these passages, however, God's use of evil is prompted by specific circumstances. Qoheleth, on the other hand, addresses life in general. Regarding Qoheleth's conception of God, Egon Pfeiffer has accurately summarized Qoheleth's theology, concluding that Qoheleth believes in the existence of God, that God is involved in some way in the world, yet he is distant and unknowable, and that God's acts are unpredictable and inscrutable (Pfeiffer, "Die Gottesfurcht im Buche Kohelet," in *Gottes Wort und Gottes Land: Hans-Willhelm Hertzberg zum 70. Geburtstag* (ed. H. G. Reventlow; Göttingen: Vandenhoeck & Ruprecht, 1965) 133–36; cf. T. Frydrych, *Living under the Sun* (VTSup 90; Leiden: Brill, 2002) 219; W. J. Dumbrell, *The Faith of Israel* (Leicester: Apollos, 1988) 242–43. See above, p. 95, for more discussion.

55. Bernon Lee, "A Specific Application of the Proverb in Ecclesiastes 1:15," *JHS* 1 (1997) article 6.

lowing the way of wisdom. Qoheleth, it seems, has acquired sufficient wisdom to qualify him to conclude that in many respects he would have been better off without it. This clearly correlates well with the epilogist's warning against the wisdom movement.

Qoheleth 2:1–11

[1] I said to myself, "Come now, let me make you experience pleasure—enjoy yourself!" But I realized that this, too, was senseless. [2] Regarding amusement, I said, "[It is] irrational," and regarding joy, "What does this achieve?"

[3] I searched around with my mind, to entice my body with wine while my mind led with wisdom, and to grasp folly, until I could see what there is that is good for human beings to do under the sun the few days of their lives.

[4] My works were magnificent. I built houses for myself, I planted vineyards for myself. [5] I made gardens and parks for myself, and I planted all kinds of fruit trees in them. [6] I made pools of water for myself from which to irrigate a grove of saplings. [7] I acquired male and female servants, and I had home-born servants, and [I acquired] more livestock for myself—both herds and flocks—than all who were before me in Jerusalem. [8] I also accumulated for myself silver and gold, the treasure of kings and of the provinces. I trained for myself male and female singers, and the delights of men—many treasures. [9] I became increasingly greater than anyone who had been before me in Jerusalem. My wisdom also stood by me. [10] Anything my eyes wanted I did not keep from them. I did not hold myself back from any pleasure, for my mind enjoyed all my labor, and this was my reward from all my labor.

[11] I considered all the work that my hands had done and the toil at which I had labored and realized that everything is senseless and [like trying to] direct the wind. There is no gain under the sun.

The first section of chap. 2 fleshes out Qoheleth's observations and conclusions on the matters introduced in 1:12–15. Qoheleth recounts details of a vast first-person experiment, in which he indulges in anything and everything that takes his fancy, in an attempt to find the value in what is done under the sun. Specifically, he aims to experience pleasure in order to discern whether it provides an answer in his search for the value of his toil.[56] Furthermore, his efforts are successful, according to v. 10, for he does indeed find enjoyment in his toil. Nonetheless, upon further reflection, Qoheleth concludes that this

---

56. Seow notes that the preposition ב 'in, of' in the expression אנסכה בשמחה 'I will make a test of / experience pleasure' (Qoh 2:1) indicates the object of what is experienced (נסה); see Seow, *Ecclesiastes*, 126.

amounts to הבל, and—in answer to the initial question posed in 1:3—that there is no profit to be gained under the sun.

While most of the details of the experiment are quite straightforward, there are some difficulties, particularly in the final portion of v. 8. The expression שדה ושדות is usually understood as a reference to concubines,[57] although this reading is by no means certain. The derivation and meaning of the word שדה are far from certain. Most modern translations opt for the meaning 'concubine', based on the claim that the word is derived from שד 'breast' and that this fits with the description 'delights of men'.[58] This reading, however, is not free of problems. Many things could feasibly be described as 'delights of men' besides concubines, and terms related to the root ענג 'to take delight' are not elsewhere normally associated with sexual delight.[59] Early versions, perhaps following the LXX, which apparently related the term to the Aramaic root שדא 'to pour out [wine]', typically understood this expression as referring to οἰνοχόον καὶ οἰνοχόας 'a male cupbearer and female cupbearers'.

Seow has suggested that שדה should be related to the Akkadian noun *šaddu*, an apparent cognate of which appears in postbiblical Hebrew meaning 'chest, box'. The Akkadian term specifically refers to chests for treasures such as gold and silver[60]—treasure chests. Seow's suggestion is at least as feasible as any other suggestion, and in light of the difficulties of the usual English translation 'concubine', is perhaps preferable.

Furthermore, the repetition of the singular noun followed by the plural is unusual, although not unprecedented (see Ps 72:5, דור דורים 'generation after generation'; Judg 5:30, רחם רחמתים 'a girl or two'). Similar expressions elsewhere in BH generally denote plurality, so here the expression is likely best understood as a reference to many treasure chests.

Amidst all the details of Qoheleth's experiment, one significant point to note is the parallel between Qoheleth's actions here and Solomon's excesses in the Deuteronomic History (see 1 Kgs 9:15–11:40). Furthermore, Qoheleth makes it clear that his activities were not for the public good but for his own

---

57. For example, see Fox, *A Time to Tear Down*, 175, 180; Crenshaw, *Ecclesiastes*, 80–81; Longman, *The Book of Ecclesiastes*, 92–93; Ogden, *Qoheleth*, 41; R. N. Whybray, *Ecclesiastes* (NCB; Grand Rapids: Eerdmans, 1989) 54.

58. In Isa 66:11 שד 'breast' and a verbal form of ענג 'take delight' (rather than a nominal form, as found in Qoh 2:8) appear together, although there is no sense that the reference has sexual overtones.

59. See Mic 1:16; 2:9; Prov 19:10; Cant 7:7. The use of the term in Canticles should not be allowed to obscure the fact that in most instances there are no sexual connotations attached to use of this term. For related terms, see Deut 28:54, 56; Isa 13:22; 47:1; 55:2; 57:4; 58:13–14; 66:11; Jer 6:2; Ps 37:4, 11; Job 22:26; 27:10.

60. Seow, *Ecclesiastes*, 131.

ends (note the repeated use of לִי 'for myself' in Qoh 2:4, 5, 6, 7, 8, 9). In light of these allusions, it is probable that the author is impugning Qoheleth's actions just as the Deuteronomic Historian impugns Solomon's activities. Thus we find Qoheleth again at odds with the temper of the remainder of the Hebrew Bible.

Qoheleth 2:12–23

[12] I turned to consider wisdom, madness, and folly, for what will the man who comes after the king [do] with what he has already done?

[13] I realized that there is an advantage to wisdom over folly, like the advantage of light over darkness. [14] The eyes of the wise person are in his head, but the fool walks in darkness. But I also know that the same fate befalls them both. [15] And I said to myself that the fate of the fool will also happen to me, so why have I been so wise? So I told myself, "This too is senseless."

[16] For the wise person—as with the fool—will not be remembered in the future. The days are soon coming when both will be forgotten. How can the wise person die in the same way as the fool?

[17] So I hated life, because the work which is done under the sun seemed evil to me, for everything is senseless and [like trying to] direct the wind. [18] And I hated all my toil at which I had labored under the sun, because I will have to leave it to the man who will come after me—[19] and who knows whether he will be a wise man or a fool? He will have control over all [which has come from] my toil at which I wisely labored under the sun. This, too, is senseless.

[20] So then I despaired about all the toil at which I had labored under the sun. [21] When there is a person whose toil is with wisdom, knowledge, and skill, and he gives his portion to one who has not toiled with them, this too is senseless and a great evil. [22] For what is there for a person in all his toil and striving of his heart at which he labors under the sun? [23] Because all his days his task is painfully infuriating—even at night his mind cannot rest! This, too, is senseless.

This next section moves rapidly from the consideration of the benefits of wisdom over folly to the consideration of death, which eradicates all distinctions and benefits. Qoh 2:13–14a presents statements that would be at home in the book of Proverbs, and as a result some scholars have suggested that some or all of these words actually form a quotation by Qoheleth of traditional wisdom that he does not himself fully endorse.[61] Appealing as this may be, it is ultimately difficult to justify disregarding these words so easily. Qoheleth's

---

61. See Gordis, *Koheleth: The Man and His World*, 221–22; Michel, *Untersuchungen zur Eigenart des Buches Qohelet* (BZAW 183; Berlin: de Gruyter, 1989) 25–30.

comments on death in the following verses do not entirely overthrow these
proverbial assertions, although they do undermine and relativize them. Thus
Qoheleth may elsewhere recommend against excessive wisdom (Qoh 7:16)
but not against any wisdom whatsoever.

Qoheleth's reflections on death and its impact on life are unparalleled in
the Hebrew Bible. When death is discussed elsewhere, there is confidence
that God will ensure that justice is done and that the righteous and wicked receive their appropriate rewards (see, for example, Ps 49:16[15]). In these
verses Qoheleth makes a number of observations about death and its bearing
on a person's attempt to find meaning in life. First, both sage and fool share a
common fate (Qoh 2:14–15a),[62] which prompts Qoheleth to question the
value of his wisdom (v. 15). This contrasts sharply with Proverbs, where wisdom is presented as unequivocally superior (perhaps incomparably superior)
to folly (see, for example, Prov 1:7; 10:8, 14; 12:15; 14:3; etc.).

Second, not only does death bring an end to life but whatever is done during this life will be forgotten (Qoh 2:16)—regardless of whether one was
wise or foolish—and it will be forgotten quickly.[63] Qoheleth here returns to
his comments made in the first chapter (1:11), this time expanding to highlight the failure of future generations to remember either the wise or the foolish. Again, these observations stand in contrast to thought in Proverbs, which
says, "the memory of the righteous is blessed, but the name of the wicked will
rot" (Prov 10:7). Qoheleth's thought here also appears to be the target of comments in 2:4, where notions such as his are ascribed to the ungodly who reason unsoundly.

Third, Qoheleth's death will mean that the fruit of his labor will fall into
the hands of another person, one who has not earned it through wisdom but
merely inherits it regardless of his or her wisdom or worth (Qoh 2:18–21).

---

62. The noun מקרה appears outside Ecclesiastes only in 1 Sam 6:9; 20:26; and Ruth
2:3, where it means 'chance, accident'. When Qoheleth uses the term (Qoh 2:14, 15; 3:19
[3×]; 9:2, 3), it is always in reference to death. Seow claims that Qoheleth's notion of fate
is Semitic (as opposed to Hellenistic), but if this is the case there have clearly been changes
in the semantic field between Qoheleth's use and uses found elsewhere in the Hebrew
Bible. See Seow, *Ecclesiastes*, 135. For further discussion on Qoheleth's use of this term,
see Peter Machinist, "Fate, *miqreh*, and Reason: Some Reflections on Qohelet and Biblical
Thought," in *Solving Riddles and Untying Knots: Biblical, Epigraphic, and Semitic Studies
in Honor of Jonas C. Greenfield* (ed. Ziony Zevit, Seymour Gitin, and Michael Sokoloff;
Winona Lake, Ind.: Eisenbrauns, 1995) 165–70.

63. The unusual use of בשכבר 'soon' with the expression הימים הבאים 'the days are
coming' is best understood to constrain the future reference to the near future. See Fox, *A
Time to Tear Down*, 184; Gordis, *Koheleth: The Man and His World*, 222–23; Seow, *Ecclesiastes*, 136.

While elsewhere in the Hebrew Bible the notion that one participates in some form of ongoing existence through one's progeny appears to be promulgated, Qoheleth finds neither hope in this thought nor an answer to his concerns. Furthermore, Qoheleth despairs regarding the gain from his labors[64] to such a great extent that he views the fact as רעה רבה 'a great evil'.

Qoheleth concludes each of these observations with a הבל declaration, for he finds they abrogate the anticipated order of the world, an order reflected in the axioms of traditional wisdom, from which his observations and words consistently deviate. William Dumbrell has summarized well Qoheleth's understanding of the effects of death on human toil: "This fact forces us to the conclusion that we must live for the moment, accepting what God, this somewhat remote figure, gives, since nothing can be done apart from him and since he disposes as he pleases."[65] Qoheleth's conclusions here lack confidence in the beneficence of the deity and are in stark contrast to the remainder of the Hebrew Bible. Again Qoheleth's words reinforce the epilogist's warning that the reader should be wary of the wisdom movement.

Qoheleth 2:24–26

[24] There is nothing better for a person [than] to eat, drink, and find enjoyment in his toil. I saw that this, too, is from the hand of God, [25] for who can feast or who is troubled apart from him? [26] Indeed, to the person he perceives as good he gives wisdom, knowledge, and joy. But to the "sinner" he gives the task of collecting and gathering to provide for the one God perceives as good. This, too, is senseless and [like trying to] direct the wind.

Many readers of Qoheleth's words find their redemption in concluding comments such as these.[66] Here Qoheleth speaks of enjoyment in toil, eating, and drinking, all of which come from God. What is more, he notes that these things *only* come from God.[67] Finally, Qoheleth writes that God gives these things to the 'one who is pleasing to him' (לאדם שטוב לפניו), together with wisdom and knowledge, while on the 'sinner' (חוטא) he places the burden of gathering for someone else. Consequently, in his conclusion Qoheleth agrees

---

64. The word יאש 'despair' appears elsewhere in 1 Sam 27:1; Isa 57:10; Jer 2:25; 18:12; and Job 6:26 always in the Niphal, whereas here Qoheleth uses the Piel.

65. Dumbrell, *The Faith of Israel*, 242–43.

66. See references above in n. 38 (p. 124); as well as Derek Kidner, *The Message of Ecclesiastes: A Time to Mourn, and a Time to Dance* (Bible Speaks Today; Leicester: Inter-Varsity Press, 1976) 35–36; Zuck, "God and Man in Ecclesiastes," in *Reflecting with Solomon* (ed. R. B. Zuck; Grand Rapids: Baker, 1994) 217.

67. The MT reads ממני 'from me', which makes little sense in the context. The reading of the LXX, Syriac, and some Hebrew MSS of 'from him' is thus to be preferred.

with both traditional wisdom thinking and the general theological underpinnings of Yahwism. Put simply: good things happen to good people; bad things happen to bad people.

A closer reading of these verses, however, reveals serious difficulties with this interpretation. The words of Qoheleth here are not as positive as some think. The expression אֵין־טוֹב בּ 'there is nothing better than . . .' in v. 24 falls far short of introducing either a satisfactory or a pleasing answer to the questions that Qoheleth has examined. It merely states that this is the best one can hope for; anything else is worse than this.[68] The rest of the Hebrew Bible hardly suggests that there is no more to life than feasting and finding enjoyment in toil. Furthermore, the fact that Qoheleth acknowledges that these things come from the hand of God speaks only of God's omnipotence, not his beneficence.

The fact that Qoheleth is ambivalent regarding the goodness of God is supported by further evidence. First, in v. 25 Qoheleth notes: כִּי מִי יֹאכַל וּמִי יָחוּשׁ חוּץ מִמֶּנּוּ [מִמֶּנִּי]. The key term here is יָחוּשׁ, usually rendered 'enjoyment' or the like in modern versions. This interpretation is uncertain, however. It is probably correct to say that the verb derives from חוּשׁ 'to feel, experience', also found in Job 20:2 and attested in postbiblical Hebrew as well as in cognate form in Aramaic; however, it probably should be understood negatively rather than positively. This is certainly the case in Job 20:2, where the meaning 'fret', suggested by the Akkadian cognate *ḫâšu*, fits well.[69] Seow also notes that the verb always carries a negative connotation in later texts.[70] Thus it stands in contrast to the אכל dispensed by God in the first clause. In this

---

68. See Mark Sneed ("The Social Location of the Book of Qoheleth," *Hebrew Studies* 39 [1998] 49–50), who writes, "The *carpe diem* ethic ('There is nothing better than . . .') found throughout is best described as an ethic of resignation (not joy, *contra* R. N. Whybray) to the fact of life's absurdity."

69. Seow (*Ecclesiastes*, 140) argues against this connection because, in order to create the expected antithesis between חושׁ and אכל, "*'kl* must be interpreted to mean 'to enjoy' or 'to have pleasure.' This interpretation is forced." Seow opts for an Arabic cognate, *ḫâša* 'to gather', despite the fact that this would more properly be cognate with a Hebrew verb of the form חושׁ not חושׁ. Contra Seow's assessment that interpreting אכל positively is forced, I consider it likely that the word is similar in meaning to its use in Qoh 10:16, where Seow does translate אכל as 'feast'. Whitley summarizes the manner in which ancient versions understood חושׁ: "The Septuagint, Theodotian and the Peshitta read יׁשׁתה (will drink) for יחושׁ, as in v. 24. So the Vulgate paraphrases *et deliciis affluet ut ego* (and abound in delights as I). On the other hand, Aquila, Symmachus and Syro-Hexaplar presuppose יָחוּשׁ 'to experience pain.' So, likewise the Targum reads חֲשָׁשָׁא, 'feeling' or 'anxiety'" (C. F. Whitley, *Koheleth* [BZAW 148; Berlin: de Gruyter, 1979] 28).

70. Seow, *Ecclesiastes*, 139–40; cf. Fox, *A Time to Tear Down*, 189; Longman, *The Book of Ecclesiastes*, 108–9.

context, the verb אכל probably serves for the full expression יאכל ושתה in the previous verse, so it may be understand broadly as 'feast'. Consequently, Qoheleth here ascribes both good and bad to God.

Second, v. 26 appears superficially to endorse traditional religious categories by labeling the beneficiary of God's good will as שטוב לפניו, one 'who is good before him', and the one upon whom God places burdensome labor for no reward as a חוטא 'sinner'. However, there are good indications that Qoheleth's use of these labels, particularly the latter, is not quite as straightforward as many claim. The primary obstacle to understanding Qoheleth's use of this terminology is the influence of the predominantly moral nuance associated with חוטא elsewhere in the Hebrew Bible. The root meaning of the word itself, 'to miss the mark', indicates that a moral sense is not endemic to the term. The word appears to denote something offensive about the person described.[71] In the immediately preceding passage, Qoheleth described himself as one who labored, only to find the fruits of his labor ultimately benefiting another person; thus he has aligned himself with the חוטא in v. 26. Further justification for this reading comes from the closing הבל refrain, for it would make little sense to say that both the rewarding of the morally righteous and the punishment of the morally wicked are הבל.

Verse 26 is correctly understood as merely acknowledging that the fate of human beings rests firmly in God's hands. To the one whom God finds pleasing, God provides wisdom, knowledge, and joy. To the one whom God finds displeasing, there is only toil, from which the rewards proceed to one whom God does find pleasing. There is here a strong assertion of the sovereignty of God—all aspects of human life are under God's control and beyond the control of men and women. What is completely absent from Qoheleth's observations here is an awareness of how to ensure that one falls in the first category and not the second. Indeed, as noted above, Qoheleth himself appears to believe that he falls in the category of חוטא (see Qoh 2:16). Qoheleth knows of no way to determine who is pleasing or displeasing to God.[72]

---

71. Seow (*Ecclesiastes*, 141–42) notes that "it is important to observe that *ḥôṭeʾ* is not a religious category in the wisdom tradition. The word *ḥôṭeʾ*, etymologically meaning 'one who misses, lacks,' refers to one who makes mistakes and bungles all the time, who cannot do anything right (Prov 8:36; 13:22; 14:21; 19:2; 20:2; Eccl 7:26; 9:2, 18; cf. Job 5:24)." See Fox, *A Time to Tear Down*, 189–90; Shields, "Ecclesiastes and the End of Wisdom," 120; Longman, *The Book of Ecclesiastes*, 109–10.

72. In Qoh 4:17–5:6[5:1–7] Qoheleth offers advice on vows that includes references to angering God. This is not, however, inconsistent with the point made here that there is no way to ensure that one is pleasing to God, for in that passage Qoheleth is merely advising the reader not to deliberately set out to offend God. See pp. 157–163 below for more discussion of this passage.

Thus Qoheleth's theistic framework differs significantly from that of the
remainder of the Hebrew Bible. While Qoheleth agrees with it on both the existence of God and the fact that the fate of human beings rests in God's hands,
he knows of no way to earn God's favor. In stark contrast to this, much of the
remainder of the Hebrew Bible explicitly identifies behaviors and attitudes
that are either pleasing or displeasing to God. Indeed, one particularly significant point to note about the search that Qoheleth undertakes in these opening
chapters is that he fails to look to any of the religious doctrines of Yahwism
for answers. For the readers who claim that Qoheleth is thoroughly orthodox,
his apparently agnostic attitude to any of the major biblical traditions is, at the
very least, troubling. For those who claim, with Eaton, that Qoheleth presents
two distinct perspectives—life without God and life with God—his failure to
turn to any identifiable religious tradition for answers to his questions seriously undermines the case for the second perspective, life with God.

Qoheleth 3:1–15

[1] For everything there is an appointed time;
> there is a time for every matter under the heavens.
[2] A time to give birth,
> and a time to die;
a time to plant,
> and a time to uproot what has been planted;
[3] a time to kill,
> and a time to heal;
a time to break down,
> and a time to rebuild;
[4] a time to weep,
> and a time to laugh;
a time to mourn,
> and a time to dance;
[5] a time to throw stones,
> and a time to gather stones;
a time to embrace,
> and a time to avoid embracing;
[6] a time to search,
> and a time to give up for lost;
a time to keep,
> and a time to throw away;
[7] a time to tear apart,
> and a time to sow together;
a time to keep silent,
> and a time to speak;

[8] a time to love,
   and a time to hate;
a time for war,
   and a time for peace.
[9] What gain is there for the worker in that at which he toils?
[10] I have seen the task that God has given human beings to be occupied by.
[11] He has made each thing appropriate in its time. He has also placed eternity in their hearts, without which people could not discover the work that God has done from beginning to end.
[12] I came to know that there is nothing good for them except to have pleasure and to do good during their lives. [13] Furthermore, [I know that] for all who can eat and drink and see good in all their toil—it is the gift of God. [14] I know that everything that God does will remain forever—there is nothing to add to it, nor is there anything to take from it. God has done this so they will fear him. [15] Whatever is now has already been, and whatever will be has already been. God will seek that which is pursued.

Some of the aspects of Qoheleth's theism introduced in the previous section are expounded more fully in the opening portion of chap. 3. Read in isolation, the poem about the appropriate time in Qoh 3:1–8 is ambiguous enough with regard to the role of God and the task of the sage to be compatible with traditional wisdom thinking. Wiersbe, for example, offers this interpretation: "In fourteen statements, Solomon affirmed that God is at work in our individual lives, seeking to accomplish his will. . . . The inference is plain: if we cooperate with God's timing, life will not be meaningless."[73] The presupposition that every event has its appropriate time underlay the task of the sages, who sought to identify that time so that they might live accordingly.

Although the poem itself makes no direct reference to God's role in relation to the appropriate time, Qoheleth's subsequent commentary does. Qoh 3:11 begins by ascribing to God the allocation of events to their appropriate times, once again underlining Qoheleth's affirmation of the sovereignty of God. However, Qoheleth does not find this truth comforting, as the remainder of the passage makes clear.

The second clause of v. 11 is one of the book's most difficult verses to interpret. The key problem lies in understanding the word עלם. Numerous suggestions have been offered regarding the possible significance of this word in this context, most of which are not convincing. Perhaps the most common interpretation for עלם offered by modern scholars is that it means 'darkness';

---

73. Warren W. Wiersbe, "Time and Toil: Ecclesiastes 3," in *Reflecting with Solomon: Selected Studies on the Book of Ecclesiastes* (ed. Roy B. Zuck; Grand Rapids: Baker, 1994) 264.

thus Qoheleth contends that God has deliberately prevented human beings from discovering his work by implanting darkness in their hearts. Justification for this interpretation comes from the use of the root עלם in Qoh 12:14; Job 28:21; and 42:3 in verbal forms that mean 'hidden', as well as in Ugaritic and Phoenician parallels. [74]

However, Qoheleth here uses a nonverbal form of the word in a context that clearly deals with temporal matters. In v. 14 (only three verses beyond this occurrence) the noun עולם can only have a temporal sense ('eternity'). Seow has demonstrated that the supposed Phoenician parallel does not in fact mean 'darkness' but, rather, 'eternity'. [75] Finally, the meaning and etymology of the supposed Ugaritic cognate *ǵlm* is not entirely clear. [76] These considerations suggest that 'eternity' is the more likely meaning of the term in this instance.

Whybray objects, however: "it makes little sense in Hebrew to say that God put (or, more probably, puts) either eternity or the world into man's mind, since the Hebrew language hardly allows such an expression to be understood as an ellipsis for 'the *notion* of eternity'." [77] But the evidence is not as unequivocal as Whybray suggests. In BH, something is said to be put (נתן) into a heart in only a relatively small number of places (Exod 35:34; 36:2; 1 Kgs 10:24; Ps 4:8[7]; Qoh 3:11; Ezra 7:27; 2 Chr 9:23), so the expression is not particularly common. Furthermore, nowhere else does BH parallel Qoheleth's words here. Some sense can be made of the expression when it is translated 'eternity' (as will become clear).

The use of עולם elsewhere in Biblical Hebrew is generally in a clearly temporal sense. Consequently, Seow's suggestion that 'eternity' is that which "transcends time" does not accord with the use of the term elsewhere in Biblical Hebrew. In the present context the term most likely has roughly the same meaning in v. 14 and so refers to the entire expanse of time—from beginning to end. This understanding is further confirmed by the preponderance of temporal language in v. 11 and throughout this portion of the work.

Precisely what it is that Qoheleth means by the statement that God has placed 'eternity' in people's hearts is also not immediately clear. The point is probably that God has given human beings a grasp of history that stretches beyond the immediate and permits them to probe the arena in which God operates in an attempt to comprehend it.

---

74. See Crenshaw, *Ecclesiastes*, 97–98; Whitley, *Koheleth*, 33.

75. Seow, *Ecclesiastes*, 163.

76. See John Huehnergard, *Ugaritic Vocabulary in Syllabic Transcription* (HSS 32; Atlanta: Scholars Press, 1987) 99, 164–65.

77. Whybray, *Ecclesiastes* (NCB), 73.

In spite of these difficulties, the words of Qoheleth in the remainder of
v. 11 help to illuminate the meaning and to highlight the frustration that Qoheleth identifies in the sages' task. The crux is the phrase מבלי אשר לא (lit.,
'without which not'), which links the conclusion of the verse with the preceding clause but is found nowhere else in BH. Elsewhere מבלי commonly functions to negate whatever follows, and sometimes it also includes a notion of
causation, purpose, or result.[78] Whitley points out that elsewhere in BH מבלי
is followed by the negative אין (and preceded by the interrogative ה), which is
formally a double negative that has a negative meaning. Based on this parallel
construction, he concludes that the expression here should also be understood
as a negative.[79]

Furthermore, the major versions and most modern scholars interpret the
expression as a negative purpose or result clause.[80] Qoheleth's point in this
view is that God has placed עלם in human hearts so that they *cannot* discover
what he has done from beginning to end. Clearly this interpretation does not
make sense if עלם is understood as 'eternity', for it makes nonsense of the
passage. How can God's having placed 'eternity' in human hearts result in
human inability to grasp God's actions through time? Proponents of this interpretation must then propose alternative but less probable meanings for עלם.

The other common interpretation of the expression מבלי אשר לא is that it
functions to highlight the contrast between God's having placed עלם in human hearts and their inability to grasp what he has done from beginning to
end. Longman, for example, renders the verse: "He also places eternity in
their hearts. But still no one can discover what God is doing from beginning
to end."[81] This understanding also requires the double negative to be read
with a negative meaning.

While both of these interpretations can be argued as fitting well with Qoheleth's thought, they still face definite problems. The theory that the double
negative expression מבלי אשר לא should be understood as a negative similar
to the expression המבלי אין, as suggested by Whitley, fails to note the significant differences between the expressions. Qoheleth's words effectively place
the second negative in a subordinate clause by interposing the relative אשר

---

78. See BDB, 115b.

79. Whitley, *Koheleth*, 33. The expression המבלי אין 'there are/were no' appears only in
Exod 14:11; 2 Kgs 1:3, 6, 16. Crenshaw also states that "the two negatives strengthen rather
than cancel each other" (Crenshaw, *Ecclesiastes*, 98).

80. So the LXX, Vulgate, Targum, Syriac, and numerous modern scholars, for example, Seow, *Ecclesiastes*, 163.

81. Longman, *The Book of Ecclesiastes*, 112, 121. Cf. Gordis, *Koheleth: The Man and
His World*, 156; Fox, *A Time to Tear Down*, 192.

between the two negative terms. Where similar constructions (negative followed by relative followed by negative) appear elsewhere in BH, the second
negative retains its negative force, logically negating the first (see, for example, Exod 12:30; Num 27:17; Deut 3:4; 11:2; 17:15; Josh 8:35; etc.).

Furthermore, understanding the expression as conveying a purpose or a result is problematic. If the term עלם is understood in a temporal sense (as 'eternity'), as the context strongly suggests (in Qoh 3:11 alone we find עת and the
expression מראש ועד סוף, and the meaning of עולם in Qoh 3:14 is clearly temporal), it becomes virtually impossible to make sense of these words with a
negative construction. How can God's having placed עלם in human hearts result in a human inability to grasp what God has done from beginning to end.

The impetus for these various readings of the text is probably the notion
that a "literal" reading does not accord with Qoheleth's argument. Literally,
the text can be rendered: 'Also eternity he has put in their heart, without
which human beings cannot discover the work that God has done from beginning to end'. Read this way, Qoheleth appears to be asserting that human beings ought to be able to discover the work that God has done from beginning
to end precisely because God has placed עלם in their hearts. In spite of the
fact that many apparently reject this idea, it does actually make good sense of
the text. Indeed, Qoheleth proceeds to summarize what God does from beginning to end, in vv. 14–15. According to Qoheleth, it is precisely this God-
given human ability to contemplate God's work beyond the immediate that
allows him to conclude that whatever is has already been and that God's work
remains immutable. These references apparently circumscribe the limits of
what Qoheleth is able to "find" regarding the work of God from beginning to
end. Clearly he could not have meant that human beings are able to attain a
full understanding of what God has done and plans to do, because elsewhere
he has denied that we can. Nonetheless, Qoheleth does demonstrate some
awareness of what God has done beyond the immediate, from beginning to
end, as it were.

Qoheleth closes this section by relating two conclusions about what he
knows (each introduced by the words ידעתי כי 'I know that' in vv. 12 and 14).
The first—that there is nothing better than to enjoy one's life whenever possible—recalls the conclusions stated in 2:24–26, although some scholars understand him to be extending the enjoyment of work to everyone, not the
select few to whom God bestows this gift. This stems from the reference to
כל האדם 'every person' in v. 13.[82] Nonetheless, it is better to understand the

---

82. See the NIV: "That every man may eat and drink, and find satisfaction in his toil—
this is the gift of God."

relative clause in a restrictive sense: the reference is not to all people but to all the people whom God allows to find enjoyment.

The second conclusion—that God's work is immutable—reinforces for Qoheleth the senselessness of existence. Because nothing can change what God has done (see Qoh 7:13) and there is nothing new, all human endeavor ultimately comes to nothing.

Qoheleth proceeds to another observation about the work that God has done from beginning to end: God ensures that his work is immutable in order to guarantee that human beings fear him.[83] The fear of God is characteristic not only of the Wisdom Literature of the Hebrew Bible but of all genres of biblical literature. The fact that Qoheleth specifically refers to fearing God (see Qoh 3:14; 5:6; 7:18; 8:12, 13), then, is widely understood as an indication that he aligns himself with the mainstream of biblical thought. However, closer inspection reveals a substantial gulf between his meaning for this term and its meaning elsewhere, even in the epilogue (12:13). Qoheleth's fear of God is the fear of a largely unknown but all-powerful deity, in whose hands lies the fate of human beings who do not know what they are required to do in order to obtain the deity's favor.[84]

Qoheleth's claim that God ensures that there is nothing new under the sun may also appear to correlate well with statements about God's immutability such as those in Ps 15:4; 110:4; Jer 4:28; and Mal 3:6. Once again, however, Qoheleth's point differs significantly from the point in other passages. Qoheleth insists that God prevents new things from happening in the universe. The remainder of the Hebrew Bible affirms that God remains constant in nature, that he is not unpredictable or erratic (God's immutability, however, is never extended to creation). Indeed, the prophets insist that God will do something new (see, for example, Isa 43:19). Here, once again, Qoheleth stands at odds with the remainder of the Hebrew Bible.

Qoheleth 3:16–22

In the remainder of chap. 3, Qoheleth moves to a consideration of justice. Qoheleth's desire for justice and his hope that God will impose justice when human justice fails are undermined by death. Consequently, Qoheleth can only reiterate his previous conclusion—that there is nothing better than to enjoy one's toil, if possible.

---

83. The relative particle here is best understood as introducing a result or purpose clause (see GKC §165b).

84. For a more-detailed treatment of this topic, refer to pp. 96–98 above.

Qoheleth 3:16–17

[16] Furthermore, I saw under the sun that in the place of justice there was wickedness, and in the place of righteousness there was wickedness. [17] I thought to myself, "Oh that God would judge the righteous and the wicked— since there is a time for every matter and every deed has a name."

At first glance, Qoheleth's reflections on justice appear to mirror orthodox thought—while recognizing that human justice is corrupted by the presence of wickedness, Qoheleth appears to affirm a belief in divine justice. For readers who claim to find Qoheleth's beliefs compatible with those of the remainder of the Hebrew Bible, this statement, together with a small number of others, is cited as proof of their position. If these words do ultimately reflect Qoheleth's conclusions, the case that the epilogist uses Qoheleth's words to discredit the wisdom movement is weakened. On the other hand, exponents of the view that Qoheleth can be aligned with orthodox thought must explain the subsequent material, which calls God's judgment into question.[85]

Others find that Qoheleth's apparent affirmation of the doctrine of divine judgment is so surprising that they attribute it to a later redactor[86] or to an orthodox speaker in a dialogue.[87] These views highlight the difficulty of reconciling such an apparently unequivocal statement of faith by Qoheleth with his subsequent uncertainty over the fate of the human spirit. If, as Qoheleth has observed, justice is not found in this life (3:16), and there can be no certainty of an afterlife (3:19–21), when will God bring judgment?[88]

The best solution to this apparent dilemma, however, is neither to attribute the statement of v. 17 to a later redactor nor to assign it to a different voice. Rather, it is to recognize that the use of the nonperfective verb in v. 17 may introduce an element of contingency into Qoheleth's statement. Qoheleth's

---

85. For example, Eaton seeks to maintain a distinction in Qoheleth's thought between life "under the sun" and the life of faith, both of which Qoheleth supposedly discusses (Eaton, *Ecclesiastes*, 85). This allows him to resolve the tension here by arguing that, if "we lapse from the viewpoint of faith, the one element which distinguishes us from the animals is lost. Man *by himself* becomes a 'naked ape.'" For a discussion of the problems with this approach to Qoheleth, see my "Ecclesiastes and the End of Wisdom," 118–21.

86. E.g., A. Lauha, *Kohelet* (BKAT 19; Neukirchen-Vluyn: Neukirchener Verlag, 1978) 75, 157, 208–9. Crenshaw writes that, "in light of Qohelet's other comments about judgment, the affirmation of divine judgment appears contradictory. This verse, then, may be a later gloss" (Crenshaw, *Ecclesiastes*, 102).

87. See T. A. Perry, *Dialogues with Kohelet* (University Park: Pennsylvania State University Press, 1993) 93.

88. Longman writes, "Qohelet implies that the time of fair judgment and proper retribution is not in the present. Yet in the following verses Qohelet also does not express a concept of eternal life and a judgment day, when all things will be set right" (Longman, *The Book of Ecclesiastes*, 127), accepting that Qoheleth contradicts himself at this point.

use of the nonperfective form of the verb spans the full gamut of possible meanings, from future indicative (e.g., 5:14[15]) to hypothetical circumstances (e.g., 2:25; 4:10). In Qoh 7:23 we find the words אמרתי אחכמה which are reminiscent of Qoheleth's words here in 3:17. In that context Qoheleth's use of the nonperfective אחכמה cannot be read as a future indicative, for Qoheleth immediately states that this plan was beyond him. Rather, Qoheleth uses the nonperfective to express his desire (in that context).[89] Clearly, the precise determination of the nuance of the nonperfective form can only be determined by the context.

Applying these observations to the present context, we find that Qoheleth makes a statement regarding the activity of God using the verb ישפט. Combining Qoheleth's observation that there is no justice to be found in this life and his doubts about any possible afterlife, we find sufficient warrant for reading this verb form in an irreal mode.[90] It should not be read as a statement of fact but should be understood as presenting a situation hoped for but not necessarily realized. In light of the failure of justice in the present and Qoheleth's belief that all things have an appropriate time, he here expresses his hope that God will effect justice where none has been found. In light of his observations elsewhere, however, we know that he probably had little real hope that this desire would be fulfilled.

Qoheleth 3:18–21

> [18] I thought to myself on the matter of human beings, surely God has selected them to show that they are animals [. . .] [19] for the fate of humans and the fate of animals are the same fate: as one dies, so dies the other, and they both have the same spirit, and the advantage of humans over animals is none, for everything is senseless. [20] Both go to the same place, both come from dust and both return to dust. [21] Who knows whether the spirit of humans goes up and whether the spirit of animals goes down to the earth?

Verse 18 repeats the self-deliberating introductory words אמרתי אני בלבי 'I thought to myself' used in v. 17. Previously, Qoheleth has used similar means first to introduce an avenue of investigation and then to follow up with the results of his investigation.[91] In v. 18, the repeated clause marks Qoheleth's considerations on the situation initially noted in v. 16—that justice is

---

89. Alternatively, the verb could have a jussive meaning, 'may God judge . . .'. See Gen 16:5; 31:53; Exod 5:21; Judg 11:27; 1 Sam 24:13[12], 16[15]; etc.

90. See B. K. Waltke and M. O'Connor, *An Introduction to Biblical Hebrew Syntax* (Winona Lake, Ind.: Eisenbrauns, 1990) §31.4, pp. 506–9.

91. While the exact wording differs, elsewhere Qoheleth first states the area of study and then proceeds to make observations and reach conclusions relating to that area of study. For example, see 1:16–17; 2:1–11, 12–16.

not executed in human courts. It also follows the statement about hoping to
see God exercise judgment. What Qoheleth finds is that, once again, death
undermines his desire to find meaning (or, in this context, justice) in life.

The remainder of v. 18 is problematic. There is no finite verb, and the two
infinitives appear to make little sense as they stand. Furthermore, the meaning
of the first infinitive, לברם, is uncertain.[92] In spite of these problems, most
agree that the overall meaning of the text is as explained by Fox: "The point
of the verse is that God made humans mortal to show them that they are but
beasts."[93]

Even if the meaning of v. 18 in isolation is unclear, the context ultimately
bears out the above conclusion. Verses 19 and 20 highlight the point of Qoheleth's comparison of human beings with animals—they share the same fate
(מקרה):[94] they come from dust and return to dust (עפר). Whereas previously
death had undermined any advantage that the wise may have had over the
foolish, now the repercussions of death are expanded to undermine even a
perceived distinction between human beings and animals.

In the context of Qoheleth's concerns over justice being done, these observations regarding death serve to undermine any real hope that God will ultimately overturn the injustices that he has observed. For Qoheleth, the fact that
justice is not achieved again highlights the failure of the wisdom movement,
for where the sages sought order there is only disorder. Whereas righteousness
ought to be rewarded and wickedness punished in a universe ordered according to the presuppositions of the wisdom movement, in Qoheleth's world this
does not happen. Here again is evidence to back up Qoheleth's conclusion that
all is הבל, a point that he reiterates in v. 19.

The reference to עפר in Qoh 3:20b has prompted a number of scholars to
argue that Qoheleth is here specifically alluding to Genesis 2–3, in which the
first man is formed from 'dust' (עפר, Gen 2:7) and returns to dust after death
(Gen 3:19).[95] This dependence is supposedly reinforced by Qoheleth's fre-

---

92. Many modern versions, together with the Vulgate and Targum, relate לברם to the
verb ברר 'to purify, purge' and by derivation provide the otherwise unattested rendering 'to
test'. Others believe that the text has been corrupted and that emendation is necessary (see
Seow, *Ecclesiastes*, 167–68; Fox, *A Time to Tear Down*, 214, 216). Perhaps the most ingenious solution to the difficulties is the suggestion by A. B. Ehrlich (*Randglossen zur he-
bräischen Bibel* [Leipzig: Hinrich's, 1914] 7.67–68) to emend לברם to לא ברם, meaning
"[God] did not distinguish them."

93. Fox, *A Time to Tear Down*, 216.

94. Qoheleth has previously used this term in the context of his comparison between
the wise and fool in chap. 2. See the comments above, in n. 62.

95. For example, "It seems obvious that 12:7 and especially 3:20 allude to Genesis
3:19" (David M. Clemens, "The Law of Sin and Death: Ecclesiastes and Genesis 1–3,"

quent discussion of 'toil', a topic also addressed in Genesis 3 (although Genesis and Qoheleth use different terminology). If this were so, the deliberate reference might be evidence of his awareness and approval of the Scriptures. This might discount the thesis that the epilogist was using Qoheleth's words to discount the wisdom movement because the sages had moved to a position incompatible with Scripture. If Qoheleth appeals to Scripture, he cannot be entirely opposed to it.

In actual fact, however, the allusion to Genesis 3 here would ultimately support our interpretation. If Qoheleth is here revealing his familiarity with the Hebrew Scriptures, or at least a portion of them, then an allusion to Genesis here only serves to magnify his failure to appeal to them elsewhere in his writings. His failure, for example, to appeal to other biblical texts when he was attempting to discover an advantage in human toil suggests either that he was ignorant of them or that he did not grant authority to their teachings and deliberately avoided them. Either way, Qoheleth's opposition to orthodox thought is only enhanced. While this passage may reflect Qoheleth's awareness of some portions of Scripture, it certainly does not reflect his approval of its teachings in general.

However, the claim that Qoheleth's use of עפר here proves a link to Genesis 2–3 is not as certain as some claim. The notion that human beings were created from soil was widespread throughout the ancient Near East, and the Genesis account itself is almost certainly using this nearly universal knowledge.[96] The

---

Themelios 19 [1994] 6); and "This direct linguistic connection leaves little doubt that Qoheleth was familiar with Gn. 3:17–19," and "Qohelet's dependence on the Genesis text has, for the most part, reached scholarly consensus" (William H. U. Anderson, "The Curse of Work in Qoheleth: An Exposé of Genesis 3:17–19 in Ecclesiastes," *EvQ* 70 [1998] 101, 113). Anderson goes so far as to say that "in fact, I have not come across a single scholar who denies Qoheleth's use of the Genesis material" (ibid., 99 n. 2). See also B. G. Webb, *Five Festal Garments* (New Studies in Biblical Theology 10; Leicester: Apollos, 2000) 103. Whybray (*Ecclesiastes* [NCB], 80) is not entirely correct in asserting that "the thought of the whole verse is again completely in accordance with traditional Israelite beliefs," for the context of Genesis 3 establishes a particular relationship between God and humans of which Qoheleth demonstrates absolutely no awareness; cf. Longman, *The Book of Ecclesiastes*, 129–30.

96. With reference to Gen 2:7, Gordon Wenham writes, "It is evident then that Genesis is here taking up a very ancient tradition of the creation of man" (Gordon J. Wenham, *Genesis 1–15* [WBC 1; Waco, Tex.: Word, 1987] 59–60). The fact that Akkadian literature typically depicts human creation from clay (*ṭiṭṭu*) rather than dust (*ep[e]rum*) speaks against direct literary dependence of the Hebrew Bible on Akkadian texts. However, both Genesis' and Qoheleth's use of עפר in preference to חמר ('clay'; see Job 10:9; 33:6; Isa 29:16; 45:9; 64:8) may be because עפר was associated with death both in the Hebrew Bible and in other ancient Near Eastern texts; see Delbert R. Hillers, "Dust: Some Aspects of Old

fact that Qoheleth was also aware of this information is not sufficient grounds
for positing direct awareness of the Genesis material. Conversely, because
Genesis provides an etiological explanation for the arduous toil to which human beings are subject, it would have been difficult for Qoheleth not to have
made reference to it if he knew it existed. Finally, Genesis 1–3 establishes a
clear distinction between human beings and all other animals. In contrast, Qoheleth here appears to affirm their similarity rather than their difference. Any
claim of Qoheleth's dependence upon the Genesis material or even his awareness of the material cannot be substantiated by the nature of the evidence.

The MT pointing of העלה 'goes up' and הירדת 'goes down' in v. 21 treats
both instances of the initial ה as the definite article, suggesting that the verse
ought to be rendered something like "who knows the spirit of man that goes
upward and the spirit of the beast that goes down to the earth?"[97] The appearance of another apparently orthodox statement (refer to the discussion of v. 17
above) is surprising, particularly in light of Qoheleth's comments on the lack
of difference between humans and beasts in vv. 19–20. However, most ancient
versions (the LXX, Peshitta, Vulgate, and Targum) indicate that the ה was
read as an interrogative rather than an article.[98] As such, this verse is not asserting that the destination of the soul after this life distinguishes humans from
animals but instead stating, through a rhetorical question, that no one knows
whether there is any difference of this sort between humans and animals.

Nonetheless, v. 21 introduces a surprising note of ambivalence in Qoheleth's thought. In the preceding verses, Qoheleth has made a series of definitive observations about the equivalence of the fate of humans and animals. In
v. 21, however, rather than making a statement, he poses a rhetorical question. The transition comes with a move from observing the common fate of
humans and animals—death—to what comes beyond death. For Qoheleth,
once the discussion moves beyond death, it has moved into the realm of the
hypothetical. The answer is that no one knows whether the fate of the human
spirit differs from the fate of the spirit of animals, and so there is little point
debating it. Crenshaw highlights the negative function of such rhetorical
questions throughout Qoheleth's work:

Testament Imagery," in *Love and Death in the Ancient Near East: Essays in Honor of Mar-
vin H. Pope* (ed. John H. Marks and Robert M. Good; Guilford, Conn.: Four Quarters,
1987) 105–9. Job 10:9 uses both of these terms in reference to the beginning and end of life.

97. So Eaton, *Ecclesiastes*, 87; cf. AV, NASB.

98. See Crenshaw, *Ecclesiastes*, 104; Seow, *Ecclesiastes*, 168; Fox, *A Time to Tear
Down*, 216–17. Fox goes so far as to say of reading the article that "this is grammatically
impossible and out of line with the context. The *heh* should be pointed as interrogative."

Qoheleth's use of *mî yôdēaʿ* functioned to call into question the entire wisdom enterprise. In a sense he was insisting on restraint where claims about knowledge were concerned. From his remarks one can surmise that elaborate boasts were being made by wisdom's champions. It seems that these affirmations about wisdom's potential extended beyond the older assertions about coping with daily experience, perhaps going so far as to insist on knowledge about Transcendence.[99]

In this light, it is unlikely that Qoheleth is holding onto faint hope that there may be an afterlife advantage for humans, some hope that beyond the grave lies a form of existence that may resolve the indignities and injustices of death.

Qoheleth 3:22

I realized that there is nothing better for people than to enjoy their work, because that is their lot, for who can show them what will be after them?

Qoheleth concludes the discussion of justice by reiterating his observation that the only wise advice a sage can truthfully offer is that one should enjoy one's work—if possible. Once again it is clear that this is only because he finds no sense in the world around him—all is הבל. There is no guarantee that justice will be done and, furthermore, there is no way to ensure that certain behaviors will result in predictable outcomes. Thus, for Qoheleth, the sage's task of discerning beneficial forms of conduct in life is futile because the presupposition that the universe obeys a set of predictable causal relationships is not borne out by observation. This again is at odds with the perspective of the remainder of the Hebrew Bible.

Qoheleth 4:1–16

The fourth chapter of Ecclesiastes contains five loosely linked observational units; all but the third are so-called "better" proverbs, built around the adjective טוב ('good'). The first three (4:1–3, 4–6, 7–8) develop themes already introduced in the first three chapters: injustice and toil. The fourth presents observations on the value of companionship over solitude (Qoh 4:9–12), while the last is a somewhat enigmatic comment about a foolish monarch and his apparent successors. The first three units correlate well with Qoheleth's previous position and continue to stand at odds with the remainder of

---

99. James L. Crenshaw, "The Expression *mî yôdēaʿ* in the Hebrew Bible," *VT* 36 (1986) 286. Crenshaw also notes that, in Qoheleth, rhetorical questions introduced by the expression מי יודע function "overwhelmingly as an expression of skepticism. . . . The mood accompanying the rhetorical questions is one of resigned inevitability" (p. 278).

the Hebrew Bible, whereas the final two sections require closer examination for us to understand their function in the epilogist's overall design of the book.

Qoheleth 4:1–3

> [1] Then I looked at all the acts of oppression that are done under the sun. I saw the tears of the oppressed, and there was no one to comfort them. Power came from the hand of their oppressors, but there was no one to comfort them. [2] So I acclaimed the deceased who had already died more than the living who are still alive, [3] but better than both of them is the one who has never existed, who has not seen the evil work that is done under the sun.

Here Qoheleth picks up his observation about injustice from Qoh 3:16–22 in order to focus on individuals who are victims of injustice, who are oppressed. Whereas the Psalms declare that God is not only on the side of the oppressed but will work to execute justice for them (e.g., Pss 103:6; 146:7), Qoheleth holds out no hope that the injustice experienced by the oppressed will ever be righted. For them there is no comforter, and God is certainly not held out as a source of comfort by Qoheleth. While other texts commenting on oppression (all using the term that appears here, עשק) sometimes attribute the oppression to the sinfulness of the oppressed (e.g., Deut 28:29, 33; Hos 5:11), it is clear from Qoheleth's later comment about the oppressed (5:7[8]) that he is referring to people who have been denied justice or are subject to corrupt overlords.

The conclusion that the dead are better off than the living highlights Qoheleth's belief that the sages are powerless to overturn the evil experienced in this world. His conclusion that those who have never existed and have never seen evil are better off than either the living or the dead highlights the fact that he has no confidence in any form of eschatological dispensation of justice. This thoroughgoing pessimism about the lot of the oppressed is again difficult to correlate with the theism of the remainder of the Hebrew Bible.

Qoheleth 4:4–6

> [4] Then I realized that all toil and all achievement, because it is from the jealousy of one man toward his neighbor, is also senseless and [like trying to] direct the wind.
> [5] The fool folds his hands and consumes his own flesh.
> [6] One handful with rest is better than two handfuls with toil and [trying to] direct the wind.

Qoheleth next returns to the topic of toil and its rewards. In this instance, however, rather than examining the profit to be earned from toil, Qoheleth identifies the underlying motivation in human endeavor: jealousy (קִנְאָה).[100] Although this term occasionally appears elsewhere in BH with a positive connotation, those uses are generally confined to God's jealousy with regard to idolatry (e.g., Exod 20:5, which uses the masculine noun קַנָּא) or to a husband's jealous guarding of the marriage relationship (e.g., Num 5:14–31). The majority of the other uses of the term are negative (e.g., Gen 37:11; Job 5:2; Prov 14:30; 27:4), and this is certainly the case in Qoh 4:4, where Qoheleth sees this motivation for work as yet another example of the senselessness and futility of life.[101]

The two proverbs in vv. 5 and 6, taken together, promote moderation. Verse 5 clearly condemns idleness both by attributing it to fools and by describing the result as 'eating one's own flesh', which is an image designed to highlight the fool's descent into poverty through idleness. Verse 6 advocates a moderate level of labor, which results in moderate rewards but affords the laborer some degree of rest ("one handful"). The alternative, "two handfuls," may result in greater rewards but allows one no time to enjoy the rewards, thus making the toil ultimately futile.

Qoheleth advocates moderation elsewhere (e.g., Qoh 7:15–18; see below, p. 253) for it is the logical outcome of his conclusion that the world and God do not follow any discernible logic or follow any moral order.[102] If Qoheleth had agreed with the traditional wisdom supposition that such a moral order was indeed fundamental to the operation of the world, he would have been able to offer definitive advice on the best way to live, for he could have been sure that certain behaviors (such as dedication to hard work and avoiding laziness) would lead to predictable outcomes (such as wealth and prosperity). However, for Qoheleth the absence of this moral order means that dedication

---

100. Much discussion over this verse focuses on the meaning of the term כִּשְׁרוֹן, variously rendered 'skill' (Fox, *A Time to Tear Down*, 220; NASB), 'achievement' (Seow, *Ecclesiastes*, 137; NIV), and 'success' (Longman, *The Book of Ecclesiastes*, 136). The noun only appears in BH in Qoh 2:21; 4:4; 5:10[11]. Forms of the verb כשׁר appear in Qoh 10:10; 11:6; and Esth 8:5, and 'succeed' appears to be the best understanding of the verb in at least the first two. Based on these contexts, 'achievement' appears to be the best understanding, since neither 'skill' nor 'success' fits well in an English rendering of Qoh 5:10[11].

101. See Longman, *The Book of Ecclesiastes*, 136–37. See also the excursus above on the meaning of הבל, pp. 112–21.

102. See Crenshaw's comments on the previous section: "Qohelet shares the sages' conviction that a just moral order should accompany belief in the Creator, but sees no evidence to confirm the conviction" (Crenshaw, *Ecclesiastes* 107).

to hard work does not guarantee wealth or prosperity, whereas moderation at
least maintains some hope of reaping the benefits of hard work while also
finding some enjoyment in the present. Once again, Qoheleth's advice reveals
his distance from the orthodoxy of the remainder of the canon.

Qoheleth 4:7–8

> [7] Then I considered [another] senseless thing under the sun: [8] there was a
> man who was alone, without either a son or a brother, but there was no end
> to all his toil. Yet his eyes are never satisfied with [his] wealth. So for whom
> am I toiling and depriving myself of pleasure? This, too, is senseless and an
> evil task.

Any division between this section and the previous is somewhat artificial, because here Qoheleth is effectively illustrating his previous point about moderation in labor. He describes a lone man laboring incessantly for his own
benefit, never satisfied with what he has, and consequently never able to enjoy the fruits of his toil. Not only is this an example of the excessive labor
of v. 6, but it further introduces the idea of companionship (or lack thereof),
which prompts Qoheleth's comments in the next section. This illustration,
then, serves to substantiate Qoheleth's affirmation of moderation in the previous section.

The abrupt introduction of first-person speech in the middle of v. 8 is
somewhat surprising. These words are commonly interpreted either as a question posed by the man in the story or else as a question that the man in the
story ought to have asked.[103] However, the fact that nothing identifies these
words as belonging to that man causes the reader to infer that the first-person
speech belongs to Qoheleth, who has spoken throughout in the first person.[104]
Either way, the effect here is that Qoheleth closely identifies with the plight of
the man of the story, recognizing the senselessness of his own labor.

Qoheleth 4:9–12

> [9] Two are better than one, because they have a better return from their toil.
> [10] For if either of them falls, the other will lift up his companion, but woe to
> the one who falls without another to lift him. [11] Also, if two lie down they
> will keep warm, but how can one keep warm? [12] And whereas one may

---

103. For the first option, English translations usually insert an explanatory "and he
says" to ease the transition; compare the AB, NAB, NEB, ASV, NIV, and NRSV. For the second
option, the introduction becomes "yet he never asks himself" or the like; cf. Gordis, *Koheleth: The Man and His World*, 242; KJV; RSV; NASB.

104. So Crenshaw, *Ecclesiastes*, 110.

overpower him, two could stand against him. A three-ply rope will not quickly snap.

Qoheleth moves from discussing the situation of a lone person to the benefits of companionship. The benefits that Qoheleth identifies are: greater earning power (4:9), assistance in times of need (4:10), shared warmth in the cold (4:11), and better chances when a person is attacked (4:12). While these verses do stand out against the background of Qoheleth's ambivalence (here for once he appears to make definitive statements concerning what is good), a number of scholars highlight the rather insipid nature of the benefits that Qoheleth has identified.[105] Gordis goes so far as to suggest that here he is pointing out that "the vaunted advantages of family life are exaggerated," explaining it this way: "He does so obliquely, by citing a conventional proverb (v. 9) to which he adds an ironic comment, ostensibly validating, but actually undermining, the proposition by limiting the benefits of family life to a few minor physical advantages."[106] Gordis almost certainly overstates the case here, because the context does not indicate that Qoheleth necessarily has family life in mind. Seow sensibly points out that Qoheleth's statements, while apparently positive, are still only relative in themselves.[107] The use of "better" proverbs fits well with Qoheleth's general approach to reaching conclusions—any affirmation remains relative; no absolutes are given. Qoheleth cannot say that something is best—only better.[108]

Once again this fits into Qoheleth's overall conclusion and is consistent with our understanding that the epilogist has employed the words of Qoheleth to highlight the fact that the sages cannot offer any conclusive advice on how one should live.

---

105. For example, see Fox (*A Time to Tear Down*, 222), who notes that "Qohelet recognizes benefits in friendship, albeit rather cheerless ones. Comrades can aid each other in difficulty, such as when one falls, is attacked, or is cold. Qohelet does not mention the emotional benefits of fellowship."

106. Gordis, *Koheleth: The Man and His World*, 242.

107. Seow writes, "It is not that there is absolute certainty in numbers. The benefit is, rather, only relative. All advantages are only relative to Qohelet. One may note that the noun *ḥûṭ* 'cord' is elsewhere not something of exceptional strength. . . . The three-strand cord may indeed snap, but such a reinforced cord will not snap as readily as the single-strand one. The strength is only relative. So, too, Qohelet means that it is 'better' to have others around than to be a loner." See Seow, *Ecclesiastes*, 188–90.

108. The nonperfective verbal form יעמדו in v. 12 should not be understood, as it is in many English versions, in an indicative sense (which lends an absurd certainty to the outcome of an unpredictable, hypothetical situation). It should instead be analyzed as being in irreal mode and be rendered 'two may stand against him'. The point is not that two will always prevail but that two stand a better chance than one.

Qoheleth 4:13–16

[13] A poor but wise youth is better than an old but foolish king who no longer knows how to receive advice, [14] for he came out of prison to reign. Then a poor man was also born under his reign. [15] Then I saw all the living who walked under the sun with the second youth, who had come to stand in place of [the first]. [16] There was no end to all these people before whom he went, although those who would come after would not rejoice in him. So this, too, is senseless, and [like trying to] direct the wind.

The links between the final section of chap. 4 and what has preceded are considerably more tenuous than those between the previous sections. The most obvious connection is the use of the טוב-proverb ('better'-proverb) form although, unlike the previous sections, it is difficult to identify any thematic links. The presentation of specific details about the characters has prompted numerous attempts by commentators to identify them with historical figures, but in the final analysis, the text is too enigmatic for anyone to resolve the question.[109] Nonetheless, the almost impenetrable difficulties in finding antecedents for the pronouns in the passage suggest that the original audience enjoyed some additional insight into the situation depicted here by Qoheleth that enabled them to comprehend the text. This, at least, indicates that it is possible that the characters do refer to historical figures, even if, so far, modern scholars have been unable to determine who they were.

The passage begins with an assertion that wisdom is better than folly in spite of the apparent benefits in the circumstances of the foolish: specifically here the wise youth over the foolish king (compare Prov 28:6). The difficulties in the text lie in the succeeding verses. The first clause of v. 14 indicates that one of these two characters came out of prison to become king. Opinions differ on whether this refers to the youth in v. 13[110] or the king. The old king is the nearest antecedent, and up to this point, there was no indication that the poor wise youth had become a king. On the other hand, it is not clear what any background information on the foolish king contributes to the discussion. If the prison information is provided as a rationale for the better-proverb in v. 13, then it makes better sense if the antecedent is the poor wise youth.

The second clause of v. 14 is even more problematic than the first. It is most commonly understood as stating that the youth who had risen from prison to royal office in the first clause was born poor under his (the foolish

---

109. For further discussion on the possibility of historical allusions in this passage, see above, p. 25.

110. See Longman, *The Book of Ecclesiastes*, 146; Fox, *A Time to Tear Down*, 225; Seow, *Ecclesiastes*, 183–84.

king's) reign. However, it is not clear why Qoheleth had to reiterate the impoverished origins of the youth, since they were just established in v. 13.[111] Seow ingeniously suggests that this clause provides a description of the foolish king's reversal of fortunes ("for [one] went forth from the prison to reign, while [another], though born into his kingship, is impoverished"). This bears out the advantage of the poor wise youth of v. 13, who "was in prison but went on to become king. By contrast, the king was born into the royal family but became impoverished."[112] In order to arrive at this interpretation, Seow understands רש to be a perfective form ('is impoverished') rather than a participle or an adjective ('poor'). This translation, however, rests on an otherwise unattested use of רוש, which only appears elsewhere in a perfect verbal form in Ps 34:11[10], where it retains a stative meaning.

Perhaps the best understanding of the second clause has been proposed by Fox, who suggests that it refers to a second youth born poor under the reign of the first wise youth of v. 13.[113] This resolves the problem of redundant information regarding the first youth and makes good sense of the Hebrew text, rendering רש as the subject of the verb נולד so that the clause reads "a poor man was also born under his [the wise youth's] reign." Although the introduction of a third character may initially appear unnecessary, many readers do identify a third character in v. 15, where it will become apparent that this reading of v. 14 is eminently viable.

Verse 15 speaks of הילד השני 'the second youth'. Although some scholars identify this youth with the wise youth in v. 13, the presence of the adjective שני 'second' makes this reading difficult. Fox finds here a reference to a third youth, who is "second" to the youth introduced in v. 14b,[114] yet it is not clear how this contributes to the argument of the passage. The majority of recent scholars identify this second youth as a successor to the first poor, wise youth in v. 13. However, the definiteness of this expression ('the') presents a difficulty for this view, because a definite article should be resumptive with reference to a youth already introduced. By contrast, the presence of the article fits well with the suggestion made above that a second poor youth is introduced in v. 14b, a second youth who is also referred to here as the one who replaces (or succeeds) the first youth. Understood this way, v. 15 suggests that this second youth has replaced the first wise youth (the most likely referent of תחתיו 'in place of him'), who himself had replaced the foolish old king in v. 13. It is

---

111. See Fox, *A Time to Tear Down*, 225.
112. Seow, *Ecclesiastes*, 184–85, 191.
113. Fox, *A Time to Tear Down*, 225.
114. Ibid., 226.

noteworthy that Qoheleth makes no comment on the wisdom or foolishness of this second youth.

The opening clause of v. 15 introduces a new element into the text, an apparent reference to the popularity of the characters (a notion that is lent support by the reference in v. 16 to those who no longer "rejoice in him"). Whereas Qoheleth began this passage by focusing on the contrast between wisdom and folly, vv. 15–16 appear to change focus. This shift may be an indicator that Qoheleth is not overwhelmed by the benefits of wisdom over folly; he recognizes that any benefits are both relative and temporary.

The meaning of v. 16 is again obscured by ambiguity regarding the antecedents of its pronouns. The first reference to 'all the people' (לכל העם) is best understood as a resumptive reference to the people mentioned in the previous verse who are "with" the second youth. The second phrase, לכל אשר היה לפניהם (lit., 'to all that he went before them'), is sometimes understood as a reference to past generations, but this makes little sense in the context. It is better understood as a reference to the same multitude mentioned previously, with the singular subject of the verb היה 'went' being the king who parades before the multitude. This phrase thus ought to be rendered 'to all before whom he went'.[115] Consequently the first part of v. 16 builds on the notion of popularity introduced in the previous verse, suggesting that the second youth enjoyed popular acclaim in a way that the first wise youth did not.

The second part of v. 16 appears to indicate that this popular acclaim is itself transient, for later generations (האחרונים) will, according to Qoheleth, not support this second youth as did the people first mentioned in v. 15. This reading of the text thus suggests that both wisdom and popularity are of only relative benefit and that they are only transient at best. Although wisdom is better than folly according to v. 13, the benefit for the wise youth is that he becomes king in place of the old foolish king. Yet this benefit is relativized, for this wise youth will himself be replaced by another. Furthermore, wisdom and public acclaim are apparently unrelated, for the wise youth's own successor is not wise but is popular. Finally, even this popularity is temporary. Thus the benefits of wisdom, so unambiguously affirmed elsewhere in the Hebrew Bible, are again relativized and diminished by Qoheleth.

This exegesis confirms Fox's comments on this passage: "The multiplicity of possibilities for resolving the ambiguities has given rise to a considerable variety of interpretations. . . . Nevertheless, most commentators agree that the point of the story is that wisdom's practical value is limited and transient."[116]

115. See Seow, *Ecclesiastes*, 185; Fox, *A Time to Tear Down*, 227; Longman, *The Book of Ecclesiastes*, 147.

116. Fox, *A Time to Tear Down*, 224.

This rather subdued and equivocal attitude toward wisdom from one who (both by his own testimony in chap. 1 and by the testimony of the epilogist in chap. 12) is the foremost among the sages can only serve to undermine the standing of the wisdom movement in the eyes of the reader.

Qoheleth 4:17–5:6[5:1–7]

[17] Tread carefully when you go to the house of God. Draw near to listen, unlike the fools [who draw near] to offer a sacrifice, for they do not know they are doing evil. [1] Do not be quick with your mouth, and do not let your heart rush to bring a matter before God, for God is in heaven and you are on earth. Therefore let your words be few. [2] Will a dream come with much effort? But the voice of a fool comes with many words.

[3] When you make a vow to God, do not be slow to fulfill it, for there is no delight in fools. Fulfill your vow! [4] It is better that you never make a vow than that you make a vow and fail to fulfill it.

[5] Do not let your mouth bring harm to your body, and do not say to the messenger that it was a mistake. Why should God become angry because of your voice and destroy the work of your hands? [6] For with many empty dreams words multiply. But fear God!

Up to this point Qoheleth has made only passing reference to God, and no reference at all to the cultic institutions that accompanied the religion of ancient Israel. Against this backdrop, Qoh 4:17–5:6[5:1–7] is in stark contrast to the rest of his discussion not only about God but also about the temple, sacrifices, vows, and fearing God. It is unsurprising that this passage is viewed by some writers, such as Barry Webb, as verification of the claim that Qoheleth does ultimately agree with the world view of the writings of the remainder of the Hebrew Bible.

> But there are strong suggestions here that human beings have not been left altogether in the dark about what this God requires of them. Foolish behaviour is not simply a matter of talking too much (5:7), but of failing to *listen* (5:1), which implies revelation. Furthermore, the exhortations about vow-keeping here presuppose the instruction on this matter in the Torah.[117]

If this proves to be true of this passage, it weakens our thesis that the epilogist is using Qoheleth's words to demonstrate the bankruptcy of the wisdom movement.

---

117. Webb, *Five Festal Garments*, 97; see also G. D. Salyer (*Vain Rhetoric* [JSOTSup 327; Sheffield: Sheffield Academic Press, 2001] 375), who, referring to the epilogue's exhortation to obey the commands of God, writes that "the implied author stresses what Qoheleth himself stressed; that the commandments of God are important (cf. 5.3–5)."

There is danger, however, in reading too much into references such as these. Because Qoheleth's words are bound in a broader literary context to the remainder of the Hebrew Bible, readers tend to project biblical concepts into Qoheleth's references here that are not necessarily justified by Qoheleth's idiosyncratic use of these terms. Thus, it is necessary to tread warily and to understand the precise significance of these words within their present context. Furthermore, we must be careful not to extrapolate perceived orthodoxy from small portions of Qoheleth's work to the rest of the work and thereby gloss over significant difficulties highlighted elsewhere in this book. Nonetheless, the fact that this short passage deals directly with these themes makes it of central significance in determining whether we think that Qoheleth was aware of some form of authoritative divine revelation (or believed in the possibility of divine revelation).

In my view, this passage focuses on how one is to approach God, primarily advocating caution: guard your steps (4:17[5:1]); watch your speech (5:1–2[2–3]); do not make vows hastily (5:3–5[4–6]). Although this advice is mirrored elsewhere in the Hebrew Bible, the motivation behind this advice in this context is what must be examined. It will become clear that for Qoheleth the reasons behind the warnings are tied to God's transcendence (5:1[2]) and God's sovereignty (5:5–6[6–7]), both of which have already been seen to form the foundations of Qoheleth's theism.

The opening exhortation, to guard one's steps when going to the house of God (4:17[5:1]), functions as an introduction to the entire section. The first specific warning is to go to the temple to listen rather than be a fool and sacrifice (מתת הכסילים זבח). The advice to listen correlates with the subsequent proverbial advice against hasty speech (5:1[2]).[118] Is the implication of this advice that there is discernible divine revelation to which one is encouraged to listen? Qoheleth does not say so explicitly, so inferring it would only be justified at this point if we can show that Qoheleth believes that only divine revelation is worth listening to or that the only discourse taking place in the house of God is revelatory. The first proposition is clearly false; Qoheleth at least expected the reader to pay attention to his words and demonstrated no awareness that his speech was in any way divinely inspired. The second point presumes too much about the type of speech that took place in the temple. These words are best understood as a warning against speaking rather than as an implicit affirmation of the existence of divine revelation in the temple.

---

118. The verb שמע is unlikely, in this context, to convey the notion of obedience (contra Fox, *A Time to Tear Down*, 228; Longman, *The Book of Ecclesiastes*, 150)—see Seow, *Ecclesiastes*, 194. The emphasis in this context lies in the contrast between listening and being quick to speak rather than between obedience and disobedience.

Qoheleth contrasts the advice regarding going to the temple to listen with the advice to avoid acting like a fool by offering a sacrifice (מתת הכסילים זבח). Precisely what this refers to is debatable. The common rendering in modern English versions, 'the sacrifice of fools', does not represent a literal understanding of the Hebrew text, in which the reference to 'the fools' precedes the noun זבח 'sacrifice'.[119] If the meaning were 'the sacrifice of fools', the word order would be reversed. It is unlikely that Qoheleth is condemning all sacrifices by suggesting that all who offer them are fools; instead, he is pointing to those who participate in the cult, giving the appearance of being upright. However, they are fools and are doing evil (as evidenced by the final clause).

Qoh 5:1[2] offers the motivation for keeping silent when approaching God: "God is in heaven, and you are on earth." Qoheleth's emphasis on God's position in heaven highlights both God's transcendence and his sovereignty. Although this in itself is not at odds with assertions made elsewhere in the Hebrew Bible, Qoheleth offers no hint that this distance is moderated by any special interest that God may have in human affairs. Indeed, the exhortation to abstain from speaking to God (presumably either in prayer or in the making of vows) suggests that Qoheleth may believe that God has little or no interest in the concerns of individuals.

Qoh 5:2[3] is also difficult, although it almost certainly condemns fools through the association with excessive speech (because Qoheleth has just counseled in favor of speaking few words). The first clause is more difficult, reading literally, "for the dream comes with much toil." Most modern commentators and versions either appear to ignore the article on 'dream' (החלום) or describe it as "generic."[120]

A better solution is to read the ה as an interrogative, so that Qoheleth is posing a rhetorical question, expecting a negative answer: "Will a dream come with much effort?"[121] Qoheleth's point is then that one cannot bring about dreams through sheer effort (here it is important to note that the biblical use of 'dream' does not correspond to the English idea of "something hoped for"). The second colon of this aphorism regarding the voice of a fool is thus highlighting the futility of "many words" by paralleling them with "much toil"— neither of which ultimately achieves a great deal from Qoheleth's perspective.

---

119. See the NASB, NIV, KJV, and ASV. Longman (*The Book of Ecclesiastes*, 149) offers this translation but admits the necessity of having to adjust the Hebrew text.

120. Those who appear to ignore the article include Fox, *A Time to Tear Down*, 229, 231–32; Seow, *Ecclesiastes*, 195; and Whybray, *Ecclesiastes*, 94. Those who describe the article as "generic" include Gordis, *Koheleth: The Man and His World*, 248; and Longman, *The Book of Ecclesiastes*, 149.

121. See BDB, 209, §1b.

The remainder of this section deals specifically with one form of speech to God: the making of vows. Many readers have noted that Qoheleth's advice on making and keeping vows resembles the advice given in the Pentateuch, and they maintain that it demonstrates Qoheleth's familiarity with and, at least in this instance, endorsement of that teaching. Indeed, the language that Qoheleth uses in 5:3[4] is strongly reminiscent of Deut 23:22, as can be seen:

Qoh 5:3[4]   כאשר נדר אלהים אל־תאחר לשלמו
                    When you make a vow to God, do not be slow to fulfill it
Deut 23:22[21]   כי־תדר נדר ליהוה אלהיך לא תאחר לשלמו
                    If you make a vow to the LORD your God, do not be slow to fulfill it

This similarity has been used in attempts to refute the claim that Qoheleth has no familiarity with the Torah and the charge that the words "fear God and keep his commandments" in Qoh 12:13 are wholly foreign to the thought of Qoheleth.

There are, however, a number of significant—if subtle—differences between Qoheleth's words and the words in Deuteronomy and elsewhere.[122] Besides avoiding use of the divine name יהוה, Qoheleth's advice is deeply rooted in his belief in the transcendence and capriciousness of God. This is manifest in a number of ways.

First, it is reflected in the consequences of failure to fulfill a vow. In Deut 23:22[21] we are told that this failure results in: כי־דרש ידרשנו יהוה אלהיך מעמך והיה בך חטא 'for the LORD your God will certainly hold you accountable, and you would incur guilt'. In this context the emphatic expression דרש ידרשנו מעמך appears to amount to 'he will certainly hold you accountable'.[123] Although Deuteronomy fails to elaborate on this outcome, it is presented as inevitable and clearly undesirable. Qoheleth, however, who consistently maintains that there is no way to know or predict God's behavior in a specific matter, is more circumspect. He avoids making claims about inevitable consequences of breaking a vow and merely states that it *may* result in God's disfavor, and it should be avoided. Seow has summarized Qoheleth's warnings thus: "Qohelet's motive clause is, by contrast, typical of the wisdom tradi-

---

122. These differences were noted by A. Lauha (*Kohelet* [BKAT 19; Neukirchen-Vluyn: Neukirchener Verlag, 1978] 96–102) and have since been highlighted by a number of other scholars. See, for example, Murphy, *Ecclesiastes*, 50; Seow, *Ecclesiastes*, 200.

123. Compare the use of the verb דרש 'require a reckoning' in Gen 9:5; Deut 18:19; Ps 9:12.

tion's tendency to avoid any language of divine causality. He does not say that God will intervene in history to hold human beings accountable. Rather, he resorts to circumlocution."[124] Qoheleth warns of two possible consequences of failing to fulfill a vow: being considered a fool (presumably by God, although the text itself merely states that 'there is no delight in fools', כי אין חפץ בכסילים) and angering God, with the result that the works of one's hands are destroyed. The second consequence, which is God's anger in response to injudicious speech, ultimately serves to substantiate Qoheleth's warning against hasty speech of any type—including vows—in the presence of God.

Second, Qoheleth emphasizes God's transcendence ("For God is in heaven and you are on earth," 5:1[2]), whereas Deuteronomy emphasizes God's immanence (see Deut 4:39). Qoheleth's God stands apart from the human world and operates independently and unpredictably. Furthermore, God has not revealed any rationale behind his actions, thus thwarting the sages, who seek to discover how students of wisdom can prosper. God's unpredictable nature means that the best advice available to the sage is to say little, lest one offend God with one's words. The repercussions of this reach beyond the making of vows, as Longman points out: "Qohelet advises people to approach God in prayer only rarely, and then only briefly, as if the danger is taking too much of God's precious time. Qohelet warns his readers to be cautious in approaching God with words because *God is in heaven and you are on earth.* We take this statement not as an assertion of divine power, but of divine distance, perhaps even of indifference."[125]

Third, Qoheleth's injunction to fear God appears to be distinguished from similar comments elsewhere by his deeply held belief in the remoteness and transcendence of God.[126] Qoheleth's fear is not of a God whose responses are known and predictable but of an unknowable God, who operates freely and independently, not answering to the sages or their wisdom.

Finally, in Qoh 9:2 we read a quite contradictory assessment of the necessity of keeping one's word. In this verse Qoheleth suggests that there is ultimately no difference between the one who swears an oath and one who does not, because all share the same fate: death.[127] Thus, once again, death attenuates Qoheleth's advice to the point of almost nullifying it. Although Qoheleth advises that it is wise not to infuriate God needlessly by promising and not

---

124. Seow, *Ecclesiastes*, 200; cf. p. 66.

125. Longman, *The Book of Ecclesiastes*, 151.

126. For further discussion on this subject, see above p. 97.

127. Although an oath (שבע) ought to be distinguished from a vow (נדר), they are closely related and are both based on spoken words. Their close relationship is made apparent in Num 30:2[3].

delivering, wise behavior will not change the fact that everyone will ultimately die, regardless of his or her choices.

The existence of these differences between Qoheleth's discussion of vows and the various relevant passages in the Pentateuch does not in itself prove Qoheleth's independence. It is important to note, however, that a discussion by Qoheleth of this sort does not inevitably mean that he was familiar with the pentateuchal material or that he endorsed it as divine revelation. Vows were made throughout the ancient Near East,[128] so the practice in Israel (or wherever Qoheleth was located) in Qoheleth's time need not have been governed by the stipulations made in the Pentateuch. Indeed, the regulations covering the making and breaking of vows in the Torah presuppose an awareness of behavior regarding vows in general.[129] Furthermore, the very fact that Qoheleth makes these warnings suggests that vows were being made recklessly, without regard for the possible consequences.

Qoheleth's warning regarding keeping vows, then, need not be founded on an awareness of the instructions found in the Pentateuch. The discussion of vows by Qoheleth is in keeping with his general understanding of the transcendence and inaccessibility of God. While it may be impossible, according to Qoheleth, to discover how to win God's favor (certainly Qoheleth has observed that wisdom does not secure it), it would be foolish indeed to enrage God by making promises and failing to fulfill them. Furthermore, the fact that Qoheleth is in essential agreement with the Pentateuch on this point does not prove his direct familiarity with it. It is telling that this passage is, for some, the most direct reference to the Torah in the words of Qoheleth. Christian-

---

128. In the *Epic of Kirta*, for example, Kirta attempts to enlist the aid of the goddess Asherah by vowing (*ndr*) a gift to her but forgets to fulfill the vow and is afflicted with a fatal illness; see Simon B. Parker (ed.), *Ugaritic Narrative Poetry* (SBLWAW 9; Atlanta: Scholars Press, 1997) 1 IV 36–37; 2 III 22–30. Edward Greenstein's summary of Kirta, that "in the final analysis, it's a god's world—beyond our control—and it is their rules by which the game of life is played" could also apply to Qoheleth, except that Qoheleth exhibits no awareness of the rules. See also Lambert, *Babylonian Wisdom Literature* (reprinted; Winona Lake, Ind.: Eisenbrauns, 1996) 116, lines 1–4, regarding oaths. Seow (*Ecclesiastes*, 62) points out a fragmentary text from Ugarit that also parallels Qoheleth's comments on vows. This text reads:

> One who acknowledges no guilt rushes to his god,
> Without thinking he raises his hands (in prayer) to the god.
> . . . his guilt . . .
> A man in ignorance rushes to his god.

(See Lambert, *Babylonian Wisdom Literature*, 116, lines 10–13.)

129. Vows are made in Genesis (see Gen 28:20; 31:13) well before the record of rules governing them. When rules were explicated regarding vows, it was a clear prerequisite that the reader understand what a vow is, how it functions, and what it achieves.

son's comments on 5:3–6[4–7] are thus noteworthy: "This could hardly be summarized as 'Fear God and keep his commands.' Indeed, this passage emits a strong 'aroma of paranoia' out of keeping with the very positive effects that fearing God is meant to engender elsewhere, not the least of which is the beginning of knowledge (Prov. 1.7; cf. 1 Sam. 12.24; Prov. 3.7–8)."[130] Finally, even if it were possible to sustain the argument that Qoheleth was explicitly referring to the teaching regarding vows found in the Torah, it is apparent that he did not entirely agree with that teaching (as seen from the differences identified above). At the very least, he did not view it as conveying any form of divine revelation. Indeed, the fact that Qoheleth nowhere refers to the teaching of the Torah or any other supposed divine revelation only underlines the argument that he knew of no alternative to the senseless life that he consistently depicts.

This section of Ecclesiastes concludes with remarks that are critical of the many words that arise out of empty dreams: "For with many empty dreams words multiply."[131] In the Hebrew Bible, חלום 'dream' refers either to normal dreams as a part of sleep or, more commonly, to prophetic dreams. This fact, together with the warning against offering sacrifices in Qoh 4:17[5:1], raises the possibility that Qoheleth is here criticizing the various religious institutions of ancient Israel by associating their activities with fools.[132] Although it is not clear that Qoheleth directed this warning against all who sacrificed, had prophetic dreams, or spoke in the temple, the presence of criticism sets Qoheleth at odds with the religious hierarchy of his time. To the reader of Qoheleth's words who is familiar with the remainder of the Hebrew Bible, this only enhances the impression that this supreme sage has reached a position that is incompatible with the canon. Once again, Qoheleth's words further the epilogist's case against the wisdom movement.

Qoheleth 5:7[8]

[7] If you see oppression of the poor and removal of justice and righteousness in the province, do not be surprised at the matter, for there is bureaucrat over bureaucrat, [and] bureaucrats watch over them.

---

130. E. S. Christianson, *A Time to Tell* (JSOTSup 280; Sheffield: Sheffield Academic Press, 1998) 116; cf. F. Zimmerman, *The Inner World of Qohelet* (New York: KTAV, 1973) 37–41.

131. Understanding חלמות והבלים 'dreams and emptinesses' as a hendiadys; see Seow, *Ecclesiastes*, 197.

132. I am indebted to Ian Young for suggesting this possibility.

This brief section returns to the subject of injustice and oppression (compare Qoh 3:16; 4:1–3). However, in contrast to the previous section, here Qoheleth offers no advice regarding ways to avert the condition of injustice; instead he merely warns his audience not to be surprised by its existence. Following these relatively clear statements is what appears to be Qoheleth's explanation for the injustice and why it should not be surprising. Unfortunately, his explanation is particularly difficult to interpret, and few attempts by modern scholars are wholly satisfying.

The most common understanding of 5:7b[8b] is that it refers to layers of bureaucracy in which corruption is hopelessly entrenched, as bureaucrats on various levels exploit their positions at the cost of their subordinates. Ultimately, the greatest cost is borne by the most vulnerable members of society. This interpretation understands the adjective גבה to be functioning as a substantive, referring to some type of government official.[133]

Kugel has objected to this interpretation of the term גבה because it does not have this meaning anywhere else in BH.[134] Rather, when it is used elsewhere as a substantive, it generally refers to "an arrogant person" or "a haughty person" (see 1 Sam 2:3; Job 41:26[34]; Ps 138:6; Isa 10:33; Ezek 21:31[26]). Furthermore, Kugel notes that the idiom "to watch over" should be שמר על, not the words used by Qoheleth, which are שמר מעל. Kugel proposes deriving גבה from the root גבה/י 'to collect [a bill, taxes, a mortgage]', a root well attested in Mishnaic Hebrew but not elsewhere attested in BH.

Both Kugel's interpretation of the text and his objections to the more common reading are themselves problematic, however. Kugel must emend the text at a number of points in order to produce a sensible reading. Although it is true that the idiom "to watch over" does generally use the preposition על rather than the compound form מעל, this in itself does not justify Kugel's solution; it merely calls into question the assumption of many modern readers that Qoheleth is here employing this idiom. In favor of the traditional interpretation that Qoheleth is referring to a form of bureaucracy is the fact that he opens with a reference to the arena in which injustice and oppression are to be found: the province (מדינה).

It is thus likely that Qoheleth is using the adjective גבה, not elsewhere associated with bureaucracy, in a pejorative sense (as the English term *bureau-*

---

133. Some scholars have suggested that גבהים may be a reference to God (see BDB, 147a, which refers to H. Ewald and O. Zöckler as proponents of this interpretation), thus suggesting that corruption goes all the way to God. However, גבה is nowhere used to refer to God in Biblical Hebrew, which makes this interpretation unlikely.

134. See J. Kugel, "Qohelet and Money," *CBQ* 51 (1989) 35–38. Seow comments that Kugel's objections to the traditional interpretation are valid; see Seow, *Ecclesiastes*, 203.

crat has itself acquired a pejorative sense). In this context, this is appropriate because of the focus on the injustice perpetrated by these officials. Nonetheless, the clause division in the MT remains difficult, and Seow's revision of the clause and word breaks is perhaps the least intrusive reading of the text that also offers a sensible interpretation.[135] The text is usually read:

כי גבה מעל גבה שמר
וגבהים עליהם

Seow proposes this reading:

כי גבה מעל גבה
שמרו גבהים עליהם

The changes are minor: the ו is no longer read as a conjunction but is attached to the verb שמר, which is now read as a plural, the subject of which is גבהים, and which now appears in the expected idiomatic form, שמרו . . . על. The text can then be translated 'for there is bureaucrat over bureaucrat, [and] bureaucrats watch over them', referring to the layers of officials who were supposed to ensure justice in the province but served only themselves and protected only their own interests.

The hierarchy of injustice and oppression that Qoheleth describes again reveals his disillusionment with the traditional world view of the sages, for rewards in this life are not dispensed in proportion to worth or merit. Furthermore, Qoheleth's failure to offer a solution to this inverted justice highlights the powerlessness of the sages in the face of a world that does not operate according to the presuppositions upon which their thinking rests. Once again, Qoheleth furthers the epilogist's argument that the wisdom movement is ineffectual and to be avoided.

Qoheleth 5:8[9]

[8] The profit of [the] land is [for] all of them; even the king is served by a field.

This verse is linked to the preceding verse by most versions and commentators. The difficulties inherent in this verse, however, preclude certainty. Literally, the text reads something like 'and an advantage of land is in all of it, a king for a cultivated field'. Perhaps the only point that most modern commentators agree on regarding this verse is that no entirely satisfying understanding of the verse exists. Crenshaw, for example, writes that the "meaning of

---

135. Ibid.

this verse is totally obscure."[136] Ogden notes that "this is one of those verses whose interpretation we may never ascertain."[137] Seow again proposes altering the word breaks but retaining the consonants (with the *qere* reading), changing from:

ויתרון ארץ בכל הוא מלך לשדה נעבד

to:

ויתרון ארץ בכלה ואם לכל שדה נעבד

> But the advantage of the land is in its provision, that is, if the field is cultivated for provision.

He associates both בכלה and לכל with the root כול/כיל 'to measure, measure out', explaining the text as making the point "that the land ought not to be accumulated for its own sake but is to be cultivated for what it produces—its yield." Nonetheless, he recognizes that this solution is not entirely adequate, admitting that this text may be "hopelessly corrupt."[138]

Clearly, the problems posed by this verse are great, and while we could analyze it a great deal, we still would be unlikely to shed light on its meaning. The previous verse makes good sense without additional material, although we cannot be entirely certain that v. 8[9] did not somehow modify the sentiments expressed in v. 7[8], which simply reflects (in its present context) the inevitability of injustice in society.[139] Nonetheless, the interpretation of Ecclesiastes as a whole certainly cannot be said to hang on this one verse.

Qoheleth 5:9–6:9[5:10–6:9]

[9] The lover of money will not be satisfied by money, and whoever loves wealth will not [be satisfied] with income. This, too, is senseless. [10] When prosperity increases, those who consume it multiply. So what advantage is there for its owners except to see it with their eyes?

[11] The sleep of the laborer is sweet, whether he eats a little or a lot, but the wealth of the rich person does not allow him to sleep. [12] There is a sickening evil I have seen under the sun: wealth safeguarded by its owner to his harm. [13] Suppose that wealth was destroyed in heinous circumstances and he had

---

136. Crenshaw, *Ecclesiastes*, 119.

137. Ogden, *Qoheleth*, 81.

138. Seow, *Ecclesiastes*, 204.

139. Some scholars have understood v. 8[9] to modify v. 7[8]. Scott, for example, suggests that מלך 'king' ought to be appended to the previous verse, which thus designates the king as the high end of the bureaucratic hierarchy (see Scott, *Proverbs, Ecclesiastes*, 228). For other possibilities, see Eaton, *Ecclesiastes*, 101–2.

fathered a son; there would be nothing left to him. [14] Just as he came naked from his mother's womb, he will go again as he came, and he will not take anything from his toil that he could carry in his hand. [15] This, too, is a sickening evil; just as he came, so he will go. What gain is there for him, because he toils for the wind? [16] Furthermore, all his days he eats in the dark and [with] great irritation, sickness, and anger.

[17] Here is what I have observed to be good: that it is appropriate [for a person] to eat, drink, and enjoy his toil throughout all his days during which he labors under the sun for the few years of his life that God has given him, for that is his lot. [18] Furthermore, to every person to whom God has given riches and wealth and enabled him to consume it and to take his portion and to enjoy his labor, this is the gift of God. [19] For he will not often remember the days of his life because God keeps him occupied with the joy of his heart.

[6:1] There is an evil which I have seen under the sun, and it weighs heavily on human beings: [2] a man to whom God has given riches and wealth and honor, so he does not lack anything he desires, but God does not enable him to consume it because a foreigner consumes it. This is senseless and a sickening evil. [3] If a man fathers one hundred children and lives many years— very many years, but he has no satisfaction from his prosperity nor even a proper burial, I would say that a stillborn child is better off than he, [4] for it comes in senselessness and goes into darkness, and with darkness its name is covered. [5] It never even sees or knows the sun, but it has more rest than he—[6] even if he were to live a thousand years twice over but not see prosperity. Do not all go to the same place?

Qoheleth once again returns to the topics of wealth, toil, and the benefit one can expect from them. The conclusions and arguments found here are strongly reminiscent of his previous discussions of these matters, reflecting the inability of those who toil for their wealth to enjoy it (5:9–15[10–16]; 6:1–2, 7), and the manner in which death undermines any possible benefit in life (5:14[15]). The opening verse is reminiscent of Qoheleth's words in 1:8b and 4:8. The fact that a similar thought is expressed again in 6:7 suggests that these references delimit this present section, which revolves around the inability of human beings to find satisfaction in whatever they seek, with particular reference to wealth. Strengthening this case further is the fact that Qoheleth elsewhere introduces investigative discourse with a summary conclusion and הבל statement, as found here in v. 9[10].[140]

---

140. Aside from the opening summary statement in 1:2, there are more specific instances found in 1:12–13 and 2:1. For discussion on the significance of הבל here, refer to p. 119.

Qoheleth follows his summary statement with three examples of the failure of wealth to satisfy the wealthy: 5:10[11], 11[12], 12–16[13–17]. The precise meaning of the *first example* is not entirely clear. The identity of the אכלים, the 'consumers' of the wealth, could be parasitic relatives, expenses associated with managing and administering the wealth, or even the wealthy themselves, who are the ultimate consumers of their own wealth.[141] However, the precise identity is unimportant (and perhaps Qoheleth has no specific group in mind but is simply highlighting the fact of increased consumption), for the point is simply to identify the correlated increase of wealth and consumption.[142]

It is in the light of this observation that Qoheleth poses the rhetorical question in v. 10b[11b], a question that must be answered negatively: there is no benefit in wealth for the owner apart from the "sight of his eyes." Once again the meaning of this expression is disputed, but perhaps Seow offers the best explanation: " 'what the eyes see' refers to what is present and enjoyable. . . . What Qohelet means is that wealth is good only when it is enjoyed in the present, and that satisfaction should not be postponed in anticipation of some greater benefit in the future."[143] Qoheleth's focus, however, is not on the possibility of enjoying wealth but on the very limited manner in which it may be enjoyed, if at all. Furthermore, those with increased wealth must also endure more consumers (whoever they may be). This presentation of the very limited value of wealth is borne out by the two remaining examples of the failure of wealth to satisfy the wealthy.

The *second example*, 5:11[12], may be summarized as "if you have nothing, you have nothing to worry about," together with the inverse statement. Qoheleth here argues about wealth similarly to the way he argued about wisdom in 1:18. In Proverbs, both good sleep and wealth are the result of paying heed to wise teaching (e.g., Prov 3:24; 8:18, 21); for Qoheleth, wealth and good sleep do not go together.

Qoheleth's *final example* of the inability to benefit from wealth comes under the description of 'a sickening evil' (רעה חולה).[144] Here it is the loss of wealth, and ultimately the loss of wealth through death, that is the problem. Yet again, Qoheleth is making the point that death undermines any advantage one may have had in life, specifically from wealth. A life of labor and toil that generated vast wealth ends with nothing in death just the same as a life of much sleep and little toil.

---

141. See Seow, *Ecclesiastes*, 219–20.
142. See Longman, *The Book of Ecclesiastes*, 165.
143. Seow, *Ecclesiastes*, 220; cf. Fox, *A Time to Tear Down*, 236.
144. See the discussion above, p. 118.

Qoheleth's observations again stand in stark contrast to the thoughts found in Proverbs, where wisdom and toil are commended, and wealth is the objective reward for wise labor. Longman has also identified this anomaly: "This conclusion [that the inability of the wealthy to enjoy their wealth is meaningless] is in tension with the predominant attitude of Proverbs toward wealth. There wealth is something that can result from wise behaviour, is a gift from God (Prov. 3:9–10, 16; 8:18; 13:21; 14:24; 15:6; 19:4; 21:21; 24:3–4), and is worthy of pursuit."[145] In light of his observations, Qoheleth records his conclusion regarding what is good in vv. 17–19[18–20], as he has done previously in 2:24–26; 3:12–13, 22. The primary distinction between this passage and those previous declarations of what is good lies in the unequivocal affirmation of finding satisfaction in one's toil in this chapter—previously Qoheleth could only half-heartedly say that there was nothing better. Nonetheless, here he also quickly undermines any attempt to interpret his words positively by highlighting the fact, in the next section (6:1–6), that he considers it evil that God gives wealth but not the opportunity to enjoy it.

Furthermore, the person that Qoheleth considers to be gifted by God, who can enjoy his or her work, is so occupied that he or she seldom has time to reflect on life (5:19[20]). Clearly, then, this person is no sage, for the sage is occupied with precisely this reflection (compare 1:18). Indeed, Qoheleth is essentially recommending avoiding the very activity in which he has partaken and which—as we have seen—results in his ultimate conclusion that life is הבל. From this perspective, the only wealthy people who have any hope of enjoying life and benefiting from their wealth are those who spurn the life of the sage! Once again, Qoheleth's point perfectly serves the purpose of the epilogist in warning the reader against the wisdom movement.

Having stated what is good, Qoheleth moves to considering the alternative: what is evil (רעה). Indeed, what is described as evil in Qoh 6:1–6 is precisely the inability to achieve the good described in the immediately preceding section: satisfaction in work and enjoyment of the fruits of one's toil. Furthermore, the blame for this is laid squarely at the feet of God (6:2, "but God does not enable him to consume it").

The magnitude of this problem in Qoheleth's mind is raised in 6:1 and is amply illustrated in the two examples cited in vv. 2–6. Qoh 6:1 highlights the problem through the use of the phrase ורבה היא על האדם. The expression literally reads, 'and it is a great [evil] on mankind', probably not referring so

---

145. Longman, *The Book of Ecclesiastes*, 165.

much to the number of people affected by this evil as to the severity of this situation for all humanity (the adjective רבה here modifies רעה, not האדם).[146]

In the first example (6:2), Qoheleth describes a person to whom God has given wealth but whom God prevents from enjoying that wealth. Without the ability to enjoy what God has given, the recipient can receive no benefit from the gift. Qoheleth declares the fact that God gives wealth but prevents the recipient from enjoying it both senseless (הבל) and profoundly evil (... רעה ורבה היא, 6:1; חלי רע, 6:2).

Qoheleth's strong language does not abate in the following verses. Here he illustrates this evil of being unable to enjoy the good things God has given by declaring that, no matter how long our lives may be, if we are unable to enjoy life, then a stillborn child is better off than we are.[147] With all due respect to Crenshaw, this text does not reflect a "wholly positive view of death in certain circumstances"; rather, Qoheleth's view of death is consistently negative.[148] That death could be viewed as better than something else does not mean that death is good—even relatively good. Rather, it highlights the horror of the alternative.

To the reader familiar with the theism of the remainder of the Hebrew Bible, these statements made by Qoheleth are deeply troubling. Ascribing evil to God and calling God's justice into question (by declaring God's actions to be both רעה and הבל) is at odds with the presentation of the God of Israel as benevolent and just. Qoheleth depicts a God who, for no apparent reason, torments humans by providing all they need to enjoy life but depriving them of the ability to enjoy it. Here again the reader is affronted by the conclusions of this sage, who is presented as the wisest of all, yet so clearly contradicts the familiar teachings of the other scriptures. If this is truly representative of the thinking of the wisdom movement in Qoheleth's time (whenever that may have been), it is clear that the wisdom movement had moved far from the theological roots reflected in the book of Proverbs. It is clear that this text strongly supports the contention that the epilogist has employed Qoheleth's words to undermine the authority of the wisdom movement.

---

146. Contra Longman, ibid., 163, 169; Ogden, *Qoheleth*, 90; NASB; but in agreement with Fox, *A Time to Tear Down*, 241; NIV.

147. Compare Job 3:16 for a similar reference to the status of a stillborn child (נפל). The only other place this term is used is Ps 58:9[8].

148. James L. Crenshaw, "The Shadow of Death in Qoheleth," in *Israelite Wisdom* (ed. J. G. Gammie; Missoula, Mont.: Scholars Press, 1978) 208. Crenshaw's reading leads him to conclude that "suicide offers a compelling alternative to further living. Its lure would seem irresistible for one who hates life and falls into despair's vice-like grip" (p. 210). The fact that Qoheleth does not reach this conclusion ought in itself to be sufficient warning that his view of death is not even vaguely positive.

Qoheleth 6:7–9

[7] All the toil of a human being is for his mouth, yet [his] appetite is never satisfied. [8] For what advantage does the wise person have over the fool? What advantage has the poor person who knows how to go before the living? [9] What the eyes see is better than wandering desire. This, too, is senseless and an attempt to direct the wind.

Although some readers recognize in Qoh 6:7 a new section largely unrelated to the previous discussion of wealth, toil, and the ability to enjoy the returns of one's labors, it is better to understand this verse as a more comprehensive application of the same principles expressed earlier. Qoheleth is making a sweeping statement regarding the inability of human beings to find satisfaction in anything they desire, a statement that closely parallels the words of 5:9[10], which opened this section, but here the statement is applied more generally than to dissatisfaction with money. Although the language used here by Qoheleth literally relates to hunger (note the use of פה 'mouth', and נפש 'appetite'[149]) it is likely that it should be understood figuratively to refer to any desire rather than just the desire for food.[150]

The relationship of v. 8 both to the immediately preceding verse and to the broader context is considerably more difficult to determine, as is the meaning of the second part of the verse. Fox, for example, understands the verse to be at best parenthetical and at worst a misplaced intrusion into the supposedly more coherent argument that Qoheleth makes if this verse is omitted.[151] The first question posed in v. 8 is in itself straightforward: "for what advantage has the sage over the fool?" The primary difficulty lies in its relationship to the preceding material, which has not mentioned wisdom or folly but has focused on material wealth and deriving enjoyment from toil. The best understanding of the function of this clause is that Qoheleth is continuing to expand the conclusions reached by (1) moving from a desire for wealth to all desire (v. 7) and (2) moving from the acquisition of wealth by toil to the skills that lie behind the ability to accumulate wealth, the skills that are traditionally associated with the wise (v. 8). If the appetite is never sated, what value is there in even possessing the skills? What advantage does a sage have? The answer to Qoheleth's rhetorical question is "none"—for, although the sage may have the skills to feed the appetite, it will nonetheless never be satisfied.

---

149. The word נפש has a particularly broad semantic range that includes 'desire' and 'appetite'. The latter meaning is appropriate both here and in Qoh 6:9. See BDB, 660b.

150. So Fox (*A Time to Tear Down*, 245), who writes that "'Mouth' and 'appetite' ... do not, of course, refer to the hunger for food alone (5:11), but rather to a diffuse yearning for possessions of all sorts. This nagging desire is never assuaged by actual possessions."

151. Ibid.

The second question posed in v. 8 has long presented problems for interpreters.[152] The identity of the עני is not clear, nor is the knowledge that is
theirs. The adjective normally refers to a poor or afflicted person,[153] yet here
this person is placed in opposition to החיים 'the living', an expression that is
almost exclusively used elsewhere in Biblical Hebrew in contrast to those
who are dead.[154] This observation undermines Seow's understanding of the
clause as making the point that the afflicted need to learn to cope with life—
to get on with living—because nowhere else does the definite plural form of
חי refer to life in the sense that Seow understands it here.[155]

Probably the best guide to understanding this second clause is the previous
clause, for there are strong indications that the two are parallel. Both are questions introduced by the interrogative מה 'what'. Both contrast two groups, the
first being introduced in each case by the preposition ל. In light of this, it is
likely that there is an ellipsis of the term יותר between מה and לעני.[156] Understood this way, the second clause, like the first, is questioning the value to the
poor or afflicted of having knowledge about associating with other people;[157]
any advantages that they might have would be subject to the same futility as
the advantages of the wise in the first clause.

Qoheleth closes with a final aphorism and then concludes by again declaring that this is הבל. The aphorism serves to summarize Qoheleth's observations by stating that one is better off being satisfied with what he or she has
(מראה עינים) than yearning for more (מהלך־נפש).[158] Fox limits the meaning of
the expression מראה עינים 'what the eyes see' to "the immediate experience of
pleasure."[159] The expression is elsewhere no more than a reference to vision
(see Lev 13:12; Deut 28:34, 67; Isa 11:3; Ezek 23:16) and is used once more

---

152. The LXX, which generally follows the Hebrew in Qoheleth quite literally, appears
to have difficulties here as well, rendering the second מה in Qoh 6:8 by διότι and the plural
החיים with the singular τῆς ζωῆς.

153. The adjective is not used elsewhere by Qoheleth, although it does appear a number of times in Proverbs (see Prov 3:34; 14:21; 15:15; etc.). When Qoheleth has previously
referred to the poor, in 4:14; 5:7[8], he has used the Qal participle of רוש. Seow (*Ecclesiastes*, 214) notes attempts to interpret עני differently here, but there is little support for these
readings; see also Whitley, *Koheleth*, 59.

154. The term החיים (definite article + m. pl. adjective) appears 15 times in BH. Three
times it refers to 'running water' (Lev 14:6, 51, 52); otherwise, it is only in Qoh 4:15 that
it appears in a context that is not directly contrasting the living and the dead.

155. Seow, *Ecclesiastes*, 214.

156. See Longman, *The Book of Ecclesiastes*, 173.

157. Fox suggests that the reference may be to leading other people; see *A Time to Tear
Down*, 245–46.

158. See the discussion of the meaning of נפש above in n. 149.

159. Fox, *A Time to Tear Down*, 246.

by Qoheleth in 11:9. In Isa 11:3, מראה עינים is contrasted with צדק 'righteous' as a basis for passing judgment. The context here, however, suggests that Qo-heleth's focus is not on heightening the value of what is experienced in the present but on undermining the value (or highlighting the valuelessness) of what one might long for but have no guarantee of achieving.

This aptly brings Qoheleth's discussions in this section to a close, for he has previously stated that desire is never satisfied (Qoh 5:9[10]; 6:7) and that the ability to be satisfied with what one has is good and is a gift from God (5:17–19[18–20]; 6:3). This insatiability of desire has been the theme of this entire section and is here the subject of the closing הבל declaration in v. 9.

Thus, we see that Qoheleth's observations and conclusions in 5:9[10]–6:9 consistently stand at odds with normative doctrine in the remainder of the He-brew Bible. In this section, he states that there is no value in wealth and ques-tions the value of wisdom. He ascribes evil acts to God, and he questions God's justice. Thus, the reader familiar with and committed to the orthodox teaching expressed in the Hebrew Scriptures would find these honest revela-tions of this exponent of the wisdom movement deeply troubling and thus be inclined to accept the epilogist's advice to be wary of the sages' words.

Qoheleth 6:10–12

[10] Whatever happens has already been designated, and what a person is [now] was [already] known. He cannot dispute with one who is stronger than him. [11] If many words increase senselessness, what is the advantage for the person [who speaks them]? [12] For who knows what is good for a person in his life—the few years of his senseless life? He will live them like a shadow, because who can tell a person what will happen after him under the sun?

These verses mark the middle of the book and introduce themes that, although anticipated in earlier passages, are expanded upon throughout the remainder of the work. As such, they function as a transition between the previous sec-tion (and, more broadly, the entire first half of the book), where Qoheleth's thoughts have been dominated by themes such as death and the senselessness of the world, which confounds any attempt to comprehend it (thus, undermin-ing the very task of the sages), and the subsequent section, which records a series of "better"-proverbs.[160]

Qoheleth's fundamental belief in determinism is reaffirmed in v. 10, where it is appropriate to infer that God is the subject of the two Niphal forms of ידע 'know' because the subsequent reference to one who is stronger than a human being is almost certainly a reference to God. The first clause asserts that God

---

160. Ibid., 247.

has predetermined everything that is happening in the present,[161] this being expressed in the idea that God (as unstated subject) has "named" these events. Naming denotes knowledge of and familiarity with something, an awareness of its characteristics, and, frequently, control over what is being named.[162] Here it is God who has ordered current events and, consequently, there is nothing a human being can do about the way the world is.

Verse 11 literally asserts that there are many words that increase הבל 'meaninglessness' (suggesting that not *all* words increase הבל).[163] Many modern translations opt for a broader meaning, wherein the focus falls not on particular words but on the volume of words.[164] However, both these readings present difficulties, divorcing the words from the context and thus making little sense or contribution to the meaning of the text.

The best way to account for Qoheleth's reference to 'many words' in the present context is to follow Fox and understand the entire verse as a conditional sentence: "if there are many words, הבל is multiplied."[165] This ties the verse to the preceding clause's reference to a dispute, for there it had been made clear that entering into a dispute with God is futile; those words are wasted and thus senseless. They offer no advantage, as Qoheleth states, to the person who proffers them. Furthermore, Qoheleth's repetition of אדם in vv. 10 and 11 serves to tie these verses together.

In v. 12, Qoheleth returns to examine what is good by posing two rhetorical questions: "who knows what is good for a person?" and "who can tell a person what will happen after him?" These questions must be answered negatively: no one knows what is good during a person's life, and no one knows what will come after him or her. In view again are the transience and senselessness of life, the meaning of which is nullified by death, and the inability of anyone to control what will ultimately become of his or her legacy.

---

161. It is preferable to understand מה־שהיה more broadly than merely 'what exists' and to translate it in present tense rather than past tense. For discussion, see Seow, *Ecclesiastes*, 230.

162. For a discussion on the significance of naming in the Hebrew Bible, see my *Man and Woman in Genesis 1–3* (M.Th. thesis, Sydney College of Divinity, 1995) chap. 4; G. W. Ramsey, "Is Name-Giving an Act of Dominion in Genesis 2–3 and Elsewhere?" *CBQ* 50 (1988) 24–35.

163. See Seow, *Ecclesiastes*, 233. Longman's translation, "for there are many words that increase meaninglessness," reflects this literal reading, but his comments on the subsequent page reflect an understanding more in line with mine; see Longman, *The Book of Ecclesiastes*, 176–77.

164. For example, "the more words, the more vanity" in the NRSV. See also the NIV.

165. Fox, *A Time to Tear Down*, 248. Although Fox calls this an unmarked question, כי can have a conditional force (e.g., Gen 4:24; Exod 12:48; Lev 4:2).

Qoheleth's assertion here that no one knows what is good further serves to undermine the wisdom movement. Determining what was good for a person was a fundamental concern of the sages, a concern readily expressed in the material found in most wisdom collections from the ancient Near East, including Proverbs.[166] Qoheleth's declaration that no one knows what is good for a person explicitly undermines the *raison d'être* for the wisdom movement and ultimately serves to substantiate the claim that the epilogist is aiming to warn prospective sages against involvement with the movement.

Qoheleth 7:1–12

[1] As a good reputation is better than fine lotion,
    so the day of [one's] death [is better] than the day of one's birth.
[2] It is better to go to the house of mourning
        than to the house of feasting,
        because it is the end of all people, and the living should take [it] to heart.
[3] Irritation is better than laughter,
        because a scowl is good for the heart.
[4] The heart of the wise people is in the house of mourning,
        but the heart of fools is in the house of pleasure.
[5] It is better to listen to the rebuke of a wise person
        than to listen to the song of fools.
[6] For like the sound of thorns [burning] under a pot,
        so is the laughter of fools.
        This, too, is senseless.
[7] For extortion can render a wise person foolish,
        and a bribe corrupts the heart.
[8] The end of a matter is better than its beginning;
        patience is better than pride.
[9] Do not let yourself be quickly angered,
        for anger resides in the lap of fools.
[10] Do not ask, "Why is it that the former days were better than these?"
        For it is not out of wisdom that you would ask about this.
[11] Wisdom is good with an inheritance,
        and a benefit to those who see the sun.

---

166. Zimmerli felt that the question about what is good for a person reflected the fundamental concern of Israelite wisdom (Walther Zimmerli, "Zur Struktur der alttestamentlichen Weisheit," *ZAW* 51 [1933] 177–204; cf. Crenshaw, *Ecclesiastes*, 131). Qoheleth has here tied this question closely to the issue of advantage, with which he opened his work (Qoh 1:3; cf. 7:11 and discussion above, p. 122), which Ogden argued was the fundamental concern of the wisdom movement. Ultimately, there is little difference between the two points, and for Qoheleth the answers to both questions undermine the wisdom movement; he finds no advantage in toil and no one who knows what is good.

¹² For the shadow of wisdom is like the shadow of money,
>   but the advantage of the knowledge of wisdom is that it preserves the
>   life of its possessors.

Surprisingly, Qoheleth's despair at not being able to determine what is good in life leads directly into a series of "better"-proverbs that make a number of assertions about what is good (or, at least, which is the better of two alternatives). Furthermore, not only do a number of the statements made by Qoheleth sound thoroughly orthodox, they seem to contradict the position that he has taken elsewhere. This is particularly true of v. 12 which appears to assert that wisdom guarantees long life.

This section opens extolling the virtues of a 'good name' (טוב שם), a sentiment reflected in Prov 22:1. The typical form adopted for aphoristic proverbs such as this and the sayings common in the book of Proverbs conditions the reader to anticipate some form of parallel observation in the second line. Although Qoheleth obliges by adhering to this form, it is the content of the parallel assertion that is surprising, even shocking, to the audience. Qoheleth's statement that the day of death is better than the day of birth is unparalleled in Hebrew Wisdom Literature—even in Job.[167] This radical inversion from an apparently typical wisdom theme to an affirmation of death, sorrow, and mourning heightens the potential discomfort and offense of Qoheleth's words.

The nature of the link between the two halves of this proverb is unclear. Robert Gordis suggests that "a man's reputation is subject to decline throughout his life, so that only after he is dead is his 'name' secure."[168] Qoheleth's statement, however, carries this notion to an extreme by concluding that the day of death is better than the day of birth. Seow argues that Qoheleth's intent is to demonstrate the absurdity of the initial statement by taking it to this extreme.[169] However, Qoheleth proceeds to reinforce this assertion in the sub-

---

167. Sir 41:11–13 is reminiscent of Qoheleth's words, and may well have been inspired by them:

The human body is a fleeting thing,
>   but a virtuous name will never be blotted out.
Have regard for your name,
>   because it will outlive you
>   longer than a thousand hoards of gold.
The days of a good life are numbered,
>   but a good name lasts forever. [NRSV]

Seow goes so far as to note that, "unlike the first *ṭôb-saying* about one's name (v 1a), the second saying is without parallel anywhere in the wisdom literature of the ancient Near East" (Seow, *Ecclesiastes*, 244).

168. Gordis, *Koheleth: The Man and His World*, 266–67. This interpretation may also be reflected in Sir 11:28.

169. Seow, *Ecclesiastes*, 245.

sequent verses, stating that mourning and sorrow are better than feasting and laughter (vv. 2–4). This indicates that Qoheleth is not merely seeking to undermine the credibility of the orthodox saying with which he began by demonstrating that it produces an absurd result when pushed to its logical conclusion; he is actually affirming the logical extreme to which the saying can be taken. For the reader and the epilogist, however, the effect of Qoheleth's logic is only to emphasize the fact that the wisdom movement could provide no positive answers to the problems of life and thus lacked any compelling value to the community or individual.

Having noted that the wise prefer mourning to mirth, Qoheleth proceeds to make some observations on the benefits of wisdom. Qoheleth has previously discussed wisdom and folly in chap. 2, there concluding that while there is some advantage to being wise the advantage is undermined by the common fate shared by both sage and fool.[170] Here Qoheleth also notes benefits to wisdom, most notably in v. 12, where he states that wisdom preserves the life of its master. However, Qoheleth's praise of wisdom is again qualified.

This qualification arises out of Qoheleth's observation that continued possession of wisdom is not guaranteed, a point made explicitly in v. 7: "for extortion can render a wise person foolish."[171] For this reason, Qoheleth can again announce that even the apparent benefits of wisdom in vv. 1–6 are ultimately הבל (7:6), for any advantage the wise person may have is fragile and readily undone.[172] Indeed, the merits of wisdom are further called into question in the subsequent sections—in 7:13–14 the amount of knowledge available to the sage is constrained by the actions of God, and in 7:15–18 the reliability of wisdom as a guarantee of a good life is disputed.

Verses 8–12 again denigrate folly and extol wisdom, ultimately stating that wisdom has the advantage because it preserves the life of its master (7:12). It is this conclusion by Qoheleth that is perhaps the most surprising, given the

---

170. Refer to the discussion on p. 133.

171. The term עשק appears in Qoh 4:1 and 5:7[8] with the more general meaning 'oppression'. However, there are instances of עשק in BH in which the more specific meaning 'extortion' appears to be intended (such as Lev 5:23[6:4]; Ps 62:11[10]), a meaning that is preferable here in light of the second line of the aphorism.

172. Some writers have raised questions about the integrity and structure of these verses, considering that the הבל statement often concludes an argument in Qoheleth, whereas here the discussion continues into the next verse. However, the best understanding of the text is to see the particle כי at the beginning of v. 7 as indicating that this verse is indeed an explanation for the הבל statement, precisely in the same way that this particle is used in the beginning of v. 6. Thus the הבל statement is connected to what has preceded it but is further elucidated by Qoheleth's subsequent comments. For a more complete discussion, see Seow, *Ecclesiastes*, 237.

consistency with which Qoheleth has qualified all his statements regarding any advantage in life. This verse warrants more detailed attention.

The first clause of v. 12 appears to equate wisdom with money. The key to this clause is the meaning of the expression בצל 'in the shadow of'. This expression usually refers to the shelter or the protection that is offered by whatever is casting the shadow.[173] Seow suggests that the preposition ב should be understood as *bet essentiae*, and צל 'shadow' should be understood as it is elsewhere in Qoheleth's words (see Qoh 6:12; 8:13), so that "one should understand him to emphasize not the protective power of wisdom and money, but their unreliability. If anyone should think of these things as a permanent shelter, then they must learn that wisdom and wealth can only provide a shade—like a shadow. They are not a lasting shelter. . . . They provide no permanent protection."[174] Although this is an attractive interpretation, it is unlikely. Elsewhere, Qoheleth has used the expression כצל when proclaiming something is like a shadow in that it is fleeting and ephemeral (see Qoh 6:12; 8:13), and in those instances צל cannot be read as *regens* in a construct.[175] Here he uses the preposition ב, and offers a *rectum* to the *regens* צל; thus, the form here corresponds to statements elsewhere about protection and shelter. Perhaps the most that could be said is that, by using a term that has had such negative connotations elsewhere in his work, Qoheleth is injecting this phrase with a degree of ambiguity.

The ancient versions do testify to some confusion over the prepositions in this verse. Some attest to reading כצל in both instances (compare the Vulgate, Symmachus, and the Peshitta), while the LXX appears to have read בצל in the first occurrence and כצל in the second. Retaining the MT presents some difficulties, for even reading two instances of *bet essentiae*, the reader must infer a great deal to arrive at a viable meaning. Whereas the versions opt for a slightly smoother simile, the MT presents a rougher but more emphatic metaphor, in which the shadow of wisdom *is* the shadow of wealth. The fact that the MT proceeds to highlight a difference suggests that emending the second בצל to כצל is probably warranted.

Qoheleth closes the comparison between wealth and wisdom by announcing that wisdom has an advantage over wealth:[176] it preserves the life of its

---

173. The word בצל occurs elsewhere in the Hebrew Bible 21 times and has the meaning of 'shelter, protection' in Gen 19:8; Judg 9:15; Isa 30:2, 3; 34:15; etc.

174. Seow, *Ecclesiastes*, 250. See also Zimmerli (cf. Crenshaw, *Ecclesiastes*, 138–39).

175. The LXX renders both בצל and כצל by ἐν σκιᾷ in Ecclesiastes. While this could be interpreted as support for reading כצל in 7:12, it should be noted that כצל is only rendered this way in the LXX of Ecclesiastes; elsewhere, other prepositions are used.

176. It appears best to understand דעת and חכמה as essentially synonymous; see Longman, *The Book of Ecclesiastes*, 191.

owner. Although this appears to be quite in keeping with the teachings of other wisdom traditions, there is a danger in divorcing these words too quickly from Qoheleth's observations and conclusions elsewhere. There is no warrant for extracting this statement from Qoheleth's words and using it to argue that he unequivocally endorses the value of wisdom. Seow recognizes the impact that the broader context has when he writes: "The point is not that wisdom assures life, or is life-giving. . . . Qohelet does not mean that wisdom's advantage is its life-generating power. He means that wisdom allows one to live. . . . It allows one the possibility of survival. It helps one cope. Wisdom, for Qohelet, affords one no permanence, it gives one no control over life itself."[177] Qoheleth qualifies wisdom again in his assessment of the availability of life-preserving knowledge and in his subsequent reminder that wisdom may be lost and the sage may become a fool. Although Qoheleth may concede here that wisdom preserves the life of its possessor, he immediately proceeds to state in 7:14 and 8:17 that the knowledge actually available to a sage is quite limited. He later adds that the possession of wisdom itself is fragile and easily lost (see Qoh 9:17–10:1). Nonetheless, here in 7:12 Qoheleth does acknowledge that there is some value in wisdom.

For the reader of Ecclesiastes, it is difficult to see how Qoheleth's affirmation of wisdom here provides much comfort or encouragement. Wisdom has repeatedly led Qoheleth to reach conclusions that are thoroughly contrary to the teaching of the remainder of the Hebrew Bible. Although wisdom may help one to live, it does not guarantee a good life or a profitable one. Rather, it seems to provide only a life distant from God and his commands, a senseless existence in a senseless world. Qoheleth may affirm wisdom, but the epilogist has chosen Qoheleth's words well, for the reader would not want to follow where Qoheleth's wisdom leads.

Qoheleth 7:13–14

[13] Consider the work of God, for who is able to straighten what he has made crooked? [14] On a good day, enjoy it, but on a bad day, consider: God has made one as well as the other, and concerning this a human being cannot discover anything that will come after him.

Qoheleth now turns his attention to God and his work. Once again, Qoheleth holds up the work of an omnipotent but mysterious deity whose actions deliberately impede and constrain the scope of human knowledge, thus limiting the wisdom of the sages (compare 3:18–21). Qoheleth's opening words here, that God is responsible for making things 'crooked' (עות), once again stand in

---

177. Seow, *Ecclesiastes*, 250.

stark contrast to conventional wisdom as expressed by Bildad in Job 8:3:
"Does God pervert (עות) justice? / Or does Shaddai pervert (עות) what is
right?"[178] Qoheleth's words highlight the powerlessness of human beings in
the face of a God who has indeed made things crooked, who has made both
the good times and the bad (v. 14), and before whom human beings are powerless to alter the course of their lives. Qoheleth does not counsel that when
times are bad certain actions can bring about a reversal of fortunes or earn
God's favor. Rather, he merely exhorts his audience to remember that God is
responsible for both good and bad.

Finally, it is this crookedness in the world that results in the inability of
mortals to understand what will happen. For Qoheleth, these limits on human
knowledge undermine the value of wisdom, for the limited wisdom that is
available to human beings cannot ultimately improve the life of a sage; for
him, good and bad still come from the hand of God. He must still live in a
world that God has perverted and that no human endeavor can rectify. Consequently, הבל is inescapably part of this world.

For the reader of Ecclesiastes, however, these words further undermine the
integrity of the wisdom movement. In addition to the troubling assertion that
God has made things irredeemably crooked, Qoheleth's insistence that human
wisdom cannot alter one's fortunes before an omnipotent God again enhances
the epilogist's argument that the wisdom movement has nothing to offer and
ought to be shunned in favor of the religious observation of God's commands.

Qoheleth 7:15–8:1

The remainder of chap. 7 focuses on the consequences of the limitations of
human knowledge and the resulting unpredictability of God's response to human actions.

Qoheleth 7:15–24

> [15] I have seen both of these things in my senseless days: there is a righteous
> person who perishes in his righteousness, and there is a wicked person who
> lives long in his evil. [16] Do not be overly righteous and do not be extra wise—
> why ruin yourself? [17] Do not be overly wicked, and do not be a fool—why
> die before your time? [18] It is good that you grasp one without releasing the
> other, for the one who fears God goes forth with both of them.

---

178. See also Elihu's words in Job 34:12. Crenshaw notes that Qoheleth's view of the
universe also differs from that of later Israelite sages: "This attitude to the order of nature
and human society differs sharply from later claims that a harmonious universe encourages
virtue, a view that surfaces in Sirach and Wisdom of Solomon" (Crenshaw, *Ecclesiastes*,
139). Aside from its use in Isa 50:4, עות always carries a strongly negative connotation (see
Amos 8:5; Ps 119:78; Job 19:6; Lam 3:36).

[19] Wisdom helps the wise more than ten rulers in the city.

[20] Indeed, there is no person who is righteous on earth, who [always] does good and never sins. [21] Furthermore, do not take to heart all the things they say lest you hear your servant cursing you, [22] for your heart knows that you, too, have cursed others many times.

[23] All this I tested with wisdom. I said, "I will become wise"—but it is far from me. [24] Whatever happens is far off and very deep—who can discover it?

In Qoh 7:15–24, Qoheleth elaborates on the limitation of human knowledge introduced at the close of the previous section. The first verses are an exhortation to moderation unparalleled elsewhere in the Hebrew Bible. The rationale behind Qoheleth's warning against being 'overly righteous' (צדיק הרבה), 'extra wise' (תתחכם יותר), 'overly wicked' (תרשע הרבה), or a 'fool' (סכל) in vv. 16–17 is stated in v. 15: sometimes the wicked prosper and the righteous suffer. Although Qoheleth unequivocally advises against folly, it is his failure to similarly disavow wickedness in favor of an unqualified affirmation of righteousness that sets him apart from the remainder of biblical literature and further diminishes the reputation of the wisdom movement for the audience.

Whybray has argued that Qoheleth's warning here is not against excessive righteousness but against self-righteousness.[179] However, there are problems with this argument. First, it fails to account adequately for the fact that prompted this warning, which is that Qoheleth has seen an inversion of justice wherein the righteous perish and the wicked enjoy long life (see v. 15). If v. 15 refers to self-righteousness, then the succeeding observation that sometimes the wicked prosper is a non sequitor. Second, Whybray's claim that the Hithpael תתחכם in v. 16 may indicate pretense when used here in reference to being wise is unlikely, given the fact that it is not used in this manner anywhere else in BH.[180] Third, the subsequent warning against excessive wickedness clearly parallels this warning about being overly righteous. However, it cannot easily be qualified as a specific form of wickedness, and this parallel fact further supports our case against qualifying righteousness. The claim that Qoheleth here refers to "self-righteousness" cannot be sustained, and we are

179. Whybray, *Ecclesiastes* (NCB), 120–21; cf. Eaton, *Ecclesiastes*, 114; R. J. Kidwell, "Ecclesiastes," in *Ecclesiastes and the Song of Solomon* (ed. R. J. Kidwell and D. DeWelt; Joplin, Mo.: College Press, 1977) 174–75; Hubbard, *Ecclesiastes, Song of Solomon*, 170; W. C. Kaiser, *Ecclesiastes: Total Life* (Chicago: Moody, 1979) 85–86; George R. Castellino, "Qohelet and His Wisdom," in *Reflecting with Solomon: Selected Studies on the Book of Ecclesiastes* (ed. Roy B. Zuck; Grand Rapids: Baker, 1994) 39–40.

180. See Seow, *Ecclesiastes*, 267; Wayne A. Brindle, "Righteousness and Wickedness in Ecclesiastes 7:15–18," in *Reflecting with Solomon: Selected Studies on the Book of Ecclesiastes* (ed. Roy B. Zuck; Grand Rapids: Baker, 1994) 310–11.

left with the clear but disturbing warning by Qoheleth against strenuously seeking to be righteous.

Qoheleth's declaration that excessive wickedness should be avoided has also troubled commentators because it appears that Qoheleth is approving of wickedness in moderation. Thus Eaton, for example, argues that the inclusion of the term הרבה in reference to wickedness functions primarily to preserve the parallelism with the previous stich.[181] However, Qoheleth's failure to qualify the term סכל 'fool' in order to preserve the parallelism with תתחכם יותר in v. 16 undermines the argument, for it indicates his readiness to violate strict parallelism when it serves his purpose. The fact that sometimes the wicked prosper, as Qoheleth has repeatedly observed (most recently in v. 15), serves as justification for his point that, so far as personal gain is concerned, it is impossible to say that wickedness must be shunned absolutely.

Qoheleth's point here follows logically from the fact that human beings cannot know what the future holds (7:14), and observation shows that sometimes the righteous perish while the wicked live long lives. Thus it is impossible for anyone to know what the ultimate outcome of his or her behavior will be, and so Qoheleth can only offer a rather agnostic, and certainly very unorthodox, piece of advice. In contemporary parlance, one might offer advice such as "hedge your bets" or "don't put all your eggs in one basket."

The final clause of v. 18 makes reference to the one who fears God. Although modern readers are generally conditioned by the use of this phrase in Proverbs and elsewhere to infer that Qoheleth is introducing a note of piety here, the immediate context makes it clear that such a reading is inappropriate. For Qoheleth, the one who fears God is the one who manages to balance righteousness and wickedness, wisdom and folly and who will have the best chance of preserving his or her life. This fear is not reverence that leads to piety but the dread of the person who acknowledges that there is no reliable means of determining how God will act in a given situation.[182]

Verses 19–22 serve to offer further comment on the themes of wisdom and righteousness raised in the preceding section. The appearance of the verb עזז 'to be strong' in the MT of v. 19 presents a few difficulties, for the transitive meaning ('make strong') adopted by most scholars to make sense of this text is problematic, as is the use of the preposition on the object ('to the wise').[183]

---

181. Eaton, *Ecclesiastes*, 114.

182. See J. Jarick, *Gregory Thaumaturgos' Paraphrase of Ecclesiastes* (SBLSCS 29; Atlanta: Scholars Press, 1990) 178.

183. In support of the transitive meaning for עזז, both Ps 68:29[28] and Prov 8:28 are cited. The understanding of עזז in these passages is not entirely clear, however (see Seow, *Ecclesiastes*, 256). Furthermore, עזז is only used with a subsequent preposition in Ps 52:9[7] (with ב 'in'), nowhere with ל 'to'.

Consequently, it is preferable to follow the reading of 4QQoh[a] and several Hebrew manuscripts of תעזר (from עזר 'to help'), a reading also supported by the LXX, which renders the verb βοηθήσει.[184] The verb עזר is frequently followed by the preposition ל to indicate what is being helped, so it fits well here.

Thus this section begins with an assertion regarding the great value of wisdom: it gives the sage more help than ten rulers in a city. Taken in isolation, this saying could be understood to be an unequivocal affirmation of wisdom—that is, of course, assuming that ten rulers lend more aid to a city than one ruler would (a point that could be disputed on historical grounds) and assuming that Qoheleth is not actually saying that wisdom is of more benefit to the sage than ten rulers in a city are of benefit to him. The fact that these words permit such diverse possibilities ought to warn us not to reach conclusions too quickly and not to jump to conclusions that rely unduly on modern inferences.

Read in context, any interpretation of these words as an affirmation of wisdom must be qualified. Wisdom may strengthen the wise, but Qoheleth has already made it clear that wisdom may be lost (7:7), and he proceeds to state that the wisdom he sought was ultimately unattainable (7:23–24). Indeed, some commentators regard v. 19 as a quotation that Qoheleth subsequently undermines.[185] Whether this is true or not, clearly Qoheleth's claims about wisdom cannot be reduced to the positive affirmation that this verse taken in isolation may appear to be advancing.

Verses 20–22 move from wisdom to righteousness. Qoheleth states his argument—that perfect righteousness is unattainable—in v. 20 and follows this with an illustration to justify his position in vv. 21–22.[186] Qoheleth's point, that one should choose to ignore some of what is said by others (v. 21) because no one is without sin (v. 22; cf. v. 20), applies the warning not to be too

---

184. See Fox, *A Time to Tear Down*, 257.

185. See Gordis, *Koheleth: The Man and His World*, 278. Although Seow does not describe the verse as a quotation, he does argue that it is used by Qoheleth as an example of overvaluing wisdom, against which he has commented already in vv. 15–18: "Qohelet's purpose is not to praise wisdom. Qohelet is not extolling the virtue of wisdom himself. Rather, he is illustrating the kind of overconfidence against which he warns in v. 16" (Seow, *Ecclesiastes*, 268–69).

186. Ogden disputes the link between vv. 19–20 as a statement of principle, and vv. 21–22, as an illustration, because vv. 21–22 do not address the theme of wisdom (Ogden, *Qoheleth*, 117). Ogden's objection rests on the structural disjunction he imposes between vv. 15–18 and 19–24. However, there are strong thematic ties between these sections that support the reading. Those who endorse the link between vv. 20 and 21–22 include Lauha, *Kohelet*, 135; W. Zimmerli, *Das Buch des Predigers Salomo* (ATD 16; 2nd ed.; Göttingen: Vandenhoeck & Ruprecht, 1967) 211; Longman, *The Book of Ecclesiastes*, 199.

righteous (v. 16) to a specific situation. This ties all of his words on righteousness neatly together.

The thematic alternation between wisdom and righteousness continues as Qoheleth returns to the theme of wisdom in vv. 23–24. The precise relationship of these words to what precedes them and what follows them has been disputed,[187] but they are clearly tied to the preceding material by their focus on wisdom. The words themselves announce the unattainability of wisdom: despite Qoheleth's desire to be wise, the wisdom he sought eluded him. This is not to say that he possessed no wisdom at all but that the wisdom he sought—wisdom that would undo the הבל that he found wherever he looked—was beyond his reach. Furthermore, he is not asserting that this inability is merely a personal shortcoming that perhaps other people could overcome. Qoheleth makes it clear that the wisdom he desired was deliberately concealed from him by God himself.

Qoheleth's words here function to diminish further any merit the epilogist's audience may have assigned to the wisdom movement by reinforcing the limitations of wisdom and its incompatibility with the religion of the Hebrew Bible.

Qoheleth 7:25–29

> [25] My heart and I turned to understand, to explore, and to seek wisdom and a solution, and to know that evil is folly and folly is irrational. [26] I found that more bitter than death is the woman who is a snare; her heart is a trap, her hands are fetters. Whoever is pleasing to God will escape from her, but a sinner will be captured by her.
>
> [27] "See this I have found," said Qoheleth, "[working] piece by piece to find a solution—[28] which I am still seeking. I could not find one man among a thousand, nor could I find a woman among them all. [29] Indeed, I found only this: God made human beings upright, but they seek many schemes."

The remainder of chap. 7 is notoriously difficult. As a unit, it is tied together by repeated combinations of seeking (בקש) and finding (מצא).[188] The opening verb, סבב ('turn'), marks a new turn in Qoheleth's discussion.[189] The text itself

---

187. Longman treats vv. 23–24 as a separate subsection but acknowledges their links to the surrounding material (ibid.). Whybray includes them with the following material (Whybray, *Ecclesiastes* [NCB], 123). Gordis ties them to the preceding material (Gordis, *Koheleth: The Man and His World*, 280–82).

188. The verbs appear in sequence in vv. 25–26 and 28–29. Elsewhere, they are combined by Qoheleth only in 8:17 and, in a different form, by the epilogist in 12:10.

189. Ogden interprets v. 25 as suggesting that Qoheleth "gave up wanting to know wisdom in order to devote himself to the study of evil and folly" (Ogden, *Qoheleth*, 119). It is

is both difficult and confusing—vv. 27–29 in particular—as Qoheleth vacil-lates between finding and not finding, and stating that he could not find some-thing, although he did find something. However, what is most troubling—at least for modern readers—is Qoheleth's apparently misogynistic remarks in vv. 26 and 28.[190]

It is initially surprising that Qoheleth should now state that he is seeking wisdom, after previously stating that the wisdom he sought was unattainable. The strength of this apparent contradiction is ameliorated somewhat by the assertion that this new direction of investigation lay within a specific realm: "to know wickedness to be folly and foolishness to be irrational." In spite of this, Qoheleth's discoveries—or rather failure to make discoveries—do ulti-mately reinforce the previous conclusion about wisdom's elusiveness.

From this introductory statement describing his task, Qoheleth immedi-ately turns to the description of a particular type of woman. That the referent is not *all* women is made clear by the singular noun אשה, by the presence of the definite article, and by the restrictive phrase following the relative par-ticle—the referent is restricted to *the* woman who is a snare, whose heart is a trap, and whose hands are fetters.[191] The presence of the definite article on האשה cannot, however, be reliably construed as evidence that Qoheleth has in mind a specific individual (whether real or metaphorical), for similar con-structions elsewhere unequivocally specify groups of individuals.[192] Long-man objects that a reading of this verse that restricts the reference to only some women cannot be reconciled with v. 28, where no woman is found among many.[193] However, v. 28 is itself beset with difficulties and even if it is asserting that there were no good women in Qoheleth's experience, this would not mean that they were all "more bitter than death."

How do we understand the expression מר ממות 'more bitter than death'? The masculine adjective modifying 'woman' is surprising but not unprece-dented.[194] Of greater semantic significance is the suggestion of Dahood and

---

not clear how he arrives at this reading, because the text clearly states that Qoheleth was 'seeking wisdom' (ובקש חכמה).

190. Fox writes, "Despite the valiant efforts of some exegetes, this passage remains ir-reparably misogynistic" (*A Time to Tear Down*, 266).

191. The Hebrew has plurals for מצודים 'snares' and חרמים 'traps' that are explained by Seow as plurals of complexity (*Ecclesiastes*, 263).

192. See Ps 1:1; 40:5[4]; 94:12; 127:5. This is, of course, not to say that the presence of the article excludes the possibility that a specific individual is in view.

193. Longman, *The Book of Ecclesiastes*, 204; Fox, *A Time to Tear Down*, 268–69. Fur-thermore, the grammatical points noted above indicate a restricted referent in this context.

194. See Exod 17:12. The word order may also have been significant, since the mascu-line noun מות 'death' follows the adjective.

others that מר should be given the meaning 'be strong' as attested for the root *mrr* in Aramaic, Ugaritic, and Arabic.[195] However, Seow has effectively demonstrated that the usual understanding of מר as 'bitter' fits best in this context.[196]

Who, then, is this woman? The fact that Qoheleth is discussing a woman or women at all at this point, following the introduction in v. 25, is surprising. It is not at all clear how any woman or women could somehow function to prove that evil is folly and foolishness is madness, as set out in v. 25. The alternative is that אשה here serves as a metaphor, an option that has been adopted by a few commentators. Ogden, for example, argues for a meaning of 'untimely death' based on the association made in Qoh 9:12 between a snare and mortality.[197] This suggestion, however, faces too many difficulties to be viable. First, unlocking the metaphor depends on a discussion that has not yet taken place in the book. The meaning would not be apparent to the reader until *after* reading chap. 9, and even then there is no clear explanation of the metaphor here in 7:26—merely some vaguely parallel language. Second, as Ogden himself admits, 7:28–29 does not make sense if the metaphor of untimely death is carried throughout the passage.

Seow offers a more reasonable explanation for the metaphor by associating האשה 'the woman' with הסכלות 'folly' in the previous verse—the only noun there that is also marked by the article.[198] Seow also notes that this is the interpretation of the early Greek translators of this text. In spite of the appeal of this interpretation, v. 28 remains problematic, a difficulty that Seow overcomes by arguing that the difficult portion is a later insertion.

Ultimately, the best understanding of this passage must arise out of a decision about (a) whether the reference to women is so out of place that it must be read metaphorically and, consequently, that v. 28b must be emended or expunged; or (b) whether the abrupt and surprising introduction of women following the stated task of v. 25 makes best sense of the text. Clearly, the metaphorical interpretation makes good sense of the relationship between vv. 25 and 26, but the lack of manuscript support among the versions for excising v. 28b means that we depend heavily on our understanding of Qoheleth's logic here to justify the excision. However, as will become clear below, v. 28 can be understood within the context of v. 25, so the case for a

---

195. See M. Dahood, "The Phoenician Background of Qoheleth," *Bib* 47 (1966) 275–76.
196. See Seow, *Ecclesiastes*, 261–62.
197. Ogden, *Qoheleth*, 120–21.
198. Seow, *Ecclesiastes*, 271–72.

metaphorical reading of these verses is weakened. Thus, it is best to understand Qoheleth to be speaking of a group or category of real women.[199]

Note Qoheleth's view of God that is revealed by the conclusion to v. 26: it is not the one who escapes this woman who is found to be pleasing to God but the reverse. The one who is pleasing to God will escape the woman, while the "sinner" will be ensnared by her. This subtle wording reinforces Qoheleth's conclusion that human beings are not masters of their own destiny, no matter how wise they may be. It is clear that Qoheleth has no idea how to find God's favor, yet a favorable outcome in life is here entirely contingent upon finding favor with God. As such, the task of the sages is undermined by God's apparent unwillingness to conform to their rules, and the value of wisdom, at least the wisdom of Qoheleth and his contemporaries, is undermined.

Attempts to interpret the final three verses of chap. 7 have been confounded by the failure of Qoheleth to explicate precisely what it is he was searching for among the thousand in v. 28. The most common interpretation is to infer, based on the use of the adjective ישר 'upright' in v. 29, that Qoheleth was seeking an upright person (finding that among men an upright person is rare, but among women an upright person cannot be found at all).[200] Although this apparent misogyny frequently offends modern readers, on one level it may be appropriate to retain something offensive within Qoheleth's words. If my argument is valid that Qoheleth's words were specifically chosen to offend and in offending to deter the original audience from becoming aligned with the wisdom movement, then there may be value in preserving something that is offensive to the modern reader of the work. These words could then function in the modern context as a clear reminder that Qoheleth's words were not chosen in order to sit comfortably with the audience.

There are some difficulties with the common interpretation outlined above, however. Aside from the fact that the misogyny it attributes to Qoheleth offends many modern readers, Qoheleth proceeds in v. 29 to report the *only* thing that he has found. If he has found *only* what is revealed in v. 29, it makes little sense for him to state in v. 26 that he had already found something else. Furthermore, Qoheleth recently noted that there were none who always do good (7:20) and will proceed to imply in v. 29 that men (אדם, the same term used in v. 28 in contrast to אשה 'women') have strayed from God's initial creation of

---

199. This is in keeping with other passages within the Wisdom Literature in which women are disparaged; see, for example, Prov 7:5–27.

200. For example, see C. D. Ginsburg, *The Song of Songs and Coheleth* (New York: KTAV, 1970) 388–89; Gordis, *Koheleth: The Man and His World* 284–85; Longman, *The Book of Ecclesiastes*, 206–7.

them as upright. Why would he be suggesting now in vv. 27–28 that occasionally there is a man who can be considered upright?

One solution to these difficulties is to read the relative particle that opens v. 28 ('which') as having as an antecedent the statement about having found one man but no woman. This relegates the offensive portion of the verse to the level of an aphorism that Qoheleth sought, unsuccessfully, to verify.[201] The beauty of this reading is that it makes sense of the text as it stands, and it overcomes the confusion introduced by the interpretation described above. Against it is the fact that this use of אשר ('which') is both unusual and unexpected.

Another solution is to emend the text and delete the second of the three occurrences of מצאתי ('I found') in v. 28 as a possible dittography, perhaps motivated by a desire to assuage Qoheleth's emphatic statement. The opening clause of v. 28 is then associated with the preceding material by the relative אשר, so that Qoheleth asserts that he has discovered one thing during his unsuccessful search for חשבון 'a solution'. Before revealing what he has found, he notes what he has not found: he has not found one man among a thousand, nor a woman among them all. The Hebrew of the last part of v. 28 would read thus: ולא מצאתי אדם אחד מאלף ואשה בכל אלה לא מצאתי. This reading then overcomes the contextual problems facing the traditional reading, for the conclusion of v. 29, which contrasts the way that God made people with their subsequent actions in seeking out many חשבנות 'schemes', is reinforced by the observations of v. 28, rather than being contradicted by them. The obvious difficulty for this reading is the lack of any manuscript support for excising the second מצאתי.

On balance, however, this last interpretation presents the fewest difficulties and offers the most consistent understanding of the passage as a whole. It anticipates the conclusion in v. 29 (rather than contradicting it, as the first interpretation does) by maintaining that Qoheleth could find no man or woman who could be called "upright."[202] But we still need to determine the precise

---

201. See Murphy, *Ecclesiastes*, 77; N. Lohfink, "Der Bibel skeptische Hintertür: Versuch, den Ort des Buchs Kohelet neu zu bestimmen," *Stimmen der Zeit* 198 (1980) 17–31; D. Michel, *Untersuchungen zur Eigenart des Buches Qohelet* (BZAW 183; Berlin: de Gruyter, 1989) 225–38; Johan Y. S. Pahk, "The Significance of אשר in Qoh 7,26: 'More Bitter Than Death Is the Woman, *If* She Is a Snare,'" in *Qohelet in the Context of Wisdom* (ed. A. Schoors; Leuven: Leuven University Press, 1998) 373–83. Fox presents a number of arguments against the approaches of these scholars (*A Time to Tear Down*, 266–67).

202. There have been numerous suggestions about what precisely Qoheleth was searching for in v. 28. If vv. 28 and 29 are to be connected, it seems reasonable to infer that the quality defined in v. 29 (ישר) was the quality for which Qoheleth was searching (see Longman, *The Book of Ecclesiastes*, 206; Murphy, *Ecclesiastes*, 77). Michael Fox suggests that Qoheleth's use of the generic אדם 'human beings' here creates an implied contrast between

nuance of this term (ישר) as well as the meaning of חשבנות, in order to understand the only discovery that Qoheleth claims to have made, in v. 29.

Fox argues that ישר "refers not to the quality of moral integrity but to intellectual directness or simplicity,"[203] based primarily on the understanding that
חשבנות carries no inherently moral connotations but merely refers to 'solutions', reflecting the human tendency to seek answers. Although Fox is clearly
correct in recognizing that חשבנות is usually a morally neutral term, this is insufficient warrant for denying any moral component to Qoheleth's use of ישר.
This term is used elsewhere in Wisdom Literature almost always with a moral
meaning, most famously perhaps in the description of the character of Job (see
Job 1:1, 8; 2:3). The contrast in the last phrase of Qoh 7:29 thus transfers to
חשבנות some moral overtones, although it is also likely that Qoheleth's choice
of this term was strongly influenced by the description of his task in v. 27 as a
quest for a חשבון. He has ascertained that the reason he was unable to find upright people cannot be attributed to God but must be attributed to the human
predilection for scheming.

Read within the context of Qoheleth's words, these comments function as a
record of Qoheleth's conclusion. For the audience of Ecclesiastes and the epilogist, however, Qoheleth's task itself becomes further evidence that the activities of the sages were not compatible with the religious ideals of Israel: the
activity that destroys humans' upright quality (בקשו חשבנות רבים 'they seek
many schemes') is strongly reminiscent of the very task that Qoheleth himself
has undertaken (ובקש חכמה וחשבון 'and to seek wisdom and a solution').[204]

One final matter is worthy of note. In v. 27 we find the sudden intrusion of
the epilogist into the words of Qoheleth—the only such intrusion within the
frame created by the opening words and the epilogue itself. This is a reminder
of the distance between Qoheleth and the reader, for we are hearing Qoheleth
through an intermediary; we are not directly engaging Qoheleth himself. Qoheleth's words are coming to us by way of extended quotation, and the function of this quotation itself will only be revealed when the epilogist speaks
again. We are thus reminded that the conclusions of Qoheleth here may not
reflect those of the epilogist.

---

humans and "dumb animals" (see Fox, *A Time to Tear Down*, 271). This contrast, however,
is not implied in the use of אדם unless the context explicitly specifies it, and so it is unlikely
here.

203. Ibid., 272.

204. See Qoh 7:25. Others have also highlighted this link, for example, Whybray, *Ecclesiastes* (NCB), 127–28.

Qoheleth 8:1

[1]Who is so wise, and who knows the meaning of anything?
A man's wisdom illuminates his face,
    but the obstinacy of his face changes it.

The relationship to the surrounding material of the wisdom sayings that open chap. 8 is not immediately clear. Although some read them as an introduction to the following section on behavior in the royal court,[205] they appear more closely tied to the preceding material thematically.[206] However, the rendering in many versions introduces an unexpectedly positive assessment of wisdom, contradicting (in particular) the observations made by Qoheleth in 7:23–24. For example, the ESV reads:

Who is like the wise?
And who knows the interpretation of a thing?
A man's wisdom makes his face shine,
and the hardness of his face is changed.

Not surprisingly, this unusually positive evaluation of the wise has resulted in a number of explanations, some going so far as to assert that this is a later gloss.[207] Adding to the problem is the unusual retention of the definite article between the preposition 'like' and the adjective 'wise' in the word כהחכם.[208] In an attempt to resolve these difficulties, Longman concludes that Qoheleth must be employing sarcasm at this point.[209] However, a more tenable understanding alters the word divisions for the beginning of the verse from (MT) מי כהחכם to read מי כה חכם. This understanding was adopted by some early commentators and may well lie behind the rendering found in the LXX.[210] This results in a rather more negative phrase, with Qoheleth asking the rhe-

---

205. Especially the second saying, which could be understood to mean that one ought to conceal one's feelings in the royal court (see Crenshaw, *Ecclesiastes*, 149; Seow, *Ecclesiastes*, 277–78). For other arguments in favor of linking Qoh 8:1 with the following material, see Panc Beentjes, "'Who Is like the Wise?' Some Notes on Qohelet 8,1–15," in *Qohelet in the Context of Wisdom* (ed. A. Schoors; Leuven: Leuven University Press, 1998) 305.

206. Beentjes (ibid., 305 n. 12) lists a number of scholars who opt for this understanding.

207. Lauha, *Kohelet*, 144.

208. Such forms are attested in BH (although rarely and then often in contested readings themselves), but nowhere else in Ecclesiastes.

209. Longman, *The Book of Ecclesiastes*, 208–9.

210. The LXX reads τίς οἶδεν σοφούς 'who knows the wise'. Although οἶδεν has probably been influenced by the appearance of this term in the second line, Euringer has argued that it masks an original ὧδε 'in this way, so' reflecting the Hebrew כה 'so'. Modern proponents of this reading include Fox, *A Time to Tear Down*, 272; and Seow, *Ecclesiastes*, 277.

torical question "who is [so] wise?" rather than "who is *like* the wise?"[211] The answer to the question has already been revealed in the previous chapter. Wisdom is elusive and out of reach, so do not strive for it too hard (see Qoh 7:16). Yet again, Qoheleth undermines the wisdom tradition, and the epilogist's revelations regarding the sages are borne out.

In the final two lines of this verse, Qoheleth appears to make some positive comments on the value of wisdom. However, in light of the previous conclusions (as well as what is still to come), they sound rather hollow. Longman regards them as sarcastic, but even if taken at face value, they indicate little more than that wise people know when to conceal their true feelings, particularly their anger.[212]

Furthermore, although these two lines are usually taken as affirming the value of wisdom, this understanding probably misrepresents Qoheleth's meaning. The translation common in modern versions treats עז פניו 'hardness of his face' as the object of the verb שנא 'change'. However, the absence of the object marker את counts against this and lends support for understanding עז פניו as the subject. Furthermore, Fox has proposed that the anomalous pronoun אני should better be appended to the verb here as an object suffix, reading ישנאנו.[213] This is a minimal change and offers the most straightforward resolution to the difficulties of the next verse. The suffix then refers (most likely) to the face that had previously been illuminated by wisdom—in this verse, wisdom is changed by the same person's עז פניו 'hardness of face'.[214]

The expression עז פניו appears elsewhere only in Deut 28:50 and Dan 8:23 but finds close parallels in various expressions that employ synonyms for עז (such as קשה, חזק) in passages such as Jer 5:3 and Ezek 2:4 and 3:8. It has strong negative connotations of stubbornness and even insolence; here, too, these characteristics counteract the benefits of wisdom. Qoheleth is asserting that the benefits that may be gained from wisdom are undone or reversed by the greed and stubbornness of human beings. Once again, Qoheleth portrays wisdom as fragile and readily overturned, undermining its value for the epilogist's audience.

---

211. The former ('so') is also a possible reading of the MT as it stands, because כ 'like' sometimes loses much of its comparative sense. For examples, see Gen 1:26; Num 11:1; 1 Sam 20:3; 2 Sam 9:8; and Neh 7:2.

212. For Seow, this phrase leads into the royal advice section, making the point that it is wise to conceal one's anger in the presence of the king. See Seow, *Ecclesiastes*, 277–78.

213. Fox, *A Time to Tear Down*, 273.

214. Fox renders these words thus: "A man's wisdom illuminates his face, while the impudence of his face changes it" (ibid.).

Qoheleth 8:2–17

The remainder of chap. 8 initially turns to offering advice regarding behavior in the royal court, but this train of thought quickly reverts to further consideration of the elusive nature of wisdom and the inherent injustice in God's universe.

Qoheleth 8:2–8

> [2] Observe the command of a king.
> On the matter of an oath before God, [3] do not be in a hurry. Leave his presence; do not remain in a bad situation, for he will do whatever he wants.
> [4] Since the command of a king has authority, who will ask him, "What are you doing?" [5] The one who observes [such] a command will not experience a bad situation.
> [Regarding the] appropriate time and a just outcome, a wise heart knows [6] that for every matter there is an appropriate time and a just outcome; that the evil of humanity is a burden on them; [7] that no one knows what will happen; and that when something will happen, no one can tell.

> [8] As there is no man with power over the wind to restrain the wind,
>   so there is no one who has power over the day of death.
> As there is no discharge during the battle,
>   so evil will not release those who practice it.

This section opens with advice regarding behavior before those in authority—both human and divine—before focusing more specifically on the human realm.[215] Although a number of modern versions and scholars have attempted to link the second half of v. 2 (ועל דברת שבועת אלהים 'on the matter of an oath before God') with the first (פי מלך שמור 'observe the command of the king'), these attempts have proved to be awkward.[216] The second half of v. 2 is best read with what follows, producing a warning against making oaths before God reminiscent of the advice given in Qoh 5:3–5[4–6].[217] The opening clause of v. 2 then stands alone and may serve as a title introducing the section. In context, it is likely that the 'oath before God' should be understood as an oath made in the royal court, where God is entreated as the witness to the oath. The antecedent in v. 3 is then the king, not God.

---

215. The opening pronoun, אני, should be read with the preceding verse; see above for discussion.

216. See the NASB; NRSV; Seow, *Ecclesiastes*, 279; Crenshaw, *Ecclesiastes*, 150. As noted above, the initial אני of v. 2 should be appended to v. 1.

217. So Fox, *A Time to Tear Down*, 276–78; Longman, *The Book of Ecclesiastes*, 211. The primary difficulty with this interpretation lies in the ambiguity of the subsequent pronouns, usually understood to refer to the king but possibly also here referring to God.

The advice relating to behavior in the royal court culminates in v. 5 with the statement about consequences: the one who takes Qoheleth's advice and obeys the royal command will not experience trouble. Following this, a transition to the discussion about עת ומשפט 'time and judgment' appears. Although many interpreters understand Qoheleth to be affirming that the 'wise heart' (לב חכם) knows the "proper time and judgment,"[218] Qoheleth's subsequent statements (v. 7) about the inability to know the future suggest that an affirmation of knowledge here is unlikely. Consequently, Seow's reading of the text is to be preferred, treating the initial reference to ועת ומשפט rather like a title introducing the discussion: "Regarding the appropriate time and a just outcome, a wise heart knows: [6]that for every matter there is an appropriate time and a just outcome."[219] Understood thus, Qoheleth is not asserting that the wise know the time and judgment, just that there is such a time. This belief that there is some underlying order to the world, after all, lies at the heart of wisdom and serves to justify the task of the sages. Qoheleth's point, however, is that knowledge of this underlying order is not available to human beings—not even to the wisest sage. In making this point, Qoheleth is reiterating what he has already concluded in chap. 3 (and elsewhere).

Qoheleth does offer a modification to the conclusions already stated in earlier chapters by including the expression ומשפט.[220] The majority of modern commentators and versions render this term with such words as 'procedure' (NASB, Fox), 'custom' (Longman), or 'way' (Whybray) rather than the more common 'judgment, justice'. While all of these suggestions make sense, Qoheleth's subsequent statements may be used to suggest an alternative understanding. In v. 7b, Qoheleth states that no one can predict the future—either what will happen or when something will happen. Because the observation that no one knows when something will happen probably relates directly to the עת 'appropriate time' in vv. 5–6, one could reasonably argue that the ignorance regarding what will happen may extend to the משפט. This suggests a meaning something like 'appropriate verdict' or 'outcome'; thus, although Qoheleth acknowledges that there is both an appropriate time and an appropriate outcome for all things, any knowledge regarding this time and outcome is unavailable to human beings.

---

218. See the NASB; NIV; Fox, *A Time to Tear Down*, 273; Longman, *The Book of Ecclesiastes*, 210, 213.

219. Seow, *Ecclesiastes*, 276. Seow's solution is itself not free from difficulties. For one thing, it destroys the chiastic symmetry apparent in v. 5.

220. Several Hebrew MSS, with support from the LXX, omit the ו and simply read ועת משפט (or, for the LXX, καιρὸν κρίσεως) 'a time of judgment'. However, the fact that this expression appears with the conjunction in the next verse suggests that the reading of the MT ought to be retained.

Structurally, this clause in v. 6 is the first in a series of four that describe what the wise heart knows. Each clause is introduced by the particle כי,[221] the first being the assertion that there is an appropriate time and judgment, as discussed above. The second piece of knowledge is that human evil imposes a heavy burden on human beings.[222] The third clause asserts that human beings do not know what is to come, a fact linked to the previous clause by the pronominal suffix of איננו and further explicated by the final כי clause, which states, via a rhetorical question, that no one knows when future events will occur.

The section closes with proverbial sayings that function to reinforce the powerlessness of human beings to change their predicament (v. 8). The four lines are probably best understood as two couplets; each couplet consists of two parallel lines, of which the first is a concrete example, and the second, the actual point of the proverb. The lack of specific markers to indicate such links (beyond context and verbal parallelism) is typical of other wisdom material (e.g., Prov 11:22; 26:14; 27:19). Thus, the first proverb could be rendered: "As there is no man with power over the wind to restrain the wind, *so* there is none who has power over the day of death." Although a number of scholars understand רוח ('wind, spirit') here to be a reference to 'life force' or the like based on the parallelism with the second line,[223] this form of proverb requires that the first line provide a concrete example that is not entirely synonymous with the second. 'Life force' is certainly too abstract a notion, whereas 'wind' is perfectly apt. Furthermore, the second couplet clearly does not exhibit as high a degree of parallelism as would be demonstrated if רוח were understood in such an abstract sense.

The second couplet is a less-ambiguous example of this proverbial form because the reference to discharge from battle is not easily understood in ab-

---

221. Seow treats the four instances of כי as introducing a series of points about the knowledge possessed by the wise heart (Seow, *Ecclesiastes*, 276). However, this reading is difficult, considering the way these four clauses are tied together (as an example, see the pronominal suffix of איננו in v. 7). Rather than being four distinct points, it appears that (at least some of) these statements function to develop the earlier statement's idea. The relationship between the clauses is better reflected in Fox's rendering of this text (*A Time to Tear Down*, 273).

222. The LXX reading γνῶσις 'knowledge' suggests that דעת was in its Vorlage rather than רעת 'evil', a reading that could easily be correct because it would fit with Qoheleth's comments elsewhere regarding knowledge (see 1:18). However, because the MT makes good sense without alteration, there are no compelling grounds for altering it here.

223. Those opting to understand רוח as 'life force' or something similar include Fox, *A Time to Tear Down*, 273, 280; Eaton, *Ecclesiastes*, 120; Gordis, *Koheleth: The Man and His World*, 290. Others see some (deliberate) ambiguity in Qoheleth's use of רוח; see Seow, *Ecclesiastes*, 276, 282; Whybray, *Ecclesiastes* (NCB), 133.

stract terms, contra Seow, who appears to read this metaphorically: "it is probably correct to relate the 'battle' here to the day of death mentioned in the previous line."[224] Seow further argues that משלחת should be understood to mean 'substitution' and notes the practice during the Persian period of sending substitutes to war in one's place. This undermines the supposed metaphorical meaning, however, because the literal meaning of the text is then nonsensical (claiming that there is no 'substitution' when in reality there was).

The meaning of the term משלחת is difficult. It occurs only once elsewhere in BH (Ps 78:49), where it clearly has a different nuance. Given the root meaning, together with the fact that the situation depicted is a battle, it seems best to understand the reference here as release from battle.[225] The point then is plain: as a soldier cannot be released from service in the midst of a battle, so evil does not release its master.

Although Qoheleth set out to provide some advice on behavior in the royal court, he quickly reverted to a reflection on the powerlessness of human beings over their lives and deaths. Once again, the value of wisdom is inherently undermined, for although it may offer assistance in relatively trivial matters such as court etiquette, it cannot provide any means to control the unruly aspects of existence. So once again Qoheleth's words substantiate the conclusions of the epilogist—the path of the sages is not the best path, for it cannot fulfill its aim of determining how to ensure a better life.

Qoheleth 8:9–17

[9] All this I saw when I set my mind on every deed that is done under the sun, when these people exercise power over others to their detriment.

[10] Thus I saw the wicked brought from the holy place to graves, but those who acted justly were forgotten in the city. This too is senseless: [11] because the sentence against an evil deed is not carried out quickly, the hearts of people are intent on doing evil. [12] For a sinner does evil a hundred times but lives long, although I know that it should go well for those who fear God, because they are afraid of his presence; [13] and that it should not go well for the evil person—and his days should not lengthen like a shadow—because he does not fear the presence of God.

[14] There is something senseless that happens on the earth: there are righteous people to whom it comes as though they had done the deeds of the evil, and there are evil people to whom it comes as though they had done the deeds of the righteous. I say that this too is senseless.

[15] So I commended joy, for there is nothing better for human beings under

---

224. Seow, *Ecclesiastes*, 283.
225. So Longman, *The Book of Ecclesiastes*, 214–15, and others.

the sun than to eat, drink, and enjoy. This will stay with them throughout the
days of their lives that God has given them under the sun.

[16] When I set my mind to know wisdom and to see the task that is done on
the earth (for even by day and by night there was no sleep in my eyes, [17] and
I saw every work of God) [I saw] that people are not able to discover the
work that is done under the sun. Insomuch as people seek earnestly, they
will not find [it]. Even if the sage intends to know [it], he will not find [it].

Verse 9 is frequently associated with the preceding section,[226] although it
more likely functions to link the preceding material with the material in the
remainder of the chapter.[227] Consequently, any disjunction at this point is
somewhat artificial.

As with much of the text in these chapters, v. 9 presents a number of difficulties. Most significant are the identity of the antecedent of the pronominal
suffix ('their') on the preposition closing the verse, and whether אדם 'man,
humans' should be understood as a singular reference or a collective reference. Unfortunately, the referent of the suffix is both grammatically and con-
textually ambiguous, possibly referring to either the one oppressing or the
one being oppressed. The only factors to guide us are the proximity of the suffix to the second אדם, together with the logical conclusion that the one subject
to the oppression of another is the one most likely to be hurt.[228] One other
consideration supporting this reading is that it then agrees with Qoheleth's
previous statements on the topic of oppression (see 4:1–3). Although these
are hardly decisive arguments, they do suggest that the best understanding is
that the אדם under the dominion (or domination) of the first אדם is the one
who experiences the hurt.

The identity of the אדם is commonly considered to be one of the individuals who were in the situation that Qoheleth was describing. The noun is also
used in a collective sense, however, and this usage has prompted some to see

---

226. See, for example, Gordis, *Koheleth: The Man and His World*, 291–92; Longman,
The Book of Ecclesiastes, 215; Fox, *A Time to Tear Down*, 280–82.

227. Note the repetition of ראיתי from v. 9 in v. 10, indicating that Qoheleth is expanding on his observations in v. 9. Among those who see this as an introduction to a new section are Murphy, *Ecclesiastes*, 84–85; E. W. Hengstenberg, *Commentary on Ecclesiastes*
(Philadelphia: Smith, English, 1860) 199. Although most scholars do recognize some shift
to a new section following v. 9, the transitional function of v. 9 ultimately suggests that the
entire chapter should be recognized as a stream of thought. Seow is thus correct in treating
the entire section as a unit (see Seow, *Ecclesiastes*, 276–95).

228. This assumption, however, is not necessarily well founded. Elsewhere among Qoheleth's words, the verb שלט is used without either explicitly positive or negative overtones
(see 2:19; 5:18[19]; 6:2), so it is not immediately clear in this context that the domination
described is implicitly detrimental.

collective references here.[229] More puzzling still is the use of the article 'the' on the first instance of אדם in v. 9. Aside from a possible but unprovable historical referent for האדם, it appears likely that the article is anaphoric, pointing back to the previous verse, which stated the limits of authority for any person (אדם). As such, האדם here may refer collectively to those said to practice evil in the previous verse.

Perhaps the best understanding of this statement is that, wherever (or perhaps *whenever*, given the use of עת 'time') anyone is in a position of power over another person, hurt is the inevitable outcome.[230] Thus, Qoheleth recalls the instability and uncertainty associated with positions traditionally held to be good: wisdom, authority, and righteousness (see 7:15–18).

The Hebrew text of v. 10 also appears to have suffered some corruption. As it stands, it is difficult to decipher, a fact that has prompted a number of suggested emendations. The most widely accepted is the rendering of a number of ancient versions,[231] which alter the MT. The MT reads:

ראיתי רשעים קברים ובאו וממקום קדוש יהלכו

The suggested emendation is:

ראיתי רשעים קבר[ים] מובאים וממקום קדוש יהלכו

Read this way, the text records Qoheleth's observation that the wicked received a burial appropriate for the righteous person (they were brought from the holy place to a tomb), while the honest (אשר כן עשו) were forgotten in the city. Thus, we again see Qoheleth highlighting the inversion of the principles espoused by traditional wisdom, according to which good people are usually rewarded.

The verse appropriately concludes with another הבל ('senseless') statement—appropriate because it is once again associated with the failure of the real world to adhere to the principles of wisdom. However, it is not immediately clear whether the statement is retrospective or prospective. Although both the preceding material in v. 10 and the subsequent material in vv. 11–13 deal with inversions of the sage's world order, the fact that v. 11 opens with the relative אשר 'because' suggests that perhaps the הבל clause ought to be

---

229. E.g., Longman, *The Book of Ecclesiastes*, 210; Seow, *Ecclesiastes*, 276.

230. GKC §118i notes that עת functions as an accusative of time, allowing the translation 'when'.

231. This emendation is suggested by the LXX, SyrH, and Copt. The Coptic version and Syro-Hexapla suggest the singular קבר ('grave'), whereas the LXX reading (εἰς τάφους εἰσαχθέντας 'carried into tombs') supports the plural form. Modern scholars who adopt this alteration include Seow, *Ecclesiastes*, 284; and Fox, *A Time to Tear Down*, 282–84.

read as introducing the material in vv. 11–13.[232] Furthermore, since Qoheleth would then be stating that vv. 11–13 are *also* (גם) הבל, the reader should understand that v. 10 describes something that is implicitly הבל.

Verses 11–12a describe another situation in which the expectations of traditional wisdom fail to be reflected in the real world—the execution of justice. However, the greatest difficulty in this section is the outright contradiction introduced in vv. 12b–13, in which Qoheleth apparently affirms belief in the validity of the principle of retribution immediately after having noted that there are clear instances in which it is violated. This has prompted various solutions, the statement either being assigned to a pious glossator or else being viewed as a quotation of the traditional wisdom position rather than an affirmation of it.[233] The difficulty with these approaches is the arbitrariness with which portions of Qoheleth's words are assigned to other sources. Because of this, I find it preferable to adopt Michael Fox's explanation, which offers an acceptable understanding of the text:

> There is no sign that 8:12b–13 are the words or opinion of another person or party. . . . Rather, v. 12 says: "It is a fact that . . . and I also know that. . . ." Although Qohelet "knows" the principle of retribution and nowhere denies it, he *also* knows there are cases that violate the rule. It is because Qohelet holds to the axioms of Wisdom that he is shocked by their violation and finds the aberrations absurd.[234]

Thus, in stating the traditional wisdom belief, bracketed by his observations on real life, Qoheleth effectively undermines the value of that wisdom. In this context, v. 14 functions to close the record of observation: any sensible view of the world would maintain that the righteous should be better off than the

---

232. See ibid., 284–85.

233. Crenshaw (*Ecclesiastes*, 155), along with C. C. Siegfried (*Prediger und Hoheslied* [HKAT 2/3; Göttingen: Vandenhoeck & Ruprecht, 1898]), E. Podechard (*L'Ecclésiaste* [Paris, 1912]), and K. von Galling ("Der Prediger," in *Die Fünf Megilloth* [HAT 18; Tübingen: Mohr, 1969] 111–12) argue that this is a later gloss. Gordis (*Koheleth: The Man and His World*, 297) argues that this ought to be treated as a quotation of traditional wisdom.

234. Fox, *A Time to Tear Down*, 286; see also Seow (*Ecclesiastes*, 288), who writes, "Most translators and commentators assume that Qohelet is unwilling to give up this knowledge, despite what is said in vv 11–12a. But this concession is merely parenthetical, it seems, and without much conviction, for he quickly returns to note the injustice in the treatment of the just and unjust in v 14." Isaksson argues that Qoheleth uses perfective forms of ידע when referring to knowledge that he has derived from personal experience and research, but his use of the participle here refers to what he knows to be traditionally accepted wisdom (B. Isaksson, *Studies in the Language of Qoheleth* [Stockholm: Almqvist & Wiksell, 1987] 67).

wicked, but any real view of the world undermines the sensible view—the world is הבל.[235]

Qoheleth then restates his conclusion in v. 15, agreeing with what he has said earlier (refer to the discussion of 2:24–26 on p. 135 above). If God permits us to enjoy life, then that is as much good as we can hope for.

The final two verses of chap. 8 again show evidence of corruption, although fortunately here the meaning of Qoheleth's assertion is relatively transparent: human understanding of the world is limited, and some things simply cannot be discovered. The difficulties in v. 16 lie primarily in the clause referring to lack of sleep. The antecedent of the third-person suffix on בעיניו ('in his eyes') is not clear, and the expression 'to see sleep' is not found elsewhere in BH.[236] Furthermore, the entire clause is intrusive and, regardless of its precise interpretation, almost always treated as a parenthetical comment.[237] These observations suggest that some minor emendation may be warranted in order to make sense of the text. One reasonable proposal is to drop the final וראה and to restore an original י, based on the theory that the extant text was formed through dittography with the opening וראיתי ('and I saw') of v. 17.[238]

The rendering of Qoh 8:17 in most modern English translations of the book appears to lend support to the case that the sages of Qoheleth's day deliberately undertook to mislead the public by claiming access to knowledge they could not, in reality, access. For example, the NIV renders the verse as follows: "No one can comprehend what goes on under the sun. Despite all his efforts to search it out, man cannot discover its meaning. Even if a wise man claims he knows, he cannot really comprehend it." The crucial part is the final line: וגם אם־יאמר החכם לדעת לא יוכל למצא. Although it would be appealing to claim support from this passage for the interpretation of Ecclesiastes expounded in this book,[239] to do so would be premature. Forms of the verb אמר ('say') followed by the preposition ל and an infinitive construct verb often express an intention or plan (e.g., Exod 2:14; Josh 22:33; 1 Sam 30:6; 2 Sam

---

235. M. Sneed ("The Social Location of the Book of Qoheleth," *Hebrew Studies* 39 [1998] 48–49) correctly notes that, in doing this, Qoheleth questions "a fundamental tenet of Hebrew faith."

236. See Longman, *The Book of Ecclesiastes*, 222.

237. Other commentators prefer to drop the clause entirely; see Seow (*Ecclesiastes*, 289), who argues that it ought to be moved to follow the next verse.

238. This proposal goes slightly further than Fox, who argues only for the alteration of the third-person suffix to a first-person (*A Time to Tear Down*, 288–89).

239. Such as the understanding of this verse expounded by Eaton that "wise men may make excessive claims; they too will be baffled" (*Ecclesiastes*, 124).

21:16; 1 Kgs 5:19; 2 Chr 13:8; 28:10, 13).[240] Read this way this text suggests
only that the sage is planning to find out what goes on under the sun rather
than actually claiming to possess such knowledge. While not all instances of
the verb אמר + ל + inf. cs. can be read this way, there are good contextual indications that it should be read this way.

First, the fact that the prefix conjugation of אמר is used tends to indicate
that the word should not be understood as a reference to a specific claim made
by the sage in question (such as that he knows the meaning of what goes on
under the sun) but instead as a reference to an incomplete task that preoccupies him. Second, the parallelism with the previous statement suggests that,
like the אדם who labors to discover the meaning of what goes on under the
sun, the חכם also seeks this information but is unable to discover it.

In light of these considerations, I conclude that this text should be rendered: "Although the sage intends to know [about what goes on under the
sun], he is unable to find out." The point of this section is to emphasize the
enigmatic nature of this sort of knowledge, a point that is central to Qoheleth's conclusion and ultimately to the epilogist's argument. Qoheleth finds
that there is no way a sage can find the answers to the questions he has raised,
and any who set out to discover the answers (as Qoheleth himself has done)
will ultimately fail in the task. The epilogist draws warnings from this against
becoming immersed in the tasks of the sages, for as Qoheleth discovered for
himself, the answers they seek are unattainable.

There may also be a degree of deliberate ambiguity in Qoheleth's statement. Qoheleth's focus is on the impossibility of successfully concluding the
search for knowledge regarding what goes on under the sun, even though he
himself tried to earlier in the book. People do not want to hear that these answers do not exist, and no one wants to waste life searching, only to discover
that the entire endeavor has been a waste of time. The temptation to conceal
this truth—even from oneself—would no doubt be immense, and it is quite
possible that the epilogist had untruthful sages in mind when he wrote that
Qoheleth corrected the work of others and that he preferred to write the truth
rather than "pleasing words."[241]

---

240. See Gordis, *Koheleth: The Man and His World*, 299; Fox, *Qohelet and His Contradictions*, 255–56; Seow, *Ecclesiastes*, 290, 295. Seow renders the expression 'desire to
know' (p. 290) which is perhaps not the best understanding. 'Desire' would better be expressed using some other verb, such as חפץ or אוה. The use of this expression in BH tends
more toward expressing an intention or plan without implying anything about the desirabil-
ity of the outcome.

241. Refer to the previous chapter for full discussion of these matters.

Qoheleth 9:1–10

[1] For I put all this to my mind to explain all this, because the righteous, the wise, and their deeds, are in the hand of God, as are both love and hate. People do not realize that everything before them is [2] senseless, as there is one fate for all: for the righteous and for the wicked, for the good [and for the evil], for the clean and for the unclean, for the one who sacrifices and for the one who does not; as for the good person so for the sinner; as for the one who swears an oath so for the one afraid to swear. [3] This evil is in everything that is done under the sun, that there is one fate for everyone. Furthermore, the minds of human beings are full of evil; irrationality is in their minds while they are alive, and afterwards [they go] to the dead!

[4] Indeed, whoever is joined to all the living has a certainty (for a live dog is better than a dead lion): [5] the living know that they will die, but the dead do not know anything, and they no longer have any gain, for they are forgotten. [6] Also, their love, their hatred, and their jealousy have already perished. They will never again have a share in all that is done under the sun.

[7] Go, eat your food with joy and drink your wine with a glad heart, when God has already approved of your works. [8] Let your clothes be white all the time, and do not let oil lack on your head. [9] Experience life with [the] woman whom you love all the days of your senseless life that he has given you under the sun, for that is your share in life and in your toil at which you toil under the sun.

[10] Everything your hand finds to do, do with fervor, for there is no doing or planning or knowledge or wisdom in Sheol, which is where you are going.

Qoheleth's observation of the failure of wisdom's anticipated outcomes for the righteous and the wicked in his previous chapter leads into reflections on the universality and finality of death—a theme that Qoheleth has previously treated in 3:18–4:3. The chap. 9 passage contains a number of difficulties. The expression הכל ('all this') at the beginning of v. 2 is often emended to הבל ('senselessness') and associated with the final clause of v. 1 to read "everything before them is senseless," largely because of the difficulties in understanding הכל לפניהם ('everything before them') in v. 1.[242] Nonetheless, a number of modern commentators argue that sense can be made of the MT without resorting to emendation (minor though it may be) and that the final clause of v. 1 refers either to the fact that "people do not know everything that

---

242. See the LXX; Symmachus; Syriac; Fox, *A Time to Tear Down*, 291; G. A. Barton, *A Critical and Exegetical Commentary on the Book of Ecclesiastes* (ICC; Edinburgh: T. & T. Clark, 1908) 158; Alan H. McNeile, *An Introduction to Ecclesiastes* (Cambridge, 1904); the NRSV.

is before them" or that "no one knows whether love or hate awaits them."[243]
Deciding between the options is not easy and ultimately has little bearing on
the overall thrust of the passage, but the emended reading attested in some
early versions and adopted by a number of modern commentators does result
in a more readable text.

Another problem in the text lies in the list of categories of people who
share the same fate in v. 2. Although most are presented in contrasting pairs
("righteous and wicked," "clean and unclean," "those who sacrifice and those
who do not sacrifice," "those who swear an oath and those who do not"), the
MT includes an extra לטוב 'for the good', which disturbs the symmetry. The
LXX completes the pairing by reading τῷ ἀγαθῷ καὶ τῷ κακῷ 'for the good
and for the evil', suggesting a missing ולרע in the Hebrew text. This addition
is also reflected in other early versions (Syriac, Vulgate, Syro-Hexapla).

In spite of these and various other difficulties, the meaning is itself reasonably clear and is ultimately stated most directly in v. 3.[244] The opening words
of this verse are probably best translated: "This evil is in everything that is
done under the sun. . . ."[245] Qoheleth's point here is that death, the "one fate"
for which all are destined (as noted in v. 2), contaminates every action under
the sun, because it undermines the sage's hope that somehow the inherent order in the universe will result in justice in the lives of human beings. Instead,
the righteous may suffer and die exactly as the wicked, rather than see any reward or profit for their righteousness.

Amid these reflections on the universality of death, the words of v. 4 in
many English versions appear to offer some relief: "whoever is joined with all
the living has hope" (NRSV).[246] This translation obscures the difficulty in precisely defining the meaning of the term בטחון, which is commonly rendered
'hope'. The term appears in BH only here and in the synoptic passages 2 Kgs
18:19 and Isa 36:4, where it refers to the belief on which Hezekiah bases his

---

243. See Seow, *Ecclesiastes*, 296; and Longman, *The Book of Ecclesiastes*, 224, re-
spectively.

244. See Seow (*Ecclesiastes*, 302–3), who writes: "The beginning of the passage is difficult. There are all kinds of textual, syntactical, and interpretive problems. Nevertheless,
the issue that these verses raise seems clear enough: it is the fact that there is a common fate
for everyone." Some of these problems are touched on in the notes that follow.

245. There is considerable discussion over the precise understanding of these words,
and a number of emendations have been offered. Alteration to the text is unnecessary, however, as can be seen from the exegesis above.

246. The term יחבר (translated 'joined' above) is the *qere* and is followed by the ma-
jority of modern commentators as well as ancient versions (LXX, Symm, Syriac) and 20
Hebrew MSS. The *kethib* reading, יבחר (a form from בחר 'to choose') is followed by Seow
(*Ecclesiastes*, 300).

rebellion against Assyria. In that context the term is probably not semantically distant from the idea of 'hope', although it perhaps conveys a greater degree of certainty than other similar Hebrew terms. The appearance of the term
in only one other context in BH does not provide a good basis for fully defining its semantic field. Nonetheless, whether or not the term בטחון could have
conveyed the essentially positive nuances present in the English word 'hope'
is ultimately beside the point.[247] The fact is that this context does not readily
admit this sort of understanding, for no such hope is offered by Qoheleth. Instead, Qoheleth is stating that the only difference between the living and the
dead is that the living know they will die, while the dead know nothing (v. 5).
Thus, the meaning of the term that is used in its other occurrences fits the context well here, for this would have Qoheleth asserting that the living are *certain* of only one thing: that they will die.[248]

Having restated his observation on the way in which death undermines life
and what happens in life (and thus also undermines the fundamental assumptions of the sages), in vv. 7–10 Qoheleth reiterates the only advice he can then
give: enjoy what you can of life (compare 2:24–26; 3:13–14, 22; 5:17–19[18–
20]; and 8:15, where similar recommendations are made). In this passage, it
is the reference to God's action in v. 7 that is most puzzling, for Qoheleth
writes: כי כבר רצה האלהים את מעשיך. Fox argues that the expression כבר רצה
should be understood as a "future perfect" form, which could be translated
crudely as "will have favored."[249] This, however, is not the way this construction has functioned elsewhere in Qoheleth's writing (compare 1:10; 2:12, 16;
3:15; 4:2; 6:10; 9:6), and there is no compelling reason here to understand
God's approval of one's actions as taking place in the future.

Although the text could be construed as implying that God has given un-
conditional approval to all possible actions, it is likely that this overstates
Qoheleth's point. In each of the similar passages in which enjoying life is
commended by Qoheleth, the ability to enjoy life is said to be contingent
upon provision by God (see 2:24; 3:13; 5:18[19]; 8:15). Here, then, it is likely
that Qoheleth's point is that, if life is enjoyable, it is only because God has
allowed it to be so, and if God has so permitted it then presumably God is
favorably disposed toward those who can enjoy life. This notion is better
brought out in translation by rendering כי as 'when' or even 'if', suggesting

---

247. It should also be noted that Qoheleth had at his disposal a number of other Hebrew
terms more commonly understood to convey the idea of 'hope'; for example, מקוה, תקוה,
and תוחלת.

248. See Fox (*A Time to Tear Down*, 287–88), who correctly understands the aphorism
כי לכלב חי הוא טוב מן האריה המת to be parenthetical.

249. Ibid., 294.

that the enjoyment is contingent upon divine approval.[250] The thrust of the verse is thus summarized by Crenshaw: "Since one's capacity to enjoy life depends on a divine gift, anyone who can eat and drink enjoys divine favor. (The corollary is that persons who lack the means or the disposition to enjoy life lack that favor.) Divine approval precedes human enjoyment."[251]

Qoheleth concludes this section in v. 10 by broadening this advice, suggesting that the reader make the most of all opportunities. In doing so, he states unequivocally that there is nothing to come following death and thus no opportunity for justice, for rewards, for punishment, or for judgment. In death one loses all that life could offer, so Qoheleth's advice is to make the most of life because it will soon pass.

Once again, for the reader familiar with the teachings of the remainder of the Hebrew Bible, Qoheleth's words here are disturbing: death is the common fate of the righteous and the wicked; the only certainty in life is death. Consequently, the only two pieces of advice Qoheleth can offer are entirely self-serving: enjoy yourself whenever you can, and experience whatever you can. This advice makes no reference to any overarching moral order in which some deeds can be said to be right and some said to be wrong. Qoheleth's conclusions are diametrically opposed to the religious ideals espoused throughout the remainder of the Hebrew Bible, and the fact that they are is by this point patently obvious to the reader.

Qoheleth 9:11–12

[11] I turned and saw under the sun that the race is not to the swift, and the battle is not to the strong, nor food to the wise, nor wealth to the discerning, nor favor to the knowledgeable, for a timely mishap could happen to any of them. [12] Moreover, [that] man does not know his time. Like fish caught in an evil net, and like birds trapped in a snare, so human beings are ensnared at an evil time when it suddenly falls on them.

Qoheleth essentially recaps his conclusions about life under the sun in these two verses. In v. 11, Qoheleth poetically states that the outcomes one would expect from a world undergirded by wisdom do not always come to pass (compare 8:14). These expectations go beyond predicting that the wise would always have food (see Prov 12:11; 20:13; 28:19; 30:8) and wealth (see Prov 3:16; 8:18; 22:4; 24:4), for an appropriately ordered universe would also dictate, for example, that the race ought to be to the swift. Indeed, each of the lines of the aphorism reflect an inversion of the outcomes expected from an

---

250. See BDB, 473a.
251. Crenshaw, *Ecclesiastes*, 162.

ordered universe. Qoheleth's observations undermine the world view of the sages and lead him to conclude that "a timely mishap could happen to any of them."[252] These words temper the previous affirmation of enjoyment by reminding the reader that the circumstances in which one may enjoy life are beyond the individual's control.

Although v. 12 is usually understood to refer to death in the words כי גם לא ידע האדם את עתו 'moreover, that man does not know his time', this reading is probably more heavily influenced by English idiom than Hebrew, and the context points in a different direction. Fox appeals to the use of עתך in Qoh 7:17, but in that instance the context clearly determines that the time in view is the time of death.[253] This passage clearly defines the time as a time of calamity that inverts the appropriate outcome (according to conventional wisdom) and renders life ultimately senseless. The repetition of עת points back to the עת ופגע of the previous verse, and this link is confirmed by the last line of v. 12, which refers to the sudden onset of an 'evil time' (עת רעה). Consequently, while the expression probably encompasses death, it is better understood as a broader reference to any time when order is subverted and senselessness prevails. Qoheleth makes it quite clear that human beings cannot determine the path that their lives will take, no matter how wise they are, and in so doing he further enhances the epilogist's case that the wisdom movement had nothing of value to offer.

Qoheleth 9:13–16

13 I also observed this about wisdom under the sun, and it seemed important to me. 14 [Suppose there was] a small city with few people in it. A great king came to it, surrounded it, and built great siege works against it. 15 Then he found a poor wise man in it, and he could have delivered the city by his wisdom. But no one had remembered that poor man.

16 So I thought, "Wisdom is better than strength, but the wisdom of the poor man is despised, and his words are not heeded."

Qoheleth next relates an anecdote in which wisdom could, in contrast to the conclusion of the preceding verses, provide an escape in time of calamity. He tells the story of a small city besieged by a powerful king; against overwhelming odds the wisdom of one poor inhabitant of the city is sufficient to rescue the city.

---

252. Or, in Hebrew, כי עת ופגע יקרה את כלם. The words עת ופגע are probably best understood to be a hendiadys meaning 'timely incident *or* mishap' (see Seow, *Ecclesiastes*, 308; Fox, *A Time to Tear Down*, 296). The singular form of the verb governing the expression, although not decisive, does lend support to this reading.

253. See Fox, ibid., 297.

The primary issue raised by modern interpreters has been whether the wisdom of the poor man was heeded and thus the city was saved,[254] or whether Qoheleth is saying merely that his wisdom *could have* saved the city but that no one thought to consult him precisely because he was poor.[255] The second reading requires that וּמִלַּט be understood in a modal sense (here 'could have delivered') and that זכר mean something like 'think of'.

Whether or not the form וּמִלַּט can be read modally ultimately rests on the understanding of the entire episode related by Qoheleth, which is expressed as a verbless clause followed by a sequence of clauses, each introduced by a *wĕqāṭal* form. Grammatically, the modal reading has a solid foundation, for although it is commonly claimed that this verb form is used to continue the nuances of the previous verb form, Jan Joosten has demonstrated that the main function of the *wĕqāṭal* form is actually to express modality.[256] The lack of any initial verbal form (since the opening clause is verbless) lends some added credence to Joosten's understanding.

Furthermore, the context also provides compelling indicators that the verbs should be read modally. In particular, the words in v. 16b pose a significant problem if וּמִלַּט is *not* read this way. Fox argues that the first clause in v. 16 only makes sense given the "real" (as opposed to irreal) reading of the story, for if wisdom had not saved the city then wisdom would not have been better than might.[257] This is unconvincing, however, for Qoheleth has at the very least stated that wisdom *could have* saved the city had the poor man been heard. Whether the city was saved or not has no bearing on the comparative assessment of wisdom and strength. Whereas v. 16a—"wisdom is better than strength"—could reasonably be derived from the story were the city not actually saved, v. 16b—"his words are not heeded"—would not have been a valid conclusion unless the city was destroyed. If Qoheleth has recorded the proverb in vv. 14–15 in order to illustrate only the point about wisdom and

---

254. So most English versions: KJV, RSV, NRSV, AB, NAB, ASV, NASB, NIV; also Fox, *A Time to Tear Down*, 297, 299; Longman, *The Book of Ecclesiastes*, 234–35; Gordis, *Koheleth: The Man and His World*, 311–12.

255. So NEB, NJPSV, NASB margin, NET; Crenshaw, *Ecclesiastes*, 166–67; Isaksson, *Studies in the Language of Qoheleth*, 97; Seow, *Ecclesiastes*, 310–11; McNeile, *An Introduction to Ecclesiastes*.

256. Jan Joosten, "Biblical Hebrew w^eqāṭal and Syriac hwā qāṭel Expressing Repetition in the Past," *ZAH* 5 (1992) 1–14. The common assertion that the *wĕqāṭal* form continues the significance of the previous verbal form is found in (for example) Waltke and O'Connor, *An Introduction to Biblical Hebrew Syntax*, 523–25; and GKC §112.2. The context remains important, for although the primary function of the *wĕqāṭal* form is to express modality, this is not the *only* function.

257. Fox, *A Time to Tear Down*, 300.

strength, the reader would have to overlook the close ties between v. 16b and the proverb as well as the fact that the proverb disproved the point made in 16b. Consequently, the context strongly favors the modal meaning for the form ומלט.

Finally, if this verb form is read modally, it suggests strongly that the entire story should be understood in this way: thus, Qoheleth is not relating a historical event but a hypothetical tale designed to make a point—a simple parable. This reading is reflected in the LXX, where all the verbs are translated by subjunctive forms. Consequently, in English it would be appropriate to preface a translation of this story with the words "once upon a time" or "suppose there was. . . ."

Regarding the meaning of זכר, Seow suggests that it is found with meanings similar to 'think of, call to mind' elsewhere in BH (see Qoh 5:19[20]; 11:8; 12:1).[258] Fox counters, however, that in these other instances זכר still reflects an awareness of facts already known, and so they do not serve as precise parallels to the required meaning here. In the final analysis these distinctions are probably subtle enough that neither interpretation can be comprehensively ruled out on the basis of usage alone.

Here, then, Qoheleth is acknowledging that in certain instances wisdom is of great value—indeed, better than might. In support of his statement, he relates the tale of a sage who could by wisdom defeat an entire army and overcome apparently insurmountable odds. Yet even this impressive example of wisdom is undone by the simple fact that the sage was poor and was therefore ignored by those who needed to hear what he had to say. Once again, the reader is left wondering about the value of wisdom, when even this impressive example ends so impotently.

Qoheleth 9:17–10:20

The remainder of chap. 9 and all of chap. 10 record a series of loosely connected proverbial sayings, many of which reflect traditional wisdom themes and demonstrate to some extent the value of wisdom in contrast to folly. The inclusion of material such as this, which apparently offers some endorsement of wisdom, potentially poses a problem: if the epilogist really is using Qoheleth's words to undermine the wisdom movement and to deter prospective students from joining it, why does he include material that could be seen to undermine his purpose?

---

258. Seow, *Ecclesiastes*, 310. Seow also points to occurrences outside Ecclesiastes: Deut 32:7; Isa 43:18; 47:7; 57:11; 65:17; Jer 3:16; Ps 77:4[5], 7[8].

Qoheleth 9:17–10:1

> [17] The words of sages in quietness are more worth hearing
>   than the shout of a ruler among fools.
> [18] Wisdom is better than the weapons of war,
>   but one sinner can destroy much good.
> 10 [1] As a dead fly causes a perfumer's oil to stink,
>   so a little folly outweighs wisdom and honor.

These verses are obviously connected to the preceding anecdote about the wisdom that could have saved a city. Although a number of modern English versions render v. 17 as a form of "better"-proverb, the Hebrew text lacks any form of טוב and reads more as an observation than a piece of advice.[259] The comparative use of the preposition מן most naturally relates to the verbal idea expressed in the participle, making the point that the quiet words of the sages are heard more than the shouts of a ruler among fools. The primary difficulty arises from the context in which Qoheleth has just stated that the poor wise man was not heard.[260] The best resolution seems to be to follow Lauha and others, who understand Qoheleth to be saying that the words of the wise are more worth hearing.[261] This then ties in well with the preceding example, in which the value of the sage's words was apparent in their power to save the city, if only they had been heard.

The fact that the poor sage's wisdom could have saved the city also demonstrates that wisdom is better than weapons of war. Yet over against this positive appraisal of wisdom stands Qoh 9:18b and 10:1, where the frailty of wisdom is highlighted. The contrastive disjunction created by placing the subject (וחוטא אחד 'but one sinner') immediately after the conjunction highlights the limitations of the praise that Qoheleth is ascribing to wisdom in this context. Wisdom may be better than the accoutrements of war, but much good can be destroyed by just one "sinner."[262]

Qoheleth elaborates on this point in the proverb of 10:1. The text itself contains a number of difficulties. First, the expression זבובי מות that opens the verse does not mean 'dead flies', as many of the versions have it but rather

---

259. For example, the NASB, which renders: "The words of the wise heard in quietness are better than the shouting of a ruler among fools."

260. The repetition of the plural participle נשמעים ('are heard'; the only two instances of the Niphal m. pl. ptc. in the Hebrew Bible) reinforces the close link between these sections (see Whybray, *Ecclesiastes*, 149).

261. See Lauha, *Kohelet*, 178; Whybray, *Ecclesiastes* (NCB), 149. Whybray also appeals to GKC §116e in support of this understanding.

262. Regarding Qoheleth's use of the term חוטא, see the discussion beginning on p. 135 above.

'flies of death' (that is, either 'deadly flies' or 'flies in the process of dying'). Gordis points out that 'dead flies' would have been written זבובים מתים and understands the MT to refer to 'dying flies', saying that flies floating in oil are "a common sight in the East."[263] The image of numerous dying flies in oil does not, however, parallel well with the observation that it takes only a 'little folly' (סכלות מעט) to outweigh wisdom and honor in the second line of the proverb. Since neither 'deadly flies' nor 'flies in the process of dying' makes good sense in the context, it is best to emend the text to read זבוב ימות as an asyndetic relative clause functioning substantivally to refer to a single dead fly.[264] This further heightens the parallelism with the סכלות מעט in the second line of the proverb and resolves the disparity between the plural flies and the singular verb forms יבאיש 'causes' and יביע ('to stink').

Second, the word יביע presents some exegetical problems. The form is usually understood to be a Hiphil, apparently from the root נבע, which itself usually means 'pour out, emit'. Although this meaning serves elsewhere in BH,[265] it is not immediately clear to most scholars how this meaning could fit here, and so it is argued that in this context the semantic range of the term can reasonably be extended to include 'bubble forth' and thus 'ferment'.[266] However, as Fox has pointed out, while a dead fly may spoil an ointment, it does not make it ferment or bubble. Furthermore, the meaning 'ferment' is not supported for this verb elsewhere, so it remains unsupported here.

Some of the early versions lack the word altogether or else treat it as an instance of asyndetic verbal hendiadys and coalesce the two verbs into one in the process of translation (see, for example, Symmachus, Targum, Vulgate). This has prompted some scholars to resolve the difficulties by discarding the word.[267] This resolution is too easy, however. The absence of a readily identifiable equivalent in early versions does not automatically mean that the word was missing from their Vorlage. They may have failed to translate the word because it was considered superfluous, or (as already noted) they may have understood the expression as a hendiadys and rendered it with one word. Furthermore, other versions (such as the LXX) do attest to the presence of this word, or at least a similar word, in their Vorlage.

Following the LXX and Syriac, a number of scholars have concluded that the word יביע must be a noun, either taking the text unemended as representing

---

263. Gordis, *Koheleth: The Man and His World*, 314.
264. So Seow, *Ecclesiastes*, 311–12; Fox, *A Time to Tear Down*, 301.
265. See Ps 19:3[2]; 59:8[7]; 78:2; 94:4; 119:171; 145:7; Prov 1:23; 15:2, 28.
266. So Longman, *The Book of Ecclesiastes*, 238 n. 3; BDB, 615b.
267. See Barton, *A Critical and Exegetical Commentary on the Book of Ecclesiastes*, 168–69; Galling, "Der Prediger," 115–16; Lauha, *Kohelet*, 180–81.

an otherwise unattested noun,[268] or else emending the text to read גְבִיעַ
'bowl' so that it refers to the fact that the entire bowl of oil is spoiled by the
dead fly.[269]

Perhaps the neatest solution is to read the expression יַבְאִישׁ יַבִּיעַ as an
asyndetic verbal hendiadys meaning 'to emit stench', emphasizing the effu-
sive nature of the smell as the fly dies and decays in the oil. This interpretation limits the extent to which the text must be emended[270] and does make
sense. Ultimately, however, the meaning of the clause is altered little by these
various interpretive alternatives for the word יַבִּיעַ.

The second half of the proverb is also problematic, for it appears to suggest that a little folly is more precious (יָקָר) than wisdom and honor. Since this
does not fit the context, most scholars contend that יָקָר is an Aramaism meaning 'weighty'. Thus, Qoheleth is not claiming that a little folly is more precious than wisdom and honor but that it outweighs wisdom and honor.

Qoheleth begins this section by proclaiming the value of wisdom but cannot do so without commenting that wisdom is extremely fragile, and much
wisdom can be destroyed by only a little folly. It is important to note that the
value that Qoheleth assigns to wisdom is not unqualified praise but rather
constrained praise: wisdom is of value in some things, but (as has been shown
in the preceding chapters) there are important matters that even the wisest
sage cannot fathom. Furthermore, even in situations where wisdom is of
value, it is susceptible to even the slightest intrusion by folly.

Qoheleth 10:2–3

> [2] The mind of the wise person goes to his right,
>   and the mind of the fool to his left.
> [3] Even when the fool walks along the road his mind is absent,
>   and he announces to all that he is a fool.

The next two proverbs specifically focus on the disadvantage of folly. The
first proverb contrasts the fool and the wise person by simply noting that they
are headed in opposite directions. Although it is attractive to go beyond this
and seek to invest some ethical value in the association of the wise with right
and the fool with left, there is little support for doing so. In BH the vast ma-

---

268. Gordis (*Koheleth: The Man and His World*, 315) states that the context "requires
a noun." He proposes an otherwise unattested noun יַבִּיעַ meaning 'the flowing vessel'. This
is, of course, highly speculative.

269. Those who opt for this emendation include Fox, *A Time to Tear Down*, 301; and
Seow, *Ecclesiastes*, 312.

270. The absence of any conjunction is quite unusual, so it is possible that an original
ו was accidentally omitted.

jority of passages that refer to both left and right demonstrate no clear preference for either direction.[271] In the passages in which there is a discernible ethical component, the usual exhortation is to go neither left nor right but straight ahead.[272] The second proverb focuses exclusively on the path taken by the fool, announcing that "his sense is lacking"[273] and that "he says to everyone that he is a fool."[274]

Qoheleth here reflects the traditional wisdom attitude toward folly. Although this does cause some tension with his remarks elsewhere (most notably 7:16–18, but see the comments on that passage above), it remains consistent with my understanding of the epilogue (and of Ecclesiastes as a whole) proposed here, for, while the epilogist may be seeking to discredit the wisdom movement, he is certainly not suggesting that folly is a viable alternative. The epilogist is contrasting the way of the sages and the commandments of God.

Qoheleth 10:4–7

⁴ If the anger of the ruler rises against you, do not leave your post, because composure appeases great offenses.

⁵ There is an evil I have seen under the sun, that is, an error that originates with the ruler: ⁶ the simpleton is placed in important positions, but the rich sit in lowly places. ⁷ I have seen slaves on horses and princes walking as slaves on the ground.

The next proverb bears no obvious relationship to the preceding material; instead it marks the beginning of some comments relating to people in authority (v. 4 uses the term המושל 'the ruler', and vv. 5–7 use the terms השליט 'the ruler', עשיר 'rich', and שר 'prince'). Apart from this link with the following text, v. 4 appears to be independent of the surrounding material. It advises dealing with the anger of one's superior with a calm response rather than by abandoning one's position.[275]

---

271. Contra Crenshaw, *Ecclesiastes*, 169–70; J. Jarick, *Gregory Thaumaturgos' Paraphrase of Ecclesiastes* (SBLSCS 29; Atlanta: Scholars Press, 1990) 251; Ogden, *Qoheleth*, 165; and many others.

272. E.g., Isa 30:21; Prov 4:27; 2 Chr 32:2.

273. The expression לבו חסר here reflects חסר־לב, which appears a number of times in Proverbs (Prov 6:32; 7:7; 9:4, 16; 10:13, 21; 11:12; 12:11; 15:21; 17:18; 24:30) with the meaning 'lacking sense'.

274. The Hebrew ואמר לכל סכל הוא is ambiguous, meaning either that the fool reveals his own folly to everyone he meets or else that he describes each person he meets as a fool. The English rendering above seeks to preserve something of that ambiguity. See Seow, *Ecclesiastes*, 313.

275. Although מקום usually refers to a physical location, it can also refer to a post or office (see 1 Kgs 20:24; so Gordis, *Koheleth: The Man and His World*, 318).

Apparently prompted by the reference to someone in authority in v. 4, vv. 5–7 provide another example of the inversion of order in the world. Verse 5 introduces the observation by announcing that it is evil (רעה) and that it originates with someone in authority (השליט).[276] Verse 6 inverts 'rich ones' (עשירים) with 'the simpleton' (הסכל),[277] an inversion reinforced in v. 7 by reference to 'slaves' (עבדים) who occupy the place of 'princes' (שרים). The fact that this social disorder originates with an error on the part of the ruler in v. 5 probably serves once again to highlight the fragility of the ordered world sought by the wise, for it is not undone by malice or deliberate subversion but by a simple mistake.

Fox comments: "such anomalies, we should note, were observed by 'traditional wisdom' too; see Prov 19:10 and 30:21–23."[278] Qoheleth's comments stand out, however, because this focus on the source of the evil lies in an apparently innocent mistake. Qoheleth repeatedly highlights the fragility of wisdom, whereas the overall emphasis of Proverbs on the underlying order in creation suggests that these inversions are both temporary and prone to dissolution.

Qoheleth 10:8–11

> [8] The one who digs a pit may fall into it,
>> and one who breaks through a wall—a snake could bite him.
> [9] The one who moves stones may be injured by them,
>> and the one who splits logs may be endangered by them.

> [10] If the axe is blunt and it has not been previously sharpened,
>> then one must exert more force.
> However, wisdom is the advantage of the successful person.

> [11] If a snake bites before being charmed,
>> there is no advantage for the snake charmer.

---

276. It makes little sense to follow many versions that understand the preposition כ to mean 'like, as' (see the LXX, Vulgate, NASB, NRSV), particularly with the article on שליט 'ruler'. Rather, it should be understood in an emphatic sense (an asseverative or כ *veritas*). See Waltke and O'Connor, *An Introduction to Biblical Hebrew Syntax*, §11.2.9c, p. 204; Seow, *Ecclesiastes*, 314; Longman, *The Book of Ecclesiastes*, 241 n. 19.

277. The segholate noun סֶכֶל is a hapax legomenon and is usually treated as synonymous with סָכָל (see Qoh 2:19; 7:17; 10:3, 14). However, סָכָל is never used in contrast to עשיר, which would seem an odd antithesis. Seow thus appropriately suggests that 'simpleton' may be a better understanding of the segholate noun here (see Seow, *Ecclesiastes*, 314–15). The verse also contains an unusual grammatical parallelism: the first line states that the singular סכל ('simpleton') is appointed to the plural מרומים רבים ('important positions'), while the second line has the plural עשירים ('rich') sitting in the singular שפל ('place').

278. Fox, *A Time to Tear Down*, 304.

In vv. 8–11 Qoheleth again diminishes the value of wisdom by contrasting a number of situations in which wisdom is of no value (vv. 8–9 and 11) with a single instance in which wisdom does have an advantage (v. 10). The four-line proverb of vv. 8–9 counts situations in which people are unjustly injured (so, conversely, their injury is not punishment for wrongdoing) while going about their business.[279] There is no comment on whether the person performing the tasks is wise or foolish, rich or poor, or good or evil. There is no indication that any course of action could have avoided the unwanted outcome. These words are thus reminiscent of Qoheleth's previous comments in 9:11–12.

Although vv. 8–9 appear to offer no hope that wisdom could benefit the people in the accidents described, v. 10 mitigates this by providing an example in which wisdom could prove beneficial. Determining the precise meaning of v. 10, however, has long proved troublesome.[280] The protasis of the conditional sentence is relatively straightforward, although it may be better to re-vocalize קֵהָה from Piel to Qal קָהָה ('is blunt') so the clause reads 'if the axe is blunt . . .'.[281]

The second clause is probably best understood as epexegetical rather than as part of the apodosis. Although many take הוא ('he, it') to be the wielder of the axe, it is most natural to take it as the axe itself (since it is the only antecedent explicitly mentioned in the text). Although the context ought to make it clear what the referent is, the clause is particularly difficult. The word פנים

---

279. Contra Crenshaw (*Ecclesiastes*, 172), who argues that the activities in v. 8 are criminal in nature, and the outcomes are examples of retributive justice. The digging of a pit may be the action of a hunter of animals (for example, see Jer 18:22; 48:43–44; Prov 26:27; Pss 7:16[15]; 35:7; 57:7[6]; and Sir 27:26, where pits are dug as traps) rather than a criminal act, and the parallel activities in v. 9 are clearly not criminal in nature. The information in v. 8 is simply insufficient to conclude that criminal acts worthy of retribution are depicted, and the broader context counts against such a conclusion. Most commentators view these as examples of "occupational danger"—see, for example, Seow, *Ecclesiastes*, 326; Longman, *The Book of Ecclesiastes*, 244. The prefix verbs in these verses should be read modally (as in the NASB, NEB, NIV, NET; Longman, *The Book of Ecclesiastes*, 243; Seow, *Ecclesiastes*, 307) and not in a real mood (as in the LXX; KJV, RSV, NRSV), which makes little sense of the comments.

280. The ancient versions attest to this. Ginsburg (*The Song of Songs and Coheleth*, 424) provides translations for comparison—from the LXX: 'If the axe falls and it troubles a face, then he will strengthen his strength. The advantage of man is wisdom'; the Vulgate: 'If the iron is blunt and it is not as before, but if it is dull, it can be sharpened with much labor. And after industry follows wisdom'; the Syriac: 'If the axe be blunt, and it troubles the face and increases the slain, and the advantage of the upright is wisdom'.

281. The alternative is, as Seow indicates, to read the Piel impersonally: 'one has blunted' (see Seow, *Ecclesiastes*, 317). However, the absence of the object marker on the noun counts against this.

'face' is frequently understood as a reference to the edge of the axe that has not been sharpened.[282] However, the normal word used to refer to the edge of an axe or other cutting implement is פה 'mouth' (see Gen 34:26; Exod 17:13; Josh 10:28; Job 1:15, 17, etc.). Only in Ezek 21:21[16] is פנים possibly used in reference to the edge of a sword, and the meaning there is disputed.[283] Seow is likely correct to note that פנים is better understood adverbially with the sense 'before' (either temporally or spatially) along the lines of לפנים.[284]

The final term in the clause, קִלְקַל, is vocalized in the MT as a Pilpel and is presumably a denominative verb derived from קלל 'smooth, shiny'. From this the verb is said to mean 'to sharpen', based on the rapid back-and-forth movement associated with both polishing and sharpening. Understood this way, the pronoun הוא must refer to the one (not) doing the sharpening of the axe. An alternative is to revocalize קלקל as a Polpal (so קֻלְקַל), giving the verb a passive meaning and rendering: "and it has not been previously sharpened."[285]

The apodosis is expressed in the words וחילים יגבר, which imply that greater exertion is required when the condition described in the protasis occurs: when the axe is blunt, greater effort is needed to achieve the goal. The purpose for recording this proverb, however, is stated in a subsequent clause that is also difficult. The word הכשיר is the crux of the various interpretations of the verse. The MT vocalizes it as a Hiphil infinitive construct from כשר, meaning 'to succeed'. Although the Hiphil is not used elsewhere in Biblical Hebrew, it is used in postbiblical Hebrew with the meaning 'to permit, adapt, make appropriate'. Seow follows this lead, although his final rendering, "It is an advantage to appropriate wisdom," uses an entirely different meaning for the English word *appropriate*.[286] However, many Hebrew manuscripts, together with the Vorlagen of the LXX, Symmachus, and the Syriac suggest that the Hebrew should be read as a definite term with a substantive meaning "the successful one."[287]

---

282. So Fox, *A Time to Tear Down*, 305; Longman, *The Book of Ecclesiastes*, 243; NASB; NRSV.

283. Leslie C. Allen (*Ezekiel 20–48* [WBC 29; Dallas: Word, 1990] 20 n. 21.c) writes, "Heb. פניך is usually interpreted as 'your edge' (cf. Eccl 10:10), but there appears to be a directional chiasmus 'rear, left, right, front.'" Allen renders Ezek 21:21[16]: "Lunge to the rear, to the right, to the left, and wherever your front is situated."

284. Seow, *Ecclesiastes*, 317.

285. See G. R. Driver, "Problems and Solutions," *VT* 4 (1954) 232. On the morphology, see Waltke and O'Connor, *An Introduction to Biblical Hebrew Syntax*, §21.2.3a, p. 360.

286. See Seow, *Ecclesiastes*, 307, 318.

287. See Fox, *A Time to Tear Down*, 306.

In spite of these difficulties, this phrase is almost universally understood to be asserting that there is an advantage in wisdom, at least when it comes to the situation described in the proverb.

Thus Qoheleth is maintaining that the situation for the wise is not entirely hopeless—for, while there are unavoidable calamities in life (as described in vv. 8–9), there are also times when wisdom is of benefit to the wise, and this is one such example. The wise person would know to sharpen the axe and thus would benefit from the reduced effort required to finish the task (although this is not, in the scheme of things, saying much for the wise).

Yet even when one has a beneficial skill in a particular circumstance, success is not guaranteed. This is the point of v. 11. The fact that the ability to charm a snake is a skill places it within the broad compass of what can be referred to in BH as wisdom.[288] Qoheleth further diminishes the value of wisdom by noting that this skill is also contingent on circumstances that are beyond the control of the sage. As Seow notes, "Wisdom may have its advantage, but wisdom guarantees one nothing."[289]

Qoheleth 10:12–15

[12] The words of the mouth of a sage are gracious,
   but [the words of] the lips of a fool swallow him.
[13] The beginning of the words of his mouth is folly,
   and the end [of the words of] his mouth is wicked irrationality,
[14] but the fool speaks many words.
No one knows what is going to happen,
   and as for what will come after him, who can tell him?
[15] The toil of a fool wearies him
   because he does not know when to return to town.

Although this section begins by referring to the words of the wise,[290] its focus is directly on folly and its perils. Verses 12–14 begin by using the fact that the

---

288. See Isa 3:3. The description of the one who charms the snake as בעל הלשון 'master of the tongue' in place of the more usual מלחש (see Ps 58:6[5]) may draw attention to the broader role of this person as one who is an expert at incantations. Seow supports this with reference to a cognate Akkadian expression (*Ecclesiastes*, 318–19). He goes on to say that Qoheleth "may be alluding to the verbosity of the wisdom teachers, those who are ever ready to offer catchy advice on how to handle every situation in life" (p. 327).

289. Ibid.

290. Qoheleth states that the words from the mouth of a sage are חן. The only other instance of this noun in Ecclesiastes is 9:11, where Qoheleth observes almost the reverse—grace does not belong to the knowledgeable.

instruments of speech (mouth and lips) are also used for eating and builds an image of the (words of)[291] the lips of a fool as consuming him.

After thoroughly deriding the words of fools in these verses, Qoheleth re-states his observation in v. 14b that no one knows what will take place in the future (compare Qoh 8:7, 17). The relationship of this statement to the preceding material is not immediately clear. The absence of the conjunction could be taken as an indication that a new proverb is being introduced at this point with no direct relationship to the preceding material, and v. 14a is the third line in the proverb begun in v. 13.[292] However, because this observation is both preceded and succeeded by material denigrating folly, it is reasonable to infer that Qoheleth includes these words here because they do relate in some way to the subject of this passage. Consequently, Qoheleth is probably implying that much of the fool's verbosity relates to prognostication about the future, and because no one knows the future, this sort of talk is a supreme example of the evil irrationality ascribed to fools in v. 13.

The association made here between the speaking of many words and the future (words that Qoheleth implies are futile, based on his certainty that the future is unknowable) suggests that Qoheleth may be referring to prophets.[293] The fact that he essentially describes them as fools further places him, and the wisdom movement he speaks for, in opposition to the representatives of ancient Israelite religion. For a reader familiar with those beliefs, this further tarnishes the reputation of the wisdom movement and enhances the epilogist's argument.

Another reason that Qoheleth included foretelling here may stem from his earlier assertion that the sages desired to know the future (see 8:17). Taken together, these two passages imply that the fool and the sage are not as different as one might first suppose. It is even possible that Qoheleth was quietly attacking the sages who made great noise about preparing for the future and ensuring that the future would bring rewards and profit to their students. This was, after all, an underlying aim of the wisdom movement.

Verse 15 moves from discussing the fools' speech to discussing their toil (עמל). However, this verse contains a number of difficulties, a fact that

---

291. An ellipsis of the word דברי appears at the beginning of the second stich in the proverb of v. 12; thus, the meaning is 'words of the lips of a fool . . .'. This same ellipsis appears again in v. 13.

292. Compare with Proverbs, where separate collections of proverbs are often listed asyndetically, but the lines of each proverb are joined with the conjunction ו; for example, Prov 19:1, 3, 4, 5, 6.

293. See above, p. 163, for another possible critique of the prophets in Qoh 5:6[7].

prompted Fox to state that "the text is undoubtedly corrupt."[294] There is lack of agreement in both number and gender (הכסילים תיגענו) which is awkward, and the meaning of the final clause is unclear. The various emendations proposed by scholars either fail to resolve all the difficulties or are unconvincing, so the only alternative is to attempt to reconstruct the sense of the original. For this task, there is relatively widespread agreement that the text continues the denigration of fools from the preceding material by stating that they are so wearied by their toil that they cannot find their way to town.[295] Although this clause is often assumed to mean the fool(s) do not know *how* to go to town (the אשר is probably causal), the text literally only says, "because he does not know to go to town." Thus, it is equally possible that a temporal sense could be attributed to the clause (since both readings are equally difficult), which would have the entire verse stating that fools are wearied by their toil because they don't know *when* to go to town, perhaps meaning they do not realize when it is time to finish work for the day and return home.

Regardless of precisely how the difficulties are to be resolved, the clear condemnation of the fool in this context may recall the ideas expressed in 10:3 that the fool demonstrates his folly to all and in 10:10 that wisdom assists the wise in reducing their workload.

Qoheleth 10:16–20

> [16] Woe to you, O land, whose king is childish
>> and whose princes feast in the morning.
> [17] Blessed are you, O land, whose king is from the nobility
>> and whose princes feast at the appropriate time,
>> to become strong and not in drunkenness.
>
> [18] Through laziness the roof sags,
>> and through idle hands the house leaks.
>
> [19] They make a feast for laughter,
>> and wine makes life enjoyable,
> but money preoccupies everyone.
>
> [20] Even in your thoughts do not curse the king,
>> and in your sleeping rooms do not curse a rich man,
> for a bird of the sky might carry the sound,
>> a winged creature may report the matter.

---

294. Fox, *A Time to Tear Down*, 307.

295. See Longman, *The Book of Ecclesiastes*, 248; Seow, *Ecclesiastes*, 320; Fox, *A Time to Tear Down*, 308.

The remainder of chap. 10 consists of four short proverbs that do not appear to have much to tie them either to the surrounding material or to one another. Although some have sought to find a common thread connecting the sayings, the thematic links are too vague to be entirely convincing, particularly with regard to v. 18; furthermore, v. 20 counsels against criticizing the rich and the powerful—which is precisely what Qoheleth does in v. 16.[296]

Verses 16–17 form a single proverb regarding the behavior of the government of the land, lamenting the situation in which an incompetent ruler and government are in power and extolling the inverse. The term נער, which stands in antithesis to בן חורים 'nobles' is generally accepted as referring not merely to a 'youth' (compare this with Qoh 4:13, which uses the noun ילד 'child' for such a person) but to someone who is in some way disreputable (some suggestions include 'minor, immature [person], slave, childish [person]').[297] The activity of the others who are in power is also highlighted because they בבקר יאכלו ('eat in the morning'). Although the context clearly indicates that this activity is regarded negatively, it is not immediately clear how "eating in the morning" could be inherently negative. What is specifically negative is not the eating itself but apparently the timing, for it is contrasted with בעת יאכלו 'they eat at the [appropriate] time' in v. 17. As a result, most commentators agree that Qoheleth is referring to more than merely eating and reason that the reference is to feasting or some similar indulgent activity that is inappropriate early in the morning but acceptable at other times (see Isa 5:11–13; 21:5).[298]

---

296. While the repetition of some ideas in these verses is suggestive of a degree of unity (i.e., the reference to a king in vv. 16 and 20, the references to eating in vv. 16–17 and 19), these repetitions are sufficient only to support the claim that the proverbs may have been grouped together because they touched on similar topics but not the claim that there is a logical flow to the verses. Some who argue for thematic unity include K. A. Farmer, *Proverbs and Ecclesiastes* (ITC; Grand Rapids: Eerdmans, 1991) 189; Ginsburg, *The Song of Songs and Coheleth*, 442; G. Wildeboer, *Der Prediger* (KHC 17; Tübingen, 1898); Hertzberg, *Der Prediger*; Fox, *A Time to Tear Down*, 308–11.

297. See Seow, *Ecclesiastes*, 328–29; Fox, *A Time to Tear Down*, 309; Longman, *The Book of Ecclesiastes*, 249.

298. Biblical Hebrew usually employs more specific terms when referring to feasting, such are חג, משתה, or כרה. There are, however, a few instances where אכל alone (i.e., without explicit use of the more specific terminology) appears to be used in reference to feasting of some type; compare 1 Kgs 4:20; 18:42; and Amos 6:4. Interestingly, Ps 101:8 records a promise from the king that he will dispense justice (by destroying the wicked) every morning (לבקרים), and 2 Sam 15:2–6 suggests the same thing. Concluding that this indicates that mornings were traditional or appropriate times for dispensing justice based only on these references would be rather tenuous, however.

The final clause in v. 17 breaks the parallelism by qualifying the eating of the rulers who bring blessing to the land. The meaning of בגבורה is difficult, the expression appearing only elsewhere in Jer 10:6; Ps 65:7[6]; and 90:10, where it means 'in *or* with might, strength'.[299] Accordingly, the expression appears to indicate that the rulers are eating for their well-being rather than for enjoyment, an understanding followed by the majority of interpreters. An alternative meaning is 'manliness' (see Jer 51:30), prompting suggestions that the qualification here is that these rulers eat with maturity,[300] the primary difference between these interpretations being that the first presents the goal of the eating while the second presents the manner in which they eat.

One indication of the meaning of this term can be derived from the subsequent term, against which it is contrasted. Although the word שתי is a hapax legomenon, it is generally understood to mean 'drunkenness' and is derived from the root שתה ('drink').[301] Because this appears to exclude becoming drunk as being the aim of the eating of the second type of governors, it is probably better to understand בגבורה as also making reference to the goal of the eating, that is, 'to become strong'. This group is feasting not merely for self-gratification but for sustenance, presumably to govern the land better.

At face value, the proverb in v. 18 refers to the perils of laziness by illustrating the consequences of a lack of household maintenance.[302] Although the claim that this proverb functions here to illustrate the dangers to the land of the type of government depicted in v. 16 by understanding "house" to be a metaphor for the land has some merit, the connections are too vague to permit any degree of certainty.[303] A more likely reference for הבית is the royal

---

299. These are the only places where בגבורה is found without a suffix or without being in construct.

300. See Seow, *Ecclesiastes*, 330; Fox, *A Time to Tear Down*, 308. Symmachus renders the term ἀνδραγαθία 'bravery, manly virtue'. This understanding of the word here in v. 17 would provide an effective contrast to the use of נער in v. 16.

301. Seow suggests that this is a variant form of שתיה (Esth 1:8; and post-BH) and provides some morphological analogies (*Ecclesiastes*, 330). The LXX renders the Hebrew בשתי as αἰσχυνθήσονται 'to be ashamed', thus reading the Hebrew word as a derivative of the root בוש.

302. This verse contains a number of difficulties: the apparently dual adjectival form עצלתים is a hapax legomenon and is unique in that nowhere else in BH do adjectives appear in a dual form (so Seow, ibid., 330–31). This has prompted a number of different explanations of the form. Furthermore, מקרה is also a hapax. In spite of these difficulties, scholars generally agree on the meaning of the proverb, at least on the surface level.

303. Seow (ibid., 331) admits that the link is possible, while Fox (*A Time to Tear Down*, 309) recognizes the link but admits that v. 18 is "slightly out of line with the context and was probably not written for this place." Gordis (*Koheleth: The Man and His World*, 327) overstates the case when he says that any such connection is "far-fetched."

house, prompted by the previous verses. Thus, the point of the aphorism is that, through the inappropriate feasting of the members of the government, the government decays, and the land itself suffers.[304]

Verse 19 recalls the words of vv. 16–17 by focusing on food and drink, which, according to this proverb, provide enjoyment in life. The crux comes, however, in the meaning of the third colon, in particular the meaning of the verb יענה. Many modern interpreters understand this to be a Qal form of the root meaning 'answer, respond'.[305] The meaning of the proverb then is that money answers all the requirements for enjoyment: it is with money that one obtains the food and wine that in turn provide enjoyment to the living.[306] Most lexicons, however, recognize a number of semantically distinct homomorphic roots with meanings such as 'be occupied', 'be bowed down, afflicted', and even 'sing' in addition to the common 'answer'.[307] These variations are reflected, to some extent, in the versions.[308] However, Qoheleth has elsewhere only used terms associated with ענה II 'be occupied' (see 1:13; 3:10; 5:19[20]), suggesting that this is the appropriate reading here as well. Consequently, Qoheleth's point is that money occupies (or preoccupies) everyone.[309]

Consequently, this apparently innocuous proverb about enjoyment becomes a subtle attack on the wealthy, who are preoccupied with money, as Seow says: "Thus, 10:19 can be read as an affirmation of pleasure—perhaps that was the original use of the saying—but it can also be taken as an indictment of the lifestyle of the rich: all they do is prepare food for parties, including the most intoxicating wine, and they are all preoccupied with money."[310] If Qoh 10:19 is actually an attack on the wealthy, then the next verse functions as a warning against exactly the sort of criticism in which Qoheleth has just indulged. The opening particle גם need not indicate an explicit connection with the preceding material; instead, it is better understood as stressing

---

304. My thanks to Ian Young for suggesting this line of interpretation.

305. See ענה I in BDB, 772a.

306. So Longman, *The Book of Ecclesiastes*, 251–52; Gordis, *Koheleth: The Man and His World*, 328; Whybray, *Ecclesiastes* (NCB), 157. Fox argues that the leap from 'answers' to 'provides' (for which Hos 2:23–24 is commonly cited) is invalid (*A Time to Tear Down*, 310).

307. See BDB, 772b–777a.

308. The LXX and Vulgate reflect ענה I 'answer, respond', while the Syriac reflects ענה III 'afflict'.

309. So Fox, *A Time to Tear Down*, 310; Seow, *Ecclesiastes*, 332–33. Both Fox and Seow parse the verb here as Hiphil in reading it with this meaning, rather than associating it with a distinct homomorphic root, despite the fact that Seow recognizes the existence of ענה II in Qoh 1:13 (*Ecclesiastes*, 121).

310. Ibid., 340.

the following word. The most obvious meaning for that word, מדע, is 'knowledge', which many extend to mean 'thoughts'. Seow, however, objects that the word never has this sense elsewhere and that the meaning 'thought' is not as easily derived from 'knowledge' as many would argue.[311]

On the basis of the parallel expression בחדרי משכבך 'sleeping rooms', it has been suggested that מדע be emended to מצע 'couch', although there is no manuscript support for this alteration.[312] Others argue that the term may implicitly refer to sexual knowledge and so, by extension, is a reference to 'bedchamber'.[313] This explanation, however, requires a substantial amount of extrapolation on the part of the reader in order to arrive at the supposed meaning, given the starting point, even under the influence of the parallel reference to "sleeping rooms" in the following clause.

Ultimately the best solution is to understand מדע as a reference to one's thoughts. In spite of Seow's objections, Fox has demonstrated that there are instances in which מדע does mean 'mind' rather than 'knowledge', so this clearly was not too difficult a derivation.[314] Qoheleth's warning is in line with his previous comments on the corruption of those in power, as suggested by both the desire to curse them and the danger of having the curse reported to them.

Throughout this section are examples of apparently orthodox wisdom sayings from Qoheleth, a fact that raises the question why the epilogist would have included material of this sort if his aim was to undermine the wisdom movement. A few points can be made in answer to this question. First, if the epilogist's presentation of Qoheleth's words bore no correspondence to the wisdom materials with which his audience was familiar, the claim that Qoheleth represented the sages would be less credible.

Second, these sayings are clearly rather limited in their scope. For example, some of this advice extends only to the value of wisdom over folly and is even then mitigated by the stated inability of anyone, sage or fool, to know the future. Qoheleth's other advice appears to be aimed at avoiding danger from authorities operating in a world where good had no guarantee of reward

---

311. Ibid., 333.

312. Felix Perles, *Analekten zur Textkritik des Alten Testaments* (Munich, 1895) 71–72; cf. W. Zimmerli, *Das Buch des Predigers Salomo* (ATD 16/1; Göttingen: Vandenhoeck & Ruprecht, 1962); Lauha, *Kohelet*, 196.

313. L. Koehler and W. Baumgartner, *Lexicon in Veteris Testamenti Libros* (Leiden: Brill, 1958) 497; NASB. Seow (*Ecclesiastes*, 333) uses similar logic to arrive at the rendering 'intimacy'.

314. Fox, *A Time to Tear Down*, 310 writes: "*Madda⁽* means 'mind' (rather than 'knowledge') in 1QS 7.3 (if a man 'gets angry in his *madda⁽*') and 7.5 (if a man commits deceit 'in his *madda⁽*'; similarly 6.9). In Aramaic, it sometimes means 'thoughts' or 'mind' (rather than 'knowledge', its usual sense), e.g., Tg-Ps 34:1."

and evil no guarantee of punishment. As such, Qoheleth's advice here derives from a world view that is fundamentally at odds with that which underpins much of the remainder of the Hebrew Bible.

Third, my interpretation of the epilogue is not that there is absolutely no value in anything the sages ever said but that their type of wisdom, which sought to provide answers to the more difficult problems of life, was either fraudulent or futile. It is not surprising that wise material should be found in the words of Qoheleth as recorded by the epilogist. Verses 16–20 are reminiscent of traditional wisdom sayings, thus locating Qoheleth firmly among the sages. They also do not say or claim very much, so conforming to Qoheleth's assertion that the knowledge of the sages is limited.

Qoheleth 11:1–6

The opening verses of chap. 11 are loosely bound together by the common theme of the inability of human beings to control their environment and their ignorance of the future (reflected in the repeated reference to 'not knowing' in vv. 2, 5, and 6).

Qoheleth 11:1–2

> [1] Cast your bread on the surface of the water,
>   for after many days you may find it.
> [2] Give a portion to seven, or even to eight,
>   for you do not know what evil may come upon the earth.

The traditional understanding of v. 1 is that it extols alms-giving or charity. This interpretation is evident in the Targum as well as in Gregory Thaumaturgos, Rashi, and Rashbam. It is also reflected in an Arabic proverb: "Do good, cast your bread upon the waters, and one day you will be rewarded." Although this proverb is almost certainly influenced by Qoheleth's words, it does reflect the common understanding that this saying refers to charity.[315] On this view, Qoheleth is exhorting his readers to perform charitable acts with no justifiable expectation of a return (so the לחם refers to the charitable acts, and sending it on the surface of the water refers to giving with no apparent hope of a reward). The consequence then is the possibility that some benefit may flow from this act in the future. Aside from the antiquity of this interpretation, further support is found in some remarkably similar advice in the Egyptian *Instruction of Onkhsheshonqy*, which reads: "Do a good deed and throw it in the water,

---

315. See Gordis, *Koheleth: The Man and His World*, 329–30; Seow, *Ecclesiastes*, 343; Michael M. Homan, "Beer Production by Throwing Bread into Water: A New Interpretation of Qoh. XI 1–2," *VT* 52 (2002) 275.

when it dries up you will find it."[316] However, modern critics of this interpretation argue that it is out of place among Qoheleth's words.[317]

The primary alternative understanding among modern scholars is that Qoheleth is speaking of maritime trade.[318] In this view, לחם is either a metaphor for merchandise (a precedent for which is supposedly found in Prov 31:14) or else a specific reference to "grain."[319] Verse 2 is then understood to continue this theme of commercial advice by suggesting that spreading the risk will avoid misfortune. However, this interpretation faces a number of difficulties. First, Qoheleth does not suggest that sending one's bread on the surface of the waters will result in any profit, merely that it will be found after many days. Second, the resumptive pronominal suffix on the verb מצא 'find' suggests the recovery of what was originally sent. In trade the aim would not be to have the original goods returned but to make a profit. Third, the interpretation depends on an unattested meaning for the noun לחם. The only parallel cited, Prov 31:14, does not attribute the meaning 'merchandise' to לחם; rather, it likens the actions of the woman bringing food to the actions of a merchant ship. Although it might be argued that this meaning could be attributed to לחם metaphorically, there needs to be some means for the reader to infer the metaphorical meaning, and here there is no clear basis for such an inference.

Other attempts to make sense of Qoheleth's words are equally problematic.[320] Most recently, Homan has argued that these verses refer to the manufacture and distribution of beer: Qoheleth is recommending beer-production and consumption in perilous times, similar to the advice already given in 9:7.[321] The argument is unconvincing, however, for a number of reasons. Homan appeals to Akkadian literature in which the verb *nadû* 'to throw' is used in technical language for brewing beer. However, Qoheleth uses the Piel imperative of שלח, which does *not* mean 'to throw'. Furthermore, the Akkadian texts cited by Homan list other ingredients besides bread, and the bread is a special type of 'bread' used specifically in the production of beer (*bappir*—a sweet and possibly pungent bread made from barley dough, mixed

---

316. A. Lichtheim (ed.), *Ancient Egyptian Literature* (Berkeley: University of California Press, 1980) 3.174.

317. See Gordis, *Koheleth: The Man and His World*, 330; Longman, *The Book of Ecclesiastes*, 256.

318. So F. Delitzsch, *Commentary on the Song of Songs and Ecclesiastes* (trans. M. G. Easton; Edinburgh: T. & T. Clark, 1877) 391–93; Gordis, *Koheleth: The Man and His World*, 330; Zimmerli, *Das Buch des Predigers Salomo*; Longman, *The Book of Ecclesiastes*, 256; Hubbard, *Ecclesiastes, Song of Solomon*, 223–32.

319. So the NET Bible. Understanding לחם to mean 'grain' is itself a questionable step.

320. See Fox, *A Time to Tear Down*, 311–12, for a brief summary of other approaches.

321. Homan, "Beer Production by Throwing Bread into Water," 275–78.

with malt to make mash for beer). Fully baked bread (in which the yeast is killed in the cooking process and is therefore of no use for fermentation) is not used in beer-production. In light of this, לחם 'bread' here would need to have a special meaning. Finally, Qoheleth only makes reference to wine (יין), and there is no word for beer in BH.[322]

Upon close examination, the arguments against the traditional understanding are not particularly compelling. In Hos 10:7 the expression על פני מים 'on the face of the waters' is used to describe the isolation of a stick, suggesting a parallel here, where the bread is cut off from its original owner without hope of return. Furthermore, it is unlikely that Qoheleth is suggesting that rewards are guaranteed for charitable works. The imperfective form תמצאנו should be understood modally, in keeping with the remainder of the surrounding material, and Qoheleth is advising his readers to do good, for good deeds *may* result in some benefit in the future. Consequently, this advice does not contradict Qoheleth's fundamental point that the future is unpredictable, a point quite clearly made in the second verse.

The term חלק 'portion' in v. 2 is used elsewhere, most commonly with reference to land, but also more broadly to a part of any whole, including food (see Deut 18:8; Hab 1:16). The fact that Qoheleth does not explicitly state in this verse what the portion is from suggests that he is referring to the aforementioned לחם 'bread'. This, together with the structural and semantic similarities between vv. 1 and 2, suggests that the two verses ought to be read together.[323]

For those who understand v. 1 as a piece of commercial advice, the second verse is understood as counsel to spread the risk of a commercial venture. In light of the difficulties with this interpretation outlined above, I consider it better to see this, too, as encouragement to give not merely to one or two but to many.[324]

In both of these verses the meaning of the conjunction כי is critical to their interpretation. Seow offers four possible meanings: motivational ('for'), concessive ('even though'), emphatic ('indeed'), or as a weakened asseverative

---

322. Suggestions that שכר means 'beer' based on cognates are unconvincing. See David Jordan, *An Offering of Wine: An Introductory Exploration of the Role of Wine in the Hebrew Bible and Ancient Judaism through the Examination of the Semantics of Some Keywords* (Ph.D. diss., University of Sydney, 2003), for a detailed discussion of these issues.

323. Both verses are divided by כי, following which is a reference to a future outcome or situation.

324. See W. M. W. Roth, "The Numerical Sequence x/x+1 in the Old Testament," *VT* 12 (1962) 300–311, for discussion of the significance of the numeric pattern used here by Qoheleth.

best left untranslated.[325] Although Seow argues against the motivational meaning in v. 1, if the verse is understood as a reference to charity a good case can be made that this is precisely Qoheleth's meaning. Aside from the fact that 'for' is the most common of the four possible meanings for כי in BH, the performance of charitable deeds based on the possibility of future reward is in keeping with Qoheleth's thought elsewhere. Qoheleth has argued that, because it is not clear which actions in the present could result in future benefits, it is better not to eliminate options by choosing one course of action to the exclusion of all others (see, for example, Qoh 7:16–18; 11:6). Committing to one path among many, when the outcome is unpredictable, has less chance of producing favorable results. In this context Qoheleth's point is that charitable giving in the present may result in some return in the future, but not giving in the present will certainly produce no future reward, so the appropriate advice is to give in the present.

Given the parallels between these two verses, כי probably functions similarly in both instances. The distribution of a portion to several in v. 2 is again motivated by the unknowability of the future. Together, these two verses recommend giving even when returns cannot be predicted, for the future is inherently unpredictable.

Qoheleth 11:3–4

³ If the clouds are full they will pour rain on the earth.
Whether a tree falls to the south or to the north,
   there where it has fallen it will remain.
⁴ Whoever watches the wind will not sow,
   and whoever looks at the clouds will not reap.

Verse 3 is generally understood to be describing events that are beyond human control, further underscoring the inability of human beings to understand and control their environment, and ultimately their own lives.

The repeated reference to the clouds (עבים) links v. 4 to v. 3. Most scholars understand it to be a description of a farmer who awaits perfect conditions in which to sow and harvest a crop and consequently never actually sows or reaps.[326] However, Qoheleth could well be using this aphorism to criticize the work of the sages further. It is apparent that at least one of the tasks of the sages was to observe the natural world in order to derive advice capable of

---

325. Seow, *Ecclesiastes*, 336.
326. E.g., Whybray, *Ecclesiastes* (NCB), 159; Fox, *A Time to Tear Down*, 314; Longman, *The Book of Ecclesiastes*, 257; Murphy, *Ecclesiastes*, 109; Seow, *Ecclesiastes*, 345.

enhancing one's lot in life.[327] These words may then be Qoheleth's criticism of the sages who spent their time pondering the world around them but never actually doing anything productive. They were obsessed with what was beyond their control and understanding.

Qoheleth 11:5–6

> [5] Just as you do not know the way the life-force enters the fetus in the womb
>   of a pregnant woman,
>   so you do not know the work of God, who makes everything.
> [6] Sow your seed in the morning,
>   and do not rest your hands in the evening,
> for you do not know whether one will succeed or the other,
>   or whether both alike will be good.

Verses 5 and 6 draw this section to a close. Verse 5 reiterates the limitations of human knowledge by following a concrete illustration with the point being made (a proverbial form found elsewhere; see Prov 25:3; 26:14; 27:19).[328] The first part of the proverb relates an example of something widely acknowledged as unknowable—how the life-force (רוח 'spirit') enlivens the growing fetus in the womb—to illustrate the point that the work of God is also unknowable. There is some debate over whether the first part of the proverb provides two examples or one. The NASB, for example, understands two examples, reading, "Just as you do not know the path of the wind and how bones are formed in the womb of the pregnant woman. . . ."[329] The absence of a conjunction on כעצמים 'like the bones' argues against this option.[330] Furthermore, a number of Hebrew manuscripts read בעצמים 'in the bones', which also appears to be the Vorlage of the Targum, a reading that is easily justified and makes better sense of the proverb as a whole and so is to be preferred.

Aside from merely illustrating the existence of human ignorance, this saying highlights the magnitude of this ignorance by stating that we cannot know the work (מעשה) of God who makes (יעשה) everything. If God makes everything and we are unable to know what he makes, what is there that we can

---

327. See 1 Kgs 5:13[4:33], where one of Solomon's wise activities is collecting of information about the natural world. Qoheleth also makes repeated references to the work of God (מעשה האלהים) in Qoh 7:13; 8:17; 11:5.

328. The syntax employed by Qoheleth here (כאשר 'just as' followed by ככה 'so') is only elsewhere reflected in Jer 19:11 (where the form is reversed).

329. Translations are divided in their understanding; those opting for two examples include the LXX, ASV, NASB, NIV, and NET, while those opting for one include the AB, NEB, NJPSV, RSV, and ESV.

330. See Gordis, *Koheleth: The Man and His World*, 332.

know? Clearly Qoheleth is very pessimistic about how much human beings *can* know.

In light of these limitations on human knowledge, Qoheleth draws his conclusion. It is not possible to predict the outcome of actions in the present (so vv. 1–2, 5) except perhaps to say that no action will yield no results at all. Therefore, act when the opportunity arises (בבקר . . . ולערב 'in the morning . . . and in the evening'), for you cannot know which action will be successful. Some take לערב to mean 'until evening', with the expression explicitly encompassing the whole working day.[331] However, this would normally be written either following the expression מן־בקר 'from morning' or with the preposition עד 'until' in place of ל 'to'.[332] Elsewhere, לערב means 'in the evening'—as in Gen 49:27; Ps 59:7[6], 15[14]; and 90:6. This reference to discrete times of the day is supported by the references to הזה או זה 'this or that'. This *carpe diem* advice is reminiscent, not only of the opening advice in vv. 1–2, but also of Qoheleth's conclusion to enjoy life when you can because the future is uncertain.

Once again, the themes of Qoheleth's thought in these verses run counter to the fundamental presuppositions of the wisdom movement that there is enough predictability to life to allow the sage some control over his or her lot. For Qoheleth, there is no hope of this sort of control, there is no value in the advice of those who claim to have access to predictable answers, and those who search for knowledge of this sort are ultimately unproductive. Both God's ways and, consequently, the future are unknowable, so it is pointless to attempt to understand them.

Qoheleth 11:7–12:7

The final section of Qoheleth's words concentrates on advice to the young in light of the impending onset of old age and, ultimately, death. The poem of Qoh 12:1–7 is well known, but the less well-known final verses of chap. 11 function as an introduction to that poem, providing two comments, each terminated by a הבל statement.

Qoheleth 11:7–10

⁷ The light is pleasant, and it is good for the eyes to see the sun. ⁸ Indeed, if one should live many years, let him rejoice in them all, and let him remember the days of darkness, for they will be many. Everything that is to come is senseless.

---

331. So the NET, NEB, AB.
332. See Seow, *Ecclesiastes*, 337–38.

> ⁹ Rejoice, young man, while you are young. Let your heart delight in your youth. Live by the desires of your heart and by what your eyes see, and know that on all these things God will bring you to judgment.
>
> ¹⁰ Remove anger from your heart and turn away evil from your body, for youth and young adulthood are fleeting.

Qoheleth begins this section by using light and dark symbolically to affirm life, an affirmation that appears to contradict some of his previous comments (e.g., 4:2–3). However, the immediate problem in this section is determining the precise referents of the images. The key lies in the parallelism between the light and the sun in v. 7. Elsewhere, 'seeing the sun' is clearly a reference to being alive rather than merely to the best parts of life (see Qoh 6:5; Ps 58:9[8]), suggesting that Qoheleth is contrasting life with death. However, some scholars object to this on the grounds that Qoheleth admits no knowledge of what comes after death and would not have drawn such a distinction.[333] Furthermore, Qoheleth clearly moves to speak of a contrast between youth and old age in both the remainder of this chapter and the poem that opens chap. 12.

Qoheleth's supposed agnosticism about what happens following death, however, is not an adequate basis for excluding death as the referent for the "days of darkness" or "everything that is to come." When Qoheleth contemplated the implications of death previously, he concluded that death undermines any significance to life (e.g., 2:12–26), which indicates a decidedly negative bias regarding death that goes beyond pure agnosticism. Indeed, in light of what he said in 9:10, it is clear that he cannot in any way be described as neutral about what is to come after death. Furthermore, the fact that the "days of darkness" will be many (Qoh 11:8), even though one can rejoice in all the years one lives, implies that those days will include (at least) the days when one is dead.

While a number of commentators maintain that Qoheleth's distinction is between life and death,[334] some understand the "days of darkness" to be a reference to both death and old age or unpleasant times during life.[335] This view overcomes the objections that the "days of darkness" are restricted to times

---

333. See Seow, who writes of the phrase 'all that comes' (כל שבא) in 11:8 that "it is unlikely that the author is talking about what comes after death, about which he insists no one knows anything" (ibid., 348).

334. So Whybray, *Ecclesiastes* (NCB), 161; Fox, *A Time to Tear Down*, 317; Gordis, *Koheleth: The Man and His World*, 334–45. Gordis claims that חשך 'darkness' is frequently used as an epithet for death (citing Qoh 6:4; 1 Sam 2:9; Job 10:21; 17:13; 18:18; Ps 88:13; Prov 20:20).

335. So Longman, *The Book of Ecclesiastes*, 259–60.

during life (see above) and also avoids any contradiction with the material that follows. Furthermore, it fits well with the assertion that everything to come is הבל, a statement made by Qoheleth without restricting it to the "days of darkness."

Thus Qoheleth reiterates his previous advice to enjoy life when we can. The call to remember the "days of darkness" reminds his readers that they may not always have the opportunity to enjoy life and certainly that life is limited, thus reinforcing the urgency associated with enjoying life while it is possibile to do so (compare Qoh 2:24; 3:12–13).

The exhortation to enjoy life whenever possible moves to an exhortation to the young to enjoy their youth in v. 9. Following these instructions to enjoy youth by fulfilling the desires of one's heart, Qoheleth adds a final clause that appears to warn the reader of the inevitability of God's judgment. For many, this apparent warning is so at odds with Qoheleth's thought that they assign it to a pious editor, who was seeking to mitigate the starkness of the contrast with advice elsewhere in the Hebrew Bible (see below). Salters, for example, writes: "The . . . passage so blatantly contradicts Nu 15 [39] that interpreters of the day felt that a modification was called for in the text itself, and so added the words: 'but know that for all these things God will bring you to judgment', creating a kind of irony in the passage. Since Qoheleth elsewhere doubts whether God punishes sin, this passage must be from a hand other than his."[336] Nonetheless, there is little textual warrant for removing the final clause, and the degree of piety inherent in these words is easily overstated. It is likely that within the broader canonical context the expression יביאך האלהים במשפט ('God will bring you to judgment') imports significantly more semantic baggage than is warranted by its immediate location in Qoheleth's work. Qoheleth has made it clear that it is not possible to understand the work of God, as recently as v. 5, and yet he maintains that human lives are subject to God's sovereignty (see 7:13–14). Within this context, this warning amounts to the equivalent of the comments in 7:16–18: Be wary of God, for he controls your fate. Since you cannot know what God requires or what pleases him, you need to try many things in the hope that you do something that God finds favorable.

---

336. R. B. Salters, "Qoheleth and the Canon," *ExpTim* 86 (1975) 341. See also Lauha, *Kohelet*, 205; Zimmerli, *Das Buch des Predigers Salomo*; Galling, "Der Prediger," 120–23; Ginsburg, *The Song of Songs and Coheleth*, 454–55; Crenshaw, *Ecclesiastes*, 184. Fox writes, "The sentence is indeed somewhat intrusive in the series of imperatives, and of all proposed glosses in the book this is the most likely. But the arguments are not compelling" (*A Time to Tear Down*, 318).

The contrast between Qoheleth's conclusion and the teaching of the Torah reflects the difference in perspective—for Qoheleth there is no knowledge of what can be done to please God; in the Torah God has revealed his requirements. Qoheleth here says, "Rejoice, young man, while you are young. Let your heart delight in your youth. Live by the desires of your heart and by what your eyes see, and know that on all these things God will bring you to judgment." The instructions found in Num 15:39 read, "you will remember all the commandments of the LORD and do them, and not follow the lust of your own heart and your own eyes."[337] So troubling was this to traditional readers that various minor but significant alterations were made in early versions. It is precisely this inversion of biblical teaching that strikes the readers of Qoheleth who are familiar with the remainder of the Hebrew Bible most strongly and disposes them to regard the wisdom of Qoheleth and the other sages as aberrant.

Verse 10 continues the sequence of imperatives that instruct youth how to live, offering advice that is complementary to the advice of the previous verse. The exhortations here—to expunge anger and physical pain from one's body—serve to facilitate the enjoyment of life advocated in v. 9 and are followed by a clause offering the basis for this advice: youth is הבל.[338] Here it is likely that Qoheleth is focusing specifically on the transience of youth in using this term, although the fact that youth is both desirable and 'fleeting' ultimately makes it also 'senseless', in the same way that all else has been labeled senseless by Qoheleth.

Qoheleth 12:1–7

[1] Remember your Creator in the days of your youth,
before the evil days come, and the years approach
when you will say, "I have no delight in them."
[2] Before the sun, the light,
the moon, and the stars are darkened,
and the clouds return after the rain.
[3] On the day when the keepers of the house tremble,
the strong men convulse,
the grinding women cease because they are few,

---

337. NRSV. Compare with Job 37:7–8; Christianson, *A Time to Tell*, 116–17. See also Sir 5:2, which may well be a response to these words of Qoheleth.

338. The term שחרות is a hapax and appears to have caused difficulties for early versions. Most recent commentators understand the term to mean literally 'black hair', which Qoheleth uses in contrast to שיבה 'gray hair', a term used to designate old age (see Gen 15:15; 25:8; Lev 19:32; etc.). Seow also suggests that the term may be related to שחר 'dawn' (Seow, *Ecclesiastes*, 351).

those who look through the windows grow dim,
4 and the doors on the street are closed.
When the sound of the mill diminishes,
and the bird begins to sing,
and all the daughters of song are brought low,
5 even [men] are afraid of a high place
and terrors along the road.
The almond tree blossoms,
the grasshopper drags itself along,
and the caperberry loses its effectiveness.
For man is going to his eternal home
and mourners go around in the street.
6 Before the silver cord is snapped,
the golden bowl is crushed,
the jar at the spring is broken,
and the wheel is crushed at the pit.
7 Then the dust will return to the earth as it was,
and the spirit returns to God who gave it.

The poem about old age with which the words of Qoheleth are brought to a conclusion is well known for the interpretive difficulties it poses.[339] Few examples of Hebrew poetry are quite as rich in imagery as this poem is. For our purposes, however, the most significant aspect of the poem is found in 12:1, the advice to remember one's Creator while young. On the surface, this exhortation lies firmly within the realm of orthodox thought, reflecting such passages as Deut 7:18; 8:18; and Jer 51:50 (contrast Judg 8:34, where the people failed to remember YHWH). For some scholars this verse is the final justification for their assertion that Qoheleth's aim is to drive his readers to the life of faith.[340] For others, such as van der Wal, this verse is the conclusion to Qoheleth's work, and it functions as an attempt to bridge the gap between human beings and God that has been so apparent up to this point in Qoheleth's words:

---

339. That the subject of the poem is old age is widely agreed on, although there are alternatives. H. A. J. Kruger, for example, has suggested that it presents the notion of "cosmic deterioration" represented through "a threatening global natural disaster of an apocalyptic nature" (see H. A. J. Kruger, "Old Age Frailty versus Cosmic Deterioration? A Few Remarks on the Interpretation of Qohelet 11,7–12,8," in *Qohelet in the Context of Wisdom* [ed. A. Schoors; Leuven: Leuven University Press, 1998] 411). However, most of the allusions that he identifies are too vague to evoke those notions without the reader's inferring a great deal, and they stand in direct opposition to Qoheleth's observations on the permanence and changelessness of the cosmos in the opening chapters.

340. See D. Kidner (*The Message of Ecclesiastes* [Leicester: Inter-Varsity Press, 1976] 100), who writes, "For our part, to *remember* Him is no perfunctory or purely mental act; it is to drop our pretence of self-sufficiency and commit ourselves to Him."

Qohelet's God is a remote God. Man is not capable of finding out the work
of that God (Qoh 8,17; 11,5). In Qohelet's opinion there is an immense gap
between God and man (Qoh 5,1). . . . Yet at the end of the book Qohelet tries
to bridge this gap. Just as in Israel's prophecy, in the Book of Qohelet a personal relation between God and man is indicated, although on [*sic*] only one
single place. . . . Hence this anonymous speaker with his own accents has to
be placed not too far from the mainstream of Old Testament theology.[341]

These apparently orthodox thoughts, together with the use of the plural participle of ברא 'create' (although the singular appears in a few manuscripts) and
the uncharacteristic reference to "Creator" rather than "God," have struck a
number of modern commentators as quite inappropriate when laid alongside
the other words of Qoheleth, prompting various suggested emendations. Seow
summarizes a number of solutions: "These include (a) *bĕrû'êkā* 'your well-
being' or 'your health' (Ehrlich); (b) *boryāk* 'your vigor' (Zimmerman);
(c) *bĕ'ērêkā* or *bôrĕkā* 'your well' (Graetz), a metaphor for one's wife, as in
Prov 5:15; (d) *bôrĕkā* 'your pit,' a synonym for the grave (Galling)."[342] However, the case for altering the text is not strong. The manuscript and version
evidence is consistent in reading 'Creator'. The plural form of the participle
ברא is unusual (the plural Qal participle of ברא appears nowhere else in BH,
which always uses the singular with reference to God), but this only supports
omitting the י, a variation found in a number of manuscripts and possibly supported in the early versions. However, Seow has pointed out that Qoheleth's
choice of terminology here may have been determined by the possibility of a
wordplay, a factor that was noted very early, as the words of Rabbi Akabya
ben Mahallalel (first century C.E.) indicate: "Consider three things and you
will not come into the power of sin: Know whence you came; where you are
going; and before whom you are destined to give an accounting."[343] This interpretation is based on the perception that Qoheleth's בוראיך 'your Creator'
could evoke similar words: בארך 'your source'—where you came from; and
בורך 'your pit' (where you are going), together with the obvious reference to
the Creator.

Thus there is little warrant for altering the text. Nor are alternative readings
of the extant text tenable. Although the participle may rarely be rendered by

---

341. A. J. O. van der Wal, "Qohelet 12,1a: A Relatively Unique Statement in Israel's
Wisdom Tradition," in *Qohelet in the Context of Wisdom* (ed. A. Schoors; Leuven: Leuven
University Press, 1998) 418; cf. H. Jagersma, "Het boek Prediker," in *Wie wijsheid zoekt,
vindt het Leven: De wijsheidsliteratuur van het Oude Testament* (ed. E. Eynikel; Leuven:
Boxtel, 1991) 115–16.

342. Seow, *Ecclesiastes*, 351. Scott (*Proverbs Ecclesiastes*, 253) also suggests (d).

343. Seow, *Ecclesiastes*, 352.

an English gerund (so perhaps בורא 'creating' in Isa 57:19), suggesting that it might be possible to render our verse 'Remember your creation . . .' (literally, 'the creating of you'), this interpretation is improbable for a number of reasons. First, the infinitive construct is the normal means by which this idea would be expressed. Second, the presence of the marker את suggests that it is appropriate to read the participle as a substantive, 'your Creator'. Third, the expression makes good sense as it stands (even if it does cause some readers to question the consistency with the remainder of Qoheleth's thoughts).

Nonetheless, it is worth noting precisely what the text does and does not say. We are not told why we are to remember our Creator or what benefits may befall those who do remember their Creator. Within the framework of Qoheleth's thought, it is difficult to justify reading this exhortation as a call to orthodox observance of God's commands. Likewise, van der Wal's assertion that Qoh 12:1 should be read as exhorting a "personal relationship between God and man" reads into these few words much more than is warranted by the context. Rather, the reference to the Creator could amount to little more than a reminder of one's place in the universe, subject to the unpredictable will of the remote and unpredictable God. In the immediately preceding passage, Qoheleth has exhorted his readers to remember the many "days of darkness," an exhortation that functions to remind the reader of the senselessness of life. More specifically, within the context of the poem 12:1–7, the reference to the Creator appears to serve primarily as a reminder of one's mortality, that life is in God's hands and thus beyond the control of even the wisest sage.[344]

Even the concluding reference to the spirit's returning to God cannot be construed as an expression of some form of continued existence after death or as a basis for a hope of escape from the senselessness that Qoheleth discovered. In the Hebrew Bible, the spirit is not conceived of as some sort of disembodied essence of a person; rather, it is what enlivens the person who, once the spirit is resumed by God, is dead. As Fox explains, "When the spirit is removed, the person, and not only the body, is said to go to the earth, or to Sheol, or to darkness (Ps 104:29; Qoh 6:4; 9:10; and often). Thus Qoh 12:7 does not imply continued existence of the sort that would overcome death and compensate for the miseries of life."[345] Ultimately, the traditional interpretation of the exhortation to remember one's Creator while young has been more

---

344. See Maurice Gilbert, "La description de la vieillesse en Qohelet XII 1–7 est-elle allégorique?" in *Congress Volume: Vienna, 1980* (VTSup 32; Leiden: Brill, 1981) 100; Fox, *A Time to Tear Down*, 322. Qoheleth has elsewhere sought to remind his readers of their mortality and encouraged them to dwell on it. See, for example, 7:2–4.

345. Fox, ibid., 331; cf. Longman, *The Book of Ecclesiastes*, 273; Crenshaw, *Ecclesiastes*, 188–89.

heavily influenced by Ecclesiastes' placement in the canon of Scripture than by the immediate context of Qoheleth's words. Remembering Qoheleth's Creator while young, in Qoheleth's context, is little more than remembering that life's outcomes depend not on what can be discovered by wisdom but on the apparently arbitrary whims of the remote and unknowable deity in whose hands lie the fates of all creatures.

Qoheleth 12:8

[8] "Utterly senseless," says Qoheleth. "Everything is senseless."

The epilogist closes the record of the words of Qoheleth by repeating the words with which he began. In doing this, he makes it clear that this statement is more than a favorite expression of Qoheleth's; it functions as a summary of all that he has said. Furthermore, this summary is unqualified—for Qoheleth there is no escape from the senselessness of the world. If there were any other answer, this summary could not stand. Yet stand it does. There has been no progression in thought, no caveats introduced to ameliorate this statement. As far as the epilogist is concerned, Qoheleth has not given us any means for escaping this conclusion—only evidence to substantiate it.

Conclusions

A number of pertinent conclusions may be drawn from this examination of the words of Qoheleth. First, in spite of his failure to find answers through the application of wisdom, Qoheleth does not denounce wisdom directly. Fox summarizes Qoheleth's observations on wisdom by noting that "Qohelet has nothing bad to say about wisdom, but only about what happens *to* it." He proceeds to list the four shortcomings of wisdom: it does not provide sufficient knowledge—it stops short of answering the fundamental questions of life; it is readily undone by folly; it is painful; and it is obliterated by death.[346] Fox is correct to note that Qoheleth is not critical of wisdom per se, for in spite of these shortcomings he maintains that it is preferable to folly.[347] Nowhere does Qoheleth denounce the wisdom movement. The closest he comes is in 7:16, where the warning against excessive wisdom comes because of the shortcom-

---

346. Michael V. Fox, "The Inner-Structure of Qohelet's Thought," in *Qohelet in the Context of Wisdom* (ed. A. Schoors; Leuven: Leuven University Press, 1998) 229–30.

347. The view that Qoheleth's words act as a polemic against wisdom has been relatively common among scholars (see the list provided by Fox, ibid., 230–31 n. 11). Where my interpretation differs is in the claim that it is the epilogist who effectively presents a polemic against wisdom and that Qoheleth's words are used by the epilogist to that end.

ings of wisdom outlined above not because Qoheleth is presenting a polemic against it.

The second observation worthy of note is that Qoheleth nowhere admits the possibility of divine revelation as a means for determining what is best in life. The passage most commonly held to indicate Qoheleth's approval of the cultic institutions in ancient Israel, Qoh 4:17–5:6[5:1–7], is better understood as attacking those who claimed to speak for God within the established religious institutions of ancient Israel. More often, where Qoheleth's words are reminiscent of material found elsewhere in the Hebrew Bible, he is contradicting the orthodox teaching. Any case that Qoheleth's intention (as opposed to the epilogist's) is to endorse orthodox thinking about what is right in life is seriously eroded by his failure to refer to the divine revelation that forms the basis for the expression of orthodox thought throughout the remainder of the Hebrew Bible.

Third, Qoheleth's own conclusion—that all is הבל—forces him to advise that the only viable course of action is to enjoy life whenever the opportunity presents itself. This advice is the logical result of Qoheleth's failure to find any unequivocal advantage in human toil. Although some readers consider this advice to be conclusive evidence that Qoheleth does have a positive outlook on life or that he is ultimately affirming the goodness of God, this view does not stand up under close scrutiny. For Qoheleth, the suggestion to enjoy life when you can is the result of wisdom's failure to provide conclusive answers about benefiting from life.

Fourth, Qoheleth's analysis and conclusions are incompatible with the teaching of the remainder of the Hebrew Bible. Moreover, this incompatibility is not merely benign but in many instances is confrontational and offensive to any reader who is favorably disposed toward biblical teaching. The epilogist subsequently uses the offensiveness of Qoheleth to serve as a powerful warning against the wisdom movement.

It is at this point that the distinction between Qoheleth's words and the book of Ecclesiastes becomes critical. Because Qoheleth belittles those who claim to speak for God and frequently affirms ideas that cannot be reconciled with orthodox thought, the reader knows (before hearing from the epilogist in 12:9–14) that this sage stands at odds with orthodox Israelite religion. With the epilogist's insistence that Qoheleth is preeminent among the sages and speaks honestly, together with the epilogist's more general warnings against the sages, the reader is brought to the conclusion that the way of the sages is not compatible with the way of God revealed through Moses and the prophets.

Summary

Qoheleth's words have always troubled his readers, largely because of the difficulty of reconciling them with the remainder of the Bible. Qoheleth seeks answers, but he looks neither to God nor to other scriptures for the answers. Instead he ascribes evil to God (6:2), accuses God of making things irrevocably corrupt (7:13), and questions God's justice (6:2). His ideas explicitly contradict orthodox statements made elsewhere in the Hebrew Bible (e.g., 7:15–18; 11:9). Indeed, I have argued that even the few brief sections of his work that are sometimes interpreted positively are almost certainly far less affirmative than they appear to be (e.g., 2:24–26; 4:17–5:6[5:1–7]).

In order to understand the original purpose of Ecclesiastes, I have suggested that when the work was first composed there was a particular group of readers who would also have found Qoheleth's words disturbing. These were students and prospective students of the wisdom movement. For, in spite of the fact that Qoheleth was a sage—indeed, the foremost sage—his remarks do not present wisdom in a particularly endearing light. Qoheleth describes a world bound by perpetual cycles unaltered by the efforts of the wise (1:4–11). Although wisdom may have minor, temporary advantages (7:12; 9:16), with it comes frustration and pain (1:17–18), and it is so fragile that it is readily undone by only a little folly (10:1). Then, when all is said and done, the wise person dies, just as the fool and even the animals die (3:18–21; 9:1–3). The wise person is then forgotten, and any advantage he or she had also vanishes.

Furthermore, if the task of the wise was to determine the right action at the appropriate time in order to bring about a favorable outcome, Qoheleth declares that it was futile—wisdom cannot provide this information, for the world does not operate according to any predictable moral laws (e.g., 10:14b). The world makes no sense, and no amount of wisdom can overcome this obstacle. Consequently, Qoheleth even advises against embracing the life of a sage (see 5:19[20]).

I have sought to show that it is fundamental to the purpose of Ecclesiastes that Qoheleth's words *did* trouble his audience, and in particular, those who were students or prospective students of the wisdom movement of his day. Although criticism may have been expected to come from outside the wisdom movement (and, it appears from my review of biblical material in the first chapter of this book that this criticism did occur), criticism of the movement

236

from within would have had far greater impact upon its students. Qoheleth's honest appraisal of the wisdom movement as largely futile and pointless would have served as a powerful deterrent to anyone considering the pursuit of wisdom.

In spite of Qoheleth's relatively negative assessment of wisdom, his words are not themselves presented in the form of a critique or attack on wisdom or the wisdom movement. Qoheleth merely reports his observations and conclusions openly and honestly. The implications of these comments by Qoheleth are only drawn out by the epilogist, who frames them with a warning and points out an alternative to wisdom. Thus, rather than seeking to ameliorate Qoheleth's stark message to make it less offensive to the students and prospective students of the wisdom movement (most of whom would probably have been familiar with the orthodox religious thinking on many of the matters Qoheleth addressed), the epilogist exploits the offense of Qoheleth's words to formulate a compelling critique of the wisdom movement of his day.

The epilogue begins by strongly affirming Qoheleth's credentials as a sage and asserting his integrity, as well as summarizing his activities. In commending Qoheleth, the epilogist carefully avoids endorsing the entire wisdom movement. In fact, by summarizing Qoheleth's activities, he casts aspersions on Qoheleth's contemporaries. By characterizing Qoheleth as both an impeccably honest sage and the corrector of others' wisdom, the epilogist has imputed to the wisdom movement a level of, at best, incompetency or, at worst, deceit that found expression in a preference for speaking pleasing words rather than speaking the truth. Furthermore, this affirmation of Qoheleth's integrity serves to overcome any tendency the audience may have had to dismiss his words due to their troubling nature.

The epilogist's subsequent, more explicit warnings against the ways of the wisdom movement (in particular, regarding the futility of the tasks of researching and recording wisdom mentioned in Qoh 12:12) recall Qoheleth's own findings about the inability of wisdom to answer the question of what is profitable for a person to do in life. The epilogist thus takes Qoheleth's comments on the inadequacies of wisdom and turns them into a warning against the wisdom movement.

This understanding of Ecclesiastes has a number of points in its favor. First, it accounts for the most difficult aspects of the book. The lack of any readily identifiable structure reflects the epilogist's intention of presenting a broad picture of Qoheleth's wisdom and thus the true nature of the wisdom movement. Internal contradictions become further evidence to support the epilogist's case, reflecting the failure of the sages to provide conclusive or coherent answers to the questions they pondered. Contradictions with the remainder of the Hebrew

Bible illustrate the degree to which the wisdom movement's ideas had become incompatible with the ideas and ideals of ancient Israelite orthodoxy.

Second, it provides an interpretation of Ecclesiastes that coheres with the dominant attitude toward human wisdom found in the remainder of the Hebrew Bible. The survey of biblical attitudes toward wisdom in chap. 1 of this book revealed a clear antipathy toward human wisdom. Whereas Qoheleth highlights various inadequacies with this wisdom, the epilogist builds on Qoheleth's revelations to present an evaluation of wisdom in keeping with this biblical position.

Third, this understanding of Ecclesiastes offers an answer to the perplexing question about its very presence in the canon, for this book becomes a warning directed at students and prospective students of the wisdom movement against the way of wisdom that Qoheleth had followed and a call back to a theological wisdom grounded in the fear of God and obedience to his commandments. As such, Ecclesiastes parallels the prophetic condemnation of wisdom. Unlike the prophets, however, Ecclesiastes presents a critique from within the movement.

Although we have no clear idea how the texts that make up the Hebrew Bible came to be included within the canon, I contend that this interpretation of Ecclesiastes may reflect both the original intention of the work and the reason for its acceptance in the Hebrew Bible. One reason that this understanding is not presented by any early interpreter could be that the epilogist worked in a specific historical, social context that clearly did not persist into the periods of the early interpreters for whom we have records. The existence of a wisdom movement at odds with the orthodox teachings of the Hebrew Bible must largely be inferred from what the epilogist says, for Qoheleth himself provides little specific information on his fellow sages. Any reader removed from that historical and social context could easily overlook this vital clue to unlocking the significance of Ecclesiastes. Later depictions of the wise, in texts such as Sirach and the Wisdom of Solomon, reflect a wisdom movement closely aligned to observation of the Torah, like the one that Qoheleth's epilogist endorses.

One final point of support for this thesis may be identified in the hypothetical results of critiques of the wisdom movement such as we find in Ecclesiastes. Although a purely historical reconstruction of the rise and fall of the wisdom movement in ancient Israel is impossible, given the dearth of readily datable evidence, it is possible to construct an implied or literary history based on the texts at hand. In a history of this sort, the beginnings lie in the wisdom of Proverbs, whose terse nature readily permits a naïve, mechanistic (mis)interpretation of the world. The book of Job can be understood to represent a reaction against this application of wisdom, denying the simplistic connection between suffering and wrongdoing. Qoheleth's words represent a similar reaction, although they go much further than Job. Qoheleth reveals that the notion that the world operates via an underlying moral order simply does not reflect reality: everything is senseless. Any wisdom founded upon such a presupposition is thus suspect. The epilogist exploited Qoheleth's revelations to produce a work aimed at discrediting the wisdom movement. Following this, even perhaps as a result of the composition of Ecclesiastes, wisdom underwent a reformation that resulted in a shift in focus to the study of and obedience to the Torah (as reflected in Sirach). In this sense, the book of Ecclesiastes marks the end of speculative wisdom in ancient Israel.

Against the arguments in support of my interpretation of Ecclesiastes is one clear problem—the absence of external historical or archaeological evidence to verify the thesis. Conversely, there is also insufficient external evidence to refute the thesis. This problem, however, is not unique to my thesis but is faced by many seeking to provide a Sitz im Leben for ancient Hebrew literature, especially literature with no readily identifiable historical connections. When an interpretation rests on evidence that may only have existed for a relatively brief time, as in this case, the hope of uncovering sufficiently detailed external information is small indeed. Nonetheless, the external evidence that does exist (such as the likely existence of some form of a wisdom movement, as well as the hostile attitude toward human wisdom in most of the Hebrew Bible) suggests that the claims I have made are at least viable.

Ecclesiastes records two responses to the failure of wisdom revealed by Qoheleth. The first is the response of Qoheleth who, attributing no credibility to supposed divine revelation (and perhaps even demonstrating some disdain for it in 4:17–5:6[5:1–7]), could only suggest that his students find what enjoyment they could in life, for any other hope would inevitably be undone by death. The second response is from the epilogist. In contrast to Qoheleth, the epilogist briefly but conclusively points to an alternate form of wisdom—wisdom founded in the fear of God and obedience to God's commandments. This is the only wisdom for which human beings are commended elsewhere in the Hebrew Bible outside Proverbs. In using Qoheleth's words to disclose the failings of speculative wisdom, the epilogist presents a unified work possessing a specific overarching purpose of deterring prospective students of speculative wisdom from embracing the wisdom movement and pointing them to their religious heritage, which offered a way out of the senseless and futile world of the sages.

Index of Authors

241

Index of Scripture

244

New Testament

Deuterocanonical Literature